T0314148

METAGAMING

ELECTRONIC MEDIATIONS

Series Editors: N. Katherine Hayles, Peter Krapp, Rita Raley, and Samuel Weber

Founding Editor: Mark Poster

(continued on page 380)

METAGAMING

Playing, Competing,
Spectating, Cheating,
Trading, Making, and
Breaking Videogames

STEPHANIE BOLUK AND
PATRICK LEMIEUX

University of Minnesota Press

Minneapolis

London

Portions of the Introduction and chapter 1 appear together as "Metagame," in *Debugging Game History: A Critical Lexicon,* ed. Henry Lowood and Raiford Guins, 313–24 (Cambridge, Mass.: MIT Press, 2016). Portions of chapter 3 were previously published as "Stretched Skulls: Anamorphic Games and the *Memento Mortem Mortis,*" *Digital Humanities Quarterly* 6, no. 2 (2012). http://www.digitalhumanities.org/dhq/vol/6/2/000122/000122.html. Portions of chapter 4 were previously published as "Hundred Thousand Billion Fingers: Seriality and Critical Game Practices," *Leonardo Electronic Almanac* 17, no. 2 (2012): 10–31. http://www.leoalmanac.org/vol17-no2-hundred-thousand-billion -fingers/.

Published by the University of Minnesota Press
111 Third Avenue South, Suite 290
Minneapolis, MN 55401-2520
http://www.upress.umn.edu

Printed in the United States of America on acid-free paper

The University of Minnesota is an equal-opportunity educator and employer.

22 21 20 19 18 17   10 9 8 7 6 5 4 3 2 1

Library of Congress Cataloging-in-Publication Data
Names: Boluk, Stephanie, 1979– author. | LeMieux, Patrick, 1984– author.
Title: Metagaming : playing, competing, spectating, cheating, trading,
    making, and breaking videogames / Stephanie Boluk and Patrick LeMieux.
Description: Minneapolis : University of Minnesota Press, 2017. |
Series: Electronic mediations ; 53 | Includes bibliographical references and index.
Identifiers: LCCN 2016039454 (print) | ISBN 978-0-8166-8715-2 (hc) |
    ISBN 978-0-8166-8716-9 (pb)
Subjects: LCSH: Video games—Social aspects. | Video games industry—
    Social aspects. | Video games—Design. | BISAC: GAMES / Video & Electronic. |
    COMPUTERS / Social Aspects / General. | SOCIAL SCIENCE / Popular Culture.
Classification: LCC GV1469.34.S52 B65 2017 (print) | DDC 794.8—dc23
LC record available at https://lccn.loc.gov/2016039454

For players, programmers, modders, mappers, speedrunners, streamers, competitors, commentators, spectators, gamblers, traders, farmers, cheaters, triflers, spoilsports, and all metagamers

Contents

INTRODUCTION

Metagaming

Videogames and the Practice of Play

[A] game without a metagame is like an idealized object in
physics. It may be a useful construct but it doesn't really
exist.

—Richard Garfield, "Metagames"

Humans make their own [metagames], but they do not
know they make them.

—Catherine Malabou, *What Should We Do with Our Brain?*

Let's play a game. It's a simple game. Maybe even the simplest game.
And although we could play it in any number of ways, let's play on paper. In
this context, our paper-and-pencil game consists of only a small square.
Here: □. This tiny gameboard doubles as a scoreboard with two possible
states: on and off, black and white, one and zero. It's not the most engaging
equipment for playing a game, but neither are the digital mechanisms
driving all videogames. Despite the fact that the physical attributes of
digital media are never quite digital and the possibilities for play are practically infinite,[1] the *desire* for a definitive outcome, score, or measurement will structure the play on this page.[2] Beyond their voluntary rules
and volunteering players, digital games require an observable or evident difference—a discrete state or abstract quantity with which we play.
Whether the observer is human or nonhuman, whether the evidence
occurs within the equipment or the field, a line in the sand must be drawn
and judged by someone or something. The game must have a state and
all such games are digital games. In the case of our small square, pencil
marks paper and perception is left up to the player. There is only one
rule: in order to win, just fill it in. Don't worry, we'll wait. . . . If you didn't
grab a pencil or pen or marker or crayon, you probably still have a white
square worth zero points. Game over. Please try again. However, if you

1

actually filled in the square, you just won the game with a high score of one point. Congratulations! But the game is still over. Try again?

This time, let's *make a metagame*. Instead of simply playing again, let's make a game out of a game. We'll use the same voluntary conditions and physical equipment as last time and we'll rely on the same belief in a digital difference between on and off, black and white, one and zero (at least for now). Here—have another small square: □. It looks like the last game, but it is not the same. We now have a history with these mechanics—a metagame based on mimesis, materiality, memory, and even a simple form of markets already at work on this page. Before you fill in the second square, let's agree to expand this metagame by adding an extra condition, just between us. To turn this deterministic task into a two-player game, we've hidden a *third square* somewhere in the pages of this book. Even though the mechanics are technically the same—to fill or not to fill—let's adjust the rules depending on the combined states of *both* the second and third squares. Now we have two bits, with a total of four possible outcomes that change the game. If both squares end up black, we both lose. If both squares are left white, we tie (and you can try a second round). Finally, our Prisoner's Dilemma[3] comes into play when the squares are not equivalent. If you find a black square while leafing through the remainder of this volume but neglected to fill your square here, we win and you lose. Another game over. But if you fill in your square now and find an empty white square later, you win the paper game! We've already made our move. Your turn.

Attitude, affinity, experience, achievement, status, community, competition, strategy, spectatorship, statistics, history, economy, politics: the metagame ruptures the logic of the game, escaping the formal autonomy of both ideal rules and utopian play via those practical and material factors not immediately enclosed within the game as we know it. Take our second paper-and-pencil game, for example. Beyond the mechanics for playing and scoring, questions emerge. Are we the kind of authors who would hide a black square somewhere in the pages of our book? Are you the kind of player to get a pen and mark your presence on paper? *Metagaming* is an attempt to ask these questions in the form of a true *game design philosophy*—a critical practice in which playing, making, and thinking about videogames occur within the same act.[4] Part media theory, part media history, and part media art, *Metagaming* explores videogames by practically and critically engaging the conditions of twenty-first-century play. From the embodied forms of vision required to navigate anamorphic indie games and the textual play of both blind and blindfolded players to the seriality of home console hacks and the financialization of international e-sports, each chapter of this book not only documents the histories and theorizes the practices of play but is also accompanied by original software available in the online version of *Metagaming* at http://manifold.umn.edu/metagaming. Exhibited at the end of each chapter, these playable postscripts are an attempt to further demonstrate and reinforce the game design philosophy already at work in the pages of this book. They are examples of practice-based research and our personal invitation to begin playing as a way to make metagames.

After all, metagames are not just games about games. They are not simply the games we play in, on, around, and through games or before, during, and after games. From the most complex house rules, arcade cultures, competitive tournaments, and virtual economies to the simple decision to press start, pass the controller, use a player's guide, or even purchase a game in the first place, for all intents and purposes metagames are the only kind of games that we play. And even though metagames have always existed alongside games, the concept has taken on renewed importance and political urgency in a media landscape in which videogames not only colonize and enclose the very concept of games, play, and leisure but ideologically conflate the creativity, criticality, and craft of play with the act of consumption. When did the term *game* become synonymous with hardware warranties, packaged products, intellectual property, copyrighted code, end user licenses, and digital rights management? When did *rules* become conflated with the physical, mechanical, electrical, and computational operations of technical media? When did *player* become a code word for *customer*? When did we stop making metagames?

Since the commercial release of the first home consoles in the 1970s, videogames have been complicit in the transformation of play into a privatized form of consumption. In *Games of Empire*, Nick Dyer-Witheford and Greig de Peuter (2009, xv) identify videogames as "*a paradigmatic media of Empire—*[of] planetary, militarized hypercapitalism" and, as such, a crucial site of resistance (emphasis original). Over the last ten years, scholars like Alexander Galloway, McKenzie Wark, and Mary Flanagan (along with Dyer-Witheford, de Peuter, and countless others) have argued for the radical potential of videogames as a medium for creative practice, philosophical experimentation, cultural critique, and political action. From Galloway's (2006, 109) "countergaming"[5] to Wark's (2007, 022) "gamer theorist"[6] and from Flanagan's (2009, 6) "critical play"[7] to Dyer-Witheford and de Peuter's (2009, 187) "games of multitude,"[8] each of these thinkers argue for a distinction between videogames as a platform for critical making and videogames as mere commodity. Yet a striking and shared feature of these theories is that each relegates the radical potential of games to a speculative horizon rather than a historical practice. Where are the gamer theorists making countergames? When will we critically play games of multitude? Rather than look toward some future (whether near, distant, or imagined), we think the answer is already in, on, around, through, before, during, and after videogames. The answer is the metagame.

Rather than collecting the artifacts and chronicling the history of videogames as if they were stable, static, separate objects, *Metagaming* attempts to uncover alternate histories of play defined not by code, commerce, and computation but by the diverse practices and material discontinuities that emerge between the human experience of playing videogames and their nonhuman operations. Metagames transform videogames from a mass medium and cultural commodity into instruments, equipment, tools, and toys for playing, competing, spectating, cheating, trading, breaking, making, and ultimately intervening in the sensory and political economies of those technologies responsible for the privatization of play. And although the term *metagame* has been used within many wargaming, roleplaying, and collectible card gaming communities for decades, since the turn of the millennium it has become a popularly used and particularly useful label for a diverse form of play, a game design paradigm, and a way of life occurring not only around videogames but around all forms of digital technology.

In an era of social media, cloud computing, algorithmic trading, networked surveillance, and drone warfare, the events determining the experience of quotidian life are increasingly automated and operate at speeds and scales beyond the domain of human phenomenology. Considering the microtemporal operations of ubiquitous media technologies that "we have no direct experience of, no direct mode of access to, and no potential awareness of," in *Feed-Forward: On the Future of 21st Century Media* Mark Hansen (2015, 8, 27) proposes that "the central challenges posed to us by this new reality [are the questions] concerning what becomes of consciousness: How can consciousness continue to matter in a world where increasingly events no longer need it to occur, and indeed, where they occur long before they manifest as contents of consciousness?" Recalling Marshall McLuhan's (1962, 265) observation that "sense ratios change when any one sense or bodily or mental function is externalized in technological form," in the twenty-first century, the central characteristic and defining problem of media is the grammatization, externalization, and quantification of thought. Whereas multiple neuroscientific studies have noted the enlarged hippocampi of London taxi drivers after a lifetime of learning to navigate the city's streets (what cabbies refer to, fittingly, as "The Knowledge"), the neuronal geography of Uber drivers is tuned to an entirely different network: Google Maps scrolling across iPhone screens (Maguire et al., 200).[9]

In *What Should We Do with Our Brain?*, a pithy and polemical essay on the relationship between neuroscience, phenomenology, and neoliberal capitalism, Catherine Malabou (2008, 12) asks a single, urgent question: "What should we do so that consciousness of the brain does not purely and simply coincide with the spirit of capitalism?" Echoing Marx's declaration that "humans make their own history, but they do not know that they make it," Malabou's (2008, 1) answer is that we must become aware that "humans make their own *brain*, but they do not know that they make it" (emphasis added). In other words, we must become aware of the brain's plasticity.[10] Malabou (2008, 5) deploys the term *plasticity* not only to refer the brain's capacity to be both "'formable,' and formative at the same time" but to emphasize that "the brain is a work that we cannot know." Because the nervous system (not to mention the entire bodily organism and its many extensions) is constitutive of human experience, we can only speculate on the experience and history of the brain itself. In 2017, seven billion absolutely unique and unimaginably complex moving sculptures reflect both the microhistory of neuronal processes *and* the macrohistory of ideology in the twenty-first century. We make our own brains, but we do not know it.

Following Derrida's reading of Hegel, Malabou's concept of plasticity could go by another name: *play*.[11] After all, humans also make their own *games*, but they do not know it. Even during the most banal encounter with videogames we constantly and unconsciously make metagames, but the logic of the marketplace obfuscates this form of critical practice. And just as Google invites employees to play on their campus, Pixar encourages workers to customize their cubicles with childhood toys, and Valve advertises a "flat" hierarchy where all desks are on wheels, the rhetoric of play and games has been harnessed to gamify intellectual, informatics, and affective labor both within corporate workplaces and within the homes of players across the globe. This corporate appropriation has also occurred around plasticity. Consider for example the ways in which the concept of plasticity has been co-opted within contemporary cognitive capitalism to naturalize models of economic precarity in the form of flexible, contingent labor. Noting this tendency, Malabou (2008, 46) writes, "if I insist on how close certain managerial discourses are to neuroscientific discourses, this is because it seems to me that the phenomenon called 'brain plasticity' is in reality more often described in terms of an economy of flexibility."

Flexibility, Malabou (2008, 12) declares, "is the ideological avatar of plasticity." Everywhere the brain is in chains and plasticity opens a path to freedom. At the same time, plasticity—like play—is always at risk of being employed as the "biological justification of a type of economic, political, and social organization in which all that matters is the result of action" (Malabou 2008, 31). Plasticity's radical potential, destructive capability and material history are obfuscated by the ideology of flexibility, a corporate buzzword deployed in an effort to leverage biological rationales in order to valorize the managerial techniques and labor practices of the information economy.[12] If flexibility is the "ideological avatar of plasticity," then videogames are the *ideological avatar of play* (Malabou 2008, 12). *Metagaming* attempts to become aware of this ideological avatar, to become conscious of the fact that play can never be reduced to product. We make our own metagames, but we do not know we make them . . . yet.

What's in a Game?

As with the small squares that started this book, every game must have a metagame and every metagame must have a game (although the two are not equal and are never so easily distinguished). One of the most substantive definitions of games comes from Bernard Suits, a utopian philosopher whose work has experienced a revival after his death in 2007. Written in the style of a Platonic dialogue, Suits' book *The Grasshopper: Games, Life and Utopia* (1978) transforms one of Aesop's most beloved fables into a philosophical treatise on the differences between work and play. In his utopian rereading of "The Grasshopper and the Ant," Suits turns the original fable on its head, inverting the moral order of leisure and labor by celebrating the Grasshopper's death after a summer of gaming instead of lauding the ant's preparation for the cold. "The point of the parable should not be the ant's triumph," Suits (2005, 27) writes, "but the Grasshopper's tragedy. For one cannot help reflecting that if there were no winters to guard against, then the Grasshopper would not get his comeuppance nor the ant his shabby victory." By imagining the possibility of a world without winters, a world in which "the life of the Grasshopper would be vindicated and that of the ant absurd," Suits introduces his theory of games.

Suits (2005, 54–55) defines playing a game as the "attempt to achieve a specific state of affairs [prelusory goal], using only means permitted by rules, where the rules [lusory means] prohibit use of more efficient in favor of less efficient means [constitutive rules], and where the rules are accepted just because they make possible such activity [lusory attitude]." In short, "playing a game is a voluntary attempt to overcome unnecessary obstacles" (Suits 2004, 55). At first glance this definition appears deceptively simple. Play is freely chosen and games consist of optional constraints. But, by defining games solely as useless challenges adopted by a disinterested player, Suits sets sail for a "magic circle"[13] called Utopia. Invested in an ideal, idle, idyllic play set apart from necessity, the Grasshopper's games do not perform a function, turn a profit, or satisfy a need. Any extrinsic motivation diminishes the autonomy of both game and play. For Suits (2005, 28) there is no middle ground: "either I die or I cease to be the Grasshopper." Set apart, in a world without winters, the Grasshopper's games become transcendental objects no longer constrained by time and space.

Despite Suits' dream of infinite summers, no such gameplay exists. Has there ever been a game that is absolutely unnecessary, immaterial, and ahistorical? Have there ever existed players able to resist involuntary action like the process of metabolism or the forces of gravity? Suits' rubric constitutes the utopian horizon of game and play, not their phenomenal, material, historical, economic, or political practices. The health benefits of recreational play, the technical particularities of graphics processors, the shared strategies of two opponents, or the monetization of broadcasted sports are just a few examples of the logistical and pragmatic constraints which perforate the magic circle and conflate leisure and labor, play and practice, into a hybrid form which Suits (2004, 27) might dismiss as "asshopper[y] or grant[ism]." On the other hand, Suits' (2004, 173) utopian philosophy allows any activity, like fixing the kitchen sink, to become a kind of game as long as the player is indifferent to the possible consequences or worldly exigencies involved with the task. The "magic" of Suits' games is that they require players to become Utopians by playing as if it doesn't matter.

In a world of asshoppers and grants where winter is a constant reality, the fantasy of summer—of games and play—serves as a ubiquitous, cultural logic that guides both the consumption and production of consumer electronics and digital entertainment like videogames. Whether or not Suits' utopian vision can ever be realized, videogames operate as the ideological avatar of play: a widely held, naturalized system of beliefs that conflates the fantasy of escapism with the commodity form and encloses play within the magic circle of neoliberal capital. In the same way that the British land enclosure of the eighteenth century transformed public land into private property, so too has the videogame industry worked to privatize the culture of games and play. Games have been replaced by videogames and play has been replaced by fun. This reduction of play as pure possibility to a class of consumer goods occurs at the expense of the metagame. After all, not only is a game easier to package and sell if it can be neatly reduced to its physical equipment, but any play that occurs in, on, around, or through videogames instantly becomes advertising for a product. The greatest trick the videogame industry ever pulled was convincing the world that videogames were games in the first place.

Unlike traditional games in which voluntary rules are consciously chosen to further constrain or interpret the physical properties of dice and cards, balls and bats, or track and field, videogames conflate the *rules* of a game with the *mechanics* of the equipment.[14] Nowhere in the official rulebook of Major League Baseball, for example, are the laws of physics defined, while in videogames the explicit authoring of forces like mass, gravity, friction, and momentum replaces traditional rule sets. Despite their colloquial designation and sale as *games,* videogames do not have rules. Rules are voluntary constraints and social contracts. They are pacts between players not to peek or move outside invisible boundaries. Mechanics, on the other hand, are ontological operations. Players have no choice but to work within the limitations of these involuntary systems.

Whereas rules can be broken at a moment's notice, mechanics cannot be turned off. There is no cheating in *Super Mario Bros.*[15] Editing the code is like corking the bat—the deception occurs within the equipment and changes the game itself. Like the physicality of sports equipment, the mechanical, electrical, and computational processes of videogames always operate outside the conscious experience of the player. But unlike the physics of bats and balls, the myriad technical operations of videogames and their fetishization as commodities obfuscate the practice of play. Videogames blackbox not only nonhuman processes but also human activity—the ideological avatar of play masks the metagame. Rather than continue to conflate mechanics with rules and videogames with games, what if videogames were not considered games in the first place, but *equipment* for making metagames?

No matter how small, no matter how subtle, the metagame is never insignificant. Before a videogame can ever be played—before software can be considered a game in the first place—there must be a metagame. The metagame emerges as the material trace of the discontinuity between the phenomenal experience of play and the mechanics of digital games. From the position in front of the television, posture on the couch, and proprioception of the controller to the most elaborate player-created constraints, fan practices, and party games, metagames are the games created with videogames. From popular mods to ironic parodies and from fan fiction and forum discussion to the latest trends made famous by professional players, metagaming functions as a broad discourse, a way of playing, thinking, and making that transforms autonomous and abstract pieces of software into games and turns players into game designers. Metagames reveal the alternate histories of play that always exist outside the dates, dollars, and demographic data that so often define videogames in industry magazines and encyclopedia entries.

As the sun sinks below the horizon and frost begins to creep across the once-plentiful fields, Suits' (2005, 29) Grasshopper has one, final revelation: that we "are Grasshoppers in disguise . . . that everyone alive is really a Grasshopper" and "that everyone alive is in fact engaged in playing elaborate games, while at the same time believing themselves to be going about their ordinary affairs. Carpenters believing themselves to be merely pursuing their trade are really playing a game, and similarly with politicians, philosophers, lovers, murderers, thieves, and saints. . . . but precisely at the point where each is persuaded [of this truth] . . . each ceases to exist." Suits imagines a utopian apocalypse (in the etymological sense of apocalypse as a lifting of the veil) in which the "revelation" of a worker's game-playing nature brings about the ontological annihilation of that very category. And although everyone alive may be engaged in playing elaborate games, these games remain hidden from view. We don't simply play games, but constantly (and unconsciously) make metagames.

Making Metagames

The word *metagame* does not appear in any dictionary. Although the term is used to denote a wide variety of activities related to games—from a specific subset of mathematical and economic game theory to the metaleptic slippage between in-game and out-of-game knowledge in roleplaying games to the common strategies or passing fashions surrounding competitive card games—there is no unified definition of *metagame*. Whereas there have been numerous discussions surrounding the meaning of the word *game,* the etymology and meaning of *metagame*'s other constitutive element, *meta,* is not as heavily debated. Whether used to describe a story about stories, a film about films, a game about games, or any X about X, in English (and mainly in the United States), the adjective *meta* typically suggests "a consciously sophisticated, self-referential, and often self-parodying style, whereby something reflects or represents the very characteristics it alludes to or depicts" (Oxford English Dictionary 2014a). There has also been some slippage between this general meaning of *meta* and the more specific concept of recursion.[16] These adjectival uses of the term are derived from the more universal prefix *meta-,* which signifies an abstraction from, a second order beyond, or a higher level above the term or concept that it precedes (Oxford English Dictionary 2014b).[17] For example, when prepended to a field of study, *meta-* "denote[s] another [subject] which deals with ulterior issues in the same field, or which raises questions about the nature of the original discipline," such as meta-economics, meta-philosophy, and even meta-lexicography (Oxford English Dictionary 2014b). Based on the ancient Greek preposition μετά, meaning "with," "after," "between," or "beyond," the prepositional origin of the prefix *meta-* continues to characterize its modern use even if μετα- was also combined with verbs in order to express "change (of place, order, condition, or nature)" (Oxford English Dictionary 2014b). Etymologically, the term *metagame* does not simply signify the general category of games that reference themselves or other games, but is also characterized by the deeply specific, relational quality of prepositions as parts of speech. In the same way a preposition situates the noun that it precedes, the meaning of *metagame* emerges within the context of specific practices and historical communities of a given game. Prepositions are to parts of speech as *metagames* are to games. A signifier for everything occurring before, after, between, and during games as well as everything located in, on, around, and beyond games, the metagame anchors the game in time and space.

Historically, one of the earliest concatenations of the terms *meta* and *game* occurred within the branch of mathematics known as game theory (as distinct from game studies). First formulated by John von Neumann in 1928 and then expanded with the help of Oskar Morgenstern in their 1944 book *Theory of Games and Economic Behavior,* game theory is "the study of mathematical models of conflict and cooperation between intelligent, rational decision-makers" (Myerson 1991, 1). [18] During the Cold War, von Neumann and Morgenstern's quantitative "science of decision-making" influenced both American and Soviet policies including strategies of deterrence based on mutually assured destruction between two global superpowers. Demonstrated by the small, square metagame that opened this chapter, the canonical thought experiment that simultaneously popularized and challenged the underlying premises of game theory was the "Prisoner's Dilemma." First named by Albert Tucker in 1950 as a way to thematize the ideas of RAND[19] researchers Melvin Dresher and Merrill Flood, in the Dilemma two prisoners are arrested for the same offense, held separately, and given a choice to betray one another with three outcomes:

1. if one confesses and the other does not, the former will be given a reward . . . and the latter will be fined . . .
2. if both confess, each will be fined . . . At the same time, each has good reason to believe that
3. if neither confesses, both will go clear. (Poundstone 1992, 118)

For game theorists, the Cold War represented a global Prisoner's Dilemma with potentially apocalyptic consequences. Considering the disturbing fact that the "rational" decision (i.e., confessing) will result in mutually assured destruction, the only way to win this logical paradox is to not play.

Rather than infinite deferral or rational suicide, Nigel Howard's (1971, 1, 2, 23) book *Paradoxes of Rationality: Theory of Metagames and Political Behavior* attempts to solve the Prisoner's Dilemma based on a "nonquantitative" and "nonrational" approach to game theory he calls "the metagame" or "the game that would exist if one of the players chose his strategy after the others, in knowledge of their choices."[20] This is the earliest substantive use of the term *metagame*. Whereas in the original Dilemma there are only two options—to confess (C) or not to confess (D)—according to Howard's (1971, 11) metagame theory, Player 1 can also make additional, "extensive" choices based on Player 2's *possible* actions. By projecting an opponent's *potential* behavior, the simple decision to confess or not exponentially multiplies into four new "metachoices:" confess if they confess (C/C), don't confess if they don't confess (D/D), confess if they don't confess (C/D), and don't confess if they confess (D/C)—a game theory within a game theory. Considering the implications of this metagame from Player 2's perspective, the projected possibilities exponentially branch again from a metagame with four choices to a meta-metagame with *sixteen* choices. This infinitely branching tree of possible choices "is the mathematical object studied by the theory of metagames" (Howard 1971, 55). When Player 1's "metachoices" are cross-referenced with Player 2's "meta-metachoices," additional points of "metarational" "metaequilibrium" appear and offer alternative, favorable outcomes (i.e., not confessing)—a mathematical solution to the problem of mutually assured destruction based on mutually assured metagaming (see Figure I.1) (Howard 1971, 59).

Famous for declaring "if you say why not bomb them tomorrow, I say, why not today," John von Neumann's (Blair 1957, 96) game theory mathematically reinforces his militant belief in deterrence (if not preemptive nuclear strike). The logical consequences of Howard's metagame, on the other hand, leads to a different point of equilibrium: mutual disarmament. However much von Neumann's game theory and Howard's metagame analysis may seem far afield from game studies (and even further from game design),[21] the distinction between a game defined by an individualistic, selfish form of abstract rationality and a metagame that acknowledges the collective, historical conditions of decision making parallels the self-referential and prepositional metagame—the game to, from, during, and between the game—deployed by Richard Garfield when designing *Magic: The Gathering* (1993).

	C	D
C	3,3	1,4
D	4,1	2,2

	C/C	D/D	C/D	D/C
C	3,3	1,4	3,3	1,4
D	4,1	2,2	2,2	4,1

	C/C	D/D	C/D	D/C
C/C/C/C	3,3	1,4	3,3	1,4
D/D/D/D	4,1	2,2	2,2	4,1
D/D/D/C	4,1	2,2	2,2	1,4
D/D/C/D	4,1	2,2	3,3	4,1
D/D/C/C	4,1	2,2	3,3	1,4
D/C/D/D	4,1	1,4	2,2	4,1
D/C/D/C	4,1	1,4	2,2	1,4
D/C/C/D	4,1	1,4	3,3	4,1
D/C/C/C	4,1	1,4	3,3	1,4
C/D/D/D	3,3	2,2	2,2	4,1
C/D/D/C	3,3	2,2	2,2	1,4
C/D/C/D	3,3	2,2	3,3	4,1
C/D/C/C	3,3	2,2	3,3	1,4
C/C/D/D	3,3	1,4	2,2	4,1
C/C/D/C	3,3	1,4	2,2	1,4
C/C/C/D	3,3	1,4	3,3	4,1

Figure I.1. Nigel Howard's solution to the original Prisoner's Dilemma (left) involves drafting a metagame (middle) and a second-order metagame (right) that reveals two new points of metaequilibrium (the shaded cells). According to Howard "the symbol 'W/X/Y/Z' represents the policy 'W against C/C, X against D/D, Y against C/D, Z against D/C'" (1971, 59).

Two decades after Nigel Howard's analysis, and after the dissolution of the U.S.S.R., Richard Garfield incorporated the term *metagame* into his design vocabulary not long after publishing *Magic,* the first collectable card game. In the Spring 1995 issue of *The Duelist* (1994–9), an official Wizards of the Coast magazine, Garfield offered a preliminary discussion of metagames in his column, "Lost in the Shuffle." Although the stakes are far less consequential than nuclear apocalypse, Garfield's (1995, 87) article begins with an anecdote about "backstabbing [his] allies in *Diplomacy,*" Allan B. Calhamer's wargame from 1954 based entirely on the social dynamic of the players. After treating each game as an individual, autonomous conflict (and losing more and more), Garfield (1995, 87) realized that his relationship to other players, to the larger social structure in which games are embedded, and even to the physical or economic constraints of certain rules functioned "not as ends unto themselves but as parts of a larger game" or "metagame." Following Howard, this is the second major theorization of the term *metagame.* Five years later, after presenting at the Game Developers Conference (GDC) in San Francisco, Garfield published an even broader definition of the term. Whereas metagaming in roleplaying games like *Dungeons & Dragons* (1974) usually refers to the use of out-of-character knowledge in order to make in-character decisions, Garfield (2000b, 16) expanded the definition to encompass "how a game interfaces beyond itself." In the same way Howard (1971, 59) applied the term *metagame* to describe a more pragmatic and contextual form of decision making or "policy," Garfield (2000b, 16) argues "there is of course no game without a metagame ... a game without a metagame is like an idealized object in physics. It may be a useful construct but it doesn't really exist."

Based on the metagame's actual, rather than ideal, relation to games, Garfield (2000b, 17–18, 18, 20) divides the metagame into four preposi-tional categories: "what a player brings to the game" (e.g., equipment like *Magic* decks and tennis rackets but also personal abilities); "what a player takes away from a game" (e.g., prize pool, tournament rankings, or social status); "what happens between games" (e.g., preparation, strategizing, storytelling); and "what happens during a game other than the game itself" (e.g., trash talking, time outs, and the environmental conditions of play). To, from, during, and between: hearkening back to the preposi-tional etymology of the term *meta* as well as Howard's practical solution to the Prisoner's Dilemma, Garfield's metagames describe players' lived experience and actual historical contexts in which games are played. Whereas Garfield's metagame has become synonymous with the strate-gies and changing trends within the cultures surrounding competitive games like *Magic* and videogames like *StarCraft* (1998) while also influ-encing game designers and scholars such as Katie Salen Tekinbaş and Eric Zimmerman,[22] there is an even more radical interpretation of the metagame.

In the original transcript of his GDC presentation, Garfield (2000b, 16) makes a small but significant departure from the published defini-tion of the metagame as "how a game interfaces beyond itself." While most of Garfield's (2000a, 1) talk is similar to his later article published in *Horsemen of the Apocalypse*, the earlier transcript reveals a slightly different definition of the metagame: not "how a game interfaces outside of itself" but "how a game interfaces with *life*" (emphasis added). This small change reveals Garfield's original commitment to the metagame as the only kind of game we play.[23] The metagame is not just how games interface with life: it is the environment within which games "live" in the first place. Like Mark Hansen's (2006a, 297) definition of media as "an environment for life," metagames are an environment for games.[24] Metagames are where and when games happen, not a magic circle within which unnecessary obstacles and voluntary pursuits play out, but a *messy circle*[25] that both constrains games and makes them possible in the first place. Inside this second circle, the ideological desire to distance leisure from labor, play from production, or games from life breaks down: it's metagames all the way down.

The Practice of Play

Nowhere is the ideological conflict between play and production more evident than in the relationship between videogames and metagames.[26] Although metagames have always existed (albeit subtly)[27] alongside videogames, over the past decade and with the rise of social media and sharing services such as Steam (2003), YouTube (2005), and Twitch (2011) the term *metagame* has become more commonly used to describe the practices within, around, outside, and about videogames. For example, when Narcissa Wright plays *The Legend of Zelda: Ocarina of Time* (1998) and *The Legend of Zelda: The Wind Waker* (2003), the addition of optional constraints, like a simple timer, radically changes the game. Speedruns, or "fast playthroughs of video games," are metagames that encourage the discovery and manipulation of mechanical exploits not immediately evident to the player or accepted as legitimate forms of play (Speed Demos Archive 2014). As Wright remarks, when new techniques such as "dry storage got discovered [in *The Wind Waker*] . . . I was reinvigorated to stay on top of the current metagame" (Wright 2013). Speedrunning is not only a metagame contingent on the virtuosic performance of real-time play, but is also a collaborative form of play based on discovering exploits such as geometry clipping, cutscene skipping, sequence breaking, and memory manipulation—games *within* the game.

More closely aligned with the spirit of Garfield's original definition, other players recover the histories of shifting strategies and tournament trends around competitive videogames as a playful and productive form of spectatorship—a game *around* the game. For example, Richard "KirbyKid" Terrell (2011) encodes VHS tapes to track the history of *Super Smash Bros. Melee* (2001) tournaments because "every game with a metagame worth understanding deserves a devoted video game historian," whereas Daniel "Artosis" Stemkoski (2012) studies and commentates competitive *StarCraft II* (2010) tournaments in Korea because "the metagame is not the same everywhere. . . . Korea, China, NA [North America], and Europe . . . each have their own metagame." Beyond pro gamers and their e-sports, even videogame audiences operate according to many observational metagames adopted from sports like rooting, gambling, and fantasy leagues based on the statistics produced during competitions. The metagame can even take the form of a game *outside* the game, as is the case when Alex "The Mittani" Gianturco (Goldman and Vogt 2014) expanded his *EVE Online* (2003) empire via cyberwarfare and offline espionage—what he identifies as a "metagame which doesn't require booting the program up at all."

Finally, in a blog post titled "Metagames: Games About Games," Andy Baio (2011) observes that the term *metagame* can also refer to "playable games about videogames"—a definition that recalls the use of *meta* in other media genres like metafiction but departs from the way in which Garfield and much of the gaming community apply the term. Thus, when John Romero appropriates the graphics, level designs, and gameplay tropes from Namco's *Pac-Man* (1980) in id Software's *Wolfenstein 3-D* (2008) or when Jonathan Blow references the characters and texts from Nintendo's *Donkey Kong* (1981) and *Super Mario Bros.* (1985) in his independently developed game *Braid* (2008), they are making games *about* games (see Figure I.2). From speedrunning *The Legend of Zelda* to the professionalization of competitive *Super Smash Bros.* or *StarCraft* to the elaborate espionage surrounding *EVE Online* to the hyper-referentiality of the indie game boom in the late 2000s exemplified by games like *Braid, Super Meat Boy* (2010), and *Fez* (2012), the metagame includes these player-produced games within, around, outside, and about videogames.

In their essay "Metagames, Paragames and Orthogames: A New Vocabulary," Marcus Carter, Martin Gibbs, and Mitchell Harrop (2012, 11) argue that, for players, "there is a broad, conceptually muddled use of the term [*metagame*] that encompasses a wide variety of different play types and styles for which a single term is not useful." Rather than attempting to redefine the word or privilege a narrower definition, the prepositional character of the term *meta* and Howard's and Garfield's definitions of *metagame* linguistically and conceptually perform its common use: to locate the specific cultural practices, material configurations, and historical transformations of twenty-first-century play. Beyond both its etymology and various definitions, metagames are not

Figure I.2. John Romero references the early history of arcade games like *Pac-Man* (left) in *Wolfenstein 3-D* (right) not only for nostalgic effect, but to make a metagame about the conventions, culture, and connectedness of videogames.

simply self-referential games about games or recursive games inside games. They are not just games we play before and after, to and from, or during and between other games. They are not just games in, on, around, above, between, beside, below, or through games. Instead, the metagame expands, as a truly broad label for the contextual, site-specific, and historical attributes of human (and nonhuman) play. What the metagame identifies is not the history of the game, but the history of play.

Meta-Metagaming

Beyond this introduction, *Metagaming* begins with a survey of six metagames. Far from a complete account, the six short stories that make up chapter 1 explore the interleaved and expanded ecology of videogames within the increasingly diffuse circuits of twenty-first-century play. The chapter includes an analysis of normative indie games and feminist art games *about* 1980s videogames, the glitches and exploits that both speedrunners and fighting game competitors find *within* home console games, the cultures of spectatorship and shoutcasting that thrive *around* international e-sports, and the espionage and intrigue that occur when massively multiplayer online (MMO) communities begin to play *without* games. While subsequent chapters feature deeper explorations of specific metagaming practices and their relation to concepts of visuality, disability, seriality, and economy, chapter 1 offers an overview of how play functions as a critical practice and how players have transformed videogames into platforms for making metagames.

Following this survey of six metagames, chapter 2 examines the pursuit of graphic realism through the development of increasingly powerful and complex modeling, rendering, and animation technologies—one of the central rules of the standard metagame that the videogame industry continues to play. In the same way that the restrained naturalism of perspectival rendering in the Renaissance was followed by a more self-conscious and reflexive Mannerist period of visual art, this chapter explores how the nascent discourses of computer-generated imagery in videogaming leads to metagaming practices that experiment with alternative spatial and optical regimes indigenous to digital environments. Adopting the same metagaming strategy deployed in *Braid*, *Super Meat Boy*, and especially *Fez*, anamorphic games such as Valve's *Portal* (2007), Sony's *Echochrome* series (2008–10), Julian Oliver's *levelHead* (2007), and Mark ten Bosch's *Megakure* (forthcoming) technically, aesthetically, and conceptually metagame computer graphics. They are games not only about games, but about *aboutness* itself: games that play with the aesthetic conventions of videogames as a visual medium and intervene in genres that emerged as a consequence of specific graphic technologies. By extending gameplay into new spatial dimensions, these metagames question the very possibility of perspective and in doing so cast anamorphosis as the rule, not the exception, of the embodied experience of vision.

After this analysis of anamorphic vision, chapter 3 examines the practices of blind players and the concept of disability in videogames. From Hideo Kojima's *Metal Gear Solid V: The Phantom Pain* (2015), a graphic spectacle that begins with extensive cutscenes of a limping, hook-handed veteran, to the *The Helen Keller Simulator* (circa 2005), an unpopular Internet meme typically consisting of a black screen with no feedback, chapter 3 considers metagaming in the context of critical disability studies. On one extreme, the hospitalized hero in *The Phantom Pain* allegorizes the hypertrophy of the graphics industry—his single eye standing in for single-point perspective and his hook hand recalling the limited articulation of a game controller. On the other extreme, *The Helen Keller Simulator* represents the atrophy of experimental games without gameplay—a failed simulation that cannot articulate the phenomenal experience of deaf and blind persons, but ultimately serves as a commentary on the impoverished representational capacity of videogames as a medium—the *withoutness* of all games. In contrast to the cinematic spectacle in *The Phantom Pain* and the minimal mechanics in *The Helen Keller Simulator,* chapter 3 concludes with a discussion of alternative approaches to playing *The Legend of Zelda: Ocarina of Time.* Around the same time speedrunners like Narcissa Wright first experimented with temporal constraints in *Ocarina of Time,* Jordan Verner and Drew Wissler began developing metagaming practices through which both blind and blindfolded players navigate videogame spaces and invent new games according to alternate sensory economies. Rather than attempt to represent disability or make games more accessible, these practices reveal that there are always more ways to play.

The recombinatory potential of play is further articulated by the title of chapter 4. "Hundred Thousand Billion Fingers" is a reference to Raymond Queneau's iconic *Hundred Thousand Billion Poems* (1961), a sonnet generator capable of producing 10^{14} unique texts—a quantity that no one reader (or even a million readers) could parse in a lifetime. In the same way that *Hundred Thousand Billion Poems* gestures toward the impossibility of accessing the totality of its many reading paths, videogames like *Super Mario Bros.* limit the player to one isolated, incomplete perspective among an enormous (but finite) set of possible playthroughs emerging from those repetitive, procedural, and discrete elements that drive computational media. Following Jean-Paul Sartre's notion of seriality framed against twenty-first-century theories of network culture by Steven Shaviro and Sherry Turkle, this chapter examines metagaming practices that reveal the serial logics always operating within videogames (a *withinness* that is never fully accessible to human forms of play). From remakes of ROM hacks to speedruns of sequencers, this survey of player-created modifications of *Super Mario Bros.* traces alternative histories of play that escape the seriality of the software itself and reveal the contours of otherwise invisible processes. In the same way that *Project M* (2011) modifies *Super Smash Bros. Brawl* (2008) according to a community metagame and Dustin Browder's game design philosophy responds to the way Korean pros play *StarCraft,* serial games like agwawaf and Jay Pavlina's mashups or Andi McClure and Robin Baumgarten's montages turn play into a form of media production that captures the material traces of play. Whether reading Queneau's book or playing games, the technical constraints of the poem or program reduce play to a range of repetitions. Rather than subjecting the player to the mechanisms of control as defined by the rules of the game (and the Nintendo Corporation), the techniques documented in this chapter metagame their own serial constructs to model the movements of a hundred thousand billion fingers.

The enumeration of a million Marios might be better represented in statistics. Beginning with the history of statistical play—from the wargames of eighteenth-century Germany to the fantasy themes of *Warhammer* (1983–) and the real-time strategy (RTS) action of *Warcraft* (1994–)—chapter 5 investigates the metagaming practices emerging around *Dota 2* (2013), a player-made mod of Blizzard Entertainment's *Warcraft III* (2002) that has evolved into an international e-sport with the help of Valve's digital distribution services, social networks, and virtual economies. Like wargaming, *Warhammer, Warcraft,* and even *StarCraft* and *EVE Online,* the mechanics governing *Dota 2* explore the informatic play of probability. It is no wonder then that the management strategies of Gabe Newell, the co-founder and managing director of Valve, are contingent on the proletarianization of the player. Since the late 1990s, Valve's moneygames have harnessed vectors of information to derive value not from gameplay as such, but from the metagames that operate outside and around computer screens. From simply purchasing and playing videogames to modding, selling, spectating, trading, and predicting future markets, for the past decade metagaming has become synonymous, in these cases, with an untapped ocean of informatic and affective labor around videogames—an *aroundness* that we call the *undercurrency.* As play accretes within this digital undertow, different forms of metagaming are made exchangeable and flattened into one monolithic unit of measure that Valve calls "productivity." Chapter 5 explores the undercurrency through an in-depth analysis one of the most famous plays in the history of *Dota 2,* a sea change in which the statistical play of two tide hunters transformed the metagame.

If anamorphic games *about* games, nonvisual games *without* games, serial games *within* games, and economic games *around* games are sometimes considered cheating or trifling because they play well beyond the standard ways we engage videogames, the metagamers discussed in chapters 2, 3, 4, and 5 are nevertheless granted some leniency within online and offline discussions. Yet some metagamers that stray further from the standard are not shown the same courtesy. Johan Huizinga's (1949, 11) term for the seditious player, or the one who profanes the magic circle and "shatters the play-world" of the game, is the "spoilsport."

Chapter 6 argues that feminist critics of the games industry unwittingly find themselves playing the part of not only what Sara Ahmed (2010) calls the "feminist killjoy" but, more accurately, that of the *feminist spoilsport*. And although Eric Zimmerman (2012) has argued that the naive belief in the magic circle is one of the most pervasive strawmen in game studies (going so far as to suggest that the myth of the magic circle has been replaced by the myth of a "magic circle jerk"), the strident and ongoing vilification of feminist work on videogames indicate that even if the magic circle does not exist, the desire for an ahistorical, escapist gamespace continues to govern the standard metagame and the ideological avatar of play. If the metagame is an environment for life, then it can also be a way to make life hell. So how do you break the metagame? How do you end the aboutness, withoutness, withinness, and aroundness that makes metagaming possible in the first place?

In *Metagaming,* stretched skulls, blind spots, billions of fingers, and turning tides are each followed by a postscript. In the tradition of Katie Salen Tekinbaş and Eric Zimmerman's *Rules of Play* (2003), N. Katherine Hayles' *Electronic Literature* (2008), or Steve Swink's *Game Feel* (2009), each chapter of *Metagaming* not only ends with a call to critical practice—to make metagames—but demonstrates the practice of play through the production of original software designed explicitly alongside this book. Like Ian Bogost's (2013, 92) concept of "carpentry" or "the practice of constructing artifacts as a philosophical practice," each unit of *Metagaming* results from the entanglement of philosophical concepts, the craft of game design, and the cultures of play that surround videogames—a game design philosophy. *Metagaming* begins with the assumption that making criticism does not stand far from critical making, and that the arguments and concepts developed throughout each chapter are a form of play and a form of game design in and of themselves.

To this end chapter 1 includes *Triforce,* a retro-remake of *The Legend of Zelda* that visualizes the topologies of Hyrule in three dimensions. Chapter 2 concludes with *Memento Mortem Mortis,* an impossible puzzle game in which recursively nested skulls from Hans Holbein's *The Ambassadors* (1533) are stretched using a graphics technique called texture mapping. Chapter 3 is accompanied by *It is Pitch Black,* a text-based action-adventure game in which a non-visual 3D space is illuminated only by the quickly scrolling thoughts of two women—Patricia Wilcox, a caver married to Will Crowther before he made *Colossal*

Cave Adventure (1975–76), and Karen Green, a character from Mark Z. Danielewski's novel *House of Leaves* (2000). Chapter 4's *99 Exercises in Play* is inspired by Raymond Queneau's *Exercises de style* (1947) and the constrained writing of the Ouvroir de littérature potentielle or "Oulipo." The game uses World 1–1 from the original *Super Mario Bros.* as a constraint for producing ninety-nine different metagames. Chapter 5 features *Tide Hunter,* a data visualization designed to repurpose the statistical output collected with the help of Bruno "Statsman" Carlucci's replay parser during The Turn of the Tide, a seventeen-second upset regarded as one of the most important plays in the history of *Dota 2.* Each original metagame can found in the online version of the book and downloaded directly at http://manifold.umn.edu/metagaming/ games. Alongside these five metagames, the first and last chapters of the book conclude with a small paper game—our attempt to implicate *Metagaming* itself within a larger metagame. Following the small metagame played at the beginning of this chapter, our first paper game ends right here: ■.

Did you win?

ONE

About, Within, Around, Without

A Survey of Six Metagames

Sooner or later, all our games turn into Calvinball.
—Bill Watterson, *Calvin and Hobbes*

For one thousand and one nights, Scheherazade delayed her execution at the hands of the Shahryar by telling him a never-ending story. Adapted for European audiences by French archaeologist and orientalist Antoine Galland in 1704, textual compilations of Scheherazade's tale of tales were translated from Arabic, edited to remove some of the more erotic elements (along with most of the poems), and supplemented with oral folklore that had no literary precedent such as "Aladdin, or the Wonderful Lamp" and "Ali Baba and the Forty Thieves." Although there are many versions of *One Thousand and One Nights,* Scheherazade's frame narrative is their common feature. Since the conclusion of Galland's twelve-volume publication in 1717, *One Thousand and One Nights* not only continues to fuel an entire genre of orientalist fantasy but also serves as an archetypical example of metanarrative: stories about stories. From oral storytelling in West and South Asia to literary fairy tales in Europe to concert halls, ballet stages, theaters, and silver screens around the world, Scheherazade eventually found herself depicted within the collectible card game *Magic: The Gathering* (1993) (see Figure 1.1).

After the initial release of *Magic* on August 5, 1993, the game's creator and lead designer, Richard Garfield, worked on a strict deadline to finish its first expansion by Christmas that year (Garfield 2002). Authored entirely by Garfield and based explicitly on *One Thousand and One Nights,* the *Arabian Nights* expansion set included new cards based on myths and legends like "Flying Carpets," "Mijae Djinns," and "Ydwen

Figure 1.1. "Shahrazad," a card designed by Richard Garfield and illustrated by Kaja Foglio, first appeared in the *Arabian Nights* expansion of *Magic: The Gathering* in December 1993.

Efreets." Other cards in the collection reflected the cultural imaginary of post–Gulf War America, for example "Army of Allah," "Bazaar of Baghdad," and "Jihad."[1] Finally, *Arabian Nights* portrayed classic characters from Galland's *One Thousand and One Nights* such as Aladdin, Ali Baba, and, of course, Scheherazade. Illustrated by Kaja Foglio and printed for a limited time between December 1993 and January 1994, the game mechanics of the "Shahrazad"[2] *Magic* card match her myth. When the card is played,

> players must leave game in progress as it is and use the cards left in their libraries as decks with which to play a subgame of *Magic*. When subgame is over, players shuffle these cards, return them to libraries, and resume game in progress, with any loser of subgame halving his or her remaining life points, rounding down. (Garfield 1993)

With "Shahrazad," stories within stories become games within games. Thematically and mechanically, the figure of the storyteller stands in for *Magic* itself, a card game Garfield designed to both cultivate and capitalize on previously ancillary aspects of gaming not usually included within the rules like collecting, competition, and community. After all, the "Golden Rule" of *Magic* is that the rules printed on the cards take precedence over the rules printed in the manual—one thousand and one ways to play (Wizards of the Coast, 2014). One of the only cards banned in official tournaments (and one of the more valuable cards in *Arabian Nights*), "Shahrazad" is Richard Garfield's (2002) favorite *Magic* card and represents the game within the game that he calls the "metagame."

As discussed in the introduction, the term *metagame* has been deployed in Nigel Howard's game theory, in Garfield's game design, and by the players of roleplaying games like *Dungeons & Dragons* (1974) and collectible card games like *Magic: The Gathering*. However, over the past decade the term has been increasingly used within the networked communities who make, play, and think about videogames. Beyond Garfield's (2000) examples of games "to," "from," "during," and "between" games, the word *metagame* has become a common label for games about games, games within games, games around games, and games without games. The referentiality of pixelated indie games and Atari-based art installations is a mimetic metagame *about* videogames. The glitches exploited when speedrunning *The Legend of Zelda* (1986) or competing in *Super Smash Bros.* (1999) are material metagames *within* videogames. The psychologies of professional *StarCraft* (1998) players and their audience's reactions during international tournaments are metagames *around* videogames. And the espionage and economy both in and outside *EVE Online* (2003) is a metagame of markets that operate *without* the videogame itself. If videogames conflate the magic circle of social ritual, the white cube of autonomous art, the black box of technical media, and the commodity form of capital into the *ideological avatar of play,* then these six examples of metagaming articulate a ludic practice that profanes the sacred, historicizes art, mediates technology, and de-reifies the fetish.

Difficult to design, impossible to predict, deeply collaborative, and always ephemeral, metagaming undermines the authority of videogames as authored objects, packaged products, intellectual property, and copyrighted code by transforming single-player software into materials for making metagames. This chapter undertakes a survey of six specific metagames that emerge about, within, around, and without videogames. And although these six examples represent some of the popular practices and vocal communities making metagames today, they are by no means taxonomic or complete. Instead, the six case studies introduced in this chapter illustrate the broad range of overlapping practices that characterize twenty-first-century play. If the greatest trick the games industry ever pulled was convincing the world that videogames were games in the first place, then these metagames peek behind the curtain, unmask the magician, and spoil the illusion in the process of inventing new ways to play with loaded dice, fake coins, trick decks, and magic cards.

Indie Game: The Movie, the Industry, the Genre

Walking through Winnipeg in early 2010, Lisanne Pajot and James Swirsky stumbled across a striking image (see Figure 1.2). Buffeted by the winds above some strip mall parking lot or beyond the chain-link perimeter of a pea gravel playground, a piece of vintage videogame equipment swayed overhead. Instead of sneakers strung up by their shoelaces, a Super Nintendo Entertainment System (SNES) controller dangled from a telephone line. How had it got there? Who had thrown it? And why would someone cast their controller up onto the wire? Whether celebrating the end of a school year or toasting the start of a marriage, whether marking the entrance to a crack house or memorializing the site of a street murder, the predominantly North American folk gesture of flinging footwear up onto unreachable public spaces sends a singular message: once crossed, certain thresholds cannot be uncrossed. When old shoes have seen too many steps, they are retired to an afterlife among the power lines. But in Winnipeg, someone had decided to play a different kind of game. Perhaps a bored player had hurled their old equipment up on a lark. Maybe the SNES controller was no longer seen as useful without the now-ubiquitous USB connection. Or it could be that the peripheral had simply been repurposed as raw material for a piece of street art. Whatever the reason, the intersection of mass telecomm with Nintendo equipment signifies the ways in which the aesthetic of retro videogames has been revivified within contemporary networks and networked culture. Swirsky made sure to return to film the abandoned SNES controller, not knowing that the found image would become the title card and iconic logo for his and Pajot's documentary, *Indie Game: The Movie* (2012).

Indie Game: The Movie follows the production of three independently developed videogames and the people who made them. Instead of fea-

Figure 1.2. The image of a Super Nintendo controller tethered to a telephone line appears both at the beginning of Pajot and Swirsky's *Indie Game: The Movie* and in the film's logo.

turing big-budget AAA software and the corporate culture of large studios, Pajot and Swirsky (2012a) focus on "the underdogs of the video game industry . . . who sacrifice money, health and sanity to realize their lifelong dreams." Beyond the stories of Jonathan Blow and David Hellman's *Braid* (2008), Edmund McMillen and Tommy Refenes' *Super Meat Boy* (2010), and Phil Fish and Renault Bédard's *Fez* (2012),[3] *Indie Game: The Movie* marks a historical moment in which the term *indie game* ceased to function solely as a label for a particular mode of independent production or digital distribution and became the common designator for a *genre* of videogames with a shared history and common aesthetic.[4]

Of the three games featured in the film, Pajot and Swirsky frame *Braid* as the successful forerunner. At the time of the filming, *Braid* had already shipped, garnered critical acclaim, and more than repaid Jonathan Blow's personally financed, $200,000 wager. A relatively slow-paced, contemplative platformer that at least initially deemphasizes reflex action in lieu of puzzle solving, *Braid*'s pastoral, painterly landscapes are complicated by the player's ability to pause, rewind, replay, and manipulate multilinear and multiscalar time. While a few games have incorporated the ability to reverse mistakes in real time,[5] *Braid* requires the player to *game the game* and use time manipulation not only to overcome precise platforming hurdles but also to navigate complex temporal puzzles and piece together the narrative of the main character, Tim. Through the Mario-like figure of Tim (an embodiment of the concept of *Time*), *Braid* weaves together three forms of obsessive, masculine desire: the ludic challenges of retro videogames, the courtly love quest for an unattainable princess, and the scientific models of technological progress that drive the military industrial complex.[6] The game explores the relationship between digital media and the atomic age, and between gamer culture and consumer behavior—a critique of in-game item collection, level grinding, and achievement hunting as well as the repetition of buying into the same videogame franchises year after year.

While Blow reflects on his success in the film *Indie Game*, Edmund McMillen and Tommy Refenes race to the release date of *Super Meat Boy*, a frenetic and fast-paced platformer driven by the twin logics of seemingly insurmountable difficulty and instant, infinite replay.[7] The eponymous Meat Boy, an anthropomorphic cube of meat with black button eyes and a toothy grin, leaves a trail of viscera as players maneuver him past saw blades and salt. Whether stopping on a dime or drifting along screen-wide parabolic jumps, Meat Boy's rapid, repeatable actions stress the interplay among real-time control, spatial simulation, and "polish" that Steve Swink (2009, 8) calls "game feel."[8] Like *Braid, Super Meat Boy* explicitly references (and shares an acronym with) *Super Mario Bros.* (1985)—an obvious metagame. In their game, McMillen and Refenes recast the classic love triangle between Mario, Princess Toadstool, and Bowser with their own Oedipal trio: the phallic hero, Meat Boy; the prophylactic damsel in distress, Bandage Girl; and the preemie home-wrecker, Dr. Fetus.

Alongside Blow's tranquil reflection and McMillen and Refenes' impending release depicted in *Indie Game,* Phil Fish's five-year legal, technical, and emotional struggle to make *Fez* provides as much dramatic conflict and anxiety as is possible for a documentary about computer programmers. Whereas *Braid* innovates in terms of time manipulation and *Super Meat Boy* profits from speed, difficulty, and repetition, *Fez* begins with a simulated computer crash that transforms Fish's idyllic 2D pixelscapes through the mathematical logic of 3D rotation, translation, and projection (an anamorphic technique that appears in games like *Echochrome* [2008] and is further examined in chapter 2). Piloting Gomez, a small pixelated sprite wearing the titular fez, players wander through an eccentric world in which rotating the viewpoint does not simply shift the 3D perspective, but also reconstitutes the landscape according to the logic of the 2D screen.

Despite the headaches and heartaches dramatized in *Indie Game: The Movie,* all three games were each wildly successful[9] and, although certainly not the first independently produced games, *Braid, Super Meat Boy,* and *Fez* represent the boom and subsequent gold rush in the late 2000s in which many independent game developers attempted to cash in on the emerging market for small-scale games that combine nostalgic graphics with novel mechanics distributed via online marketplaces like Microsoft's Xbox Live Arcade, Sony's PlayStation Store, Nintendo's Wii Shop Channel, and Valve's Steam. While the stories of Blow, McMillen, Refenes, and (eventually) Fish's successes inspired other first-time game devs, *Braid, Super Meat Boy,* and *Fez* have something else in common in addition to the logistics of their independent production, digital distribution on Xbox Live Arcade, and massive sales: explicit references to the mechanics and aesthetics of the Nintendo Entertainment System in the mid- to late 1980s. Indie games, as an aesthetic genre, recover a history of play in the form of a metagame that represents, references, or otherwise cites the graphics and gameplay of other games. They are games *about* games (see Figure 1.3).

As mentioned in the introduction, Andy Baio's description of metagames as "playable games about videogames" is distinct from the more common use of the term to describe the history of play or the current popular strategies. In his blog post entitled "Metagames: Games about

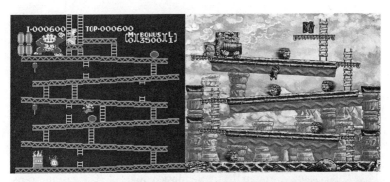

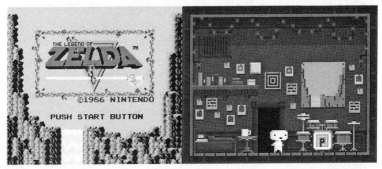

Figure 1.3. *Braid* (top right), *Super Meat Boy* (middle right), and *Fez* (bottom right) explicitly reference videogames from the 1980s like *Donkey Kong* (top left), *Super Mario Bros.* (middle left), and *The Legend of Zelda* (bottom left) respectively.

Games," Baio assembles a long list of examples, noting that "most of these, like *Desert Bus* [c. 1995] or *Quest for the Crown* [2003], are one-joke games for a quick laugh. Others, like *Cow Clicker* [2010] and *Upgrade Complete* [2009], are playable critiques of game mechanics."[10] Echoing Baio's definition of *metagame,* in *Indie Game: The Movie,* Fish calls *Fez* "a game about games," and the same logic could be applied to *Braid* and *Super Meat Boy* (Pajot and Swirsky 2012b). In *Braid,* Tim runs and jumps along faux *Donkey Kong* (1981) platforms, stomps Goomba-like enemies, and evades piranha plants from *Super Mario Bros.* (1985). At the end of each world, he encounters Mario's signature flagpole flying an international maritime signal that attempts to warn the player against progressing further and a Yoshi-esque dinosaur who subverts the "I'm sorry, but the princess is in another castle" trope through an endless deferral.

Like *Braid*'s Mario-isms, McMillen and Refenes' game is packed with Flash-animated parodies in which Meat Boy, Bandage Girl, and Dr. Fetus play out Oedipal versions of cutscenes from classic titles like *Street Fighter* (1987), *Castlevania* (1986), *Adventures of Lolo* (1989), *Ninja Gaiden* (1988), *Mega Man 2* (1988), *Pokémon* (1996), *Ghosts n' Goblins* (1985), *Bubble Bobble* (1986), and, of course, the original *SMB, Super Mario Bros.* On top of its many explicit shoutouts, *Super Meat Boy*'s various "warp zones" temporarily adopt the resolution and palette constraints of vintage platforms like Nintendo's handheld GameBoy, feature Meat Boy–inspired art by other game designers, and, when completed, unlock characters from other independently developed games[11] like Michael O'Reilly's hyper-referential *I Wanna Be the Guy* (2007), Anna Anthropy's "masocore" platformer *Mighty Jill Off* (2008),[12] and even McMillen's original animations for Tim in *Braid* (graphic assets that Blow ultimately decided to remake with Hellman). While these quotations appear to celebrate the cross-platform community of successful independent game developers, they also further establish indie games as a genre with similar graphics and gameplay, canonizing a cohort of other successful 2D platformers released in the late 2000s.

In the same way that *Braid* and *Super Meat Boy* remix retro mechanics and reference more than a few old games, *Fez* begins in Gomez's bedroom, a pixelated square adorned with a low-resolution poster of the landscape from the original *The Legend of Zelda* (1986) title screen. After the player has climbed to the top of a tetromino town (made of various arrangements of *Tetris* [1989] blocks) and acquiring the ability to rotate space, the world "crashes," freezing the game on a glitchy kill screen before rebooting to a Polytron Corporation version of a motherboard's BIOS readout. As the player goes about "defragmenting" the gameworld by shifting perspective to gather pieces of a monolith-like hypercube, another game emerges from within the game. The collectathon in *Fez* functions as a prelude to a cryptographic puzzle that initially required a massive, collaborative effort on the part of the players to first decode then deploy the hypercube's instructions within the gameworld. More than just a coincidence, the fact that each of these indie games recalls and reinvents games like *Super Mario Bros., The Legend of Zelda,* and *Tetris* reveals the personal history of these three designers and how play becomes a building block for a metagaming practice.

Over the course of thirty years, *Super Mario Bros., The Legend of Zelda,* and *Tetris* have become platforms for making new games. If Jonathan Blow, Edmund McMillen, Tommy Refenes, and Phil Fish are any indication, these are the games with which Nintendo "zapped an American industry, captured your dollars, and enslaved your children" (Sheff 1993).[13] After the North American home console market was first saturated and then expunged in the early 1980s, Nintendo rebooted the medium by marketing their "entertainment system" as a children's toy while designing the hardware to mimic those appliances already at home in the American den. As Jamin Warren observes in *Indie Game,* "for anyone that grew up basically after 1975, 1980 or so, we were the first generation to grow up with our parents giving us games . . . the first generation that grew up with videogames but not as an active purchasing choice" (Pajot and Swirsky 2012b). As indicated by the fact that no other women aside from Ed McMillen's spouse, Danielle McMillen, is interviewed in the documentary, the unquestioned "us" in Warren's statement is historical, geographic, and gendered. These indie games are not simply the byproduct of an independent or self-funded production or the result of the success of digital distribution platforms in 2008, but also reflect an aesthetic paradigm based on the history of North American men growing up in the eighties and nineties. From parking lots and playgrounds to early publications and consumer phone lines, the oral and transmedial history of playing console games lives on as a nostalgic memory, a design platform, and (according to the sales of these games) a successful marketing strategy.

While at the time of their release *Braid, Super Meat Boy,* and *Fez* distinguished themselves according to their unique graphics, inventive gameplay mechanics, and the personal histories of their developers, these differences are underwritten by a structural homogeneity based on their relation to the North American videogame industry in the late 2000s as well as a much longer history of cultural colonization and commodification of precarious labor. As Simon Parkin (2014) notes, "stories of sudden indie-game riches are appealing. They have a fairy-tale quality, the moral of which is often, 'Work hard and you will prevail' (even though this kind of overnight success is often the result of an un-replicable recipe involving privilege, education, talent, toil, and timing)." It is hardly a coincidence that Pajot and Swirsky's three primary examples of indie games were each personally funded projects produced by two-person teams of young white men. It is also no coincidence that these examples were all 2D platformers with clever mechanics and retro references. And finally, it is no coincidence that they made millions on Microsoft's digital distribution service. These coincidences coalesce in *Indie Game: The Movie* because the film itself mirrors the logic of the marketplace by deploying the term *indie game* as a way to valorize only certain kinds of precarious labor practices—the ones that paid off. The very concept of indie games circulates as a form of cultural imperialism that both colonizes profitable forms of independent production and sanitizes them for mass consumption. Adopting the term *indie games* from the much wider spectrum of creative and experimental labor, then applying it as a general descriptor for a specific form of game making, reduces *all* independent development to this particular aesthetic and mechanic genre of videogames and also reduces *all* independent developers to those white, North American men able to make a living developing games in the wake of the global economic collapse beginning in 2008.[14] Anna Anthropy's (2012) blunt summary of the film is more direct: "White guys who grew up playing *Super Mario* sacrifice every part of their lives to the creation of personal but nonetheless traditional videogames."

In terms of geographic space, Pajot and Swirsky's admittedly compelling narrative ignores those modes of independent game development occurring in the gray-market releases of ROM hacks and language mods in China or the *doujin* fan games repurposing graphics from anime and videogames alike in Japan or the small, mobile games produced after hours with the borrowed resources of American and Japanese companies outsourcing to India (Shaw 2013, 184–85).[15] In terms of a longer timeline, independent game development did not begin with "indie games"—a point Bennett Foddy convincingly argues in his historical survey of independent game development during the 2014 "State of the Union" address at IndieCade East. As Foddy (2014) contends, the notion that *Braid, Super Meat Boy,* and *Fez* inaugurate the emergence of independent game development is a myth bolstered by the common historical narrative that the videogame crash of 1983 and subsequent commercialization of games for home consoles arrested independent production until the late 2000s. A longer history might start with the level editors shipped with *Lode Runner* (1983) and *ZZT* (1991) or the all-in-one game creation systems like *Garry Kitchen's GameMaker* (1985) and the various *Construction Kits* of the 1980s. Mark Overmars' re-release of *GameMaker* in 1999 and ASCII and Enterbrain's *RPG Maker* in 2000 became viable platforms before the production of games within Macromedia's Shockwave and then Flash took off throughout the 2000s. Ironically, the emergence of the term *indie game* as a label and genre in the late 2000s signals the moment independent game development became dependent.

Still swinging somewhere overhead, the purple and lavender buttons of a specifically *North American* Super Nintendo controller blend in with the cloudy Winnipeg sky. In Japan and Europe, the brightly colored, red, blue, yellow, and green buttons mimetically mirrored the Super Nintendo's logo—a set of four circles, offset from one another in the signature colors of Nintendo's mascot (the blue-and-red-clad Mario sporting a yellow cape and straddling a green dinosaur). By contrast, the buttons on the American, Canadian, and Mexican counterpart were replaced with more subdued hues. The logo itself, appearing on cartridge packaging and game manuals in North America, was converted from the RGB color scheme to grayscale hatching that aped the look of CRT interlacing. Although some criticized Pajot and Swirsky for their choice of interface, arguing that the red, black, and gray controller from Nintendo's previous console, the NES, would have been a more appropriate icon for a movie about three eighties-inspired indie games, this distinctly regional controller is poetic in a different way. The sight of those purple buttons in the sky not only signifies the historical relocation of videogames from the home console to the networked clouds, but reveals a particularly North American form of ideology naturalized in the production of indie games. Whereas folk culture is often assumed to somehow exist outside of or historically predate capitalism, the acts of both shoe tossing and controller tossing signify the emergence of a postconsumer and aftermarket practice—a form of metagaming built not before or without, but after and within those discarded technical, historical, and cultural systems cast off the beaten "upgrade path" of global capitalism (Harpold 2007, 3).

A Giant Joystick: Alternative Control
and the Standard Metagame

Before the Super Nintendo controller swayed in the breeze overhead, there was a giant joystick. Whereas controller tossing in *Indie Game: The Movie* signifies the metagame of a privileged group of designers that has since become a standardized aesthetic and software genre, there are countless other metagames that circulate outside the normative structures of play and production represented in Pajot and Swirsky's film. What other interfaces swing alongside Nintendo's classic controllers on telephone poles across America? The knobs, dials, and joysticks of the pre-D-pad era[16] of Odyssees, Fairchilds, and Ataris float alongside Sony's and Microsoft's now-ubiquitous USB devices (though many must also pile up on the ground, cordless). Mice and keyboards, balance boards and dance pads, Virtual Boys and Oculus Rifts, and scores of light guns also sway in the breeze. Beyond mass-produced interfaces, imagine all the mods, custom builds, and one-off oddities hanging on the wire. Imagine a quadriplegic controller with a series of sip-and-puff sensors mounted to a mouthpiece or a chin-controlled joystick assembled by hand and supported by a homemade PVC pipe and plywood stand.[17] Imagine an eye writer built by an international community to aid an L.A. graffiti artist with ALS.[18] Imagine wearable accessories for intimate, two-player performance art[19] or repurposed rumble packs for cybersexual encounters.[20] Imagine a giant joystick.

The controllers shipped with consoles, individually sold in stores and even remade within the aftermarket economies trailing the release of most mainstream videogame hardware, are designed to function as a standard interface between player and game. The Super Nintendo controller hanging in Winnipeg is just one part of a larger technological platform. In their study of the Atari VCS, *Racing the Beam,* Ian Bogost and Nick Montfort (2009, 2) define a platform as "a particular standard or specification before any particular implementation of it." Within these standards, play is generalized in two interrelated dimensions. First, Super Nintendo games, for example, are explicitly designed in terms of a control idiom based on the states of twelve binary RAM values that map the states of twelve buttons.[21] In this sense, videogames standardize play by responding only to the changes within this set of discrete values. The umpire is automated within the mechanics of the software and every pitch is always already in or out, fair or foul, strike or ball—there is no in-between. Second, as a result of these binary buttons, players are standardized. Universal control assumes a universal body, and since the Super Nintendo controller was included as the default input for the platform, most games designed for the SNES anticipate bi-dexterous players (with two mobile hands able to act independently). Whereas standardized control standardizes play and produces normative players, alternative interfaces do not simply make videogames accessible, but radically transform what videogames are and what they can do.

From 9-volt AC adapters to North American controllers (and even the various chips within cartridges and consoles alike), the equipment packaged with and advertised as part of a videogame platform encourages players to conflate "official" hardware with the rules of the game—what could be called the *standard metagame*. As with "indie games," the standard metagame operates as an unquestioned ideology structuring twenty-first-century play and comingling what happens in front of the television screen with a specific commodity. Despite the submarket of turbo controllers and Game Genies, in many cases using the "official" controller becomes an unspoken rule restricting play rather than one of many possible preferences. Games scholar and HobbyGameDev founder Chris DeLeon (2013, 7–8) boils this standard way to play down to five "meta rules":

Rule 1. The game is to be interacted with only by standard input controllers . . .

Rule 2. The physical integrity of the hardware is not to be violated . . .

Rule 3. The player should be directly and independently responsible for the actions made during the game . . .

Rule 4. If playing against other players, the other players should not be disturbed outside the game . . . nor unfairly distracted within the game by meta commands that are not part of the core gameplay . . .

Rule 5. The computer game should be played as released and/or patched by the developer.

Unlike the speed and scale of a videogame's mechanical processes (e.g., the height of Mario's jump or width of his hitbox), nothing is stopping the player from breaking DeLeon's meta rules. Though it goes unsaid, this standard metagame structures the lusory attitude players unconsciously assume when picking up a controller and powering on a console. These meta rules are not a deterministic or involuntary mechanic but a completely voluntary result of a set of assumptions about videogames as a cultural commodity and mass medium. It is precisely through the popularization of the standard metagame that videogames begin to operate as the ideological avatar of play in the twenty-first century. Play as a synonym for possibility is replaced wholesale by the standard metagame. DeLeon (2013, 8) writes, "to return to [Bernard] Suits' notion of rules as forcing inefficient play by making a golfer rely on the golf club to achieve the goal, the central rule of computer games is then that the player is supposed to rely only on the controller during play to achieve the goal state." Change the controller, change the game.

Two decades after the Atari VCS, or "Video Computer System," defined a generation of 8-bit, cartridge-based home consoles, Mary Flanagan built *[giantJoystick]* (2006). According to Montfort and Bogost, Atari's "rubber-coated black controller with its one red button [had] become emblematic of the Atari VCS and of retro gaming, if not of video games in general" well before Nintendo invented the D-pad (Montfort and Bogost 2009, 22). True to its name, Flanagan's *[giantJoystick]* is a ten-foot-tall working version of Atari's classic controller—a game *about* videogames in general (see Figure 1.4). Originally a commission for the Game/Play exhibit at the HTTP Gallery in London, *[giantJoystick]* looms large in the white cube, denaturalizing both Atari's games and the site of play through a massive scale change. After climbing the three steps running alongside the left side of *[giantJoystick]*'s boxy base, players find themselves suddenly on a different kind of platform, wrestling the hexagonal, seven-foot-tall, anthropomorphic stick. The joystick is so large that no single player can easily manipulate both it and its accompanying red button. With Flanagan's *[giantJoystick]* the privatized, domestic play of the home console era is made public and collaborative not through the networked connectivity of some massively multiplayer online game like *Second Life* (2003) or *World of Warcraft* (2004) but through a local, multiplayer metagame. Rather than leveraging official hardware, default controllers, or nostalgic representations of retro games to reinforce the standard metagame on contemporary platforms, Flanagan breaks the unspoken rules of that game through a scale change that activates play as a site for critical practice. The diminished, "childlike scale" not only invokes a culture of 8-bit nostalgia and child's play, but deliberately attenuates the control and power of individual users (Flanagan 2006a). Instead of engaging in a fantasy of individual mastery or

Figure 1.4. Players collaboratively control Flanagan's *[giantJoystick]* (left) at the opening of Game/Play at the HTTP Gallery in 2006 (right). Photographs by Mary Flanagan, 2006 (left), reproduced with permission; and Régine Debatty, 2007 (right), reproduced via Creative Commons Attribution-ShareAlike 2.0 License.

one-to-one input and output, communities of players adopt an arduous controller and challenge the ableist discourse structuring the ideology of the standard metagame.

Before building *[giantJoystick]* at DMC Fabrication in Brooklyn, Flanagan's artistic practice explored play through academic research and social activism. A year prior to *[giantJoystick]*'s debut at the HTTP Gallery, Flanagan theorized a feminist game design philosophy through the concept of "playculture," the title of her 2005 dissertation for the University of the Arts in London. In contrast to DeLeon's five normative meta rules, in the catalog for *Game/Play* Flanagan (2006b) defines playculture as

> first, the way in which participants engage in acts of subversion of many computer systems, and second, the way in which players perform and play *with, in,* and *on* such sites. Play is a social act, and computerised play makes actual technologies into "locations" for play. (Emphasis added)

Playculture articulates the time and space of what Flanagan (2009, 6) later calls "critical play." Like playculture, metagames cannot be reduced to general, standardized modes of play. The metagame is not only the social, local, and performative site that Flanagan marks "with, in, and on" videogames, but also constantly (even if unconsciously, or only minimally) subverts the ideological assumptions that condition the culture of play. Although there is always a friction between the historically contingent acts of play and the abstract rules of institutionalized games, how can intervention occur within a standard platform when it is constructed, either physically or socially, in such a way that denies access to significant populations of people? How can change occur within a medium that many players never have access to in the first place? How can we become conscious of the fact that we are always playing, making, and breaking metagames (even when we do not know it)? Flanagan's response to the lack of consciousness and inclusivity has been to change not only the controller, but the players.

In 1999 Flanagan founded TECHarts, "a community action project that encourages girls from the city of Buffalo and Erie County to receive an affordable hands-on education in computers, technology and media literacy" (Squeeky Wheel 2014). This was one of the early examples of the ways in which women are working together to reprogram the standard metagame. A decade later, groups like Dames Making Games in Toronto (est. 2012) and Code Liberation in New York City (est. 2013) regularly arrange meetups, workshops, classes, and spaces for women to learn how to code and make games.[22] These feminist organizations are designed as cultural platforms oriented less around the production of playable objects and more around community play, support, and solidarity. The result of such activities is a reinvestment in playculture as a practice that breaks all the rules of the standard metagame. Feminist game spaces (and the games they design) challenge not only the supposed individuality of play, the sanctity of hardware and software products, the authority of the original developer, and the generality of the standard controller, but also the lack of diversity that exists in contemporary game design, both independent and industrial.

Establishing the link between feminist theory and disability studies, Rosemarie Garland-Thomson (1997, 19) shows that "many parallels exist between the social meanings attributed to female bodies and those assigned to disabled bodies. Both the female and the disabled body are cast as deviant and inferior; both are excluded from full participation in public as well as economic life." Along with the emergence of feminist cohorts, organizations like AbleGamers, AudioGames, and Switch Games have approached issues of access and embodiment from a different angle. As AbleGamers write in their manifesto on inclusive game design, "for the mainstream gaming markets, the best practices of universal design cannot be applied" (Barlet and Spohn 2012, 8). When it comes to bodies, there are no universals. The growth of relatively affordable[23] physical computing and 3D fabrication makes it possible for videogame controllers to be individually tailored through both DIY customizations and microeconomic models targeting specific bodies, not general audiences. Alongside custom fabrications like Flanagan's *[giantJoystick]*, individually or specifically modeled alternative controllers destabilize the distinctions between able and disabled bodies by demonstrating the radical specificity and irreducibility of both people and play that has always existed alongside the discursive abstraction of the normative player. The standard way to play is a matter of cultural and historical production—a not-so-lusory attitude toward videogames that privileges a normative, or standardized, body. Metagames like *[giantJoystick]* (as well as the blind and blindfolded playthroughs of *The Legend of Zelda: Ocarina of Time* [1998], discussed in chapter 3) disrupt the dominant way we play, reveal the invisible rules guiding play, and offer an alternative to the standard metagame. Nonstandardized players use nonstandardized interfaces to play nonstandardized games. Disability is the rule, not the exception, and radical accessibility means individualized or specific—not standardized—control. There is no standard player and, in some form, every player is always already disabled.

Operating *within* Flanagan's *[giantJoystick]* are the guts of another joystick: a Jakks Pacific plug-and-play, all-in-one controller-console. Not simply a USB device for Atari emulators like Stella or an aftermarket peripheral for the original 2600 platform itself, in 2002 the American toy company Jakks Pacific produced this stand-alone version of Atari's iconic controller. Like Atari's own Flashback series of plug-and-play consoles that can output to most televisions and projectors through a simple AV cable,[24] Jakks Pacific's Atari-like joystick came with ten licensed games including arcade classics like *Breakout* (1978) and *Asteroids* (1979) alongside titles first released for home console like *Yar's Revenge* (1981) or *Adventure* (1980).[25] Beyond solving practical problems related to the display and exhibition of retro videogames,[26] the joystick within *[giantJoystick]* conflates controller, cartridge, and console into a single object—literalizing the popular metonymy between interface and media. Matthew Kirschenbaum (2008, 36) calls this conflation a "medial ideology" that "substitutes popular representations of a medium, socially constructed and culturally activated to perform specific kinds of work, for a more comprehensive treatment of the material particulars of a given technology." This is not "screen essentialism," a term Kirschenbaum

(2008, 31) borrows from Nick Montfort, in which graphics stand in for computing in general, but perhaps a kind of "controller essentialism" or an even more general "interface essentialism." Interface essentialism means that all manner of interfaces, from standard controllers to a product's packaging and even television commercials, not only represent but also reduce and replace their constitutive media platforms. Neither an official controller nor an Atari 2600, Flanagan's *[giantJoystick]* compresses the platform to a single interface, and, in doing so, effaces the particularities of the Atari Video Computer System. *[giantJoystick]* is not a metagame about Atari's popular controller or particular software, but a game *within* a game and *about* the games that occur *around* all videogames—an intervention at the site of play.

All the Categories are Arbitrary: Speedrunning *The Legend of Zelda*

as oot any% shifts back to vc-j, my mind wanders to the ess adapters
and to the virtual console, that doesn't crash when gim is performed
and to the old kakariko route, resetting the console to save time
and to the timing method, the arbitrary start and end points
my mind wanders. (Wright 2015)

Before she quit speedrunning, before she got carpal tunnel syndrome, before she began hormone therapy, and before she wrote "all the categories are arbitrary," Narcissa Wright made a living playing *The Legend of Zelda*. On her Twitch.tv channel in 2014, video capture of home console output was accompanied by webcam footage of glittery, viridian fingernails either grabbing a white GameCube controller or clasping a plug-and-play console—not a Jakks Pacific, but a handheld, Chinese version of the Nintendo 64 called iQue. Livestreaming on Twitch to an audience of thousands, Wright monetized her time spent speedrunning the original Japanese release of *The Legend of Zelda: The Wind Waker* (2002) and a rare Chinese version of its predecessor, *The Legend of Zelda: Ocarina of Time,* released only on the iQue (see Figure 1.5).

Part an act of censorship intended to "protect the mental and physical development of the nation's youth," and part economic protectionism, at the turn of the millennium the Chinese Ministry of Culture enacted a ban "forbidding any company or individual to produce and sell electronic game equipment and accessories to China" (Clark 2013; Ashcraft 2010). With Nintendo, Sega, and Sony's consoles relegated to gray-market goods, plug-and-play controllers reminiscent of the Jakks Pacific's Atari joystick were manufactured to skirt the ban in mainland China. In 2003 Nintendo collaborated with the Chinese company iQue to build the *Shén Yóu Ji* or Divine Gaming Machine commonly known as the iQue player—a blocky, pseudo-off-brand controller-console that uses an external memory card instead of cartridges to load Chinese versions of Nintendo 64 games like *Ocarina of Time* and *Super Smash Bros*. Among many other subtle differences like a decreased number of polygons loaded at a time (which results in less lag), the display rate of Chinese text in the iQue release of *Ocarina of Time* is slightly faster than Japanese text and significantly faster than English. Whereas the Jakks Pacific installed inside Flanagan's *[giantJoystick]* was probably selected as a matter of convenience despite its architectural differences from Atari's original platform, Wright selected the iQue precisely because its various electrical and material discrepancies accelerated the *Ocarina of Time* metagame.[27] My mind wanders "to the ique player, the fast memory card, the old gamecube laser / to the ps2 disc speed, the sloppy port, the hd remaster / to the pal cartridge, the patched glitch, the japanese text speed / to the turbo controller, the rules / the rules!" (Wright 2015).

As the fifth installment of the classic series, *Ocarina of Time* represents Link and Zelda's 3D debut, a daring reinvention of the action-adventure genre on the Nintendo 64 overseen by the original team members of Nintendo's infamous R&D4: Shigeru Miyamoto, Takashi Tezuka, Toshihiko Nakago, and Koji Kondo.[28] Released when Wright was nine years old, *Ocarina of Time* defined that year's Christmas and, along with *Super Smash Bros.*, would occupy her time growing up in Steven's Point, Wisconsin (Li 2014). After moving three hours south to study graphic design at Chicago's Columbia College in 2007, Wright also became a student of the subculture of speedrunning. Quietly lurking on the forums at Speed Demos Archive (SDA), a community hub and clearinghouse dedicated to publishing and archiving high quality speedruns or real-time attacks, Wright learned that speedruns are "fast playthroughs of video games . . . [in which players] use every method at their disposal, including glitches, to minimize time" (Speed Demos Archive 2014). From one perspective, the goal of speedrunning is self-evident: play games fast. But conceptual clarity gives way to cultural, political, and practical

Figure 1.5. On Wright's Twitch.tv channel in 2013 and 2014, *The Legend of Zelda: Ocarina of Time* (right) is accompanied by timed splits (top left) and webcam footage of glittery fingernails (bottom left).

problems. By adding an additional rule to the standard metagame, the speedrunning community not only changes the way games are played but also questions the very ontology of videogames. When does a game start and end? What is the definitive version of a given title? How do software and hardware technically operate? Why spend time playing the same game over and over? And—perhaps more immediately—who cares? Speedrunners self-consciously debate and collaboratively decide on answers to these questions which, when set in motion, function, like all metagames, as a form of game design. The voluntary rules invented by speedrunners, called "categories," are metagames adopted by players that evolve in, on, around, and through the media ecology of hardware, software, and community comprising a game like *Ocarina of Time.* "All the categories are arbitrary / perhaps marksoupial said it best: / do whatever you want, there are literally no rules" (Wright 2015).

Completing a game as quickly as possible, a category that runners call "Any%" (in contrast to 100% completion), is the gold standard of speedrunning—a simple rule that can transform almost any videogame into a complex metagame.[29] How Any% is put into practice, however, changes according to that game's community (as evidenced by the difference between real-time attacks and tool-assisted speedruns of *Super Mario Bros.,* analyzed in chapter 4). Does the timer start when the console powers on or when the player first gains control after the main menu? Does the timer end when the last enemy is defeated, with the last input, or when credits begin to roll? What if there are no credits or final boss? What mechanics, aside from those outlined in the rulebook, can be exploited to save time? What gameplay sequences can be broken or skipped? Speedrunning categories are often more influenced by those aspects of a game that generate community interest and ludic pleasure rather than the orthodox ideologies or ontologies that define videogames in terms of authorial intent or technical operation. Instead of dogmatic adherence to hierarchical taxonomies and rigid definitions, there is a plasticity to speedrunning categories, which tend to multiply and transform as the metagame evolves through the community's collective research, discovery, and exploitation of new techniques for playing each game. "All the categories are arbitrary" (Wright 2015).

Back in Chicago in the late 2000s, Wright (2013b) became obsessed with the programming infelicities in her favorite *Zelda* game, remembering, "It was my hobby in college to discover how memory manipulation works in *Ocarina of Time,* specifically Bottle Adventure Glitch" and, years later, a technique called 'Wrong Warping.'" Most Nintendo 64 games (and many of the first generation of videogames with 3D graphics) can be mechanically exploited in terms of character movement, and *Ocarina of Time* has its fair share of collision detection failure, out-of-bounds exploration, and sequence breaking due to discrepancies between physics systems and animation states, especially at extreme velocities or angles of approach. The types of exploits that captured Wright's interest, however, were those that directly exposed the computational logic of videogames by transforming the gamespace into a programming interface capable of both pointing to specific memory addresses and replacing their values at will. Hyrule is not just an interactive 3D environment but also an integrated development environment (IDE).[30] Whereas the Bottle Adventure Glitch allows players to arbitrarily write a predetermined set of hexadecimal values to the memory addresses that represent items stored in Link's inventory (in order to produce unintended items), Wrong Warping allows players to write arbitrary hexadecimal values to memory addresses that correspond to cutscenes occurring within each geographic location in the game (in order to warp to unintended locations). Although manipulating memory is, in the broadest sense, what videogames do (like when Mario grabs a coin and the score is incremented or when he travels down a warp pipe and a new level address is loaded), exploits within *Ocarina of Time* let players update their inventory without grabbing the item or warp to a room without walking through the right door. Outside of authored sequences of combat, navigation, and dialog constructed according to the affordances of the various technical systems driving *Ocarina of Time,* unintended exploits like Bottle Adventure and Wrong Warp permit speedrunners to play the game *within* the game and invent metagames limited not merely by mechanical constraint but by the voluntary choices of players. "To warp or not to warp" becomes the question. My mind wanders "to the practice, the process, the savestate / to the gameshark, the game saver, the gecko code / to the cheating, the splicing, the policing / the audio waveform / my mind wanders" (Wright 2015).

Of course, there is no page for "Bottle Adventure" or "Wrong Warp" in the official manual shipped with *Ocarina of Time.* These exploits did not appear in strategy guides or even fan-made walkthroughs until well after Nintendo ceased production on the original cartridges.[31] Although official players' guides work to both educate players on how best to enjoy *Zelda* and legitimize certain kinds of play, the mechanics of the game extend well beyond what is outlined on carefully constructed pages. Seemingly mundane or supposedly intuitive actions like creating a save file, starting a game, using the control stick to navigate, or squeezing the Z trigger to target enemies[32] are nevertheless just one, normative interpretation of *Ocarina of Time*'s complex functions. Beyond these "intended" mechanics, the incredible speed and enormous scale of digital media guarantees the emergence of exploits—recombinatory rules operating outside both the experience of any one player and even the expectations of the original programmers. For example, if a Nintendo 64 is powered on with the control stick tilted, that angle will be calibrated as the default position, altering the value of stick's neutral position and, in the case of Nintendo 64 games such as *Doom 64* (1997), permitting an extra range of directional motion—a position faster than fast.[33] My mind wanders "to the homebrewed wii, the region freed wad, / to the replacement joystick, to the hori mini pad, / to the rubber band, tape, and grease / my mind wanders" (Wright 2015).

In *Cheating: Gaining Advantage in Videogames,* Mia Consalvo (2009, 114) explains that "exploits don't involve a player actively changing code in a game or deceiving other players; instead, they are 'found' actions or items that accelerate or improve a player's skills, actions, or abilities in some way that the designer did not originally intend, yet in a manner that does not actively change code or involve deceiving others." Adopting a similar attitude, Speed Runs Live (2014) allows all glitches because "the game merely executes the code in the way it was programmed to do. The game is the law. If you start trying to get at 'developer intentions,' then you start a game of guesswork trying to figure out what exactly was intended or not." The ideology of speedrunning recognizes videogames exclusively in terms of a discrete state space produced by the operation of specific hardware and software (usually sanctioned releases by major companies, as is the case with Nintendo's iQue). If videogames are agnostic to how they are played and every operation yields states of equal value, then there are no glitches, nothing is out of bounds, and the intentions of an author and audience are a completely arbitrary metagame in and of themselves. Furthermore, despite the fact that programmers and players alike may author algorithms to reliably arrive at a given possibility, there is both a formal and a phenomenal gap between the electrical manipulation of bits and bytes and the conscious experience of play. Although videogames operate in a cybernetic loop with and alongside human players through the contrivances of real-time control, they always execute *outside* individual experience. The possibilities of play are so immense that no one person could ever hope to access, let alone master, the range of games within these software sandboxes. *Ocarina of Time* is no different. Even after a decade of glitch hunting, there is always the possibility for new play to emerge through new discoveries, new attitudes, or new self-composed constraints. As Wright (2013c) admits,

> While I believe pretty strongly that 'you can always go faster, always,' I do see people meeting goals and saying 'I'm done! I'm done!' The closest to that happening was when I got 4:57:XX for *The Wind Waker* before dry storage. Dry storage got discovered and I was reinvigorated to stay on top of the current metagame, and I have been ever since.

And she did. Wright went from forum lurker to prolific speedrunner, glitch hunter, community organizer, and, as of July 20, 2014, the world record holder for *Ocarina of Time* with an Any% time of 18:10 on the iQue. Of course, even after months trimming seconds and saving frames, Wright's record was quickly surpassed.[34] My mind wanders to "the futility of it all. the statistical waiting game / grinding endless attempts, waiting for the outlier / never enough, suboptimal, improvable / my mind wanders" (Wright 2015).

Supported by forum posts, Internet Relay Chat (IRC) conversations, and the explosion of livestreaming in the late 2000s, speedrunning investigates the strange games already operating within videogames and expands single-player software into a massively multiplayer metagame. For the speedrunner, a live audience transforms private play into public performance, breaking up the monotony of repetitive practice through networked intimacies, gamifying the game through community feedback (and funding), and remediating everyday life into narrative. Even before Twitch.tv was launched in 2011, streaming services like Justin.tv, Ustream.tv, and even individually encoded Real Time Streaming Protocol (RTSP) feeds were being used to share speedruns. When Daniel "Jiano" Hart first pointed a webcam at his CRT screen, Wright knew streaming was the future of this metagame (Wright 2013d). In 2009, Wright teamed up with Hart to design the frontend of Speed Runs Live, a website based on a database and IRC bot Hart had programmed to register participants and record results of telematic races in real time. Suddenly, previously distinct, serial experiences of play became community events (initially called "impromptus"), through a simple network solution. Beyond publicizing "RaceBot"'s results, Speed Runs Live capitalized on Twitch's popularity (and the service's public API) to produce a stream aggregator in which any broadcaster previously registered with RaceBot is displayed on the website's frontpage according to their current number of viewers. Speed Runs Live has since become a major community hub for speedrunning and, along with Speed Demos Archive, has begun to host and publicize community events like charity marathons. My mind wanders "to the rng, the frame perfect timing, the human error / to the attempts, the streams, the splits / to the audience, the shit talk, the cliques / the fame / my mind wanders" (Wright 2015).

In contrast to electronic sports or "e-sports,"[35] speedrunning has thus far remained comparatively uncommercial. The practice itself is not as easily molded to the template of broadcast sports and the community has been resistant to attempts to mainstream the practice.[36] This is not to say that the speedrunning community has not produced its own models of monetization. One of the most common ways that geographically isolated speedrunners gather is through the organization of large-scale online charity marathons like Awesome Games Done Quick (AGDQ) and its sister marathon Summer Games Done Quick (SGDQ). Since 2010, these biannual, week-long streaming sessions have become the public face of speedrunning. The practice of livestreamed telethons is becoming more popular as smaller groups borrow this fundraising model. The GDQs showcase the most accomplished runners engaging the most active metagames with donation readings and couch commentary by their peers. Organized by Mike Uyama and Andrew "romscout" Schroeder (with the help of dozens of volunteers) on GamesDoneQuick. com, over the past four years the GDQs have raised millions of dollars in donations for nonprofit organizations like Médecins Sans Frontières and the Prevent Cancer Foundation.[37] For Wright, as well as Uyama and Schroeder, what was once a full-time hobby became a full-time job. While speedrunning has not yet adopted sponsorship models and corporate funding like e-sports, a few speedrunners have started to make a modest living by coupling Twitch's partner program with donation systems borrowed from the GDQs. With the success of both Speed Runs Live and her early Twitch partnership, in 2014 Wright quit freelancing and committed fully to a lifestyle sustained by subscriptions and donations of viewers.[38] My mind wanders "to the traveling, the marathons, / sexually harrassed, fleeing, hiding / reclusive, paranoid, getting high / playing smash, destroying my wrists / my mind wanders" (Wright 2015).

Wright's annual performances at the GDQs were celebrated not only because of her skill, but because of her charisma and in-depth commentary. At AGDQ 2013 not only was she able to complete the *Ocarina of Time* in 22 minutes 33 seconds in front of a live audience of both local and telematic viewers, but she also recounted the long history of the Bottle Adventure Glitch and the Wrong Warp. Then, at SGDQ 2013, Wright returned with her iQue to introduce a hundred thousand people to the Chinese version of *Ocarina of Time* and further historicize the community's discoveries. Scurrying past a now Chinese-speaking Saria and skipping the sword for a simple Deku stick is just the start of Link's contemporary Any% adventure. While deftly manipulating the iQue controller, Wright commentated a "Naviless Aquascape" from the Lost Woods before "Super Sliding" across Hyrule Field. Her first challenge? Collecting Cuccos in Kakariko Village to attain an item of great significance—not the Triforce, but a bottle. In the spring of 2008, the first generation of *Ocarina of Time* speedrunners would then dash to the

Temple of Time in order to prematurely "Door of Time Skip" and find a fishing pole in the future. In 2013 Wright simply "Save Warped" to the start of the game then bought a shield and "Mido Skipped" to access the Great Deku Tree. Backflipping across the empty basement after defeating the game's first boss, Link landed on the edge of the blue warp that would normally conclude the dungeon. Instead, with the help of a bottle, Wright queued an animation state nicknamed "Ocarina Items" mid-jump in order to retain control of Link and manipulate the camera during the cutscene. Warping relies on specific frame counts, so Wright had to control exactly how many frames of the warp sequence were loaded. As Wright (2013e) explained, by exiting the "Ganondoor" on one of five precise frames during this sequence, the player can load one of five cutscenes including "child day," "child night," "adult day," and "adult night" in Kokiri Forest and, serendipitously, a fifth memory address that points directly to the top of Ganon's castle seven years in the future.

Suddenly standing at the top of Ganon's tower, to complete this "link to the past" a child version of Link never meant to be played in the future must prepare for a seemingly impossible task: a "Hyper Extended Super Slide" off Ganon's tower before fighting the final boss with nothing but a Deku stick. On the way, Wright (2013e) carefully avoided burning boulders because "Princess Zelda and a burning Deku shield cannot coexist"—a time paradox that also crashes the game when two objects from different timelines occupy the same memory address. From four hours to one hour to less than twenty minutes, for hundreds of players (and hundreds of thousands of viewers) *Ocarina of Time* has changed dramatically over the last decade as the Any% metagame evolved from the standard metagame to the Bottle Adventure to the Wrong Warp. At the beginning of her SGDQ run, Wright (2013e) mentioned that "a lot of people probably remember the AGDQ run earlier this year in January . . . and in that run I was talking about how after years and years we finally solved the category. Well, turns out this game never ends." For speedrunners, the metagame never ends; you can always go faster . . . until you can't.[39]

As Wright's world record plunged from 18:56 to 18:41 to 18:40 to 18:32 to 18:29 to 18:10 throughout 2014, a game of virtuosic skill became a game of chance as play relied more and more on random events within *Ocarina of Time*. No longer a real-time attack but an attack on real time, the competition around popular speedruns are sometimes better measured in the weeks, months, and years that players spend rather than the minutes, seconds, and milliseconds each subsequent world record saves. As Wright puts it, "there's, like, a 23 percent chance of something happening. If it does, you can continue the speedrun past the first eight minutes or so. So you have to play perfectly for eight minutes, and then only 20 percent of the time or so, you'll actually get to continue" (Grayson 2016). After over 1,200 failed attempts to achieve 18:10, how long would it take to actually improve her world record? At some point, the human cost of speedrunning outweighs the desire to achieve a new record (leaving the record open for players willing to risk their time).

Shortly after getting carpal tunnel syndrome, deleting her Twitch account (temporarily), and beginning hormone therapy, Wright released a spoken word poetry on her new YouTube channel on December 17, 2015. Solemnly recited over a grainy, grayscale video of that critical moment before the "Hyper Extended Super Slide" on top of Gannondorf's tower, Wright's poem, "all the categories are arbitrary," deftly weaves descriptions of videogame hardware, speedrunning techniques, community history, personal biography, and gender identity together into another kind of metagame that challenges the default categories of the normative ways we play. My mind wanders

> to the life i poured into it all
> working in a frenzy, managing a community
> disrupting speedrunning
> building upon it, something new and greater
> and then it fell in upon itself
> jiano saw it first; i was foolish
> it couldn't be unified; all the categories are arbitrary
>
> finished painting my nails, doing my makeup
> put on some mascara, roll up my thigh highs
> all the categories are arbitrary
>
> slip on a skirt, buy a new dress
> feel the pain from the laser
> all the categories are arbitrary
>
> leaving the clinic, bottles in my hand
> spironolactone, estradiol
> all the categories are arbitrary (Wright 2015)

Kirby Kids and Master Hands: *Super Smash Bros.* as a Sandbox

Masahiro Sakurai first met Satoru Iwata at HAL Laboratory in 1989.[40] HAL was a subsidiary of Nintendo located in Chiyoda City, the metropolitan center of Tokyo, and Sakurai was only nineteen years old (Iwata and Sakurai 2008a). Whereas Iwata, a gifted programmer and project manager, would leverage his successes at HAL to become the CEO of Nintendo from 2002 through the Wii era until his much-mourned death in 2015, Sakurai was directly responsible for designing some of Nintendo's most beloved yet idiosyncratic franchises: *Kirby* (1992–) and *Super Smash Bros.* (1999–). Kirby, a soft, pink, *chibi*-esque blob, is the eponymous hero of Sakurai's first series and is perhaps best remembered for deconstructing the notion of "power-ups." A design trope pioneered in games like *Pac-Man* (1980) and *Donkey Kong* (1981) and then expanded in *Super Mario Bros.* (1985), power-ups usually grant an avatar extra abilities for a limited time after picking up a power pellet, super hammer, or magic mushroom.[41] Building on the success of *Kirby's Dream Land* (1992), a handheld platformer for the Game Boy, *Kirby's Adventure* (1993) was released for the Nintendo Entertainment System one year later and further developed Kirby's special skills. Not only could the *kawaii* character inhale air to float and suck up enemies for ammunition, but in *Adventure* Kirby could also swallow his foes to absorb a diverse array of abilities. *Kirby's Adventure* featured twenty-six power-ups like "Cutter," "Fireball," "Hammer," "Parasol," "Spark," "Stone," "Tornado," and "Wheel," to name a few. Well beyond Super Mario's suits or the weapon upgrades of Mega Man, the breadth of Kirby's potential seems to undermine the whole point of the platforming genre. Why attempt to execute a series of precise jumps when Kirby can float at will? Why try to avoid enemies when Kirby can roll or slash or burst into flames to dispatch them? In this sense, Sakurai's game design philosophy may seem too lenient in its attempt to appeal to inexperienced players but these critiques ignore Kirby's greatest feature. The variety of game mechanics (many of which either avoid or bypass whole levels)[42] allow the player to not just choose *how* to play the game, but *what* game to play in the first place.[43] *Kirby's Adventure* functions not only as a videogame with set rules in the form of mechanics, but also as a toybox that lets the player design their own metagames—a sandbox for building an assortment of castles. Beyond simply charting different paths through a given game, the metagame radically changes the game.

Almost twenty years after they first worked together, Iwata interviewed his ex-employee about the two-person prototype they had built together in 1998. Their "ultimate handcrafted project" would become *Super Smash Bros.*, one of Nintendo's bestselling franchises (Iwata and Sakurai 2008b). Charmed by Sakurai's idea for a physics-based "four-player battle royale" on the Nintendo 64, Iwata urged the young designer to pursue the game full time while personally programming the prototype on weekends (Iwata and Sakurai 2008b). *Kakuto-Geemu Ryuoh* or *Dragon King: The Fighting Game* would only become *Super Smash Bros.* after its nondescript, polygonal characters and stand-in skybox—a photograph of HAL's Ryuoh-cho neighborhood (which Iwata snapped from his office window)—were replaced with Nintendo's IP. *Super Smash Bros.* is the first game to go beyond the Mushroom Kingdom and bring Nintendo's famous first-party franchises together in one metaverse.[44] Although *Smash Bros.* is a game *about* games, unlike the indie game genre, Nintendo's metagame does not simply cite the graphics and gameplay of their earlier titles but plays with intellectual property in order to cultivate their corporate brands.[45] Following the accessible design and mechanical variety of the *Kirby* series, and featuring the company's mascots from *Super Mario Bros.* (1985), *Donkey Kong* (1981), *The Legend of Zelda* (1986), *Metroid* (1986), *F-Zero* (1990), *Star Fox* (1993), and *Pokémon* (1996), alongside characters from HAL franchises like *Mother* (1989) and *Kirby*, Sakurai's *Super Smash Bros.* became a go-to, pick-up-and-play party game in the late nineties.

Despite the success of Sakurai's self-professed approach to designing games that "first-time gamers could pick up without hesitation," as always, something unexpected occurred (Iwata and Sakurai 2008c). With the release of *Super Smash Bros. Melee* for the Nintendo GameCube in 2001, players discovered that despite (or perhaps on account of) its open-ended design and dynamic mechanics, the game operated differently than most 2D fighters. Unencumbered by the sprite-based collision and metric motion and at the intersection of physics simulations and character animations, new mechanical exploits emerged as a game *within* the game. As with *Ocarina of Time*, there is no page for "wave-dashing" in the *Melee* instruction manual, but air-dodging into the ground at an acute angle exploits the relation between the game's physics system and character animations to introduce a quick, sliding motion—an exploit that "turn[ed] a popular party game into fierce competition overnight" (Beauchamp 2011).

In *The Smash Brothers* (2013), a nine-part documentary series that pulls together camcorder footage of basement tournaments alongside interviews of a diverse, grassroots community of competitive "Smashers," Travis Beauchamp (Eastpoint Pictures 2013a) traces the decade-long history of play in this "sandbox fighting game." As Chris "Wife" Fabizak (2013, 12–3), testifies in his deeply personal autobiography, *Team Ben: A Year as a Professional Gamer* (2013), in order to win:

> First, learn to *L-Cancel*. By pressing the L button at the exact moment an aerial move hits the ground, lag following the attack is reduced. . . . Next, learn to *short hop*. Press and release the jump button extremely quickly and your character will jump half the normal height. . . . Now learn to *dash dance*. Hold the joystick to the side and your character will run . . . run back and forth within a specified distance and the turnaround is swift, giving your character flexibility in movement. Piece it together. The following maneuver should take *less than 1 second*: short hop, down air, fast fall, L-Cancel, shine, wavedash, short hop again. (Emphasis added)

Driving along the eastern seaboard, from a gym in New Jersey to a rec center in Pennsylvania to a church in West Virginia to a mall in Ohio, Fabiszak began studying, taking notes, and learning about other players in order to master both *Melee*'s microtemporal mechanics and the community's psychological mindgames before winning his first tournament based on "an unprecedented understanding of the Peach vs. Marth metagame" (Fabiszak 2013, 14). And he was not alone.[46] Across the U.S. and internationally, players began to explore the game *within* the game by chaining together mechanical exploits into combos, studying hitbox animations frame-by-frame, and analyzing the statistical data of both characters and players alike. Competitors, commentators, coaches, and even Narcissa Wright[47] banded together in city or state-wide "crews" to create a competitive game *around* the game despite Nintendo's reluctance to embrace this community metagame.

Unlike Blizzard and Valve who, since the late 1990s, explicitly tuned their PC games to foster online and offline competition and in the late 2000s began to invest in e-sports as an advertising platform, Nintendo's console games are designed to exist as islands, isolated from social networks due to lack of persistent player accounts, leader boards, and live chat.[48] Furthermore, and to the chagrin of the competitive *Smash* community, Sakurai's *Super Smash Bros. Brawl* (2008) for the Wii actively discouraged the metagame developed in *Melee* by dramatically slowing movement, removing exploits like wavedashing, and adding a new, completely random chance to "trip" (and temporarily stun the player's character) with every quick flick of the joystick—a luck-based mechanic that levels the playing field by lowering the skill ceiling. Chiding Sakurai's design for the 2008 sequel to *Melee* targeting "first time gamers" on Nintendo's family friendly Wii console, Lilian "milktea" Chen (East Point Pictures 2013b) laments the loss of *Smash*'s "duality of being able to be played as a party game and as a competitive game." Whereas games like *Kirby's Adventure* and *Super Smash Bros. Melee* allow for different styles of play, in the Wii era, Nintendo's general design philosophy and lack of online infrastructure obfuscate their metagames. In the same way speedrunners continue to play *Ocarina of Time,* smashers continue to play *Melee.* Rather than "beating" their respective games and upgrading to newer versions, these communities make and remake the metagame that itself evolves over time within and alongside these software sandboxes.

Beyond a chronicle of release schedules and review scores, metagaming indexes the material histories and community practices of play. On Critical-Gaming.com Richard Terrell (2011c) writes, "Every game with a metagame worth understanding deserves a devoted video game historian." Similar to Beauchamp's story of East Coast-West Coast rivalries and Fabiszak's personal account of a "year as a professional gamer," Richard Terrell's (2011d) "Project M-etagame" is a record of the history of competitive *Super Smash Bros.* Adopting the moniker "KirbyKid," Terrell was one of the few smashers to stick with Sakurai's signature character in competitive *Melee* (see Figure 1.6).[49] Although Kirby is widely perceived as one of the weaker fighters within the *Smash* metagame, he is also a kind of meta-character able to steal the powers of every other fighter (not unlike the "Shahrazad" *Magic* card or Rubick, the *Dota 2* hero who makes an appearance in chapter 5). Intrigued by the possibilities of Kirby's improvisational play, Terrell adopted the character as his avatar to honor Sakurai as well as assume a self-imposed constraint—a metagame of his own making (Terrell 2010).

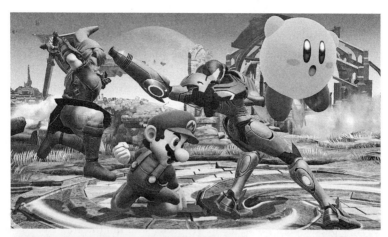

Figure 1.6. Sakurai's signature character Kirby returns in *Super Smash Bros. for Wii U* (2014) (top), a figure that "metagame historian" Richard Terrell adopted for his moniker "KirbyKid" (bottom). Photograph by Patrick LeMieux, 2014 (bottom).

In "Project M-etagame" Terrell (2011a) offers a broad definition of metagaming as the "collective learned gameplay strategies/techniques" like wavedashing or short hopping; "behavioral trends" like quitting early or suiciding as a way to forfeit a competitive match; "modded controllers" like removing the springs in the bumper buttons on GameCube controllers for quicker L-canceling; "using cheats/glitches/exploits/guides" like unplugging a router to gain an advantage in networked games; and "any larger, connecting, overarching fiction" like the metaverse of *Smash* itself and the fan fiction it inspires. Whereas Flanagan's modded Atari joystick breaks one of the rules of the standard metagame and Wright's *Ocarina of Time* speedrun on the iQue adds an additional speed constraint to DeLeon's list, Terrell identifies five aspects of competitive *Smash* that stretch the five standard meta rules through the addition of competitive play. Terrell (2011b) observes how "metagames are very cultural in that they reflect the trends, discoveries, behaviors, and beliefs of a group of people" but despite forum discussion, tournament videos, and livestreams, the history of the metagame does not leave a mark within the software. There are no footprints in the sand.[50]

While the mechanical, electrical, and algorithmic constraints of *Super Smash Bros.* as an assemblage of technical media may not change according to how people play, the homebrews, hacks, and modifications of Nintendo games transform the metagame into an explicit game design practice, codifying historical play into bits and bytes. Terrell's "Project M-etagame" is a cheeky citation of *Project M* (2011–2015), a community-built, "piracy-free" mod that attempts to rebuild *Super Smash Bros. Melee* inside the *Super Smash Bros. Brawl* engine for home console. Terrell (2011c) calls *Project M* a "*Melee-Brawl*-hybrid" which means a metagame historian must "take into consideration the development of *Melee* and *Brawl's* metagame to best understand the start of *Project M's* development." However, the reverse is also true. *Project M* also preserves the history of the metagame within the patch updates and change logs stored on the *Smash Boards* forums and in each version of the software itself.[51] Play and practice converge in *Project M,* a digital artifact that captures the metagame in each software update like insects trapped in amber. From a corporate game *about* games to the glitchy game hidden *within* the game to the competitive game *around* the game to *Project M,* the hands of players move from manipulating characters, to discovering mechanics, to organizing tournaments, to designing a videogame.

Super Smash Bros. begins and ends with its own "Master Hand." The disembodied white glove with a mind of its own first appears in the opening cutscene of the original *Super Smash Bros.* before serving as a cursor icon within the game's graphic user interface (GUI). Throughout the series, Master Hand returns as the final challenger that must be defeated to complete the single-player campaign. Circling an Edenic mise-en-scène of a child's suburban bedroom, Master Hand begins *Smash Bros.* by reaching into a toy box to retrieve one of eight different dolls—

miniature versions of Nintendo's intellectual property represented as playthings for the idle hands of a global corporation.[52] Dumping a limp Mario, Link, Kirby, etc. onto the nearby desk, a snap of the fingers brings the characters to life as the books, lamp, and windowsill morph into a scene from the Mushroom Kingdom. Ready? Go! Representing Sakurai, Iwata, and the game's other creators at HAL Laboratory and Nintendo, Master Hand's magic recalls the long tradition of the hand of the animator that appears at the birth of film itself.[53] Whereas this first, cinematic Master Hand enacts a metaleptic leap between *Super Smash Bros.'* diegesis and its designers, control is soon shifted to the interactive hand of the player.

Having breathed life into Nintendo's action figures, the hand of the animator becomes animated in *Super Smash Bros.'* character selection menu. While the metaleptic Master Hand in the opening cutscene recalls classic cinematic tropes, the metonymic Master Hand in the GUI recalls Susan Kare's "clicker" icon that first appeared in Apple's HyperCard software in 1987. As with *Mario Paint* (1992) and *Mario 64* (1996), players manipulate *Super Smash Bros.'* menus by guiding a miniature version of Mario's hand, the Master Hand, to point, pinch, and place data in the form of a cursor icon. While the hand of the animator becomes the hand of the player, the darted glove included in Nintendo's games (and eventually replacing Kare's original icons in Apple's operating systems) is itself an iconic figure in the history of animation. Both Mario and the Macintosh's white, right-hand glove not only intentionally signify Mickey Mouse but also, unintentionally, the much longer racial history of cartoons (see Figure 1.7).

Disney's mouse belongs to the "funny animal" tradition of comics and animation in which the addition of ears and tails to black bodies sanitized the genre of comedy inspired by the tradition of blackface and minstrel shows. Although Mickey's gloves are easy to disavow as merely a contrivance of the technical limitations related to articulating fingers in early animation, Bimbo and Betty (1930), Oswald and Ortensia (1927), Foxy and Roxy (1931), and, of course, Mickey and Minnie (1928) are anthropomorphic animals that whitewashed their relation to racist caricatures inspired by minstrelsy and vaudeville. This racialized history was further obfuscated as these hands found a new home within the GUIs of contemporary operating systems like Mac OSX. Whereas the manicule, a pointing finger directing a reader's attention, has been used

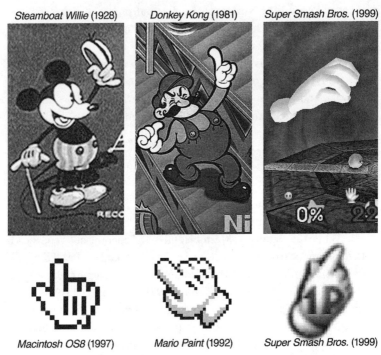

Figure 1.7. After the popularization of the talkie in the late twenties, in *Steamboat Willie* (1928), the first ever "Merry Melody," Mickey Mouse adopts gloves and a lilting voice of Al Jolson's *Jazz Singer* (1927). From there, Mickey's gloves eventually find themselves in both Mac OS8 (1997) and *Mario Paint* (1992) in the nineties before they are conflated with the hand of the animator in *Super Smash Bros.* (1998).

for a millenium in chirographic and print texts, its transformation from hand to glove in both Mac OSX and *Smash Bros.* recontextualizes the medieval pointer according to the context of twentieth century animation and twenty-first century computing (Sherman 2008).

Although Charles Pratt (2013) observes that, compared to other game genres and player demographics, the fighting game community assembled around software like *Super Smash Bros.* "is exceptionally international and diverse" and "the tournaments have a wider variety of racial, ethnic and class backgrounds than any other gaming event," the ubiquitous darted glove nonetheless allegorizes the ways in which "user friendly" interface design seeks to erase the racial history of computation. GUI elements like the Master Hand not only point to the discourses of twentieth century racism but, once embedded within the technical circuits of electronic forms of entertainment, they also gesture toward the largely invisible circuits of production dependent on blood and labor. From coltan mining operations in the Congo to e-waste recycling facilities in China, the labor organized around the unearthing as well as eventual reuse of conflict minerals is what enables the production, distribution, consumption, and disposal of consumer electronics like videogames. The ideological desire for an immediate, transparent, or what Apple (2009) calls "magic" interface attempts to render invisible the material, historical, and human substrate of computation for the sake of the seamless immersivity of technical mastery—what Heidegger would call *Zuhandenheit* or "readiness-to-hand." Through an ironic twist, *Super Smash Bros.'* Master Hand, of all things, exposes the ways in which the representation of computing attempts to mask or obscure its own history.

Returning as the final boss of *Super Smash Bros. Melee*, "the Master Hand awaits anyone who survives the long and difficult road to the 'Final Destination.' This symbolic link between the real world and the imaginary battlefields of *Super Smash Bros. Melee* is quite a handful in battle, and just because it wears a white glove doesn't mean it fights clean" (Hal Laboratory 2002). But this "link between the real world and the imaginary battlefields" has a significance that Sakurai could not have intended. Like Bottle Adventure Glitch and Wrong Warping in the *Ocarina of Time*, when performed correctly on the character selection screen of *Melee*, the "Master Hand Glitch" allows players to take control of the character that was never meant to be manipulated by human hands. By advancing the stage selection screen without first selecting a character, the null ID variable is automatically replaced with a 0 which represents the first fighter in the character array—not Mario but Master Hand. In the same way the *Smash* community subverted Sakurai's rules by modding their own quasi-legal game, *Project M,* the Master Hand Glitch demonstrates the way in which players refuse to settle for the token power initially handed out and the way in which the metagame resists the dehistoricizing impulse of videogames. The metagame then, does not merely signify the games we play within and around videogames, but extends to include the specific historical, gendered, classed, raced, and embodied conditions of play that can never be ignored and are in fact essential to play. After cutscenes and GUIs, mods and exploits, this "Project M-aster Hand"—a material history of play—moves from the hand of the designer and player to the clapping hands of live spectators around both local competitive games like *Super Smash Bros.* or international e-sports like *StarCraft.*

Sons of *StarCraft:* To Look is to Play is to Labor in International E-Sports

The professionalization of English language *StarCraft* (1998–) commentary began with orange chicken and Prima strategy guides, beige towers and biking to the mall in Leawood, Kansas. In the hundredth episode of his early netcast, "The Day[9] Daily," Sean Plott (2010) recalls growing up in a "*StarCraft* family" with his mother and brother, Nicholas. Living in the cross-state suburban sprawl of Kansas City in the nineties, the Plott brothers could not have predicted that *StarCraft*, a computer game and adolescent obsession, would capture their attention for decades and lead to full-time careers not as professional players but as spectators, commentators, and analysts of the (predominantly Korean) metagame. With the popularity of video playthroughs, live streaming, and observer modes in online games, the act of play can no longer be reduced to the manipulation of a keyboard, the agency of a single player, or even the operations of the software or the output on the screen. Spectatorship is not a superfluous byproduct of gaming but part of a much broader media ecology of play in which the production, performance, and perception of videogames are conflated. In the case of *StarCraft*, the game of spectatorship has flourished to become, for many, their primary form of play—a metagame *around* the game. Biking home from the mall with their first copy of *StarCraft*, Sean and Nick took turns playing, each spending half of their time watching the other as they traded off on the family's lone networked computer. The Plott brothers—better known by their online handles "Day[9]" and "Tasteless"—were two of the earliest people to recognize that watching games was as meaningful as playing them. Along with a community of dedicated players like Daniel "Artosis" Stemkoski, the Plotts embedded themselves within the economy and ecology of competitive videogame playing—a metagaming phenomenon that has come to be known as e-sports.

Following the success of Blizzard's *Warcraft* (1994–) series, *StarCraft* evolved from "orcs in space" to become one of the most popular RTS (real-time strategy) games of all time and the defining example of the genre—a type of computer wargame in which the common idioms of desktop computing are used to build infrastructure, produce military assets, and direct combat from a gods-eye perspective in real time rather than in turns (Wyatt 2012b).[54] In his "E-Sports Manifesto" Sean Plott (2011) writes

> We believe that our game, *StarCraft,* is the chess of our generation. *StarCraft* requires the dexterity of a pianist, the mind of a chess grandmaster, and the discipline of an Olympic trainee. We believe that our game, *StarCraft,* is as dynamic and exciting a spectator sport as any other. We fill auditoriums to cheer on our favorite gamers. Most of all, we believe our game, *StarCraft,* is a beautiful platform for play.

A decade earlier, in 2000, the World Cyber Games (WCG) began to leverage *StarCraft* as a platform for international competition. Funded by the Korean Ministry of Culture and Tourism, the Ministry of Information and Communications, Samsung, and eventually Microsoft in 2006, the WCG is one of the earliest, international infrastructures for competitive videogame tournaments. Since 2000, the organization has not only brought different games, communities, and cultures together for their annual "gaming olympics," but developed some of the earliest Internet broadcasts featuring live footage cameras, commentators, and cash prizes for computer games.

In "Day[9] Daily #100" Sean Plott (2010) recalls that his family "really started to gel around *StarCraft*" in 2005, the year both he and his brother made it to the U.S. qualifiers for WCG. Two weeks before the tournament, however, a cruel, almost biblical, twist of fate halted the celebrations of their "*StarCraft* family." Because the brackets were arranged alphabetically (rather than randomly seeded or organized according to overall standing), the Plotts' first game at the Hammerstein Ballroom in New York City would be against one another—best of three, single elimination. Unknown to the Plott brothers, the outcome of this particular match would determine much of the next decade of their lives. While recording "Daily #100," Sean (2010) chokes back tears remembering the inner turmoil of his 2–0 victory. Backstage at the tournament, Nick was emotionally exhausted and deeply disappointed in his performance but promised, "You know what, Sean? You're going to win this tournament." And after beating Stemkoski in the second bracket, Sean would prove his brother right and go on to get first place WCG U.S. qualifiers.

With one Plott eliminated in the first round, the brothers found themselves in the familiar situation in which one played and the other watched. Freed from the agony of competition, Nick noticed that the announcer hired for the *StarCraft* tournament was struggling to narrate the complex strategy game. So Nick asked for a mic, walked up on stage, and launched his career as a *StarCraft* commentator—a profession that did not yet exist. Gregarious and gracious, Nick was a natural. As Sean climbed from bracket to bracket to win his first major tournament, Nick's voice echoed throughout the ballroom. And whereas Sean won a chance to play in the WCG Finals, Radio ITG immediately hired Nick to cast the event in Singapore. Leveraging these experiences, in 2008 Nick dropped out of college, moved to Seoul—pink hair, piercings, and all—to become "the first Western *StarCraft* caster in South Korea" shortly followed by Stemkoski (Lien 2013).

In Korea, national television stations showcase *StarCraft* games, professional gamers live off corporate sponsorships, and *StarCraft* leagues fill stadiums with fans waving custom designed "cheerfuls" and banging inflatable "balloonstix." The Korean government proudly describes Seoul as the "Mecca of e-sports" (Korean Culture and Information Service 2012). Whereas North America and Europe have taken an increasing interest in spectator e-sports since the late 2000s, nowhere is *StarCraft* as permanently entrenched in mainstream culture than in Korea. The game changed Korea and, in contrast to the majority of Nintendo's treatment of the *Super Smash Bros.* series, the Korean metagame has changed the way Blizzard makes *StarCraft*.[55] With the release of *StarCraft II* in 2010, Tasteless traded in t-shirt and jeans for a suit and tie and a seat alongside longtime rival and fellow expat, Artosis. Branding themselves as "Tastosis, the casting archon," Plott and Stemkoski doubled down on a career with no predefined path. Since then, the duo has served as cultural ambassadors, mediating not only between Korea and English-speaking players, but also between *StarCraft* and non-*StarCraft* players.

While Plott provides color commentary, Stemkoski is known as the more analytical of the casting duo. He insists that the mindgames played between players is the most important aspect of *StarCraft*. Literally living the game, pro gamers eat, sleep, and play together in team houses, travel the world to compete in international tournaments, and transform their once leisure activities into a career. Whereas competitive *Super Smash Bros.* features a bottom-up or grassroots approach to monetizing the community metagame in church basements and rec centers, competitive *StarCraft* has always had a more complex relationship with its parent corporation in the sense that Blizzard pushes out patches, approves new maps, organizes tournaments, and funds prize pools. And, just as the metagame is captured in the updates of *Super Smash Bros.: Project M,* the history of e-sports becomes part of the design history at Blizzard as *StarCraft*'s patches and maps respond to the ongoing playstyles of professional gamers.

As Stemkoski (2012) remarks, "One of the most beautiful things, (in my eyes, at least), is the intricate dance the strategies and build orders take around the current Metagame." From their commentators box at Gretech Corporation's GOMTV in the Gangnam district of Seoul, Tastosis translates the Korean metagame (see Figure 1.8). In contrast to Richard Terrell uncovering the *Smash* metagame in retrospect, Plott and Stemkoski interpret the history of the metagame in real time. In her analysis of the narratological structure of sports commentary, Marie-Laure Ryan (2006, 79) argues the live broadcast may be compared to a "computer program operating 'in real time': it is a time-consuming process that receives its input from another process running at the same time." The practice of watching and narrating a game is a form of play that requires learning how to read the screen, interpret the action, and translate the strategy into a legible narrative for a larger audience—another kind of RTS game. As Tracey Lien (2013) observes, "When Tastosis casts a match, it's not a matter of Zerg versus Protoss or Marines versus Zerg, it's NesTea versus MvP along with their history." Lien (2013) wagers that "Stemkoski spends more time on *StarCraft 2* than most professional gamers."

Whenever he is away from Korea, Stemkoski (2012) must "sit down and watch every game," meticulously taking notes to document the shifting build orders, strategies, and mindgames that make up the metagame. Pausing, rewinding, and analyzing dozens of games, Artosis takes color-coded notes detailing every "Fast Forge Expansion" to "Fast Harass" with warp prism and sentries. He logs each "Three Base Double Robotics Core" and every "Timed Fourth Base Stargate" meant to anticipate Zerg's "Hive Upgrade." Whereas professional players must spend their time practicing, professional commentators like Stemkoski invest in a metagame that turns watching the game into a game. On a typical day of research Stemkoski might watch every PvZ (Protoss vs. Zerg) match up occurring at a specific tournament, in a specific region, on a specific map. Daybreak,

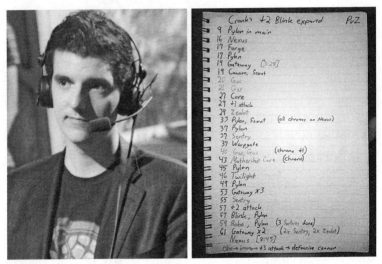

Figure 1.8. Casting and commentating for GOMTV, Daniel "Artosis" Stemkoski (left) translates the Korean metagame according to his thorough research and playful chemistry with Nicholas "Tasteless" Plott. Pages of Artosis' notebook (right), for example, track the evolution of *StarCraft* build orders over time. Photographs by Nick Pettit, 2011 (left), reproduced via Creative Commons Attribution-ShareAlike 2.0 License; and Daniel Stemkoski, 2014 (right), reproduced with permission.

for example, is a half-terraformed asteroid floating in space originally designed by Winpark, a member of the Korean map-making team Crux. After the Global StarCraft II League (GSL) discovered the asteroid in the summer of 2011 via an online poll, Daybreak replaced Xel'Naga Caverns in the league's map pool and was eventually colonized by Blizzard a year later. Daybreak drifted from the local metagame in Korea to become an official part of *StarCraft* itself. Whereas Masahiro Sakurai developed a sequel that stripped the game of those components that made it most compelling for tournament play, Dustin Browder, the director and lead designer of *StarCraft II*, "watches Tastosis every morning" (Lien 2013).

As T. L. Taylor (2012, 213) argues, "Computer games presume, at their very core, direct actions and as such rarely conceptualize a spectator role." However, as she demonstrates in her impressive history of e-sports, *Raising the Stakes: E-Sports and the Professionalization of Computer Gaming*, watching games is (and has always been) a core aspect of playing games. From the spectacle of competitive play in *Tennis for 2* in 1958 to the *Spacewar!* Olympics sponsored by *Rolling Stone* in 1972, video-games have always had spectators.[56] From watching *Indie Game: The Movie* in theaters across North America to viewing Mary Flanagan's *[giantJoystick]* in an art gallery in London, spectating games is also a form of metagaming. Speedrunning races occur regularly on Twitch and competitive *Smash* (and *Project M*) has now filled arenas of its own. Even *Colossal Cave Adventure* (1975–76), Crowther and Wood's inaugural text adventure game, was played collaboratively on time-shared PDP-10 mainframes in the late seventies. The "YOU" who was described "STANDING AT THE END OF A ROAD BEFORE A SMALL BRICK BUILDING" was less of a second-person singular and more a second-person plural as one player would input the aggregate commands of a group.[57] Yet, when the academic field of game studies was in its infancy, the ludological aspects of videogames became the primary criteria through which scholars could differentiate and critique the medium without relying on earlier print- or film-based methodologies.

Espen Aarseth's (1997, 1) book, *Cybertext: Perspectives on Ergodic Literature,* coined the term "ergodic" to describe the "nontrivial effort" required to engage games. Adopting a similar approach, in *Gaming: Essays on Algorithmic Culture,* Alexander Galloway argues that a different theoretical apparatus must be constructed for analyzing videogames based on the fact that games are not representations of events, but actions. Galloway (2007, 104) writes, "The activity of gaming . . . only ever comes into being when the game is actually played . . . [and is therefore] an *undivided* act wherein meaning and doing transpire in the same gamic gesture" (emphasis original). Even though these definitions account for a broad understanding of "effort" and "doing" and can include nonkinetic activity, Aarseth and Galloway's game theories are often conflated with either the physical gestures needed to interact with most games or the discrete decisions that directly impact the experience of a work. These forms of engagement are qualitatively distinguished from others, such as film spectatorship. However, as evidenced by the examples of metagaming discussed so far, activities such as spectatorship cannot be easily differentiated from conventional definitions of play. From Twitch to transmedia television, both watching people play and playing with the practice of watching are forms of ludic spectatorship. Whether sitting shoulder-to-shoulder in stadium seats or watching over someone's shoulder at the local "BarCraft," spectatorship is an ergodic, gamic action in and of itself.

As players share more and more gameplay by trading demo files, posting videos, and livestreaming, videogames increasingly incorporate recording, hosting, sharing, and even analytic services in a race to redirect the work of watching (and sensing more broadly) back into economic circuits. In the expanded ecology and economy of videogames, spectatorship operates as a form of play and production in and of itself. Although metagaming practices that use game engines to produce "machinima" and "Let's Plays" might make use of YouTube's creation, distribution, and monetization systems to produce new genres of video,[58] the expansion of livestreaming services like Twitch, HitBox, and UStream have created new genres of play and production. Beyond broadcasting and archiving gameplay, Twitch has become a platform that enables real-time, collaborative forms of play. Salty Bet, for example, is a popular Twitch channel in which viewers not only watch the nonhuman combat of various fighting game AIs but also place fictional bets with virtual money via the IRC channel running alongside the spectacle. Whereas the gameplay driving every Salty Bet operates according to the calculations of computerized opponents, *Spelunky* Death Roulette is another IRC-based betting service in which viewers wager how *Spelunky* (2009) players will meet their demise. A fast and furious *Rogue*-like platformer, one of the central pleasures of both playing and watching Spelunky is the novelty of each procedurally generated level and the unexpected ways in which those levels conspire to kill the player. Rather than betting on the fortunes of autonomous bots or guessing what procedurally generated game over awaits, Twitch Plays *Pokémon* combines a single-player game and the real-time input of a hundred thousand spectators to produce a new type of crowd-sourced, massively collaborative videogame. First, IRC commands collected on Twitch are pumped into a Game Boy emulator running Nintendo's famous *Pokémon Red* (1996) via a simple LUA script. The result is an average of 80,000 people watching and sending dozens of commands a second to a befuddled Pokémon trainer who ended up spending 16 days, 17 hours, 45 minutes, and 30 seconds to complete the first entry in the Pokémon series in only 122 million unique inputs—not quite *Hamlet*, but nonetheless an accomplishment at the hands of a million monkeys (or Mankeys). Within this expanded field of play, companies like Blizzard, Valve, Microsoft, and Sony are developing their own in-game spectatorship clients, one-click streaming consoles, and even real-time biometric sensors to both quantify and capture the attention of spectators and players alike. Following Google, Facebook, Twitter, and other social media giants, the videogame industry has begun to acknowledge attention as an alternate form of currency—an *undercurrency* (discussed in depth in chapter 5).

Aside from experimental approaches like Salty Bets, Death Roulettes, and various Twitch Plays channels, e-sports like *StarCraft* reveal the relationship not only between spectatorship and play, but between spectatorship and work. As Jonathan Beller (2006, 78) argues in *The Cinematic Mode of Production,* "to look is to labor." Whereas the work of watching a Hollywood film does not necessarily translate into an exchangeable commodity (yet), likes, upvotes, and hearts transform the qualitative experience of attention into quantitative values in the form of PageRanks and consumer profiles. Circulating within contemporary information economies, attention is expropriated when "one 'buys' a commodity and 'sells' one's labor in the same act of spectatorship, thereby bypassing the mediation of money" (Beller 2006, 3). In the context of global capital, spectatorship has become a new site of free labor, another gear in the "social factory" that recognizes the "value-productive dimensions of sensual labor in the visual register" and thus flattens the distinction between playing and viewing a videogame (Beller 2006, 3). In the "ludic century,"[59] one could revise Beller's claim by arguing that *to look is to play is to labor,* and that even games operating *without* games become a form of metagaming.

RIP Vile Rat: Digital Diplomacy and Electronic Monuments in *EVE Online*

At 12:54 p.m. on September 11th, 2012, the Goonswarm Federation CEO, Alex "The Mitanni" Gianturco, received an IRC message from his Chief Diplomat, Vile Rat: "Assuming we don't die tonight. We saw one of our 'police' that guard the compound taking pictures" (Gianturco 2012). Gianturco was responsible for the largest alliance of players in *EVE Online,* a massively multiplayer space simulation first launched by Crowd Control Productions (CCP) in 2003. CCP (2014) calls *EVE* "The Sandbox" due to the fact that "the game world . . . combined with the persistent actions of thousands upon thousands of players . . . [produces] emergent gameplay where a single shot, business deal or even just a word can determine the destiny of thousands." But on this particular occasion Vile

Rat was not talking about *EVE*. A few hours later, in a parallel universe, Sean Smith typed his last recorded words from the U.S. consulate in Benghazi:

> [vile_rat 9/11/12 2:40 PM]: FUCK
> [vile_rat 9/11/12 2:40 PM]: gunfire (Óskarsson 2012)

Well before any international news outlets were aware of the Benghazi attack, members of the Something Awful Forums and the *EVE Online* community were already mourning the loss of their friend alongside Smith's family. In the early hours of September 12th, Gianturco's heart-wrenching farewell letter, "RIP: Vile Rat," unintentionally broke the story of both Smith's death and the attack, which also claimed the lives of Ambassador J. Christopher Stevens, Tyrone Woods, and Glen Doherty.

Two days later, standing in the hangar at Joint Base Andrews on September 14th, Hillary Clinton (2012) remarked,

> Sean leaves behind a loving wife, Heather, two young children, Samantha and Nathan, and scores of grieving family, friends and colleagues. And that's just in this world. Because online, in the virtual worlds that Sean helped create, he is also being mourned by countless competitors, collaborators and gamers who shared his passion.

While Smith worked as information management officer in Libya, he led not a double or alternate but an augmented life as one of the most powerful and respected diplomats in *EVE Online,* a figure whose word did "determine the destiny of thousands." His longtime friend and partner, Gianturco (2012), testifies that "if you play this stupid game, you may not realize it, but you play in a galaxy created in large part by Vile Rat's talent as a diplomat." Contrary to Clinton's distinction between worlds, for Smith and others who play metagames about, within, around, and even without videogames, there is no IRL: it's all RL.[60]

Six years before the attack in Benghazi, when Vile Rat was still a rookie spy for the newly formed Goonfleet's Intelligence Agency, the twenty-eight-year-old Foreign Service officer began his ascent as a virtual diplomat. Without even logging into *EVE,* Vile Rat manipulated the metagame occurring across IRC channels, discussion forums, and VOIP chats—a game *without* a game. During the third year of the "Great

War," in which tens of thousands of players struggled against a massive conglomerate called Band of Brothers, Vile Rat staged a public split from the Gianturco and the Goons in order to infiltrate an enemy subsidiary and gain the trust of key players outside the game itself. By fomenting internecine conflict and persuading the smaller group of mercenaries to declare their independence from Band of Brothers, Vile Rat engaged in the millennia-old strategy of divide and conquer in order to disable an entire institution without having to sacrifice ships or squander ISK (i.e., not Iceland's Króna, but *EVE's* in-game currency, "Interstellar Kredits"). Under the new order of the Goonswarm Federation, the dominant form of power within New Eden shifted from space battles to high-stakes diplomacy, a game of espionage, counterespionage, and counter-counterespionage. Vile Rat had helped to engineer an economic and political metagame made in the image of the real-world military and governmental institutions in which he also served as a U.S. diplomatic officer.

Remembering Smith's influence on the metagame both inside and outside New Eden, Gianturco fondly recalls,

> Sean was not just some guy in *EVE Online,* he was the Chief Diplomat of the largest alliance in the game. He also created a diplomatic corps that was based upon the State Department itself . . . So now instead of having one diplomat which is what most alliances have we have a Chief Diplomat, we had several diplomatic directors, and we had attachés who were liaising with the various entities who they were focused on. (Goldman and Vogt 2014)

Vile Rat's influence on the Great War, the creation of the Jabberlon5 chatroom "where every nullsec personage of note hangs out and makes deals," and the formation of Goonswarm's *Corps Diplomatique,* all function in terms of a "metagame which doesn't require booting the program up at all" (Gianturco 2012; Goldman and Vogt 2014).[61] Ned Coker, a spokesperson for CCP, acknowledges the crucial role of *EVE's* metagame, stating, "The metagame is anything you're not actually doing in the game itself; the social aspect of it, and the politics . . . because the defeat penalty is so high; the people you trust become so much more important and the metagame arises out of that" (Ungerleider 2014). The world of New Eden is a sandbox, but one in which only some players get their hands dirty. By definition, all metagames have real consequences and *EVE* makes this patently clear. As such, the history of play in *EVE*

Online—the handprints, castles, and lines drawn in the sand—are circumscribed by the diplomatic metagame. Vile Rat did not just play the game; he had a hand in making the game. Along with many others he developed managerial systems, institutions, governmental agencies, schemes, and schemes-within-schemes. The stories of these exploits propel play as much as they are generated by the history of New Eden, both a sandbox and a book of sand.

According to Jim Rossignol (2008), "what has perhaps been most fascinating about the continuing war is the stream [of] war stories—the tales of commitment and tenacity from both sides, over the months. Whoever you talk to, they'll have a story of how their fleet mounted a 48-hour continuous defense of a single system, or how they set alarm clocks at 4 a.m. so they could be up to finish off an enemy installation when the time came about, or how they tricked the enemy into losing some priceless piece of hardware." The folklore of *EVE* and other massively multiplayer online games is captured in logs, screenshots, forum discussions, and, now more than ever, recorded video—calcified forms of metagaming documenting the player-produced narratives and histories.[62] In an attempt to harvest this storytelling ethos and profit from the history of play in *EVE*, CCP is now working on both a comic book series and a television series based explicitly on the "true" stories told by players that could potentially exceed the political intricacies of *Game of Thrones* (Graser 2014). CCP's transmedia experiment harnesses the generative literary potential of EVE's players in order to recirculate their stories back into the game's commercial operations. These player-produced narratives attempt to memorialize those unrepeatable events that would otherwise disappear in the dustbin of digital ephemera.

In the days, weeks, and months that followed Smith's death, the name "Vile Rat" echoed throughout *EVE*. Players posted condolences like "fly safe, Vile Rat," and "shoot blues, tell Vile Rat," both inside and outside the game. No matter their alliance, the words "RIP Vile Rat" temporarily appended the majority of space station IDs throughout Null Sec, blending serial numbers with sympathetic notes as thousands of players engaged in an exercise in constrained poetry:

BKG-Q2 VIII—Moon 1—BKG0dspeed Vile Rat
JU-0WQ VII—JU-st the Vile Rat Memorial
U-SOH2 VII—U-SOH2 Soon for V1le Rat

EOY-BG III—EOY did it have to be Vile Rat
U-HYZN VI—U-HYZNo Replacement For Vile Rat
MZ1E-P IX—MZ1 Moment of Silence 4 Vile Rat
CU9-T0 IV—CU On the other side Vile Rat
FO8M-2 III—FO8M-2soon for Vile Rat
UMI-KK VII—UMIss Vile Rat
F-88PJ VII—F-88 Ways We'll Miss Vile Rat
LBGI-2 III—LBGI-2 Good to be gone Vile Rat
MA-VDX VII—MAny hearts to Vile Rats Family
5S-KXA XI—5Shattered worlds RIP Vile Rat
RO90-H VIII—RO90oz poured out for VIle Rat
C-C99Z III—C-Can't Believe Vile Rat is gone
60M-TG I—60Ways Vile Rat Changed EVE

As Vile Rat's name dotted the stars and appended space stations, players produced other spontaneous memorials, "creative appropriations of game mechanics that hybridized and translated traditional and contemporary tropes for grieving, commemorating and memorializing" (Gibbs et al. 2013). A repository of empty cargo containers inscribed with the common slogan "RIP Vile Rat" were launched into uninhabited virtual space, eerily recalling the flag-draped caskets at the transfer-of-remains ceremony at Andrews Air Force Base. Players painstakingly arranged matrices of warp bubbles to produce a celestial rendering of "RIP Vile Rat," a starlight vigil to which many networked pilgrims traveled (see Figure 1.9) (Gibbs et al. 2013). As Gregory L. Ulmer (2005, xiv) explored in the context of DIY digital memorials after 9/11 in *Electronic Monuments*, these digital shrines are not only testament to Vile Rat and his impact on the community of players, but they were testament to the entangled history of the metagame in *EVE* with the history of geopolitics: two war-torn worlds to which Vile Rat had dedicated substantial effort toward peaceful conflict resolution. Even prior to Vile Rat's last message on Jabber, these two worlds had never been truly distinct from each other. Just as Gianturco signed his commemoration, the rules of engagement both inside and outside the rules of the game continue to be "shoot blues, tell Vile Rat."

Interplay

From indie games and artworks to speedrunning, shoutcasting, e-sports, and espionage, the six metagames surveyed in this chapter emerge

Figure 1.9. Electronic monuments commemorate the life of Sean "Vile Rat" Smith in *EVE Online,* a space simulator and digital sandbox in which Smith's virtual diplomacy still plays out in the form of a metagame.

from different material platforms, social settings, geographic regions, and historical contexts. They cannot, however, be distinguished entirely from one another. These examples of metagaming expand Richard Garfield's (2000) original list of prepositions from the temporal contexts of playing "to," "from," "during," and "between" games of *Magic: The Gathering* in the mid-1990s to the spatial contexts of playing games about, within, around, and without videogames in the 2000s. These prepositions are to speech as metagaming is to videogames: they situate their subjects in time and space. And just as prepositions as parts of speech fail to signify without a subject, performance, or context, metagames cannot operate in a vacuum and cannot be entirely distinguished from one another. Behind can be about, without can be around, during can be within, and along can be throughout. Time and space converge. Here, there, this, that. Like Wittgenstein's "language games," metagames interact, overlap, sustain, and inspire each other as they mediate videogame play. As stated at the beginning of this chapter, metagaming is a broad, aesthetic practice that characterizes not the histories of games, but the histories of play itself.

Prior to speedrunning on Twitch, Narcissa Wright—along with many of the founding members of Speed Runs Live—played competitive *Super Smash Bros.* Recalling Richard Terrell's moniker, "KirbyKid," Wright's first online handle was "KirbySSB," a reference to Masahiro Sakurai's signature character. Expanding the intersection between speedrunning and *Smash* to indie games, Edmund McMillen and Tommy Refenes' *Super Meat Boy* does not simply reference retro games like *Super Mario Bros.*, but encourages players to race through each level. Like the timer splits used by speedrunners to track their progress and compare results, *Super Meat Boy* recognizes the history of play through an in-game visualization of every failed attempt (an idea McMillen and Refenes credit to Andi McClure and her "Many Worlds Emulator," discussed in chapter 4). An obvious choice to run and race within, *Super Meat Boy* is regularly featured at various charity marathons, and Team Meat regularly participates. At AGDQ 2012 and 2013, McMillen and Refenes called in to commentate their game and support the charity. The duo also offered what speedrunners refer to as the "Team Meat Scholarship" to fund travel for international players like Max "coolkid" Lundberg, who, at the time, held the world record for Valve's *Half-Life* (1998) (a game discussed at the beginning of the next chapter). What these sorts of expanded networks suggest is that none of the practices described in this chapter exist independent of one another. Although videogames are often imagined as solitary or antisocial activities in popular culture, the richest forms of play are deeply communal and form a broader media ecology in which the practices of independent designers, media artists, speedrunners, modders, e-sports commentators, virtual diplomats, and metagame historians cannot easily be untangled. Games like *Super Meat Boy, [giantJoystick], The Legend of Zelda, Super Smash Bros., StarCraft,* and *EVE Online* are hardly unique in their overlapping communities of play. In the twenty-first century, all games have metagames and metagames always move, morph, mutate, and meander.

Beyond the references to indie games and art games *about* retro gaming, the glitches used to gain an advantage *within* speedrunning and competitive games, the audience activities *around* international e-sports, the online and offline espionage *without* massively multiplayer games, and even the many economies both produced by and producing videogames, there are countless other metagames. From *Magic: The Gathering* to *EVE Online,* metagaming also includes *Final Fantasy* FAQs[63] and *Pokémon* fanfic, *Skyrim* mods and *Doom* maps, *Halo* machinima and *Minecraft* Let's Plays, Game Boy chiptunes and Speak & Spell circuit bending, Kickstarting and Greenlighting, accessible designs and alternative interfaces, total control hacks and constructing computers within computer games, and the millions of minute activities occurring before, during, and after as well as in, on, around, and through videogames. The following chapters undertake a closer analysis of the prepositional paradigms outlined here. From the embodied forms of vision required to navigate anamorphic indie games in chapter 2 and the techniques of both blind and blindfolded players in chapter 3 to the seriality of *Super Mario* mods in chapter 4 to the evolution of player performance in international e-sports in chapter 5 to the gamified harassment discussed in the final chapter, this book attempts to document, theorize, and, finally, make metagames.

Metagame 1

Triforce

In *The Legend of Zelda* (1986), there are two locations that explicitly defy the logic of the Cartesian grid: The Lost Woods and The Lost Hills. When traveling through these single-screen mazes, Link finds himself endlessly looping, temporarily arrested by a classic gaming trope. Like *Asteroids* (1979) and *Pac-Man* (1980), if the player's avatar exits the edge of the screen, it seems to appear on the opposite side as if teleported from one side of the screen to the other—a counter rolls over from 255 to 0. The mathematical certainty and programmatic simplicity of The Lost Woods and The Lost Hills generates complex and sometimes paradoxical topologies. Whether the player realizes it or not, each looping space maps not to the flattened grid on which the rest of Hyrule is organized, but instead to the three-dimensional topology of a torus. *Triforce* is an original piece of software that explores the topology of *The Legend of Zelda* by visualizing the 8-bit game in three dimensions (see Figure 1.10). To download *Triforce,* go to http://manifold.umn.edu/triforce.

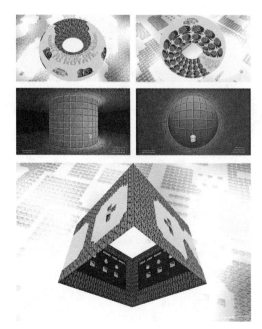

Figure 1.10. *Triforce* is an original metagame by Patrick LeMieux and Stephanie Boluk that maps the two-dimensional spaces of Hyrule onto three-dimensional topologies.

TWO

Stretched Skulls

Anamorphic Games and the Memento Mortem Mortis

Their only experience of humanity was a crowbar coming
at them down a steel corridor.
—G-Man, *Half-Life 2: Episode 2*

Realism is a terrible, terrible design trope.
—Gabe Newell, "On Productivity, Economics,
Political Institutions and the Future of Corporations"

Peering out from a canyon cradled between two mesas, a series of
striated buttes punctuate the Southwestern landscape. Fat tubes of rich,
red earth jut into the sky as if extruded along the sharp contrasts of a
height map. Below, specular highlights and ray-traced reflections define
a river's surface—a sheet of frozen ripples sinking beneath banks of rust-
colored sand. Atmosphere occludes the horizon where a purple, pixelated
smear articulates the union of red and blue. The colors are odd, the shadows are off, and the entire scene is slightly stretched like the painted
panorama of a museum diorama, Hollywood backlot, or chapel ceiling.
An anamorphic image posing as perspectival space, this imaginary New
Mexico unfolds into a cruciform that wraps around the geometry of a
skybox. The smell of ozone and petrichor of the desert is replaced by the
odor of a freshly unboxed graphics card or stack of memory sticks in
anti-static wrap. On a contemporary computer, the sharp cliff faces and
stiff bipedal figures that populate the foreground are rendered at a much
higher resolution than those twenty-year-old, interpolated buttes in
the background. Patrolling the cliff's edge, a lone marine from the Haz-
ardous Environment Combat Unit (HECU) idles outside the Black Mesa
Research Facility; the contours of his crisp uniform stand out against the
anti-aliased skyline. In *Half-Life* (1998), low-poly models float in the middle of a New Mexican-themed box—a cube composed of six seamless

Figure 2.1. A computer-generated New Mexican vista (top) is the result of a series of six seamless textures (bottom) that wrap the skybox to produce the background of *Half-Life*.

256 x 256 pixel textures. Wisps of cream-colored clouds, pre-baked maroon shadows, and the rippling bump map of the teal water paint a strange picture. This New Mexico may as well be Mars (see Figure 2.1).

On the surface of Mars, NASA's Curiosity rover carries a piece of New Mexico with it. Cut from some of the densest lava on Earth, a smooth basalt disk installed as part of the rover's alpha particle X-ray spectrometer (as distinct from mass spectrometers) is the control variable for extraterrestrial experiments (NASA 2012). A terrestrial tabula rasa chemically contrasting the Martian soil, basalt is used to calibrate the half-lives of materials on Mars. One such anomalous material, a 1 x 5.5-foot rock formation, was found on the 53rd Martian day of NASA's first rover mission in 2004 and nicknamed "Sandia" after the Sandia-Manzano mountain range in New Mexico (NASA 2004). When characterizing the New Mexican landscape at the beginning of *Alien Phenomenology, Or What It's Like to Be a Thing,* Ian Bogost (2012, 1) writes:

> When the weather is clear, the Sandia Mountains to the east of Albuquerque drip the juices of their namesake fruit for a spell each evening, ripening quickly until the twilight devours them. . . . In the hollowed out Manzano Mountain, the United States Armed Forces Special Weapons Command once stashed the nation's largest domestic nuclear weapons repository, some 2,450 warheads as of the turn of the millennium.

From NASA to SETI to the Trinity nuclear test site and the landfill where Atari abandoned its surplus *E.T. the Extra-Terrestrial* (1982) cartridges (among other things),[1] New Mexico offered Bogost (2012, 1) a "childhood of weird objects." In *Alien Phenomenology* Bogost (2012, 17) channels Graham Harman's "Object-Oriented Ontology" and Levi Bryant's "Democracy of Objects" in order to evoke a New Mexico in which all objects are assigned the "same ontological status." From "the guilty Manhattan project physicist, the oval-headed alien anthropomorph, and the intelligent celestial race" to "the scoria cone, the obsidian fragment, the gypsum crystal, the capsicum pepper, and the propane flame," *Alien Phenomenology* not only attempts to place all objects on equal ontological footing, but in doing attempts to *decorrelate* the human experience of the world from the larger "world of things" (Bogost 2012, 3).[2]

Somewhere in terrestrial New Mexico, no doubt near the abandoned missile testing grounds and corporate landfills of the twentieth-century military entertainment complex, is another kind of complex buried beneath the red sand: Black Mesa Research Facility, the setting of Valve Corporation's first game, *Half-Life*. From mesas on the surface of Mars in *Doom* (1993) to the Black Mesa Research Facility in *Half-Life*, both the graphics and gameplay of first-person shooters (FPS) are predicated on the mechanics of perspectival rendering.[3] In these games, aiming and firing a gun stands in for the point-and-click interface of a computer mouse. Ballistics are reduced to the path of a ray traced from the first-person camera to the geometry of the game's polygonal environment.[4] But, in the same way that the objects in Bogost's New Mexico infinitely withdraw from the domain of experience, the red planets carefully rendered in first-person shooters are always, in some way, just out of reach (or out of sight). Even before Gordon Freeman pushed the G-Man's anomalous materials into the anti-mass spectrometer in Lab X and triggered the resonance cascade linking planet Earth and dimension Xen, Black Mesa Research Facility was full of xenomorphs.[5]

Half-Life begins with Freeman's commute from the Level 3 dormitories to the Sector C test labs and control facilities via the company's automated tram. As he arrives late to work on that fateful day, a public service announcement calmly intones, "The time is 8:47 a.m. Current topside temperature is 93 degrees with an estimated high of 105. The Black Mesa compound is maintained at a pleasant 68 degrees at all times" (Valve 1998). Twenty-seven years old with a Ph.D. in theoretical physics from MIT, the player's silent cipher must wait. Unable to exit the tram, for the next five or so minutes[6] Freeman is subjected to a series of ominous vignettes occurring behind the scenes at Black Mesa that foreshadow the events of *Half-Life*: a security guard banging on a tunnel door, white-coated scientists scuttling along rusted catwalks, a concrete pipe swinging at the end of a chain, a nuclear missile in mid-transport to some unknown launch site, autonomous quadrupedal robots performing industrial labor (and sometimes blocking the tram), a black Apache helicopter on a landing pad in the New Mexican landscape, and the mysterious G-Man straightening his tie in an adjoining tram above what appears to be the neon green goo of a reactor leak. As scenes of industrial disarray and bureaucracy run amok pass by, it's no wonder Gordon is late to work. The tram is designed not for transportation but for sightseeing—for *seeing sight*. It operates as a camera obscura or anatomical theater, a lens with which to view the alien and alienating visual technics of *Half-Life* itself.[7]

A compelling but nonetheless linear experience, *Half-Life* is also on rails. The infamous tram ride not only showcases snippets of the various levels the player will soon traverse, but, in its attempt to render a seamless experience in real time, foregrounds the underlying interface metaphors and logic of control that structure the game. Even after stepping onto the platform at Sector C, Freeman is still propelled from corridor to corridor although designer, player, and even the G-Man conspire to obfuscate the linear mechanisms of algorithmic control in order to present the illusion of an immersive, interactive, and open world. At the end of the game, Freeman need not leap into the portal to dimension Xen; he is already embedded in a distorted, inaccessible, and irresolvable universe of everyday-yet-eldritch objects. That is not a nuclear missile, that is not an Apache helicopter, that is not the G-Man, and that is not a pipe (or crowbar); rather, these are demonstrations of real-time diegetic storytelling, scripted in-game events, and seamless level design. As Gordon Freeman discovers, Black Mesa is in the business not only of exploiting alien technology for monetary and military gain, but also of inventing the idioms that inspired cinematic shooters like *Battlefield* (2005–), *Modern Warfare* (2007–), and *Black Ops* (2010–). Gabe Newell (Tufnell 2011), the co-founder of Valve, remembers that "*Half-Life* in many ways was a reactionary response to the trivialization of the experience of the first-person genre." In his 1998 review, Ron Dulin (1998) attests that "a major goal in any game is to create the illusion of reality, a fact that is especially true for first-person shooters. The whole point of the genre is to put you, literally, in the role of the protagonist . . . [and *Half-Life* is] the closest thing to a revolutionary step the genre has ever taken." Or so Black Mesa would have us think. Despite the long-held desire for perspectival immersivity, there is always an anamorphic remainder lying along the monorail or the steel corridor of the first-person shooter.

If anyone can outdo the alien and alienating inventions of the Black Mesa Research Facility, it is Aperture Science, Inc. First introduced in Valve's *Portal* (2007), the corporate rivalry between Aperture Science and Black Mesa manifests through both in-game and out-of-game advertising and propaganda reminiscent of Apple's "Get a Mac" campaign, which pitted Justin Long's "I'm a Mac" against John Hodgman's "I'm a PC" from 2006 to 2009 (see Figure 2.2).[8] Aperture Science's most popular product, central to the gameplay in *Portal*, is the Aperture Science

Handheld Portal Device, or "portal gun."[9] In *Half-Life 2* (2004), Black Mesa's Zero Point Energy Field Manipulator, or "gravity gun," is transformed from a piece of equipment designed to handle anomalous materials to another perspectival technology in the hands of Gordon Freeman. Cinder blocks, oil barrels, and saw blades are first pulled to the player then positioned in front of the camera before each object can be projected along a vector traced from the player's virtual camera-eye to the geometry of the gamespace. Extending the perspectival operations of the gravity gun beyond the rays traced from various weapons, the Aperture Science Handheld Portal Device represents a game mechanic that not only references *Half-Life,* but makes a metagame about first-person shooters as a genre.

Whereas *Half-Life* attempts to present an immersive and naturalistic 3D space in which both the physics and scenery mimetically reference a New Mexican landscape and follow the conventions of filmic realism (even while bunny-hopping from asteroid to asteroid in dimension Xen), *Portal* articulates a different model of space. At the beginning of the game, another silent protagonist, Chell,[10] wakes up from a "brief detention in the relaxation vault" to discover herself a lab rat in a series of experiments run by GLaDOS, the artificially intelligent unreliable narrator of *Portal* (Valve 2007). In order to complete the AI's twenty test chambers and escape the Aperture Science Computer-Aided Enrichment Center, the player must use the portal gun to produce "intra-dimensional gates" that connect the various planes of polygonal space. Enter through one portal, exit through another one, or, as GLaDOS explains, "momentum, a function of mass and velocity, is conserved between portals. In layman's terms: Speedy-thing goes in, speedy-thing comes out" (Valve 2007). Beyond momentum and movement, these wormholes also function as screens or mirrors used to refract the player's line of sight as well as the vision of the robotic sentries and surveillance systems within the Enrichment Center. Here, the term *aperture* not only signifies a hole or portal, but it also refers to the part of a camera lens that opens and closes to regulate light levels. In *Portal,* the gun that folds and collages space is literally viewed through the lens of cinema—a piece of nonlinear editing software that remakes digital space in real time. Instead of employing the standard first-person interface, in which rays are traced according to a line of sight from the camera to a given enemy's geometry, *Portal* plays with space in the same way games like Jonathan Blow's *Braid* (2008)

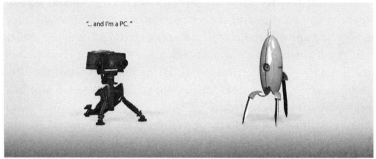

Figure 2.2. Whereas the gravity gun follows in the footsteps of *Doom's* BFG 9000, the portal gun adopts the aesthetic of Apple computers (top). This Mac-versus-PC–esque rivalry is made explicit in Valve's teaser images promoting their digital distribution service, Steam, once it was released for Apple computers (bottom).

play with time—metagames that take now-familiar genres like the first-person shooter or platformer, add a second-order challenge, and so transform action games into puzzle games *about* other games. And, as *Braid* inspired dozens of metagames that self-consciously model the temporality of videogames, there are also a host of "*Portal*-likes" or "first-person puzzle platformers" that celebrate and attempt to expand upon *Portal* as a genre in and of itself.[11] *Portal* is a game about perspective that both references and critiques the previous perspectival games that came before it.

Realism, naturalism, similitude, likeness, representation, reference, and mimesis in videogames do not index the geometry and textures of a given game to an object in the world, but instead signify a correlation between the player's expectations and the game's operations. Perspective, in this case, is a user-friendly interface meant to camouflage point-and-click mechanics and prevent the player from conceptually engaging with the technical operations of the software. Games *about* games, then, do not simply deploy perspectival rendering uncritically, as with *Half-Life,* but intentionally disrupt or distort the immediate experience of space. *Portal* offers its users an anamorphic interface and joins numerous other games discussed in this chapter that experiment with digital-born forms of vision as a means of investigating the disconnect between the phenomenology of play and the alien topologies of computational space. In order to explore this form of metagaming, this chapter first reviews how anamorphosis has been treated as a philosophical tool for exploring the relationship between human phenomenology and mimetic technologies like perspectival painting, computer-generated imagery, and even first-person shooters. From Hans Holbein the Younger's *The Ambassadors* (1533) to Robert Lazzarini's *skulls* (2001), anamorphic artworks mediate the tension between mathematical models of vision that reduce sight to a single, abstract locus. Extending the arguments of media theorists Espen Aarseth and Mark Hansen, this chapter then analyzes how anamorphosis functions in contemporary videogames. Like the discussion of Phil Fish's *Fez* (2012) in chapter 1, videogames like Sony's *Echochrome* series (2008–10), *levelHead* (2007) by Julian Oliver, and Mark ten Bosch's *Miegakure* (forthcoming) feature anamorphic techniques that mark the dissonant registers of time and space produced between human biology and digital media. By perturbing assumptions about vision in order to decorrelate body and code, anamorphic games generate what we call a *memento mortem mortis*: a reminder of the limits of human phenomenology and a tacit acknowledgment of the desire to think the unthinkable and play in the spaces that exceed the boundaries of perception.

Two Myths of Mimesis

Before the perspectival technologies of Black Mesa sank beneath New Mexican sands and before portal guns glued spaces together and operated as anamorphic lenses, Pliny the Elder (c. AD 77–79, Bk. 35, Ch. 43) recounted two myths of mimesis in his *Naturalis Historia*. In one, Dibutades, the daughter of the Corinthian sculptor Butades is saddened by the imminent departure of her lover and traces the outline of his shadow as it is cast on a wall (see Figure 2.3). Inspired by this image, Butades

Figure 2.3. *The Origin of Painting: Dibutades Tracing the Portrait of a Shepherd* (1785), by Jean-Baptiste Regnault, depicts Butades' daughter tracing the outline of her lover's shadow.

presses clay over the drawing to sculpt a relief portrait based on the silhouette. This myth, which binds drawing and sculpting, does not celebrate the originality or expressivity of the artist's hand but instead focuses on the possibility of an indexical relationship between light, sight, and representation: an ancient camera activated by the hand of Butades' daughter. Elsewhere in *Naturalis Historia,* Pliny recites another well-known tale featuring the painters Zeuxis and Parrhasius, who compete to determine the most talented artist. In the story, Zeuxis paints grapes that look so natural birds fly down to peck at them, but Parrhasius wins the competition by painting curtains that deceive even Zeuxis, who attempts to draw them aside to reveal his competitor's artwork. Like the crows clamoring for figurative fruit, Zeuxis is tricked by Parrhasius' *trompe l'œil.* The desire for mimetic representation has fueled the invention of perspectival technologies from Butades' lovelorn daughter tracing shadows on a wall to Renaissance-era drawing machines tracing light through panes of glass to contemporary ray tracing, an algorithm for rendering photorealistic computer graphics (see Figure

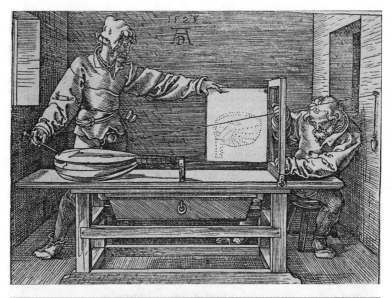

Figure 2.4. Both *Man Drawing a Lute* (1525) by Albrecht Dürer (top) and a typical example of ray tracing (bottom) represent mathematical models of light as vectors piercing a picture plane. Image by Patrick LeMieux, 2012 (bottom).

2.4). What unites these methods of simulating light is the often unexamined, mathematical process of perspective that reduces the human body to a cycloptic camera lens—an abstract optic perfectly positioned to decode perspectival data.

But what if the sun had begun to set on Butades' daughter, transforming her lover's silhouette into a monstrous grotesque? Or if Zeuxis had approached Parrhasius' painted curtains from an oblique angle, disrupting the two-dimensional illusion of depth? What if Albrecht Dürer's gridded glass "veil" had been bumped askew or if the algorithms responsible for rendering computer-generated imagery were not formulated properly? What if Aperture Science miscalculated the photographic effects of their Handheld Portal Device? Do subtle shifts in field of view or vantage point radically alter the human perception of perspectival images or is optical distortion actually a precondition for mimetic representation? Pliny's myths of mimesis remain myths because they continue to express the *desire* for a technological correlate to human sight—a technology capable of rendering a painted, projected, or backlit screen into a transparent, immaterial, or immediate window.[12] The fantasy of immediacy stubbornly ignores both the material support of an image and the embodied response of a viewer, reinforcing the notion of a lossless transmission between an abstract set of Cartesian coordinates and an equally abstract Cartesian mind. Rather than buy into the fantasy of perspective (and those industries centered around perspectival technology and the exploitation of its myths), what if anamorphosis was recast as the rule governing vision rather than the exception to "normal" sight? What if there is no central, authoritative, or natural way of seeing despite the way optical technologies simulate the effects of light on the human eye? Even after the centuries-long construction of the modern viewing subject, the most naturalistic representational technologies still suppress a strange supplement. Whether examining early painting or traversing the polygonal environments of a virtual world, an anamorphic remainder looms in the interstices between technics, optics, and human perception.

The possibilities and problems of perspectival rendering have been inherited by the computer graphics industry, a field of research whose design goals and business models are deeply wedded to the progressivist logic of mimetic technologies. Despite the fact that there are only a finite number of unique polygons, pixels, and processes perceptible to the human eye, the videogame industry, for example, continues to invest in higher and higher visual fidelity. As graphics guru and co-founder of id Software John Carmack noted at the 2011 Electronic Entertainment Expo (E3), rendering technologies are "converging at the limits of our biological systems" (McCormick 2011). Having seen the so-called "limits" of 2D displays, in 2014 Carmack took a job as Chief Technology Officer at Oculus and, along with id Software's Michael Abrash, is now exploring the affordances of VR headsets and the technical capacities of 3D gaming. With graphics technologies approaching the threshold of conscious perception, an increasing number of computer games are beginning to experiment with alternative spatial, temporal, and optical regimes indigenous to digital environments. Much like the restrained naturalism of Renaissance perspectival rendering led to a more self-conscious and reflexive Mannerist period of visual art, so have the nascent discourses surrounding computer-generated imagery and videogaming begun to internalize and amplify the codes of perspective to produce "anamorphic games." From *Portal* to *Fez* and beyond, anamorphic games are games *about* games—mimetic metagames that dramatize the relationship between sight and simulation, vision and virtual reality to reimagine what it means to see by playing with perspective.

The *Memento Mortem Mortis*

Popularized during the Renaissance, anamorphosis is a rendering technique that results in a strangely stretched, but geometrically viable image. When attempting to "decode" the distortions applied to a given anamorphic artwork, onlookers must either assume an oblique viewing angle in relation to a foreshortened image or reflect a catoptrically warped image through a corresponding conic or cylindrical mirror. In 1927, Erwin Panofsky famously characterized traditional perspective as a "symbolic form" loaded with the Western ontology of the stable, fixed, and unified Cartesian subject (Panofsky 1996). Anamorphosis, on the other hand, is regarded as a marginal visual technique, a *trompe l'œil* that operates according to a different cultural logic, covertly applying pressure to the universality of classical perspective and all its ideological assumptions. But what if these assumptions were somehow reversed? Does not perspectival rendering, despite its cultural ubiquity and long history of perceptual conditioning, also require decoding? Is it even possible to see a perfect, perspectival image without minor distortions of eye, angle, and environment intervening? Though ease of rendering and conventions of human sight privilege this particular, historically contingent instance of mimesis, what if every perspectival image is actually anamorphic? What if anamorphosis was not only considered a means of encoding secrets in images, but was itself the secret that lies at the heart of all images?

Traditionally, perspectival rendering assumes that the position of the viewer is directly in front of and oriented toward the "picture plane," a two-dimensional field that typically coincides with the material surface of an image. Conflating the picture plane with the angle and dimension of a canvas, for example, allows geometric projections representing light vectors to intersect with an unambiguous, material support (e.g., the surface of a canvas, the emulsion of a photographic plate, the phosphors of a screen, the photocells of a digital sensor, or even the pages of this book). This ideological conflation of mathematics and materiality removes the need for difficult, higher level modeling and simplifies the rendering process. The geometry of anamorphic images, however, requires nonstandard viewing angles by intentionally foreshortening the picture plane and decoupling it from the physical geometry of the painting, plate, panel, or page. This experimental and unconventional technique produces coded, mannered, and seemingly non-natural imagery. As such, anamorphosis is often regarded as a curiosity, an occasional virtuosic supplement to the catalog of classical perspective throughout the history of art. However, if the historical coincidence of the imaginary picture plane and the material surface of a painting is merely one particular case within a much larger field of possibility, then anamorphosis can be re-thought as the rule rather than the exception to perspectival image-making. In the same way that Richard Garfield observes "there is no game without a metagame," no image exists without the anamorphic distortions produced by historical context, material composition, and bodily experience interacting with and influencing vision.

From the covers of book jackets to the commercials on television to the virtual cameras of first-person shooters, contemporary visual culture is dominated by perspectival modes of representation. It is easy to forget that mimetic images, no matter how naturalistic, require a cognitive leap in order to resolve the relationship between a mathematical system of rendering and embodied vision. By explicitly denying the so-called "correct" viewing position, anamorphosis forecloses the possibility of ever resolving the human gaze to the geometric parameters of an image. Anamorphic technique foregrounds the biological complexity of binocular vision, the angle of approach, height of a viewer, surface deformations of a medium, and even the atmosphere through which light passes. These anamorphic conditions undergird human perception and demonstrate that classical perspective—what has been culturally coded as "natural"— remains a highly constructed, mathematical method of simulating light rather than an accurate model of vision. Perspective is to vision what Newton's classical mechanics are to quantum physics: a useful but ultimately inadequate approximation. Despite the popular desire for transparent, immediate experiences of media, conventional perspective is impossible to fully realize for viewer and painter alike. Whether standing in front of a canvas or grasping a controller, embodied vision is not properly

Figure 2.5. When viewed at an oblique angle, Hans Holbein's *The Ambassadors* (left) reveals a strange, stretched skull (opposite page). Image by Thomas Shahan, 2011.

perspectival but actually anamorphic, constantly modulated by embodied encounters with the material environment.

The quintessential example of anamorphosis is Hans Holbein's *The Ambassadors,* a large and meticulously rendered oil painting featuring a strange, anamorphic "smear" across the bottom of the otherwise typical portrait of two sixteenth-century European diplomats (see Figure 2.5). In *The Ambassadors,* the two men stand costumed and well lit in a carefully proportioned, perspectival space, each with an elbow resting on the foreshortened table. The painting displays a menagerie of symbolic details denoting worldly opulence including fine clothing and foreign textiles, a lute with an open book of sheet music, two globes, and various instruments for navigation and cartography: technologies of rationalism that will help provide the "correct" perspective for mapping the New World. Yet, if the viewer examines the painting from an unorthodox

position either above and to the right or below and to the left of the standard viewing angle,[13] the smear congeals into a grinning skull: a subliminal *memento mori* hidden in plain sight.

Although the inclusion of subtle reminders of mortality like skulls, timepieces, wilting flowers, or rotting fruit were common among portraits and still lifes produced in medieval and Renaissance Europe, Holbein's *memento mori* is particularly unsettling given its uncanny manifestation through the technique of anamorphic foreshortening.[14] Here, the anamorphic skull is powerful not because it looks like a skull, but precisely because it *does not* look like a skull. Consider the possibility that this "not-skull" might reveal nothing to the viewer but paint. A sixteenth-century audience, for example, might have missed the skull entirely, only subliminally apprehending a death's head upon one last, over-the-shoulder glance from the bottom of a stairwell or the threshold of an exit. Though it has the potential to trick the eye, this smear of abject materiality exists within its own ontological (and more specifically mathematical) register and casts an anamorphic doubt back into the previously perspectival world of the two diplomats. Working with the established cultural tradition of the *memento mori,* Holbein summons notions of death's alterity as a metaphor for the ultimate strangeness of both the materiality of paint and the mathematics of perspective. This fleeting glimpse of a death's head reminds the viewer not of their eventual expiration, but of the (perhaps more unsettling) fact that there exist objects and affects that exceed not only perspectival rendering but human experience altogether. The anamorphic skull renders a world of nonhuman technics that not only lies beyond the limitations of the human body, but is also completely disinterested in the affairs of man and the vagaries of life and death.

In this respect, it may be more accurate to use the term *memento mortem mortis* than *memento mori.*[15] The *memento mortem mortis* transforms the human-centered "remembrance of death" into the "remembrance of the death of death"—the realization that one day even death will die. Despite the impossibility of ever experiencing a world devoid of life, the *memento mortem mortis* invites the viewer to speculate on the radically attenuated phenomenology and starkly physical conditions of such a world. Where the *memento mori* mobilizes representations of death to challenge human vanity, the *memento mortem mortis* extends this critique beyond morbid anthropocentrisms by summoning not the representations of human death, but the nonhuman processes of technical objects. The result is not only the humbling acknowledgment of some thanatological equalizer between all human life, but also a call toward philosophical speculation. In this way, the painterly materiality of the anamorphic skull exposes a notion of cosmic indifference that is vaster, more alien, and more terrifying than the anthropocentric concerns of life and death represented through a *memento mori.* Throughout the history of painting, the skull, like other depictions of human detritus, has been used to signal human mortality. By stretching these skeletal remains across a separate, foreshortened picture plane that refuses to cohere with the geometry of the painted scene, the *memento mori* opens up the yawning abyss of the *memento mortem mortis.*

Anamorphosis, as well as those technologies that directly frame their nonhuman components in relation to human phenomenology, is just one example of a *memento mortem mortis.* In anamorphic images the subject and object never completely resolve for one another and there remains an incommensurable gap, as reflected in Holbein's painting. In this sense, the human and the skull can never see eye to eye, and *The Ambassadors* functions as an allegory for de-anthropomorphized materiality in the idiom of early modern painting. Hubert Damisch (1995, 28) has argued that mathematical perspective was the dominant mode of image making in the twentieth century (far more than in previous eras prior to the development of mechanical forms of image inscription such as photography, film, and video). Yet these chemical, mechanical, electrical, and even computational forms of perspectival rendering can still each be regarded as cases of anamorphosis. All images are anamorphic insofar as they apply the rules of perspectival projection to an arbitrary and anthropocentric picture plane. The coincidence of the picture plane and material surface of the image is popular because of the convenience of calculating only one projection, rather than the multiple abstractions necessary for anamorphic rendering. Despite the fact that all paintings could be considered anamorphic under this definition, only some, like *The Ambassadors,* form a *memento mortem mortis* by explicitly questioning the necessary relation between the human body, an image's material support, and the abstract geometries of the perspectival picture plane. Similarly, while the corridors of Black Mesa Research Facility can never entirely resolve to the player's expectations, Aperture Science, Inc. builds anamorphic technologies explicitly designed to disrupt and disorganize perspectival space. For media theorists Espen Aarseth and Mark Hansen, the concept of anamorphosis functions more broadly as a paradigm for understanding digital technology in general, from stretched skulls to stretched skyboxes.

Ergodic Resolution and the Digital Any-Space-Whatever

At the end of *Cybertext: Perspectives on Ergodic Literature* (1997), Espen Aarseth embraces anamorphosis as a metaphor for what he calls "ergodic literature" and operates from the assumption that anamorphic images posit a privileged perspective from which to faithfully reconstruct an image. Taking examples from print, computer games, hypertext fiction, and electronic literature, in *Cybertext* ergodic literature is defined as those works whose completion requires "nontrivial effort" on the part of the reader (Aarseth 1997, 1–2). By nontrivial effort, Aarseth means the kinetic as well as intellectual labor performed by a reader or player that specifically influences the outcome or effect of a given text or game. Ergodic literature is distinct from most standard forms of writing because it requires meaningful effort above and beyond, for example, turning pages or flipping to the end of a book to read the final chapter. Considering Aarseth's concept in relation to Holbein's skull, a viewer's self-conscious act of bending low to the ground in order to match the oblique angle of anamorphic distortion meets the requirements of ergodic labor. The active engagement required in any attempt to decode or decrypt anamorphic images is what leads Aarseth to make an analogy between early modern techniques of anamorphosis and certain forms of interactive media.

In the last chapter of his book, Aarseth (1997, 181) defines anamorphosis as a "solvable enigma." For Aarseth, the defining quality of anamorphosis is the moment of revelation produced when the distortion of the warped image is resolved through the viewer's effort to locate the vantage point from which classical perspective is restored. The passage from what Aarseth (1997, 91) terms "aporia" to "epiphany" connects anamorphic painting to ergodic literature (and videogames). With this in mind, Aarseth interprets the text-based games and interactive fiction of the late seventies and early eighties such as Will Crowther and Don Woods' *Colossal Cave Adventure* (1975–76) and Infocom's *Zork* trilogy (1980–84) as models of an anamorphic textuality in which the player must work in order for the mystery to be revealed. But not all ergodic texts provide puzzles with seemingly concrete answers, and Aarseth invents a second category he terms "metamorphosis" in which mastery and resolution are refused (e.g., Michael Joyce's hypertext novel *Afternoon: A Story* [1987]).

There is no need, however, for a second category in which to reroute those texts that do not appear to have singular interpretations, linear causality, or solvable enigmas waiting at the ready. As suggested earlier, rather than reifying a specific subject position in front of a painting, image, artifact, or portal, the concept of anamorphosis radically critiques all subject positions as tenuous and fraught. Even if there is a viewing angle in which an image becomes more legible, there remains no one "correct" angle, and any resolution the viewer might feel should be met with some skepticism. The anamorphic skull in *The Ambassadors* is not a *memento mori* in the sense that it reminds the viewer of her mortality as she catches a glimpse of the skull through the corner of her eye, but is actually a *memento mortem mortis* because it calls into question the very concept of a fixed subject and resolved object. Rather than simply serving as a reminder of some distant future bereft of human life, the *memento mortem mortis* demonstrates that experience itself is already composed of nonhuman assemblages imbricated within a vast network of relations never entirely legible to conscious experience.

In contrast to Aarseth, in *New Philosophy for New Media* (2006) Mark Hansen deploys anamorphic artwork to parallel those aspects of digital media that explicitly fail to visually resolve and produce bodily discomfort because of the formal incongruity between embodied space and the speeds and scales of digital media. Specifically, Hansen's close reading of *skulls*, an anamorphic sculpture by Robert Lazzarini in the tradition of *The Ambassadors*, challenges Aarseth's concept of anamorphosis. For Hansen, *skulls* produces a "digital any-space-whatever," a term he borrows from Deleuze to describe the uncomfortable, proprioceptive sensation produced in response to the disjunct ontological registers of digital media. It is precisely the failure of the human body to easily assimilate anamorphic images that Hansen finds useful for thinking about digital media. Robert Lazzarini's sculptural installation *skulls*, exhibited at the Whitney Museum of American Art's 2000 show BitStreams, serves as Hansen's central case study on the issue (see Figure 2.6).

Recalling Holbein and Aperture Science, Inc., Lazzarini's artwork engages the tension between systems of perspectival projection and the

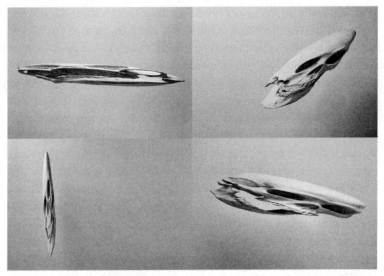

Figure 2.6. Robert Lazzarini's *skulls* is an installation of four stretched and squashed sculptures that were laser scanned, mathematically manipulated, rapid prototyped, and then cast from bone. Photographs by Robert Lazzarini, 2009, reproduced with permission.

limits of human perception. Instead of projecting smears of paint across picture planes, Lazzarini builds smeared sculptures that stretch in three dimensions and challenge the viewer to reconcile vision and bodily proprioception. Where anamorphic images are rendered onto a foreshortened picture plane, Lazzarini's sculptural process involves applying two-dimensional planar shifts (including perspectival effects) directly to the geometry of three-dimensional haptic objects.[16]

Lazzarini's digital development process begins by laser scanning or solid modeling a common object, instrument, or weapon to generate an editable polygonal mesh. The geometric points, lines, and planes abstracted from each object are mathematically bent, warped, shifted, and distorted within modeling software before being 3D printed. The resulting rapid prototypes are not finished products, but serve as templates for physically sculpting the now-deformed models from the same materials that constituted the original object (e.g., the stretched *skulls* are cast in bone). Although this complex process remains relatively consistent throughout his catalog, Lazzarini's diverse array of subjects are

selected to enhance the cognitive dissonance created between the materiality of his anamorphic sculptures and their perceptual effects. Rang-
ing from skulls to violins, hammers, teacups, telephones, telephone
booths, chairs, knives, revolvers, and brass knuckles—although, unfortunately, no crowbars yet—these objects and weapons share one thing
in common aside from their anamorphic effects: an ergonomic reference
to the human body. It is only through this remarkable conflict between
optic and haptic sensations that Lazzarini's sculptures become tools
from another digital dimension: hammers with ungraspable handles.[17]

Among this selection of digitally disfigured tools, *skulls* stands apart.
These sculptures do not share the same status as the broken, Heidegge-
rian hammer that reveals its nonhuman character only once it ceases to
function for a human operator's intended use. Like *The Ambassadors*
before it, Lazzarini's stretched *skulls* are not broken at all. Instead, the anamorphic objects operate as intended. They produce a *memento mortem
mortis* that frames nonhuman fields of experience within the register of
human utility. The horizon of unthinkability represented in *skulls* serves
as a means to philosophical inquiry. Here the very idea of unthinkability
enacted in these uncanny objects becomes a kind of technology—a
useful (and fully operational) philosophical tool for speculation. The
optical instability of Lazzarini's sculptures draws attention to this speculative horizon as a means of re-inscribing it within the sphere of
human perception. There is a certain irony to the fact that *skulls* maintains a kind of functionality despite its anamorphic tilts, shifts, twists,
and turns. The fact that viewers cannot fix their gaze on a stable optical
regime only intensifies the *skulls'* role as a *memento mortem mortis*.
Technically, *skulls* does what it is supposed to do—it enables philosophical, aesthetic, and contemplative work.

Despite their physical status and oblique reference to the history of the
memento mori in painting, in a chapter titled "The Affective Topology of
New Media," Hansen (2006b, 202) argues that Lazzarini's sculptures are
"exemplary of digital media art." Lazzarini's sculptures exist physically
within three-dimensional space and yet, no matter what angle the distorted objects are viewed from, they fail to visually resolve in a satisfying
way. Looming in life-scale and cast in bone, the digitally modeled *skulls*
renders one of the most visually recognizable parts of human anatomy
strange and uncanny. Their hollow eyes refuse to stare back. If an observer
closed her eyes and held Lazzarini's stretched skulls, the contours would

resolve to the haptic touch, but as Hansen (2006b, 202) writes, *skulls* "'makes sense' visually—only within the weird logic and topology of the computer." Because of their technical status as digital media art, *skulls* becomes a means through which Hansen describes the incommensurable ontology of a computer. Lazzarini offers an optical distortion designed to disrupt, rather than pacify, the senses. The sculptures produce a bodily experience that Hansen labels the "digital any-space-whatever"[18] (digital ASW), a proprioceptive sense akin to nausea or vertigo as the body fails to orient itself—a category of play that Roger Caillois (2001, 12) calls "*ilinx*." Hansen (2006b, 198–99) writes that in the face of *skulls* "you feel the space around you begin to ripple, to bubble, to infold . . . and you notice an odd tensing in your gut, as if your viscera were itself trying to adjust to this warped space."

Hansen (2006b, 205) concludes his analysis with the suggestion that "what *skulls* affords is, consequently, not a direct apprehension of an alien space that *is* digital, but a bodily apprehension of just how radically alien the formal field of the computer is" (emphasis original). In this sense the *memento mortem mortis* and the digital ASW go hand in hand—reminders of an expanded, nonhuman terrain driven by a necessarily incomplete (or anamorphic) apprehension of the speeds and scales of technical media. In an artwork like *skulls,* which is as psychologically unsettling as it is proprioceptively disruptive, experiential strangeness quickly transforms into existential thinking when confronted not with mortal remains, but with the irresolvable and indigestible remainder of the *memento mortem mortis.* Though Hansen's concept begins as an embodied, affective sensation, the digital ASW gestates within the same inclement ontological spaces conceptualized by the *memento mortem mortis.*

Videogames, like all digital media, are built upon mechanical, electrical, and computational process that inform, yet operate outside human experience. The nonhuman speed of switches being flipped, the mind-numbing repetition of serial data being sequenced, the irreducible materiality of magnetic platters being polarized, and even the mechanics of interdimensional portals being opened and closed at Aperture Science can never be fully represented to human sensibility. Instead, the *memento mortem mortis* emerges from the incongruity between computational and human forms of space and time that manifests as an embodied and affective response (i.e., Hansen's digital ASW) to allegorize these invisible processes. Whereas a work like *skulls* emphasizes the failure of the viewer to grasp these forever skewed and uncanny objects, most videogames do not generally make a practice of cultivating sensory discomfort. But what if a body were required to negotiate two- and three-dimensional spaces simultaneously, as with Sony's *Echochrome* software? Can muscles remember the extra-dimensional abstractions of Julian Oliver's *levelHead*? And is it possible to see four-dimensional geometries as Mark ten Bosch's *Miegakure* claims?[19]

From *Portal* to *Echochrome* to *levelHead* to *Miegakure*, the anamorphic games examined in the remainder of this chapter intentionally play within the dissonant registers produced between biological and computational systems. They produce ludic metaphors of the *memento mortem mortis* to model an engagement with an unthinkable computational space. Yet, despite their experimentation with alternative haptic and visual regimes, even these metagames about games resist pushing the implications of anamorphosis to its limits. Rather than forcing the player to stare an inassimilable digital landscape in the face, they persist in offering a fantasy of mastery through the successful completion of goal-oriented tasks and suggest that the body can be acclimated to their eccentric spaces. Flight simulators may be developed to combat airsickness, and it is with a similar logic that these anamorphic games invite players to test-drive the digital ASW, to make it safe and naturalize the body to the "incredible strangeness," "odd tensing[s]," and "weird sensation[s]" of the *memento mortem mortis* (Hansen 2006b, 198–99).[20] As GLaDOS quips in her game's trailer "now you're thinking with portals" (Valve 2006).

Echochrome: Anamorphic Architecture and Shadow Play

When the first generation of home videogame consoles supporting 3D graphics processing was introduced in the mid-1990s, the development of 2D, sprite-based games was temporarily arrested.[21] In the flush of fascination with these strange polygonal spaces, the efforts of software engineers and game designers alike were redirected from sprite sheets, parallax scrolling, and painting with pixels—or "dotting"—to domesticating and naturalizing 3D environments for mainstream consumption. Since the indie boom of the late 2000s, however, there has been a renaissance of 2D platforming games that explicitly reference the technological constraints, pixelated aesthetic, and ludic genres of 8-bit games like *Super Mario Bros.* (1985), *The Legend of Zelda* (1986), and *Tetris* (1989). The flatness of the screen and depiction of 2D space are no longer technical limitations but creative constraints—design choices that can be placed in conjunction with 3D spaces to create metagames about graphics processing and computer rendering itself. From *Super Paper Mario* (2007) to *Portal*, anamorphic games are not only metagames about graphic technologies, but about *aboutness* itself.[22] One series of games that structures its gameplay around the perspectival play of both two- and three-dimensional spaces is the "Echo" franchise, which includes *Echochrome* (2008), *Echoshift* (2009), and *Echochrome II* (2010).

Produced by Sony's Japan Studio and Game Yarouze for the PlayStation Portable (PSP) and PlayStation 3 (PS3), in *Echochrome* the player is presented with a minimal, white space featuring a centralized, floating object composed of stairs, walkways, ramps, and ramparts reminiscent of M. C. Escher's illustrations of impossible spaces and paradoxical architectures (see Figure 2.7). When the joystick is tilted, *Echochrome*'s hovering levels rotate and, unlike a hand-drawn optical illusion, reconstitute their perspectival conditions in real time. All the while, a solitary figure strolls back and forth, footsteps clacking in empty space. The lone resident of these "endless walkways" (the rough translation of *Echochrome*'s Japanese title, *Mugen Kairō*) is a white, textureless mannequin who autonomously wanders up and down the crisply contoured, isometric expanses. Both the oblique reference to Escher's artwork and the mannequin (a tool traditionally used to help model perspectival figures) are fitting considering that the game's primary mechanic involves rotating anamorphic architectures in ways that paradoxically play with the dichotomy between screen and space.

In *Echochrome*, there are five main rules governing the mannequin's movements:

1. When two separate pathways appear to be touching, they are.
2. If one pathway appears to be above another, it is.
3. When the gap between two pathways is blocked from view and the pathways appear to be connected, they are.
4. When a hole is blocked from view, it does not exist.
5. When the mannequin jumps, it will land on whatever appears beneath it. (Sony 2008)

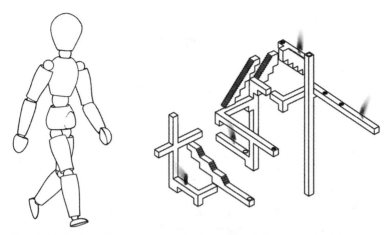

Figure 2.7. *Echochrome*'s mannequin main character and illusionistic level design reference both the traditions of perspectival naturalism and the anamorphic effects of M. C. Escher's artwork. Sony advertisements, 2008.

These five laws of perspective define the relationship between two- and three-dimensional spaces within the world of *Echochrome*. By inverting the order of perspectival rendering, the pictorial logic of the screen is given precedence over the mimetic representation of space. What you see is literally what you get.

Echochrome recalls *The Ambassadors* in the way it mixes traditional perspective with anamorphic effects. By placing both two- and three-dimensional space in conversation with each other, the game conflates the dual logic of flat "screen" and deep "window," two metaphors Anne Friedberg contrasts in *The Virtual Window: From Alberti to Microsoft* (2006). In her book, Friedberg argues that although perspective has been the historically dominant form of visuality, computer-generated imaging has dramatically transformed how space is culturally perceived and organized. She examines the graphic user interface of computer desktops and the way they are composed of multiple, overlapping windows, conflicting light sources, and purely abstract drop shadows. Although Leon Battista Alberti famously described classical perspective as a "window" onto another world, Friedberg critiques Alberti's metaphor[23] and demonstrates how computer software companies have appropriated similar rhetoric for describing the non-perspectival, nonlinear incongruities and contradictions of computer operating systems. In this sense, the flattened desktop and overlapping panes of Microsoft Windows has become a "window"—the artificial tropes and interface metaphors of operating systems have become naturalized as yet another form of realism.[24]

Echochrome stands out as a particularly intriguing example of alternative spatial organization because it knowingly plays with the tension between pictorial and sculptural space. As the player rotates the central object in three dimensions, real-time graphics processes render an illusion of depth, with the screen or monitor serving as virtual window. Near and far, broad and deep, *Echochrome's* rotating spaces appear to behave rationally. But when the motion stops, the collisions and connections of the Escher-esque architecture are ultimately determined according to the logic of the suspended two-dimensional image. The "window" into another realm flattens into an opaque screen.[25]

Adjusting *Echochrome's* perspective transforms not only the player's view, but the composition of the architecture itself. The spatial dimensions and composition of the object are not fixed in space. Instead, the in-game architecture is reconstituted depending on the angle from which it is viewed. In the tradition of Espen Aarseth's concept of ergodic literature, this is perspectival rendering structured within the logic of ludic mastery, and it operates according to fixed points of resolution— more a puzzle game than a puzzling game. If the player rotates the architecture correctly, or, more precisely, manipulates the in-game camera to the proper coordinate, the puzzle will be solved and the secret revealed. Discovering the solution to these levels and cracking their spatial codes, promotes a reductive model of anamorphosis—one that equates embodied vision with an absolute, mathematical result produced by a virtual camera. In this sense, *Echochrome* differs from a work like *skulls* in which there is no chance of ever decoding the sculptural smears into perspectival representations. The game's ludic logic acts as an interface through which the player finds herself able to assume a naive position of control and mastery of those perspectives that would otherwise be hopelessly irresolvable. According to *Echochrome's* eccentric camera, the human eye is reduced to a one-dimensional point in space, perfect for projecting and reflecting ray-traced light.

Whereas *Echochrome* creates a world built around the intersections of two- and three-dimensional space, its sequel, *Echochrome II*, adds the play of light and shadow to its predecessor's uniquely hybrid perspective of multi-dimensional objects. Once again, what you see is what you get. The mannequin's silhouette, referred to as "the cast," must traverse visual puzzles through the player's anamorphic manipulations of light. In *Echochrome II*, the cast does not walk along the physical objects, but is literally cast along the shadowy, two-dimensional projections that fall in the wake of floating blocks, stairs, and steps (see Figure 2.8).

Similar to its predecessor, *Echochrome II* was developed by Sony's Japan Studio and made for PS3 but, unlike *Echochrome,* the sequel requires the PlayStation Move, a motion-sensing hand controller spatially tracked by the PS Eye, Sony's interactive, infrared camera.[26] The Move controller is topped by a glowing sphere that flickers and changes colors when the wand is active, emitting infrared light for the PS Eye to behold.[27] This motion-tracking technology inverts the relationship between controller and camera popularized by the Nintendo Wii, which emits two infrared points of light from a stationary bar set near the screen and tracked by a camera within the Wii Remote (aka the Wiimote) (see Figure 2.9). In *Echochrome II,* this light-tracking technology is used to position an in-game light source which, when cast on the floating objects, produces virtual shadows in real time based on the player's

Figure 2.8. An *Echochrome II* advertisement features interactive illumination and promises an experience so immediate that the screen between player and game vanishes.

Figure 2.9. A comparison of Sony's PlayStation Move and Nintendo's Wii Remote reveal similar design sensibilities.

bodily gestures. These motions translate into the screen's perspectival space as the player shines the Move controller on their television like a virtual flashlight. Rays are traced from the tip of the wand at the precise angle of incidence and projected from an in-game light source behind the camera in order to "pierce" the screen and produce the appearance of an out-of-game light source illuminating in-game objects and architectures.

The shadows produced by the Move evoke the flickering lamp flame from Pliny's account of Butades' daughter. But rather than assume a visual symmetry between silhouette and object (the way in which this myth has been traditionally depicted in various paintings), the game reveals the dissonance and distortions that prevail in the world of shadows.[28] In *Echochrome II*, the player can adjust the light source in order to produce anamorphic shadow play. If a player positions the controller at a particular angle, in the same way a viewer might position her body in relation to *The Ambassadors,* the game will reveal hidden, albeit banal, images (e.g., a robot, a smiling face, a snake, etc.), simultaneously converting previously insurmountable obstacles into more conventional 2D platforms for the player-controlled "cast" to hop, skip, and jump across (see Figure 2.10). Just as Butades used the shadow traced by his daughter to cast a relief portrait, *Echochome II* conflates silhouette and sculpture to model not earthen effigies but polygonal pathways. These digital projections not only operate according to the pictorial logic of two-

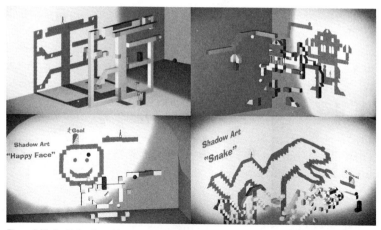

Figure 2.10. In *Echochrome II,* positioning the Move controller in relation to the screen reveals anamorphic images within the shadows.

dimensional shadow play, but are assigned an autonomous physics and materiality distinct from the original objects. The glowing orb simulates a cycloptic eyeball, projecting unique perspectives as the player learns how to alter the angle of the light source in order to play with distorted, anamorphic images.

Both *Echochrome* and *Echochrome II* produce spatial effects that are unique to the logic of the computer, but they depart from the *memento mortem mortis* by generating puzzles as "solvable enigmas." Both games encourage the player to participate in a fantasy of mastery by simulating anamorphic effects within a deterministic gamespace. Whereas anamorphic painting requires a player's body to physically adjust in relation to the object, these videogames produce anamorphic encounters through in-game camera rotation. *Echochrome* doesn't actually require a bodily perception of space, but uses perspectival rendering in a way that mimics anamorphosis. Similarly, *Echochrome 2* simulates a perspectival "eye" as a single point in space through using Sony's Move. In this sense, players only see the shadow play of *Echochrome 2* second-hand. Rather than activating perspective through vision, they render the gaze of a camera eye, adjusting the Move controller in order to project perspectival imagery onto the screen. Though the *Echochrome* games require haptic input, the mathematical transformations depicted in each polygonal space do not enliven an expanded, anamorphic field of affective, bodily experience but instead work to reinforce the hegemony of vision. Anamorphic distortions in the *Echo* series are framed in such a way that a properly perspectival solution is always the correct answer, repressing any sense of a radical encounter with the *memento mortem mortis*. Despite the play between two- and three-dimensional space, these metagames about perspectival rendering and user-friendly interfaces function merely as shadow boxes that ludically reinforce a naive fantasy of mastery by adhering, slavishly, to one-dimensional puzzles with one-dimensional solutions.

levelHead: A Multi-Dimensional Memory Palace

Echochrome II is designed to function with (and market) a specific commercial remote: Sony's PlayStation Move. In 2010 a generation of controllers, inspired by the success of Nintendo's unconventional Wii Remote, challenged the joystick-button and mouse-keyboard input combinations that have served as the industry standard in terms of interface design. Hardware like Nintendo's Wiimote, Sony's Move, and Microsoft's Kinect expand players' attention beyond their two thumbs by incorporating motion tracking and gesture recognition. Despite explicitly reframing input in terms of the body, these technologies fall under the category of "natural user interfaces," or NUIs, that ideologically reinforce the longstanding desire for a seamless and immersive form of interactivity in which the body is rendered invisible and vision is indexed precisely to the algorithmic abstractions on the screen. Amidst this turn toward so-called NUIs, media artist Julian Oliver designed a piece of software and a unique control scheme that does not take embodied forms of interaction for granted.

In 2007, Oliver created *levelHead,* an interactive installation exhibited in museums and galleries (as well as on the home computers of tenacious Linux users) (see Figure 2.11). The game combines color-coded and patterned cubes with custom, open-source software and a webcam to motion track and replace the six unique quick response (QR) codes of each cube with three-dimensional, interactive architecture. The result is a large, real-time video projection that displays the player's hands interfacing with the virtualized cubes—each facet filled with internal geometries. The cubes serve as both screens and joysticks, and, as with *Echochrome*

Figure 2.11. The installation of *levelHead* with cube-controllers, camera, and projection results in an augmented reality game at Ars Electronica 2008 in which manual manipulations are mapped to a virtual memory palace. Photograph by Otto Saxinger, 2008.

and *Echochrome II*, the player's physical gestures and positioning change the perspectival viewport to propel a small, white, humanoid silhouette who anonymously strolls through a six-sided interior space. This unassuming avatar, like the minimally designed "cast" featured in the *Echochrome* series, follows the path of least resistance based on the angle at which the player holds each QR-encrusted cube. By tilting the cube-controllers, the player indirectly steers this avatar that simply walks forward, a lost soul wandering aimlessly through shifting architecture. The three cubes work in sequence, each containing six unique rooms overlaid within the same physical space for a total of eighteen "levels." By tracking objects and actions instead of interfacing with standardized controller input and by projecting the results back on that which is being sampled, Oliver's augmented reality game extends the perspectival space of the screen to the physical environment and vice versa.

The inside of each of *levelHead's* cubes is articulated as if it were a shadow box, but when the player presents a new QR-encoded face to the camera, an entirely different space appears. The difficulty of *levelHead*, then, is to imagine six simultaneous rooms within the geometry of the single box in hand. This challenge, as Oliver has written, is complicated when one must remember the spatial organization of six discrete geometries despite the fact that they are not simultaneously present or interconnected in a way that is physically possible. The logic of the cube's architecture, therefore, must be constructed out of a different set of haptic cues, engaging with the wrist and hand rather than the screen and eye. As Oliver (2009) details on his website,

> the tangible interface aspect becomes integral to the function of recall. . . . As the cube is turned by the hands in search of correctly adjoining rooms muscle-memory is engaged and, as such, aids the memory as a felt memory of patterns of turns: "that room is two turns to the left when this room is upside down."

Although Oliver (2009) offers a walkthrough on YouTube, he notes that the game is "very difficult" and, given the two-minute time limit to finish each puzzle, it is doubtful many have fully toured what he calls "the apartment." Thus, for the vast majority of players, engagement with *levelHead* comes closer to producing an experience of Hansen's digital ASW and the existential doubt of the *memento mortem mortis* than *Echochrome*'s "solvable enigmas." The cube-controller each player holds inevitably transforms into a kind of virtual skull, a reminder of an anamorphic discrepancy between eye–hand coordination and camera–computer calculation.

When grasping the "level heads," hands and wrists immediately organize each cube into a coherent program that does not necessarily comply with the images on the screen. As Oliver points out, the body grounds the player's frame of reference even as she grapples with architecture removed from standard forms of spatial orientation. There is a palpable disconnect between what the player feels when holding each solid cube and what she sees projected on the screen. The incommensurability between haptic and optical feedback in *levelHead* recalls the phenomenological problem articulated in Lazzarini's *skulls*. Were a viewer to close her eyes and place her hands on the stretched sculptures, the digital-born objects would resolve to the touch. Yet, without haptic feedback, the visual distortions throw off the viewer's equilibrium to produce the feeling of a digital ASW. Oliver's *levelHead* makes a game out of negotiating haptic orientation with a visual and cognitive disorientation and dramatizes what Andy Clark and David J. Chalmers (1998, 8) characterize as "the externalization of thought"—a phenomenon in which level and head can no longer be separated.

In their short essay, "The Extended Mind," Clark and Chalmers cite a 1994 study by David Kirsh and Paul Maglio in which participants were asked to play the game *Tetris* (1985). In Kirsh and Maglio's (1994, 518) experiment, data was collected in three ways: (1) the unobtrusive sampling of real-time keystroke data as advanced, intermediate, and novice gamers played *Tetris*; (2) tachistoscopic tests of the same subjects performing cognitive rotation tasks related to *Tetris*; and (3) an "expert system" called *Robotetris* built as a machine control for the experiment. After comparing the results of these three groups, Kirsh and Maglio discovered that when enabled by environmental as well as bodily support, human players are far more efficient when playing *Tetris*. Using a controller, participants performed the operation in 300 milliseconds (200 milliseconds to press a button, then 100 milliseconds for the screen to refresh), whereas it took around 1000 milliseconds for the same result to be achieved mentally (measured with standard tachistoscopic tests). For Clark and Chalmers, this study empirically demonstrates how cognition exceeds not only the mind, but the hand as well—consciousness codeveloping in concert with environment and body to produce a different kind of *levelHead*.

While Kirsh and Maglio explain how prosthetic technology transforms cognition using the example of *Tetris*, few videogames explicitly attempt to trouble this relationship. Conversely, the ability to recall space in *levelHead* overtly depends on both the body and a series of external apparatuses due to the fact that the architecture produced in the game cannot be visualized accurately in three-dimensional space. As Oliver emphasizes in an artist statement, the muscle memory of the hand is indispensable for successful navigation of the game's paradoxes. Although seasoned players of almost any videogame are acutely aware of the operation of muscle memory, many games foreground the autonomy of vision (through, for example, the presence of cutscenes) and the primacy of visual memory and mental modeling (in the case of most puzzle games). By contrast, *levelHead* does not take hand, body, or cube-controller for granted or treat them as merely instruments for executing orders. Oliver's game is built around the conceit that all the interactions within a cybernetic system are a necessary precondition for comprehending and traversing the environment.

The *Tetris* study further erodes the Cartesian model of mind–body dualism, demonstrating a distributed form of cognition that puts pressure on the question of where the body stops and the rest of the world begins. Ironically, this example of situated cognition is constructed around a cognitive *aporia*. The incommensurable gulf between the processes of a computer and the embodied engagement of the human is also necessary for the system to function: the dash in *human–computer interaction* signifies this chasm. Thus, Oliver's "level heads" tilt, shift, twist, and turn into versions of the smeared skull, challenging the player to peer into an irresolvable and paradoxical architecture. Clutching this existential object, a *memento mortem mortis,* the player glimpses into a space beyond human thought, beyond the debates of "to be or not to be," into a dimension where these questions are rendered insignificant.

Beyond the simulated cameras and onscreen architecture of *Echochrome, levelHead* extends anamorphic distortion to the embodied space of the human viewer. By creating a mathematical projection in which six interconnected rooms coexist within the same three-dimensional space, *levelHead* inverts the standard notion of projection and plays with a kind of fourth-dimensional logic. According to the space depicted of the screen, these six three-dimensional rooms exist within the same cube, overlapping each other. Although only one room is visible, the player can imagine the cube functioning like a tesseract or hypercube. The player must imagine six three-dimensional cubes contained within the cube she holds in her hand, although only one set of three-dimensional coordinates is observable at any time. This conceptual abstraction stands in for the player's encounter with the alien and inaccessible ontology of the everyday technological objects with which we surround ourselves. Anamorphosis becomes a means to aestheticize this encounter with what Ian Bogost has called the "alien phenomenology" of the computer.

Miegakure: A Garden of Many Forking Dimensions

While *levelHead*'s disorienting architecture implies a fourth-dimensional space and marshals the *memento mortem mortis* to allegorize this potential, Marc ten Bosch's forthcoming *Miegakure: A Garden in Four*

Dimensions directly incorporates four-dimensional mathematics into its game design philosophy. Both *Echochrome* and *levelHead* experiment with perspectival systems in which the laws of two- and three-dimensional perspective overlap with each other. *Miegakure,* on the other hand, adds one more spatial register in order to attempt to create a four-dimensional puzzle platformer (see Figure 2.12). Although visualizing the fourth dimension stretches the very limits of imagination, it is relatively simple to represent mathematically. This is a space where the abstractions of math and physics discourse freely and the body may be able to affectively register interdimensional shifts at a subconscious level, but perspectival vision is more or less left in the dark. For this reason, the fourth dimension has been a curiosity for artists wishing to critique the ocularcentrism of classical perspective and Cartesian space.

In her work on fourth-dimensional theories of twentieth-century art, Linda Dalrymple Henderson (1984, 205) writes that "the fourth dimension was a concern common to artists in nearly every major modern movement" because it "encouraged artists to depart from visual reality and to reject completely the one-point perspective system that for centuries had portrayed the world as three-dimensional." Though many visual artists throughout the twentieth century dabbled in four-dimensional theory—from multi-point and non-perspectival Cubist

Figure 2.12. The tutorial sequence in Mark ten Bosch's forthcoming *Miegakure* introduces players to a Japanese "garden of forking paths" that operates according to not three, but four spatial dimensions.

renderings to Surrealist explorations of scientific theories like the non-Euclidean spatial geometries of Henri Poincaré—ten Bosch takes his inspiration from Edwin Abbot's *Flatland: A Romance of Many Dimensions* (1884), a nineteenth-century novel narrating a square's journey through one-, two-, three-, and eventually four-dimensional space.

Faced with the paradox of representing the unrepresentable, ten Bosch's strategy is to create a gamespace in which each three-dimensional coordinate contains not three, but four points of information. As written on ten Bosch's (2011) website, "at the press of a button one of the dimensions is exchanged with the fourth dimension, allowing for four-dimensional movement." Thus, a block situated within a three-dimensional grid will appear to magically "smear" across the screen by substituting a given coordinate for a hidden fourth point in another space. Mathematically, one can make n-dimensional objects by simply adding more and more coordinates alongside the traditional designations for width, height, and depth. What exists as a computational abstraction cannot be completely articulated on the two-dimensional screen, but the process of substituting alternate sets of data simulates the traversal among four spatial dimensions.[29]

Ten Bosch does not treat this relationship between gameplay and fourth-dimensional physics merely as a form of symbolic substitution. He proposes that *Miegakure* grants access to the fourth dimension, allowing players to "experience it first-hand, using trial and error, as opposed to being told about it" and promotes a fantasy of mastery, colonization, and control over four-dimensional space (ten Bosch 2011). Despite his ambitious claims, the deeper significance that will ultimately be gained from *Miegakure* is not "first-hand" knowledge of the fourth dimension, but knowledge of the computational processes of the videogame itself. It is in this respect that *Miegakure's* fantasy of traversing the fourth dimension becomes a metaphor for traversing the mathematical abstractions made possible by the microtemporal process and macroscalar storage of digital media. The gameplay of *Miegakure* recalls Hansen's (2006, 202) claim about the way in which the anamorphic space of *skulls* stands in for the "weird logic and topology of the computer."

In *Gaming: Essays on Algorithmic Culture,* Alexander Galloway (2006, 106) argues that videogames are "allegories of control"; they are cultural objects which rhetorically present themselves as sources of interactivity and agency, yet in doing so conceal the "protocological network of continuous informatic control" under which we now live. Video-games ultimately relegate player behavior to a strict system of rules that allegorize contemporary informatic culture at large. One might further add that videogames function not only as allegories of control, but as *allegories of the beyond*. By presenting a set of computational processes as rules for organizing play, videogames invite players to discover the constraints and affordances of a given gamespace and along the way remind oneself of the limits of the human body. To play a game is to test a nonhuman system, to uncover (and be uncovered by) the codes that will produce both experiential dissonances like the digital ASW while opening fields for philosophical speculations. In *Miegakure,* the fourth-dimensional exercises depicted in the game's diegesis and its compu-tational dynamics are interlinked. *Miegakure* establishes a homology between the fourth spatial dimension and the internal workings of a computer by placing them within the same experiential register: at the limits of human perception. By attempting to colonize computational space through the insertion of a human agency, *Miegakure* adopts the ambitious premise that the formal topology of computational space can be manipulated, controlled, and conquered absolutely (when, as Gal-loway [2006, 106] observes, videogames in fact excel at accomplishing the opposite). Ten Bosch's game delights in the telic fantasy of extending the human agency into spaces and places where it does not belong.

The gap between what is possible to represent in mathematics and what is sensible within human phenomenology is the inspiration for Quentin Meillassoux's (2008, 7) concept of "the great outdoors" in *After Finitude*. Rather than thinking of the great outdoors in the tradition of Caspar David Friedrich and those works of sublime art that situate the human subject among the overwhelming sublimity of nature, Meillas-soux (2008, 26) uses the expression to refer to a universe that persists beyond the horizon of human correlation, writing, "This is the enigma which we must confront: mathematics' ability to discourse about the great outdoors; to discourse about a past where both humanity and life are absent." The term *miegakure,* ten Bosch (2011) clarifies, is Japanese for "hide and reveal" and refers to a specific gardening technique used in Japan. The game is set within a Japanese Zen garden, evoking a space of contemplation and relaxation as the player ponders mathematical abstrac-tions and interdimensional ontologies. Like Mark Z. Danielewski's *House of Leaves* (2000), *Miegakure*'s four-dimensional gardening techniques conjure a space that is paradoxically larger on the inside than the out-side. The objects in the garden interweave with one another and expand through multiple dimensions. The gardening metaphor is particularly apt because a garden not only represents a space of contemplation, but one of control and the domestication of nature. Ten Bosch's game can be read as an attempt to domesticate a computational wilderness, to seize the great outdoors, and till the land such that it falls back under the purview of human experience and agency. By creating a homology between anamorphic techniques and the great outdoors, *Miegakure* pushes anamorphic games into the next speculative dimension by pro-cedurally rendering an allegory of the beyond.

Games of Speculation

The fascination with a computational wilderness, the great outdoors of digital space, is at play in Ian Bogost's New Mexican landscape, described at the beginning of *Alien Phenomenology* (and at the beginning of this chapter). Synthesizing the recent proliferation of philosophies that fall under the umbrella of Speculative Realism, and specifically engaging with Graham Harman's version of Object-Oriented Ontology, Bogost embraces the alien nature of quotidian objects, from microwavable cas-seroles to steel corridors and crowbars. Bogost (2012, 9) describes how the material world of things has been de-privileged in the face of the *sturm und drang* of human drama, arguing,

> If we take seriously [Graham Harman's] idea that all objects recede intermi-nably into themselves, then human perception becomes just one among many ways that objects might relate. To put things at the center of a new metaphysics also requires us to admit that they do not exist just for us.

These concealed and re-distributed relations underwrite Bogost's con-struction of an alien phenomenology. Bogost (2012, 34) declares that "the true alien recedes interminably. It is not hidden in the darkness of the outer cosmos nor in the deep sea shelf, but in plain sight, every-where, in everything." What would you do if the alien were everywhere? The answer, for Bogost, is wonder. "Despite all the science fictional claims to the contrary," he writes, "the alien is different. One does not ask the alien, 'Do you come in peace?' but rather, 'What am I to you?' The posture one takes before the alien is that of curiosity, of wonder"

(2012, 133). In *Alien Phenomenology,* Bogost attempts to reinscribe a sense of respect for the mysteries of quotidian objects—for the alien that does not arrive from a galaxy far, far away but is part of our everyday lives. "It's everywhere," he asserts, and perhaps this is most deeply felt when one is attending to what peers back from the remote space of the smart phone, the laptop, the ATM machine, or other quotidian computers (Bogost 2012, 133).

Bogost's response to this call of the wild is to practice wonder, but this is by no means the only answer philosophers have posited. On the other hand, is not horror the obverse of wonder? Horror comes closer to the feeling Hansen describes as the digital ASW and what Eugene Thacker articulates in his book *After Life* (2010). In *After Life,* Thacker explores the philosophical concept of life and living. Also informed by the recent explosion of speculative philosophies which redirect philosophical inquiry away from the human toward "a politics of life in terms of the nonhuman or the unhuman," Thacker (2010, 5) turns to the fantasy writing of H. P. Lovecraft to find creative models for thinking that which exists beyond thought. Lovecraft, he argues, "presents the possibility of a logic of life, though an inaccessible logic, one that is absolutely inaccessible to the human, the natural, the earthly, an 'entelechy of the weird'" (Thacker 2010, 23). What Thacker identifies as "weird" in Lovecraft's writing, is the same speculation at work in the anamorphic gameplay of videogames that work to test or allegorize the limits of human experience. While Lovecraft attempts to name the unnamable, these games convey the sense of playing the unplayable. As Thacker (2010, 23) writes, "the weird is the discovery of an unhuman limit to thought, that is nevertheless foundational for thought. The life that is weird is the life according to the logic of an inaccessible rift, a life 'out of space and time,' and life of 'extra-dimensional biologies.'"

Whether using terms like *weird, eccentric, alien,* or *anamorphic,* these ideas seek to resituate the place of the human within a more complex cosmology of objects, and the metagame becomes the point of contact between human sensibility and this expanded field beyond the limits of perception. The strange spaces navigated in videogames like *Portal, Echochrome, levelHead,* and *Miegakure* allegorize the incomprehensibility of a computer; they create expressive systems that point to the profoundly alien nature of the technological objects that are such an integral and often ignored aspect of contemporary culture. And they are also metagames in the sense that each are games *about* games and their various visual regimes. These anamorphic metagames play with the phenomenological disconnect between nonhuman technics and human sensibility. Yet, despite the ubiquity and embeddedness of digital logic within the economic, social, and even biological strata of everyday life (on both sides of the digital divide), the videogames examined here attempt to mobilize the affective friction produced as a result of the irreconcilable alterity of technical media.

As a way of assuaging the anxiety of discovering that one lives on an alien planet, *Portal, Echochrome, levelHead,* and *Miegakure* present defamiliarized spaces and propose that the abyss that separates humanity from the mysterious black box of technology is, in fact, navigable. In these games, the computer is not so much a Lovecraftian monster, but a kind of riddle or enigma, troubling but potentially solvable—not a black box, but a puzzle box. The fundamental paradox of these "anamorphic games" is that they ultimately subsume speculative worlds into a playable world. They present imagery and gameplay referencing the "great outdoors" but packaged specifically for human play. Their controllers fit into the palms of human hands and their screens cast wavelengths of light within the spectrum of human vision. In this respect, the videogames presented in this chapter actively resist what could be called speculative gaming. The *memento mortem mortis* is still only a reminder that tentatively motions toward a nonhuman heart at the center of all materiality. Like Holbein's *The Ambassadors* and Lazzarini's *skulls,* anamorphic games deploy a *memento mortem mortis* to create metaphors for a computational wilderness, reminding their users of both their experiential limitations and the limitations of technological understanding.

If one were tasked to develop a videogame completely indifferent to an end user, what would this speculative game look like? Would it participate in a mutual withdrawal of both player and game, or would it place both game and player at incommensurable odds with each other? In much the same way the anamorphic lens can be said to neither reflect nor refract light, but rather trap the gaze, the speculative game would serve as a black hole. Speculative games cannot have a user; they cannot be used or even thought by the player. Speculative games have no metagame. As Richard Garfield (2000, 16) reminds us, "It may be a useful construct but it doesn't really exist . . . [for us]." The "for us" added to Garfield's passage is a signifier and watchword for correlationist thinking and the metagame. However, the software discussed in this chapter challenges the viewer not to perceive the imperceptible or conquer other-worldly domains, but to begin speculating on the possibilities of video-games *without* us. The result is not speculative games, but games of speculation.

Metagame 2

Memento Mortem Mortis

Memento Mortem Mortis is an original piece of software that simulates the stretched skull from Hans Holbein's *The Ambassadors* (1533). Whereas Robert Lazzarini's *skulls* (2001) features a variety of non-perspectival topological transformations applied to 3D geometry, *Memento Mortem Mortis* conflates the displaced picture plane from traditional anamorphic projection with the polygonal planes of a human skull through a graphic technique called texture mapping (see Figure 2.13). Although the anamorphic effects of puzzle games like *Portal* (2007), *Echochrome* (2008), *levelHead* (2008), and *Miegakure* (forthcoming) often revolve around a predetermined solution, in *Memento Mortem Mortis* each skull simply reveals a new level of anamorphic distortion. From a randomly generated maze to the multiple levels of digital distortion, the puzzle may have a solution, but it is not for us. It is picture planes all the way down. To download *Memento Mortem Mortis,* go to http://manifold.umn.edu/memento.

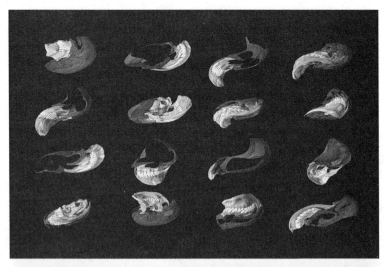

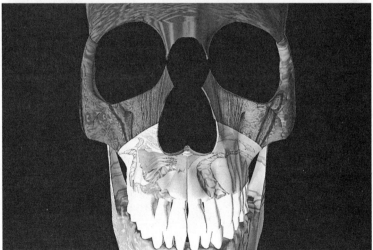

Figure 2.13. *Memento Mortem Mortis* is an original metagame by Patrick LeMieux and Stephanie Boluk that uses texture mapping to anamorphically smear an *Ambassadors*-themed maze across the surface of a human skull.

THREE

Blind Spots

The Phantom Pain, The Helen Keller Simulator,
and Disability in Games

No texture, no brushwork, no drawing, no forms, no
design, no color, no light, no space, no time, no size or
scale, no movement, no object.
> —Ad Reinhardt, "Twelve Rules for a New Academy"

One who gains the eye of truth will be able to see what is
hidden in the darkness.
> —Shadow Temple Fake Wall, *The Legend of Zelda: Ocarina of Time*

No avatar, no enemies, no combat, no collectables, no collision, no momentum, no motion, no map, no menu, no text, no cutscenes, no story, no sequels, no series, no franchise, no company, no copyright, no property, no publication, no distribution, no sale, no strategy guide, no review, no critique, no consumption, no input, no output, no controller, no console, no platform, no mechanics, no rules, no goals, no players, no game. And yet, there is a metagame. Not a game-as-platformer or game-as-shooter or game-as-simulation or game-as-puzzle or even a game-as-videogame, but a *game-as-game*—a metagame without explicit preconditions or predefined constraints (and, as such, a metagame representing the *sum total* of all preconditions and constraints). Not an inversion, but the absolute negation of the game in the form of a timeless, scoreless, ruleless, goalless, fieldless, equipmentless, playerless game-as-game. This a-game, anti-game, de-game, dis-game, im-game, il-game, ir-game, no-game, non-game, not-game, and un-game is also the only game there is. Certainly playful, although not explicitly addressing a game design philosophy, Ad Reinhardt explored this aesthetic philosophy of absolute negation in his writing, comics, and art throughout the twentieth century.

In 1966 Reinhardt exhibited his life's work at the Jewish Museum in New York. That winter and into the next year, gallery after gallery was filled with black squares (see Figure 3.1). Almost a hundred artworks hung in the museum but no one saw them. Reinhardt's five-by-five-foot black abstractions are *not* paintings, but conceptual art designed within the familiar idioms of painting in order to plumb the depths and test the limits of the ontology of art through a process of negation. In the words of Reinhardt (1991, 85), for every "tradition of abstract art, and previous paintings of horizontal bands, vertical stripes, blobs, scumblings, bravura, brushwork, impressions, impastos, sensations, impulses, pleasures, pains, ideas, imaginings, imagings, imaginations, visions, shapes, colors, composings, representings, mixtures, corruptions, exploitations, combinings, vulgarizations, popularizations, integrations, accidents, actions, texturings, spontaneities, ready-mades, stylizations, mannerisms, irrationalities, unawareness, extra-and-unaesthetic qualities, meanings, forms of any traditions of pure, or impure, abstract-art traditions" there is an "extreme, ultimate, climactic reaction to, and negation of" painting in the form of a black painting. For there to be a painting of something, there must also be paintings of nothing—a paradoxical painting both *about* painting and *without* painting. Not an art-as-painting or art-as-object or art-as-institution or art-as-market or art-as-history or even art-as-concept, but an *art-as-art*—Reinhardt's curmudgeonly term for the general, universal, ontological being of art in and of itself.[1] At the Jewish Museum, just a few months before he died on August 30, 1967, Reinhardt offered these black paintings as one possible limit point of art—a representation of art-as-art in the idiom of abstract painting: painting in the form of its blackest negation.

Of course, Reinhardt could never fully practice the art-as-art dogma he preached. Just as the magic circle, black box, white cube, and commodity form function as ideological avatars haunting the contemporary cultural imaginary, tech industries, art institutions, and global market, art-as-art can never fully materialize. Reinhardt's black paintings function pedagogically, alluding to the philosophical concept of art and operating in explicit contrast with the historical, material, institutional, or political definitions of the term. Of course, formalism in mid-century American art *was* political. In the 1950s Clement Greenberg curated art against Russian Socialist Realism; Jackson Pollock and the New York School of abstract expressionism were weaponized across Europe after

Figure 3.1. Represented here by a solid black facsimile, Ad Reinhardt's abstract paintings typically consist of a five-by-five-foot canvas trisected vertically and horizontally by almost imperceptible differentiations of blackness that result in a subtle cruciform when viewed over time.

the war; and Ad Reinhardt's black paintings were positioned were positioned against the vulgarization of art as nationalist propaganda and capitalist commodity. As Joseph Kosuth (1991, 191) notes in his short essay "On Ad Reinhardt," "Painting itself had to be erased, eclipsed, painted out in order to . . . make art itself visible through that 'other' which his painting then constituted." Since the language of art in the 1950s and 1960s was a painterly one, "draining" paintings of all their definitive qualities rendered the parameters of the discourse itself visible. In this sense, Reinhardt's black paintings function as a tool or barometer to measure the superfluous elements surrounding art-as-art and not as the construction of art-as-art in itself. Kosuth (1991, 192) argues, "assertions about art can only be made negatively; in this way, [Reinhardt's] assertion of art itself was the positive by-product of those acts of negation."

To this end, Reinhardt's (1991, 82) black paintings were meticulously constructed, stroke by stroke—"brushwork brushed out to remove brushwork." Their composition and coloring were carefully measured, almost scientifically adapted to the human eye. The five-by-five-foot Vitruvian squares were not propped up on easels or hung on walls but positioned face up on short benches to absorb the sunlight of Reinhardt's New York studio. Kosuth (1991, 191) elegantly summarizes that "the different colored blacks of Reinhardt's paintings presented an internal structure which described the square of the whole painting in relation to its larger context and discourse"—a metapainting meant to reveal the nature of painting even as it erased itself. Despite the cosmic indifference espoused by Reinhardt's art-as-art dogma, these black paintings are tuned to the perceptual capacities of the human viewer, tempered to the human body, and adjusted to the human eye (and reminiscent of the embodied operations of *memento mortem mortis* in chapter 2). Reinhardt's strategy, then, was not to render art-as-art visible, but to practice his philosophy through the medium of painting. The monochrome speaks.

Occupying a privileged relationship to language, Reinhardt's monochromes foreground the textuality of all images. In his "how to" series of newspaper comics for *PM,* Reinhardt preaches that "a painting is not a simple something or pretty picture or arrangement, but a complicated language you have to learn to read" (Reinhardt 1946). It is no surprise that many examples of language art take the form of the monochrome, and, specifically, the black painting. As Mel Ramsden notes in a letter to Charles Harrison (2003, 20–21), "It had seemed necessary, finally, that the 'talk' went up on the wall." The work of the would be members of the conceptual art collective Art & Language—such as Ramsden's *Guaranteed Painting* (1967) and *Secret Painting* (1967–68)—were black paintings directly influenced by Reinhardt's late practice. Likewise, Joseph Kosuth reproduced the size, scale, and form of Ad Reinhardt's paintings when he mounted black photographs of white dictionary definitions of words like "definition," "meaning," "idea," "art," "blank," "square," and "nothing."

Historicizing this approach, Kosuth (1991, 13) begins his 1969 essay "Art after Philosophy," with the proposition that "traditional philosophy, almost by definition, has concerned itself with the *unsaid*. The nearly exclusive focus on the *said* by twentieth-century analytical linguistic philosophers is the shared contention that the *unsaid* is *unsaid* because it is *unsayable*" (emphasis original). For Kosuth, the emergence of both Ludwig Wittgenstein's linguistic philosophy and Marcel Duchamp's readymades at the turn of the century indicated "the end of philosophy and the beginning of art" (1991, 14). In this sense, Kosuth's idea of conceptual art coincides with the linguistic proposition. Considering the relationship of metagames to prepositions—a form of Wittgenstein's "language games"—could Reinhardt's ultimately linguistic maneuver be applied to a discussion of games and play? What is a videogame without video? Or, for that matter, without audio, without interface, without computation, and without play? What is a non-video game? A non-videogame? A metagame?

For the past thirty years, and especially since the popularization of real time 3D graphics processing in the mid-nineties, the computer and videogame industry has been caught up in a graphical arms race: a dogged pursuit of ocularcentric spectacle culminating in the hypertrophy of the visual economy of games like *Metal Gear Solid V: The Phantom Pain* (2015). As considered in chapter 2, alongside the cinematic extravagances of well-funded, widely promoted AAA games, a generation of players and designers has internalized the logic and codes of videogames to produce games and game practices that engage the nonvisual conditions of the medium. These non-video games have attenuated visual gameplay as a form of critical game design resulting in examples of ludic atrophy like *The Helen Keller Simulator* (2005–), an unpopular Internet meme that consists of a black (or blank) image with no audio, promoted as a first-person videogame. Whereas the prologue of *The Phantom Pain* is intercut with unplayable cutscenes, *The Helen Keller Simulator* deploys the restriction of vision to an uncannily similar effect. In contrast to this hypertrophy of cinematic spectacle and the atrophy of minimal mechanics, this chapter will examine a little-known metagaming practice in which both blind, low vision, and sighted players navigate videogame spaces without the use of video and invent new ways of playing according to alternate sensory economies. Considering Steven Connor's

(2011, 18) *Philosophy of Sport* in which he claims that "disabled sports are the only sports there are," these blind and blindfolded metagames hold a critical lens up to not only the games industry but the design, dissemination, and consumption of software in general. By turning to questions of disability, this chapter investigates ludic experiments that challenge contemporary models of videogame production to reveal new modes of play.

[FADE IN FROM BLACK:] The Hypertrophy of Games

Fade in from black. Framed by a grid of white ceiling tiles, a perfectly rendered prosthetic hook extends upward, away from the virtual camera affixed to the face of the in-game avatar. Floating above, just out of reach, and buffeted by the parameters of whatever particle system is synced with the spinning ceiling fan, a flower petal drifts downward. Whether a hallucination brought on by medication, the piece of shrapnel protruding from the protagonist's prefrontal cortex, or some cinematic form of magical realism, the white lily petal is impossible to grasp. Carefully modeled, textured, lit, and animated within the mathematical constraints of perspectival space, the flower petal stands in for a form of naturalism which continues to propel the central desires of the videogames as a mass medium and cultural commodity: technological mastery, graphic realism, and player immersion. This petal appears as a utopian vision—a white whale to our Ahab avatar—promising a reality that can be simulated, controlled, exchanged, and consumed. That is, until another reality startles the player from her stupor: the fact that no amount of technological innovation—neither 4k displays or virtual reality headsets—will immerse anyone other than the digital subject seen on screen. As discussed in chapter 2, the mathematical abstractions necessary for this form of visual spectacle remain formally estranged from the phenomenology of the human player, although not the virtual veteran in the videogame. This digital body, with its single, cycloptic camera-eye and prosthetic controller-hand stands in for videogames as the ideological avatar of play. The hospitalized hero here is not disabled but rather perfectly adapted to the constraints of this specific visual regime, his single eye a metonymy for single-point perspective and his hook-hand recalling the limited mobility of a game controller as the dex-

Figure 3.2. The cycloptic eye and hook-hand of the virtual veteran in *Metal Gear Solid V: The Phantom Pain* allegorize the larger videogame industry and its pursuit of a kind of realism that is always just out of reach.

terity of digits is replaced with digital inputs (see Figure 3.2). Although framed in terms of missing limbs and limited vision, this representation of a disabled body is actually defined not by what is absent but by what is present in overabundance: the hypertrophic product of cinematic excess—a visual overload that weighs the camera down on the gurney.

Fade in from black. "Please try to relax." Between the rhythmic gasps of a medical ventilator and the faint beeps of a heart rate monitor, a Soviet doctor stationed at the Royal Air Force hospital in Cyprus begins to explain, "You've been in a coma for quite some time."[2] It's 1984 in a world where special forces units like "FOX" and "FOXHOUND" wield cybernetic prosthetics and magical realisms interchangeably, where private military companies like "Militaires Sans Frontières" are pawns within in a war economy driven by a hundred-billion-dollar cache called "The Philosopher's Legacy," and where bipedal nuclear-armed tanks like "Metal Gear" walk the earth. But before the postcomatose patient can equip a red, bionic arm for a Spaghetti Western-inspired, open-world special op in Afghanistan,[3] the game must fade in from black. Premiered at the Spike Video Game Awards (VGAs) on December 7, 2012,[4] the first trailer for *Metal Gear Solid V*, which mysteriously debuted as just *The*

Phantom Pain and featured footage of a disabled vet's escape from the RAF hospital, was intercut by a series of vague questions:

> What happened? Where am I? Why can't I move my body? Am I in a dream? Is this real? Something is coming! What is going on? Do they want me dead? What are they after? Do they want us all dead? Why is this happening to me? No escape? Have I gone to hell? Open your eyes. Open your eyes, already.

From the patient's first-person perspective (lying in a prone position on the floor after all hell breaks loose at the hospital), a split-hook prosthesis stretches toward the illusory lily petal. The movement from darkness to light initiates a scene of visual excess, a spectacle that disables both the player and player character while simultaneously revealing a blind spot in the logic of what Terry Harpold calls the "upgrade path" (Harpold 2009, 3). "Because technical innovation in popular computing is driven more by the allure of expanding markets," Harpold (2009, 3) points out, "commercial discourses of the upgrade path will inevitably promise consumers new and more satisfying interactions, and encourage them to see the older ones as outmoded or no longer relevant." As videogame consoles and personal computers alike evolve from 8-bit to 16-bit to 32-bit to 64-bit processors and videogames balloon from megabytes of cartridge or compact disc data to gigabytes of downloadable assets, the overabundance of graphic spectacle institutionally and phenomenologically disables other forms of sensory engagement, allegorized by the beginning of *The Phantom Pain* in which an amnesiac amputee lies paralyzed on the hospital bed.

About a year later, on March 27, 2013, Hideo Kojima unveiled that *The Phantom Pain* was in fact another entry in the *Metal Gear Solid* series (1998–) of "tactical espionage" games in a panel presentation titled "Photorealism Through the Eyes of a FOX" at the annual Game Developers Conference (GDC) in San Francisco. In the hour-long talk, Kojima and his production team[5] focused on the Fox Engine, their latest proprietary platform built to develop the "next generation" of videogames not only on consoles such as Sony's PlayStation 4 and Microsoft's Xbox One, but also, for the first time in the history of the series, personal computers via digital distribution services like Valve's Steam. Not merely part of an animation or rendering pipeline, the Fox Engine includes the editors and interfaces Kojima Productions would use to build levels, direct cutscenes, produce effects, design user interfaces, and trigger sounds—everything needed to make the next *Metal Gear*. The team spoke exhaustively on their engine's ability to simulate linear space lighting and physically based rendering, and their demos were populated with complex polygonal assets produced with techniques like photo-based scanning and photographic texture mapping. The presentation culminated in very convincing renderings of an old man's face, a shirtless Congolese boy, a wet leather jacket, and a hyperrealistic, slowly rotating stone (see Figure 3.3). Within the contemporary videogame industry (as within the flattened New Mexican landscapes enveloping the Black Mesa Research Facility at the beginning of chapter 2), all assets are equal and even the most banal subjects require graphical overkill. Technical advances in computer-generated imaging—from the original 2D *Metal Gear* in 1987 to the rebooted 3D *Metal Gear Solid* in 1998 to Kojima's last[6] *Metal Gear* game in 2015—necessitate finer and finer divisions of labor, and within this granularization of game development even granite gets its fifteen milliseconds of fame (slipping out from beneath the foot of the protagonist, forever codenamed Snake, and tumbling toward the camera as he scales a cliff face at the beginning of the GDC demo).

Months before their GDC presentation, Kojima Productions released two nearly identical pictures of a conference room from their company headquarters in the Roppongi district of Tokyo: one photograph and one

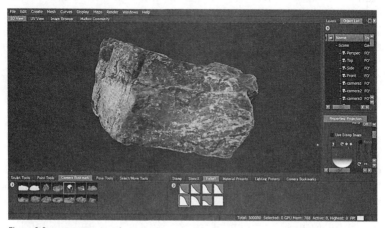

Figure 3.3. At Kojima Productions, even an object as unremarkable as a stone undergoes the same process of photo-based modeling and texturing applied to human subjects.

Is it REAL, or is it "FOX?"

The 2 sets of images below depict our Kojima Productions meeting room. One set is comprised of digital photographs, while the other contains screenshots of the scene recreated in the FOX ENGINE and rendered in realtime. Can you tell which is FOX?

A   or   B

Figure 3.4. By asking "Is it REAL or is it FOX?" Kojima challenges players to distinguish between a photograph and a Fox render of his studio's conference room.

Fox render.[7] Accompanying these images, the text invited viewers to determine "Is it REAL, or is it 'FOX?'" (see Figure 3.4). Like Zeuxis' birds pecking at painted grapes or ancient artists attempting to pull back curtains, Kojima claimed that the Fox Engine's graphic output "looks real" and that there is "virtually no difference when compared to the photograph"—a Turing Test of graphical realism (Kojima et al., 2013).[8] As with Pliny's myths of mimesis, detailed at the beginning of chapter 2, and in the case of many mainstream videogames, photorealism not only refers to the ability to accurately represent mimetic details like detailed textures and dynamic lighting but also implies the ideological desire for both mastery over and subjection to these tricks of light. Whereas Butades' indexical portraiture was designed to comfort his lovelorn daughter, and Zeuxis and Parrhasius' painterly illusions were each perpetrated on an unwitting subject, photorealism in contemporary videogames requires complicity on the part of the player in their own sensory and cognitive deception. Realism is not, as Joseph Witek (1989, 116) writes, "an essential relation between certain texts and the world of experiences" but is instead "a conspiracy between writer and reader" or between designer and player. In this respect, the contemporary gamer is more like Pygmalion (who tricks himself) rather than Zeuxis and Parrhasius (who attempt to trick each other). We are each implicated in the construction of our own gamic Galateas.

In *Rules of Play*, Katie Salen Tekinbaş and Eric Zimmerman (2003, 450–51) call this cultural logic the "immersive fallacy," or the "idea that the pleasure of a media experience lies in its ability to sensually transport the participant into an illusory, simulated reality. . . . so complete that ideally the frame falls away so that the player truly believes that he or she is part of an imaginary world." Lying along the contour of the magic circle, Salen Tekinbaş and Zimmerman's immersive fallacy (like Jay David Bolter and Richard Grusin's [2000, 31] analysis of the fantasy of "immediacy" in *Remediation*)⁹ not only critiques the very possibility of immersion as such, but also diagnoses a widely held historical desire for an escape into an autonomous zone of free play. Rather than a linear march toward absolute similitude, the graphics industries (as well as their customers) do a dialectic dance that two-steps between the science of simulating light and the superstition in an engagement so sublime that the medium becomes immediate, the body immaterial, and the representation real. Art historian Martin Jay (1988, 2, 6) describes this "resolutely ocularcentric" focus on the "alleged objective optical order" as one of the "scopic regimes of modernity," and the use of computers has only intensified the drive to produce a mathematical, rationalized space that translates three-dimensional objects onto two-dimensional screens. How has this ocularcentric conflation of graphics and realism become a fixed point around which the standard metagame orbits? Why is the ideological avatar of play so resolutely focused on the visual? Is there a nonvisual, non-video game hovering somewhere in the blind spot of twenty-first century play?

In *Gaming: Essays on Algorithmic Culture*, Alexander Galloway (2006, 73–74) differentiates between "realisticness" as a form of representation in which "images (or language, or what have you) are a faithful, mimetic mirror of reality thereby offering some unmediated truth about the world" and—following Fredric Jameson and the discourses of social realism in film—"realism" as a "technique to approximate the basic phenomenological qualities of the real world." Whereas the Fox Engine may yield higher polygon counts and more complex lighting simulations than other games, Kojima's games may nevertheless be less "real" than "those games that reflect critically on the minutiae of everyday life, replete as it is with struggle, personal drama, and injustice" (Galloway 2006, 73, 75). Although not a representation of reality, there is however another kind of correspondence between the Fox Engine and "the minutiae of everyday life": not the photorealistic representation of war, but the appropriation of the tools and techniques of Hollywood cinema. It is not a coincidence, for example, that *Metal Gear Solid V* employs motion capture and the surprisingly minimal voice acting of Kiefer Sutherland (instead of loquacious fan-favorite David Hayter).[10] Despite the PR spin, these innovations and expenses are in no way an attempt to produce a more "realistic" or "authentic" Solid Snake, but are signifiers that *Metal Gear* (and, by extension, Kojima Productions) aligns with the cultural capital, star text, and special effects standards of the global entertainment industry—a form of militarism that Tim Lenoir and Henry Lowood (2005) call the "military entertainment complex."[11] Although videogames continue to struggle toward photorealism, the Fox Engine successfully represents one social reality of war in the twenty-first century via the appropriation of the bureaucratic, budgetary, and technologies of Hollywood.

Shortly after releasing *Metal Gear Solid* in 1998, Kojima (Kent 1999) remarked, "The human body is supposed to be 70 percent water. I consider myself 70 percent film." The latchkey son of a single, working mother, Kojima spent his youth writing short stories and shooting original scripts in Western Japan (Edge 2003). Though these early interests never panned out, the influence is obvious, and Kojima has reported that he still watches a new movie every day (Parkin 2012). From sly references and direct citations of 1980s American film in *Metal Gear* on the MSX2 computer to what many have regarded as an egregious use of cinematic cutscenes in *Metal Gear Solid 4: Guns of the Patriots* (2008) for the PlayStation 3, the videogames that Kojima directs have always been implicated in the logic of film. *Metal Gear*'s primary protagonist, Solid Snake, was originally named after Kurt Russell's one-eyed, mullet-sporting Snake Plissken from John Carpenter's *Escape from New York* (1981). Released first for the MSX2 and then the NES, the game's 1987 cover art is lifted directly from promotional photographs of Michael Biehn from his role as Kyle Reese in *The Terminator* (1984) (see Figure 3.5). The direct citation of American film and science fiction is not simply a feature of the first *Metal Gear,* but common to many other Japanese games from the era like *Contra* (1987) and *Ninja Gaiden* (1988) which feature Geiger-

Figure 3.5. Many early Japanese videogames took their inspiration from Hollywood films. For example, the first *Metal Gear*'s cover (right) is clearly based on production stills from the set of *Terminator* (left).

esque monsters and other poached imagery from movies like *Predator* (1987) and *Alien* (1979). But what started as a derivative yet straightforward stealth game, an early progenitor of an entire genre of videogames based on sneaking and spying, would become a platform for Kojima's cinematic ambitions.

Since 1987, Hideo Kojima has been making *Metal Gear*. When the series turned twenty-five in 2013, Kojima was celebrating his fiftieth birthday—half his life had been spent working on the games despite his own persistent claim that each *Metal Gear* was his last.[12] With the promise of each new console generation (and additional funding from Sony in return for console exclusivity), Kojima's perpetually concluding saga always finds itself rebooted, revisioned, and retconned as he makes, remakes, and eventually demakes *Metal Gear*. Released for Sony's PlayStation consoles starting in 1998, the *Metal Gear Solid* portion of the series is best known for its complex and recursive story full of retroactive continuities and political commentary told through cutting-edge graphics, lengthy cutscenes, and professional voice acting. Set in a near future of bioengineered clones of super-soldiers and billion-dollar tanks with nuclear payloads, each title in the series expresses Kojima's fears, from nuclear proliferation to genetic cloning to the surveillance state and the war economy. Like the hyperreferential games about games discussed in chapter 1, *Metal Gear Solid* is also *Meta Gear Solid*: a self-conscious remake that literalizes the nostalgic tropes of retro gaming as a both fan service and a form of magical realism within the high-fidelity graphics and melodramatic acting of twenty-first-century Japanese videogames. The tension between platform and plot reached its cinematic apotheosis on the PlayStation 3 with *Metal Gear Solid 4,* which features over eight hours of in-game cutscenes and a DVD-style interface for pausing, playing, rewinding, fast forwarding, and even saving player progress in each animated sequence. Here input is dramatically attenuated to a form of remote control. Nevertheless, *pressing play* is still play.

Considering these moments in which human input is put on hold, in *Gaming* Galloway (2006, 12) describes the cutscene as a "grotesque fetishization of the game itself as a machine," and the record number of cutscenes in *Metal Gear Solid 4* is perhaps one of the most extreme examples of this cinematic grotesque. Adopting terms from literary and film theory to address the "semi-autonomous space that is removed from normal life," Galloway discusses two kinds of processes that occur in videogames: "diegetic machine acts" and "nondiegetic machine acts." Whereas cutscenes function diegetically to tell a story, nondiegetic machine acts include not only mechanics like "power-ups, goals, high-score stats, dynamic difficulty adjustment, the HUD, [and] health packs" but also "software crashes, low polygon counts, temporary freezes, server downtime, and network lag" (Galloway 2006, 28). Never completely separate, diegetic and nondiegetic orders overlap in *Metal Gear Solid 4.* In what little game is left outside Kojima's cinematic excesses, miniature cutscenes also proliferate throughout the gameplay, as small animation sequences not only represent the disability of the player's avatar but also enact a form of disability.

As "Old Snake" squirms through the gutters, bunkers, alleyways, and trenches within a series of undisclosed locations in the Middle East, South America, Eastern Europe, and the Fox archipelago in Alaska, he occasionally flinches or groans, stopping to rub his aching back unless the player applies a soothing compress or provides hot ramen. Autonomous actions on the part of the aging avatar disrupt gameplay through the injection of short animations—computer processes that temporarily disable play. In these instances, diegetic machine acts border on nondiegetic machine acts as the representation of impairment also impairs the players' performance within the game. The coughs and spasms of Old Snake are reminiscent of CD skips or network lags, one example of what Galloway (2006, 31) calls "disabling acts." Here representations of disability also disable player control, as is the case in the prologue of *The Phantom Pain* in which "Punished Snake" struggles to crawl across the floor of the RAF hospital in Cyprus. As with Old Snake, action no longer correlates to input.

Five years after Old Snake's debut in *Metal Gear Solid 4*,[13] an unknown Scandinavian game development team calling themselves "Moby Dick Studios" released a trailer for their first game, *The Phantom Pain*, at Spike TV's VGAs. With familiar themes, graphical excess, and "tactical espionage action" that immediately recalled the *Metal Gear* series, *The Phantom Pain*'s teaser begins with the perspective of a patient struggling to regain consciousness from his prone position on a hospital gurney. Explosions rack the room as a man in full facial bandages approaches, warning "[I've] been watching you for nine years. You can call me Ishmael." As the player's one-armed, one-eyed avatar struggles to stand and see, crawling painfully through the hospital corridors, Ishmael takes point in their two-man army. After a laborious escape on all fours as other wounded soldiers are corralled and executed in the burning building, the entire structure ignites in hellfire as a gigantic whale bursts from the ruins of the hospital, soaring across the sky and toward the patient, mouth agape. Whether the whale is the patient's drug-fueled hallucination, a trick of the light, a VR training simulation, a form of magical realism, or all four is unknown.

Players immediately knew *The Phantom Pain* was the next *Metal Gear*. The trailer, for example, not only features a protagonist that resembles Snake, with his signature mullet and ad hoc eye patch, but also recalls the graphic tropes of Kojima Productions' Fox Engine. The fiery hallucinations flickering at the ends of the hospital's dark hallways appear to take the form of Stalinist GRU[14] colonel Yevgeny Borisovitch Volgin in his rubber, anti-static combat suit and FOXHOUND's Psycho Mantis wearing his signature gas mask and floating through level geometry at will. Beyond the game's graphics, the first name of Moby Dick Studios' lead director, Joakim, is an anagram for Kojima. His last name, Mogren, includes the word *ogre,* an in-house code name for one of Kojima's forever-forthcoming projects. Finally, only two hours after the trailer first screened, fans discovered that characters spelling "METAL GEAR

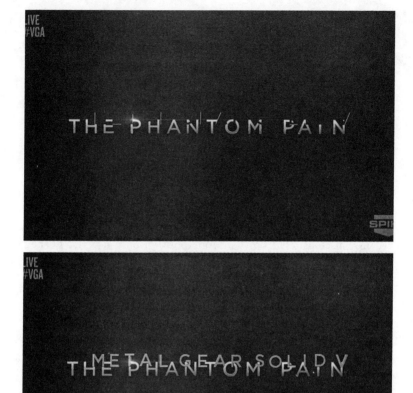

Figure 3.6. Beyond graphic similarities and ARG-like clues, the fact that "METAL GEAR SOLID V" neatly overlays *The Phantom Pain*'s logo was definitive proof of Kojima's poorly kept secret.

SOLID V" could be interleaved into a series of indentations in the game's logo (see Figure 3.6).

Despite the flurry of detective work that resolved the mystery in the early hours of December 8, Kojima continued to perpetuate the farce throughout the spring leading up to the Game Developer's Conference during the last week of March in 2013. Fans played along as games journalist Geoff Keighley booked an interview with Joakim Mogren in an undisclosed location on March 15. An odd exchange by all standards, uncertainty around *The Phantom Pain* was actually reignited when Mogren appeared on camera. Like H. G. Wells' *Invisible Man* (1897), Humphrey Bogart in *Dark Passage* (1947), and, most obviously, Ishmael in *The Phantom Pain* trailer, the Swedish man's head was completely entombed in cotton gauze as if he was disfigured in an accident, recovering from cosmetic surgery, or concealing his identity. A form of what some disability activists and theorists have labeled "disability drag" or, more aptly, "crip face"—the phenomenon of able-bodied performers acting in disabled roles—Mogren donned bandages in order to mimic the mysterious, masked guide from the hospital in *The Phantom Pain* and to disguise himself (Hadley 2014, 153).

What began as an ill-conceived PR stunt, however, took on renewed significance when multiple communities across the Internet began to speculate that the Swedish videogame director was not in fact a human, but an elaborate, computer-generated prank perpetrated by Kojima. Forum posters wondered "Is it REAL or is it FOX?" and began to document evidence of modeling, texturing, lighting, and animation errors occurring within Mogren's bandaged face (see Figure 3.7). A long list of possible problems included the following:

- The upper eyelids only half drop. The attached skin doesn't move at all (i.e., the eyebrow, the recess below the eyebrow).
- The lower eyelids simply don't move. I don't know about you, but I can't move my upper eyelids independently of the lower. More-so, when you are shocked or taken aback by something, the natural is to winch/ squint [sic].
- The point of light in his pupil doesn't move in relation to his head movement. In fact it's static within the pupil at all times.
- The shadows around the bandages on the right of the image are not consistent with the head. (Guiberu 2013)

Whether fans were in on the joke or being strung along as part of the playful advertising campaign is unclear, but online polls at Game Trailers, Giant Bomb, and NeoGAF indicated that thousands of people at least fascinated by the idea that Joakim Mogren could be computer generated.[15] Inverting the conventional logic of mimesis, players' eyes were not deceived, but *desired deception.* Instead of being tricked, maybe

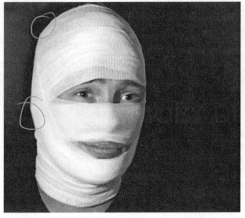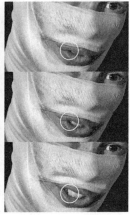

Figure 3.7. In these images, taken from Keiley's first interview with Joakim Mogren, viewers attempted to discover the polygonal edges and texture glitches that would prove the interviewee was a product of Kojima's Fox Engine.

Zeuxis was just playing along with Parhassius; maybe Pygmalion only fantasized about Galatea. This strange inversion was the product of three coinciding factors: a desire for an exponential leap in graphical similitude promised by the Fox Engine, an apophenic suspicion[16] inspired not so much by the success of Kojima's viral marketing campaign but its *failure* to fool anyone, and the dehumanizing discourse around disability brought on by Mogren's unsettling mask. Although controversy fueled debate over the ontology of Joakim Mogren, a stranger mask was about to be revealed at the Game Developers Conference.

A few weeks later, Keiley interviewed Mogren on site at 2013's GDC. As with his previous on-camera appearance, the Swede appeared with his face fully bandaged, only his mouth and eyes visible to the viewer. During this second interview, however, there can be no doubt as to whether or not Mogren is computer generated. "It's great to see you again. It's only been a few weeks since we chatted," Keiley begins, apprehensively noting that "you look a little bit different." While his mouth moves to answer, Mogren's 3D-printed, blue eyes stare out from the carefully wound bandages, unblinking (see Figure 3.8). After a few awkward moments, Hideo Kojima removed the computer-generated and rapid-prototyped Ishmael mask and put his glasses back on. By donning this uncanny mask and pretending to be a Swedish programmer cosplaying

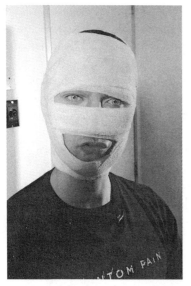 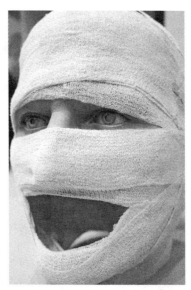

Figure 3.8. Finally, Kojima revealed *Metal Gear Solid V: The Phantom Pain,* after a bizarre performance in a 3D-printed mask at GDC 2013. Photographs by Hideo Kojima, 2013.

as an injured Ishmael, Kojima aligns his own subject position with that of the Melville-inspired narrator and Virgilian guide who shepherds Snake through the hospital's phantasmagoric inferno. Like the many iterations of Snake, Kojima has been enabled (and disabled) by his own white whale, the three-decades-long leviathan that is the *Metal Gear* series. *Metal Gear* has not operated like a game as much as it has been a platform, simultaneously enabling and disabling certain possibilities.

When the masked figure walked onto the GDC stage to begin "Photorealism through the Eyes of a FOX" and revealed both his identity and the identity of *The Phantom Pain,* the only surprise was how anticlimactic, insulting, and poorly conceived Kojima's publicity stunt actually was. Whereas companies like Microsoft and Valve have successfully produced elaborate alternate reality games to advertise new titles,[17] here, the videogame industry itself becomes an alternate reality in which the hypertrophic pursuit of graphic realism short circuits other forms of play. Kojima's mask is not simply evidence of poor taste and insensitivity, but signals the larger, disabling effects of a series like

Metal Gear Solid. Following the advertising campaign centered around the fake, Scandinavian game development team and Keiley's interviews with various blue-eyed and bandaged men, Hideo Kojima finally revealed his *Phantom Pain.*

As Vivian Sobchack (2010, 65) notes in her essay on the "phenomenology of bodily integrity," phantom pain was recognized as early as 1551 by Ambrose Pare and the term *phantom limb* first appeared in print in the work of British neurologist John Hughlings Jackson based on Silas Weir Mitchell's earlier reference to the phenomenon in 1871 as a "sensory 'ghost.'" The term was included in the *Index Medicus* in 1954 and was then popularized by V. S. Ramachandran in his book *Phantoms in the Brain,* written with Susan Blakeslee in 1999, which details his invention of novel treatments like mirror visual feedback in which a patient relieves phantom pain by placing an arm or leg in a mirror box in order to visualize its corresponding phantom and regain control of that which is no longer there—a kind of photorealism through the eyes of a BOX.[18] More recently, Cassandra Crawford's 2015 study of the history of phantom limbs articulates the term as both a medical condition and a biological concept that has structured the experience of limb loss since the Civil War, in which a large number of survivors with amputated limbs were offered prosthetic technologies for the first time.

After having her leg amputated above the knee in 1993, Sobchack (2010, 52) describes her own experience of phantom pain as an "ambiguity not only of the *reduction* of my body's boundaries and articulations of itself but also of its surprising and radical *expansion*" (emphasis original). As Sobchack (2010, 52) wryly explains, "My lived body became for me an intimate laboratory in which I could examine, test and reflect phenomenologically not only upon the sensations and dynamics of my so-called 'phantom' left leg, but also those of my 'real' leg—dare I say, in a pun that will be telling, the right leg that, now, was left." What stood out to Sobchack (2010, 56) was the contrast between her conscious experience and the psychic presence of her amputated, left leg—a phenomenon she calls "dys-appearance," based on the work of Drew Leder—and, perhaps more disconcerting, her general lack of awareness and the proprioceptive transparency of her intact right leg. So immersed and familiar was she with the geometry of her body, Sobchack (2010, 58) remembers, that she "began to focus, with as much phenomenological specificity as possible, on my transparently 'absent' (rather than 'dys-appeared') right leg" and "had to explicitly force myself to sense my right leg even as I could clearly see its objective location and shape." Just as Sobchack's phantom pain signals a constitutive lack that, paradoxically, cannot be experienced until it is absent, in the Ahabian drive from one *Metal Gear Solid* to the next, Kojima enacts his own kind of disabling act that, like Sobchack's (2010, 56–57) dys-appearing amputation, reveals the "absence of an absence" that makes games possible in the first place.

Although *Metal Gear Solid V: The Phantom Pain* promises to outdo all previous iterations of the *Metal Gear Solid* series, Kojima signals a deep ambivalence toward this project by both deploying a disabled man as the protagonist of his game and assuming a position of disability himself.[19] In one respect, this Ahab figure with his eye patch and prosthetic hook is a welcome contrast to the able-bodied white men typically cast in the leading roles of AAA games.[20] However, the figure of disability here marks not an absence, but, like Sobchack's dys-appearance, the hypertrophy of the culture and technology of videogames oriented toward an upgrade path of endless sequels, graphic spectacles, and greater and greater sales. A term for the expansion of muscle and organ tissue, *hypertrophy* can describe a medical condition and impairment, but it is also the process exploited by bodybuilders in order to inflate and sculpt their muscles. Kojima's *Phantom Pain,* then, is not the ache of a missing limb or felt absence, but the pain that comes with the overextension and specialization of one faculty to the detriment of all else. The decades-long investment in spectacular and cinematic game design technologies comes at the expense of other sensory and financial economies. In the same way that Melville deployed Ahab as a figure of nineteenth-century transnational capitalism, so too does Kojima's Ahab avatar signal contemporary cognitive capitalism and the overinvestment in a particular model of game design. Marked by the avatar's hook-hand and cycloptic eye, Kojima's pursuit of the game industry's white whale ends with the hypertrophic exceptionalism of the perfectly rendered, cinematic cutscene disabling all other nonocular forms of sensory engagement.

[FADE OUT TO BLACK:] The Atrophy of Games

Fade out to black. Before the screen goes dark and gameplay all but ends, an emaciated Russian psychic, clad in black leather and wearing a gas mask, floats in midair, suspended in the center of the commander's office at the U.S. military base on Shadow Moses Island. In contrast to the florescent lights, grated catwalks, and steel panels of the larger Alaskan compound, the officers' quarters are comfortably furnished with decorative lighting, marble floors, and wood trim. Here Psycho Mantis demonstrates his "true power": reading the player's mind (or, in other words, ascertaining personality traits based on gameplay analytics). In *Metal Gear Solid,* the player may be "very methodical . . . the type who always kicks his tires before he leaves," "a highly skilled warrior, well suited to this stealth mission," or "extremely careful with traps . . . either very cautious or . . . a coward." Probing more deeply into the player's "soul"—ludic fingerprints with which Mantis builds his "psychic" profile—the ex-KGB, ex-FBI, FOXHOUND operative may discover that "you like *Castlevania,* don't you?" or the fact that "you have not saved often, you are somewhat reckless." Transitioning from a psychic to a psychokinetic demonstration, Mantis orders the player to "put your controller on the floor. Put it down as flat as you can" before moving the controller "with the power of [his] will alone." As the player watches their PlayStation controller rumble and shake on the ground,[21] Psycho Mantis asks, "Can you feel my power now?" The most memorable boss fight in the *Metal Gear Solid* series, the Psycho Mantis battle begins in earnest only after the screen suddenly goes black and a faux video warning (spelling "HIDEO") flashes in the upper right-hand corner (see Figure 3.9).

Fade out to black. After eight and a half hours of in-game cutscenes depicting high-heeled, cyborg ninjas taking down lizard-legged, bipedal tanks, *Metal Gear Solid 4* is interrupted by a discussion of storage capacity, CD-ROM swapping, dual-layered Blu-ray discs, and the affordances of the PlayStation 3. After a tour through a series of photorealistic warzones around the globe, there is a low-poly dream sequence in which posttraumatic stress manifests as retro graphics and low-res textures ripped directly from the original *Metal Gear Solid* on Sony's original PlayStation. The pursuit of graphic spectacle is always interrupted by cracks, fissures, deficiencies, and supplements that break the illusion and highlight the medium specificity of videogames as technical objects. As a series, *Metal Gear Solid* both camouflages *and* highlights the gaming apparatus and its relation to the larger videogame industry upon which it depends and through which it circulates. Hideo Kojima is not just writing a vast metafiction but is also producing a metagame that self-

Figure 3.9. Suddenly flashing across the screen, first large, then small, this green "HIDEO" warning is just one of Psycho Mantis's metagaming maneuvers that mimics the video channel of CRT TVs in *Metal Gear Solid*.

consciously intervenes on issues of genetic engineering, virtual reality, nanotechnology, global surveillance, and the war economy by implicating the videogame itself within the world of *Metal Gear*. The diegetic machine acts that disable play through cutscenes are always in opposition to the nondiegetic machine acts that disable play through material metagames. This kind of metagaming points the way not toward hypertrophy, but toward atrophy.

As much as Kojima's games participate in a naive desire for realism, the fantasy of immersion, and the promise of technological mastery, the *Metal Gear Solid* series complicates this hypertrophy of games by including medium-specific metagames that perform the opposite gesture: an atrophy of games. Breaking the fourth wall like a kind of Brechtian metatheater, the defamiliarizing moments in *Metal Gear* foreground the platform and larger media apparatus of videogames. There are passwords hidden in the game's packaging, mind-reading mini-bosses who mock memory card data, psychic trauma in the form of fake input warnings that flash on the televisions screen, future-proofed solutions that require players to change controller ports, rapid-fire button mashing followed by controller vibrations for optional arm massages, a compromised commanding officer who orders the player to power down the console, Sony and Apple electronics that function diegetically within the game, and more than a few references to virtual missions, combat simulations, cloned combatants, cyber warfare, and games within games.

In light of Kojima's relationship with Sony and the waning power of Japanese games in the era of the massively multiplayer online game (e.g., *World of Warcraft* [2004]), the popular military shooter (e.g., *Battlefield* [2002–], *Call of Duty* [2003–]), and the rise of social games and mobile apps (e.g., *FarmVille* [2009], *Angry Birds* [2009], *Candy Crush* [2012]), games journalist and critic Leigh Alexander has proposed that *Metal Gear Solid* is not actually about legendary heroes, proxy wars, child soldiers, and military technology, but a commentary on Kojima's personal battles in the ongoing console war. In an interview with Tom Bissell (2010, 187) Alexander argues that "the war in the game is the *console* war" and that *Metal Gear 4* represents "the journey of a game designer whose methodology is out of date" (emphasis original). Although the *Metal Gear* series has historically been at the technical forefront of the videogame industry, showcasing the capacities of each new console generation, and although Kojima's storytelling style is deeply informed by the logic of photorealism inherited from the Hollywood film industry, the series is also defined by its self-reflexive embrace of videogames as a technical medium. *Metal Gear*'s fate is deeply entwined with the evolution of gaming platforms, specifically the Sony PlayStation.[22] The movie is interrupted by the menu. The immersive experience is short-circuited by electrical circuits. The cinematic spectacle is halted by the load times, frame drops, texture resolution, and soft locks of the Sony PlayStation as a material platform.

Alexander Galloway frames these kinds of nondiegetic machine acts in terms of disability. For Galloway (2007, 31) disabling acts are "any type of gamic aggression or gamic deficiency that arrives from outside the world of the game and infringes negatively on the game in some way. They can be fatal or temporary, necessary or unnecessary. . . . crashes, low polygon counts, bugs, slowdowns, temporary freezes, and network lag." Whereas the hypertrophic cutscene disables interactivity as a means to immerse the player in a diegetic storyworld, the disabling act terminates in a conceptual practice in which the player is invited to contemplate the materiality of videogames as technical media. Rather than regard disabling acts as limitations (what Galloway negatively labels "aggressions" and "deficiencies"), some games have made use of these forms of gameplay as affordances rather than constraints within a critical game design practice.

Imagine a *Metal Gear* without cutscenes, without photorealistic models, without complex terrain, without complex enemy AI, without a vast arsenal of weapons, without an inventory of Japanese sundries, without customizable camouflage, without tactical espionage action, without *Metal Gear*. Before completely fading out to black, these negations form a kind of design philosophy that challenges the never-ending progression of more processes and more polygons and more products and more payments (although not always more play). The player is left with those disabling acts that previously seemed to interrupt play. Before Psycho Mantis was born via matricide, before he burned down his village and killed his father in a telekinetic primal scene, before he became an FBI profiler and inherited the personalities of the criminals he investigated, before he encountered a one-eyed and hook-handed veteran at a military hospital in Cyprus, before he was recruited by FOXHOUND to stop Solid Snake on Shadow Moses Island, and before he faded the screen out to black, another Snake on another mission on another continent in another era encountered another kind of enemy: a ladder.

After slithering through the jungles of Southern Russia on a "virtuous" mission to assassinate "The Mother of the Special Forces" and his beloved mentor, The Boss, midway through *Metal Gear Solid 3: Snake Eater* (2004), "Naked Snake," must ascend a seemingly endless ladder (see Figure 3.10). The third release in the series but the earliest entry in the game's narrative chronology, *Snake Eater* features the first Snake in a Vietnam-inflected, Bond-inspired jungle scenario set in 1964. As Matthew Weise (2012) aptly puts it, "*Snake Eater*'s deep, convoluted, irreverent world is a magical assault on the Western spy genre, dismantling the mythological universe of 1960's James Bond and reassembling it according to the logics of Japanese post-Hiroshima pacifism." During an encounter that subverts the player's expectation of the (usually) short tunnels and climbs punctuating the game's levels, Snake's stamina meter is put to the test. These interstitial areas typically operate as loading zones to obscure the levels and manage the game's geometry (a technique pioneered in *Half-Life*) but, as Snake begins to climb the ladder in Krasnogorje Tunnel to get from the verdant jungles of Sokrovenno North to the stark and rocky base of the Krasnogorje Mountain, the next level does not immediately appear. Gripping rung after rung as footfalls clink rhythmically on metal, a whispery vocal track begins to waft through what must be the longest vertical duct in Southern Russia:

What a thrill
With darkness and silence through the night

What a thrill
I'm searching and I'll melt into you
What a fear in my heart
But you're so supreme!

Building slowly, an a cappella version of the game's title soundtrack, "Snake Eater," becomes stronger as Naked Snake continues to climb the ladder. Written by Norihiko Hibino and performed by Cynthia Harrell,[23] the theme song parodies John Barry's lounge singer ballads that appear at the beginning of Bond films. The song is barely audible at the start of the climb, but increases to full volume as Snake ascends:

I give my life
Not for honor, but for you (Snake Eater)
In my time there'll be no one else
Crime, it's the way I fly to you (Snake Eater)
I'm still in a dream, Snake Eater[24]

For over three hundred steel rungs, the only action the player can take is to sit back and push up on the analog stick for a couple of minutes, listening to the music and reflecting on the central operations and experiences of playing videogames. In a piece of software that usually lasts around sixteen hours, two minutes may seem trivial, but the time spent climbing the ladder feels like another game altogether—a game inside a game or a game without a game.

By stripping the game down to the barest gameplay, this protracted moment of climbing in *Metal Gear Solid 3* calls into question the multiplicity of material supports that both make the algorithmic operations of games possible and are also eclipsed by the spectacle of Snake's stealth missions. Ascending the ladder pulls back the curtain of cutscenes to reveal the illusion of teleological progress that level-driven and quest-driven videogames present to the player—the moment not only suggests the futility of climbing an endless ladder, but hints at the Sisyphean endeavor of the entire game. Just as Brecht's epic theater challenged the aesthetics of illusionism in order to make spectators self-conscious, *Metal Gear* defamiliarizes the gameplay experience by removing many of the standard interactive features of the series. In this moment, the ladder reduces gameplay to a form of cinema as the action of climbing begins to operate like a cutscene—but one that cannot be skipped. As

Figure 3.10. A seemingly infinite ladder challenge's Snake's determination and stamina in the middle of *Metal Gear Solid 3: Snake Eater*.

the player cranks the projector step by step there are no enemy soldiers, no codec calls, no in-engine cutscenes, no CQC,[25] no COBRA Special Forces unit, no nuclear tank—just a ladder.

Apart from *Metal Gear* there are numerous videogames that selectively deploy a minimalist aesthetic to limit the gameplay, foreground disabling acts, and reveal the medium specificity of videogames as technical media. In *Super Paper Mario* (2007), for example, when Mario re-enters World 6–1 he discovers that the level has been completely destroyed and there is nothing but empty white space and a black line running through the world (see Figure 3.11). Recalling Émile Cohl's *Fantasmagorie* (1908) or Osvaldo Cavandoli's *La Linea* (1971–86), which featured cartoon characters animated out of the gestures of a single horizontal line on the frame, the effaced world distills *Super Paper Mario* to its core gameplay as Mario walks through a monochromatic side-scroller.[26] Another minimal moment in the same game occurs earlier in World 2–3 when Mario must run on a hamster wheel for over five minutes in order to earn 10,000 rupees (a reference to the currency used in *The Legend of Zelda* [1986]). This setup gently mocks the process of grinding that is such a common feature in roleplaying games (RPGs)— and the grinding wheels of capitalism more generally. Apart from *Super*

Paper Mario, many other games have scenes where the player must climb long, seemingly endless stairs, such as *Super Mario 64* (1996), *Final Fantasy VII* (1997), and even the original *Metal Gear Solid.*

Beyond the serial repetition of minimal level design, other games have selectively deployed an aesthetic of long duration to highlight the ticking timers and flashing frames specific to computational media. In order to enter Master Belch's secret base under Grapefruit Falls in *EarthBound* (1994), your team must "say the password!" But, as one helpful Mr. Saturn reveals in Saturn Valley, the password is "stand still, wait for three minutes," forcing the player to wait patiently instead of responding with a codeword. In a similar vein, one of the infamous "8 Star" challenges at the end of *Braid* (2008) requires the player to wait for a slow, leftward-floating cloud platform to carry the protagonist, Tim, across the entire level at an almost imperceptible speed—an exercise in long duration and obsession that is significantly more intense compared to either the three minutes of waiting in *EarthBound* or *Metal Gear Solid 3*'s ladder. Elsewhere in the third *Metal Gear,* simply waiting for the aged assassin codenamed The End to die in the vast forests of Sokrovenno is a valid way to complete the boss fight. Players may also advance the clocks on their PlayStation's operating system to speed up the process in a moment typical of *Metal Gear*'s material metagaming.

A history of this kind of minimal gameplay begins with the loading screens, pause states, idle animations, and repetitive gameplay of *all* videogames. Whereas mainstream games judiciously deploy moments of aesthetic minimalism and metacommentary, over the past decade, publicly available development tools and open-source modding frameworks have allowed independent and experimental developers to produce videogames that are not necessarily targeted toward commercial markets and can be dedicated entirely to exploring minimal mechanics that attenuate gameplay. Exercises in literalism like *You Have to Burn the Rope* (2008), *Close Range* (2009), and *Cow Clicker* (2010) expose the underlying procedural operations of their respective genres—shooters, platformers, and free-to-play social games—by distilling the gameplay down to a single interaction or operation. *You Have to Burn the Rope* is a one-level platformer by Kian "Mazapán" Bashiri in which the player must walk through a level and burn the rope of a chandelier to kill the only boss—the Grinning Colossus. The level takes less than a minute to complete, but the player is rewarded with a delightfully catchy credits

Figure 3.11. Aside from its anamorphic gameplay, Nintendo's hybrid RPG-platformer *Super Paper Mario* also showcases its share of minimal moments.

track celebrating your accomplishment by ironically declaring "Now you're a hero, you managed to beat the whole damn ga-ame" (a smug sentiment that echoes *Portal's* famous ending song, "Still Alive," by Jonathan Coulton). *Close Range* is a first-person shooter released by the satirical newspaper *The Onion* in which the player does nothing but shoot a revolving series of heads at close range, from an array of human faces to the heads of a horse and an ostrich—each click is automatically a bullseye.[27] *Cow Clicker,* a *Farmville*-like parody by Ian Bogost, was initially intended as a critique of the free-to-play genre of social media games that offered little challenge but was built on a Ponzi-like structure of acquisition in which the player could either pay money for items or recruit other social media users in order to generate virtual goods. Apparently clicking cows to generate "mooney" was something players really enjoyed because Bogost's game garnered enough of a following that he had to kill it off in a "Cowpocalypse" in which the cows vanished and players were left with empty green fields. Other minimal games like Penn and Teller's *Desert Bus* (c. 1995), Neil Hennessey's *Basho's Frogger* (2000), RRRRThats5Rs' *Don't Shoot the Puppy* (2006), Auriea Harvey and Michaël Samyn's *The Graveyard* (2008), Marcus "Raitendo" Richert's *You Only Live Once* (2009), anna anthropy's *queers in love at the end of the world* (2013), Darius Kazemi's *Zeno of Elea* (2014) remove conventional game mechanics to make minimal metagames. These are games *without* games because they strip away the verbs and vocabulary to leave only the syntax.

Examining the work of artists experimenting with this negative relation to videogames, Galloway labels Jodi's *Untitled Game* (1996–2001) and *SOD* (1999), Anne-Marie Schleiner, Joan Leandre, and Brody Condon's *Velvet Strike* (2002), and Cory Arcangel's *Super Mario Clouds* (2002, 2009) "countergames." For Galloway (2006, 115–18, 107), countergaming "replaces play with aesthetics, or perhaps something like the play of signification" and, through its subtractive approach, deliberately "ignores all possibility of gameplay." Unlike the cinematic games that disable play in the service of spectatorship and visual plenitude, these types of games that labeled art games, alt games, anti-games, not games,[28] non-games, no games, null games, and "countergames" follow in the tradition of abstract painting by ignoring or removing game mechanics in the interest of expanding the conceptual field of play.[29] Yet Galloway (2006, 125) remains skeptical of countergaming practices, calling for an "avant-garde of video gaming not just in visual form but also in actional form" and "radical gameplay, not just radical graphics."

One work that takes minimalist and monochromatic gameplay to its limit while still subsuming it within the logic of an "actional form" is *4 Minutes and 33 Seconds of Uniqueness* (2009). Designed at the Nordic Game Jam in 2009 by Petri Purho, Heather Kelley, and Jonatan "Cactus" Söderström and inspired by John Cage's *4′33″* (1952), *4 Minutes and 33 Seconds of Uniqueness* features a black, monochromatic background that slowly fills from left to right with white as time passes (see Figure 3.12). Recalling Cage's infamous composition written for David Tutor which consisted entirely of four minutes and thirty-three seconds of "silence" (designated by sheets of rests), in Purho, Kelley, and Söderström's game the player must wait for exactly four minutes and thirty-three seconds for the screen to fill. *4 Minutes and 33 Seconds of Uniqueness* is like a loading bar, but nothing is loading.[30] There is no data being prepared in the background and there are no files downloading from the Internet. The bar, like Cage's sheet music, is simply a measure of time.

If another player begins the game at any time during the process, however, the application will immediately close. In the same way that Cage's performance tunes the listener to the ambient noise of the orchestral

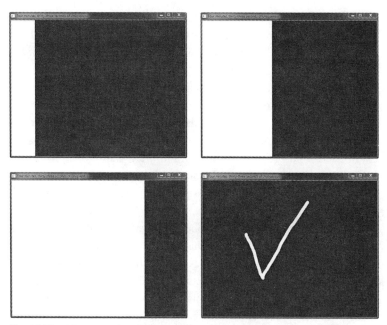

Figure 3.12. *4 Minutes and 33 Seconds of Uniqueness* begins as a black screen that slowly fills to white unless someone else opens the program.

space, *4 Minutes and 33 Seconds of Uniqueness* draws attention to the ambient interactions and alternative forms of interactivity that are the precondition for playing most videogames. This minimal metagame critiques the serialized conditions of network culture and fantasies of connectivity, as the player can only "win" or "complete" the game if another user does not log on while a playtime is in session. Only one player in the world can ever be playing this game at any one time. John Cage (1961, 102) famously described Robert Rauschenberg's white, monochromatic paintings as "airports for the lights, shadows, and particles." A similar effect is produced by staring at the slowly moving progress bar in *4 Minutes and 33 Seconds of Uniqueness*. By stripping the videogame to all but the act of waiting for a loading bar to turn from black to white, *4 Minutes and 33 Seconds of Uniqueness* does not simply excise gameplay, but it also opens the player up to the different kinds of play that are always taking place.

Much like Cage's work in which the performance allows the audience to relocate their listening from the musicians on the stage to the ambient sounds produced while sitting in a "silent" concert hall, *4 Minutes and 33 Seconds of Uniqueness* not only creates a space for the player to contemplate the mental metagame of when to boot the software and how to avoid being interrupted by another player, but also redirects focus toward the broader experience of play that takes place in, on, around, and through the network. While most massively multiplayer online games emphasize connectivity and promote online communities, *4 Minutes and 33 Seconds of Uniqueness* delivers a less optimistic diagnosis that the serialized conditions of networks ultimately work to estrange individuals as much as they bring them together. In the same way Cage's *4′33″* includes the suppressed coughs of audience members, uncomfortable shuffling of seats, and muffled sounds from outside the concert hall, *4 Minutes and 33 Seconds of Uniqueness* expands the field of play to include the microtemporal actions and exchanges that are occurring on and between the complex network of machines that make this game possible—the disabling acts that enable videogames as a medium.

Refining this concept by explicitly highlighting popups, loading errors, and plugin requirements—the computational equivalent of creaking chairs and intermittent sniffles in a crowded theater—*4:32* (2010) by Jesper Juul is a playful response to Purho's *4 Minutes and 33 Seconds of Uniqueness*. Rather than load up a game in which all the player must do is wait for a bar to fill or press up to climb a ladder (while, perhaps, taking note of the material supports that make videogames possible in the first place), Juul produces a game that is composed entirely around the metaleptic (and metaludic) practices of downloading software, installing applications, and refining user settings (see Figure 3.13). Upon loading the website Juul's game first requires the Firefox browser to run then instructs the player to install a suite of plugins like Unity, Silverlight, and Java; change the language to Spanish/Spain es-es; reduce the screen resolution to 800 x 600 pixels; uninstall Flash, etc. Through this intense and ultimately frustrating process of adjustments, *4:32* not only represents black screens and failed loading processes but directly incorporates nondiegetic machine acts into the diegesis of the game (undermining the distinction Galloway makes between diegetic and non-diegetic elements of videogames). In *4:32* play takes the form of the anticipatory process of preparing to play.

Installing a piece of software and fiddling with runtime settings is a profoundly ubiquitous and necessary part of the gaming experience (especially in the case of accessibility), yet frame rates, screen resolutions, language specifications, and key bindings are rarely discussed as part of the central pleasures of playing videogames. As such, Juul's *4:32* highlights the disabling acts that are constitutive of a player's gaming experience, yet often conceptually bracketed and rendered invisible when playing conventional games.[31] *4:32* is a metagame that incorporates all those actions that are imagined to take place outside the game, yet create the necessary conditions for play to occur in the first place. Works like *4 Minutes and 33 Seconds* and *4:32* put pressure on Galloway's claim that countergames are "progressive in visual form but reactionary in actional form" as they ask the player to reconsider what precisely constitutes the field of action in games—both experientially as well as mechanically. Not playing, it would seem, is also a viable form of play.

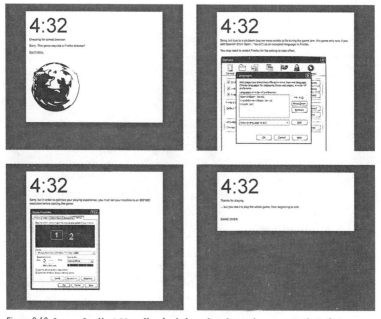

Figure 3.13. Jesper Juul's *4:32* endlessly defers play through a seemingly infinite series of compatibility checks, language requirements, plugin updates, and suggested resolutions.

Figure 3.14. *The Helen Keller Simulator* is an Internet meme that propagates in the form of a black website, video, applet, or application.

Perhaps the most extreme iteration of the minimal game is *The Helen Keller Simulator*. Propagating in the form of a deadpan Internet meme, the *Simulator* usually consists of a black screen with no other visual, auditory, or haptic feedback (see Figure 3.14). Whether produced in HTML, JavaScript, Flash, or Unity, this soundless, shapeless, colorless, texture-less, monochromatic videogame is initially assumed to be loading, paused, crashed, or nonfunctional before cognitive dissonance catalyzes into a crude punchline. Stated frankly, the faulty logic of the joke is that the experience of a blind and deaf person is illegible, unplayable, broken, and boring. The game explicitly maps what Galloway labels as "disabling acts" to disabled bodies. But, if one were to invert the joke (and Gallo-way's terminology), it is clear that *The Helen Keller Simulator* does not simulate the subjectivity of blind and deaf persons, but instead signals the failure of the medium to represent non-normative subject positions and alternate sensory economies. Despite the fact that the *Simulator* is a game about the lack of vision and hearing, it is nonetheless built around a visual regime. In explicit contrast to the hypertrophied masculine body deployed as an allegory for the videogaming apparatus at the beginning and end of *The Phantom Pain, The Helen Keller Simulator* attenuates play, preferring instead to joke at the expense of those bodies that have been historically excluded from the videogame medium.

The videogame industry designs hardware and software not only around standard models of generalizable, able bodies, but around gendered bodies as well. As danah boyd (2014) argues in her considerations of motion sickness and virtual reality headsets like the Oculus Rift, if women are unequally affected by the vertiginous effects of headsets designed around the proprioceptive capacities of a team of mostly male engineers, these simulators are not for everyone.[32] Thus, when *The Helen Keller Simulator* converts the figure of not only a blind and deaf person, but also a woman, into a meme, it reinforces not only the visual hegemony of games, but a culture of ability- and gender-based marginalization. As Susan Wendell (2006, 244) emphasizes, "To build a feminist theory of disability that takes adequate account of our differences, we will need to know how experiences of disability and the social oppression of the disabled interact with sexism, racism and class oppression." Within videogame culture, none of these issues are separate from one another and comingle in a game like *The Helen Keller Simulator*.

Helen Keller's gender is not incidental to the joke of *The Helen Keller Simulator*. Alongside Wendell, theorists like Rosemarie Garland-Thomson and the late Tobin Siebers have articulated some of the intersections between feminist theory and disability studies. Garland-Thomson (1997, 19) writes that "Many parallels exist between the social meanings attributed to female bodies and those assigned to disabled bodies. Both the female and the disabled body are cast as deviant and inferior; both are excluded from full participation in public as well as economic life." Siebers (2008, 154) further notes that "the women's movement radicalized interpretation theory to the point where repressive constructions of the female form are more universally recognized, and recent work by gay and lesbian activists has identified the ways that heterosexual models map the physique of the erotic body to the exclusion of nonnormative sexualities. Disability studies has embraced many of these theories because they provide a powerful alternative to the medical model of disability." Rather than pathologize individual bodies, the intersection of the social model of disability with issues of gender as well as class, race, sexuality, and age demonstrates how structural inequalities and ideological constructions not only privilege certain bodies at the expense and disenfranchisement of others but produce disability in the first place.[33] This overlap is manifested in *The Helen Keller Simulator*'s sexist and ableist punchline. *The Helen Keller Simulator* manipulates this iconic figure by treating her as a tool for commenting on the ontology of videogames and not as a historical agent with a distinct subjectivity in her own right.[34] In order to make their joke, the simulators reach for the lowest-hanging fruit: one of the most lionized "supercrips."

In *Feminist, Queer, Crip,* Alison Kafer (2013, 90) offers a definition of this common cultural trope: "Supercrips are those disabled figures favored in the media, products of either extremely low expectations (disability by definition means incompetence, so anything a disabled person does, no matter how mundane or banal, merits exaggerated praise) or extremely high expectations (disabled people must accomplish incredibly difficult, and therefore inspiring, tasks to be worthy of nondisabled attention)." An inversion of the figure of the poster child whose mere existence makes her both a hero and subject of pity, the figure of the supercrip represents the ableist fantasy of individual perseverance, of mind over matter, and of where-there's-a-will-there's-a-way attitude. Responding to a culture that has exploited the story of Helen Keller to create unattainable expectations and an impossible role model for persons with disabilities, Georgina Kleege's (2006a, 1) open letter to Keller, *Blind Rage,* argues that her "life story inscribes the idea that disability is a personal tragedy to be overcome through an individual's fortitude and pluck, rather than a set of cultural practices and assumptions, affecting many individuals that could be changed through collective action." Representations of Helen Keller often epitomize this pervasive ideology.

The reference to Helen Keller's name in the game's title is both a punchline and an illustration of how, in the case of the black monochrome, language fills the void. Without the name "The Helen Keller Simulator" there would be no game. Similarly, since no game is so immersive that it can ever articulate the complexity of human subjectivity (not to mention that of a blind and deaf woman born in the nineteenth century), *The Helen Keller Simulator*'s gameplay quickly migrates from the play of likeness to the play of language. Describing Keller's complex relationship to language, in a *New Yorker* article Cynthia Ozick

(2003) remarks how she was "at once liberated by language and in bondage to it, in a way few other human beings can fathom." As a result, Keller's language has been historically perceived as unmoored from the empiricism of the senses, a claim that lead to charges that her writing was not that of a human but of an automaton—a machine that recombines and remixes words into attractive combinations but is nevertheless incapable of producing "meaningful" descriptions rooted in "authentic" lived experience.

Considering Keller's lifelong struggle against plagiarism and accusations of "substituting parroted words for firsthand perception," Ozick (2003) recounts the moment when, at the age of twelve, Keller was put before an in-house tribunal at Perkins School for the Blind after being accused of plagiarism. According to Ozick (2003), Keller's own response to such charges was to declare her detractors "'spirit-vandals' who would force her 'to bite the dust of material things.'" In the wake of these accusations, Mark Twain (1917, 731) would become one of Keller's most ardent defenders, protesting that plagiarism was not the exception but rather the rule that governs all human discourse: "as if there was much of anything in any human utterance, oral or written, except plagiarism! . . . For substantially all ideas are second-hand, consciously and unconsciously drawn from a million outside sources, and daily used by the garnerer with a pride and satisfaction born of the superstition that he originated them." Despite the passage of a century, *The Helen Keller Simulator* is not only as quick to dismiss Keller's agency as her early skeptics, but also foregrounds and then demeans the textual conditions structuring Keller's experience.

As Ozick argues, Helen Keller engaged the world through language. And although neither the monochromatic painting nor the minimalist game capture this experience, these media nonetheless shift focus away from the sensual visual object toward the discourse of linguistic abstraction. *The Helen Keller Simulator* meme, across its many instances and iterations, does not effectively simulate or represent the phenomenology of being blind and deaf, but it highlights the insufficiency of contemporary videogames to offer access to this form of sensory economy. At the same time, as is evident in the comments section of the various *Simulators*, the most important aspect of these games is not the object itself (be it HTML or Java or YouTube video or bitmap image), but the conversation that circulates around it. The life of *The Helen Keller Simulator* is not discovered through the input and output of conventional gameplay, but through the discourse and language that always attends and supports play.

This move from kinetic play to conceptual, linguistic, or textual play mirrors the movement from abstract expressionism and minimalism to conceptual art in the late 1960s and early 1970s. When taken at face value, Ad Reinhardt's black squares were as much paintings as *The Helen Keller Simulator's* black screens are videogames. Both black paintings and black games attempt to empty their respective media formats in order to discover the underlying conditions that structure painting and play. In the process, they become increasingly conceptual—operating according to linguistic or textual rules rather than those of color, composition, competition, collection, or collision detection. They become blank slates, platforms for thinking about the ways we think about media as much as they signify the ends of media. In 1921, Alexander Rodchenko painted *Pure Red Color, Pure Blue Color,* and *Pure Yellow Color* as a way of announcing the end of painting. Despite claims that the monochrome was the final stroke, this end always seems to repeat. Artists like John Cage, Robert Rauschenberg, and of course Ad Reinhardt continued to end painting again and again; what was once declared an endgame strategy converted into serial practice, an art historical meme that continues to return in different contexts and conversations. In the case of the not games, non-games, no games, and null games represented by *The Helen Keller Simulator,* the end of gameplay is also serially reproduced—a poetic practice and genre of metagaming *without* videogames.

[CUT TO BLACK:] Blind and Blindfolded Play

Cut to black. No longer viridian, now azure fingernails are featured alongside a white GameCube controller on the upside-down webcam footage accompanying live streaming video of *The Legend of Zelda: Ocarina of Time* (1998) on Twitch.tv. As Link enters the vaguely Middle Eastern setting of Gerudo Valley, Narcissa Wright intones,

> One, two, three, four, five. Grab the edge, climb up the edge! Target. Roll, roll roll. Side hop, side hop, side hop, side hop, roll. Side hop, side hop, side hop, side hop, roll! Side hop, side hop, roll, roll. Side hop. Backflip, backflip, instant shield drop, roll, backflip aaaand roll! One more. And hit back. And hit backflip. Aaah! Welcome to *Ocarina of Time!* (Wright 2012)

As mentioned in chapter 1, Wright is well known for her work on Nintendo's classic 3D adventure game, *Ocarina of Time,* and for her articulate analysis and speedrunning commentary. She is also one of the great glitch hunters who discovered new ways to play games like *Ocarina of Time* by peeking and poking at memory addresses and studying the data structures of Nintendo 64 games.

After almost a decade of research, in 2013 Wright began using the iQue, a Chinese plug-and-play controller based on the Nintendo 64. As previously discussed, because the display rate of Chinese text is slightly faster than the Japanese and significantly faster than the English text, the Chinese version of *Ocarina of Time* on the iQue is advantageous for certain kinds of speedrunning. For speedrunners, the language in games is evaluated not according to its semantic value, but on its material and operational properties. Not only does Chinese text require fewer characters per word, conveying more content per pixel, but the iQue also displays text at a faster frame rate than the Nintendo 64. Beyond considerations of the text within the game, speedrunners collaborate to write "routes"—text-based instructions or directions detailing the fastest way to complete a videogame given what techniques and exploits are known at the time. For speedrunners like Wright, some of the most visually spectacular games (for their time) become reduced to sequences of input or text-based instructions.

Almost exactly one year before Wright was first beginning to make serious contributions to the *Ocarina of Time* metagame, when the game still took around four hours to beat in the winter of 2007 and spring of 2008, another player began to visit the Speed Demos Archive (SDA). After reading detailed descriptions of and technical advice about how to most efficiently navigate *Ocarina of Time* on the speedrunning forum, in 2006 Jordan Verner created a new thread titled "Can Someone Please Help Me with *OoT*?" Verner, who was born blind, recognized the relationship between his project and speedrunning and hoped to enlist the help of the community at SDA in order to complete one of the best known (and most complex) entries in the *Legend of Zelda* franchise. Initially, the responses on the forum ranged from skeptical and dismissive to flat out rude:

> Odd, a blind man who can find this site, type nearly perfectly, plays video games . . . has OoT 'for boss fights', wants the map to be there (even though

he can't see it) and expects a video to help him learn the game . . . what? (Hitaro 2006)

I'm sorry, but there are way too many complications for me to believe that a blind person can play through OoT. (Zurreco 2006)

I wasn't trying to make a useless post, but this is kind of a useless topic. (coolcwer2 2006)

A number of posters were unable to fathom that a blind person could successfully read, write, and interact on the Internet, let alone play videogames, particularly the vast, 3D world of *Ocarina of Time*. Although Verner's initial request was met with some resistance, active leaders of the SDA community like Kari "EssentiaFour" Johnson (a prolific player who, at the time, was working on the first speedrun of *Final Fantasy IX* [2000]), Andrew "andrewg" Gardikis (who had just become the world record holder for *Super Mario Bros.* at the time of Verner's post), and Drew "Runnerguy2489" Wissler (a burgeoning *Ocarina of Time* speedrunner who would become one of Verner's great allies) recognized the significance of Verner's project and its striking similarity to the practice of speedrunning.

As Wright demonstrates on her Twitch channel, although the speedrunner may be sighted, speedrunning operates at the limits of visuality. Slowly perfecting her *Ocarina of Time* world record throughout 2014, margins for error became slimmer as Wright's strategies increasingly relied on random events. As a speedrun becomes more and more optimized, play asymptotically converges with the speed and scale of digital media. When engaging in thousands of playthroughs, manual dexterity and psychological consistency become a scaffold supporting a game of chance. What are games of skill for the average player turn into a lottery as speedrunners must wait for an opportunity in which perfect execution aligns with optimal luck (usually structured by random number generators [RNG] within the game).[35] Technical consistency is achieved by mapping the kinetic motion of thumbs on joysticks to memorized input patterns—mnemonic texts discovered within the game that, if performed correctly, produce predictable outcomes.

Echoing Verner's process of creating mental maps, taking lengthy notes, and engaging in constant practice to memorize sequences and internalize haptic routines to play *Ocarina of Time,* so too does the speedrunner discover and engage, at some level, with a text-based game. Whereas many platforming games such as *Super Mario Bros.* rely on visual feedback, variable momentum, and frame-precise navigation,[36] *The Legend of Zelda* series has always included a coarser, less granular model of movement mapped directly to discrete player input. In contrast to the dynamic movement in *Super Mario 64*,[37] running and jumping in *Ocarina of Time* do not scale with speed. Link's metric motion is easier to predict, plan, and consistently perform: "Side hop, side hop, side hop, side hop, roll!" (Wright 2012). Exploiting these metrics (as well as the stereo sound afforded by the Nintendo 64's three-dimensional spaces),[38] Verner first became adept at beating dungeon bosses then began to work on a reliable method for navigating the fields, towns, and dungeons in *Ocarina of Time*.

For players who require alternative interfaces or who have low or no vision, there has been stunningly little attention paid to the issue of accessibility and to the potential of videogames beyond those sensory economies that prioritize vision. Although there are many text-to-voice adventure games designed for a nonsighted audience and a few games that have been modified and redesigned to feature nonvisual play such as *Shades of Doom* (1998) and *AudioQuake* (2003), audiogames remain a remarkably minor genre of game design. One notable exception is Jeremy "Aprone" Kaldobsky's software which includes accessibility applications like a mouse coordinate reader and a webcam color reader alongside a host of small, independently developed videogames. *Swamp* (2011), for example, is Kaldobsky's relatively popular, squad-based, survival-horror game designed primarily for nonvisual play.

Whether in film or digital media, sound often remains an ancillary, invisible aspect of production subordinate to visual media, especially in videogames. Some notable exceptions include Kenji Eno's audio-based branching romance story *Real Sound: Kaze no Regrets,* released in Japan for the Sega Saturn in 1997; Thomas Westin's award winning first-person sci-fi game featuring 3D sound design for the PC in 2002, *Terraformers*; and sound-based mobile games like Somethin' Else's *Papa Sangre* from 2010. Although these games exist, compared to the breadth of the catalog and depth of most AAA videogames, the current state of audiogaming leaves something to be desired. In many cases, contemporary audiogames appear to be decades behind in terms of production—small-scale, no-budget games made by volunteers in the idiom of arcade gaming but with audio instead of video feedback. But, as was the case with the indie game boom of the late 2000s, perhaps there will be an audiogame movement led by developers like Verner.

Before he began studying computer science and after he published video recordings of successful boss fights on YouTube, other speedrunners began to work with Verner by making audio records of their play-throughs, transcripts of specific button presses, and even specific RAM states for instant replay. The project exponentially expanded when Wissler, Mark "TurquoiseStar17" C., Roy Williams, and other runners began to work with Verner to produce a massive, hundred-thousand-word, collaboratively written plaintext file called *MasterScript.txt*. Along with a small AutoIt program that Verner developed in order to automate the otherwise difficult-to-predict angle of weapons like the bow and hookshot,[39] *Ocarina of Time*'s visual interface was transformed into texts. To navigate the Forest Temple, for example, Verner consulted this passage:

> Upon restarting, make your way forward to reach the main room. Take out your hookshot. . . . Save and reset . . . so you are facing forward when you reach the elevator. After riding it to the bottom, sidchop right twice, back flip once, sidehop right one more time, move forward. Grab the wall and push it up. Roll forward three times. Sidehop left 6 times, roll forward 3 times. Go into C-up view and start your hookshot automater. [*sic*] Move the view left 8 times then roll forward 5 times, you should land on the first switch. Wait a few seconds for the view to shift, Turn 180 degrees, wait again. Go into C-up view and move left 3 times. Roll forward 8 times, then side-hop left 2 times. Roll forward 5 times. Sidehop left once, then turn 180. Press Z. Grab the wall you're now facing and push it up. Make a step forward if you're not completely at it. Backflip 2 times, sidehop right once, backflip once, sidehop right once, backflip once, sidehop right once, sidehop left once, you will land on the second switch. Sidehop left 5 times, roll forward 7 times, sidehop left 2 times, turn 90 degrees left and push the wall. Roll forward 5 times, move a step up and grab the wall. Push it again. Sidehop left 7 times. Roll forward 8 times. Sidehop left 3 times, then hold Z and run up until you walk onto the third switch. Wait a few seconds for the view to shift, then turn 90 degrees left and press Z. Use the hookshot automater [*sic*] one more time and shift to C-up. Move right 5 times, then hold up and make your final triumphant run across the room to the boss door. (Verner et al.)

Through *MasterScript.txt*, Verner collaborated with the speedrunning community to transform a 3D action-adventure game back into a text-based adventure game. In doing so, he not only interrupted the competitive goals of those speedrunners working with him, but transformed assumptions around what videogames are and what they can do. With *MasterScript.txt,* the idea that *Ocarina of Time* is a stable object with a fixed author and an intended design is no longer obvious. Although the technical operations of the game's ROM, the system's RAM, and the serial pulses sent to and from the controller remain unchanged (there is no hacking involved in this hack), the reception and manipulation of the game occur according to an alternate logic, a different kind of game design philosophy. At the level of the material interface and the phenomenal experience of play, it was not the involuntary mechanics of videogames, but the voluntary rules of a community metagame that transformed Nintendo's closed product into an open platform for making new games, sharing new experiences, and writing new texts.

Although a number of Speed Demo Archives community members worked with Verner to produce scripts, save states, and compile strategies for navigating *The Legend of Zelda,* there was one runner in particular who was drawn to Verner's metagame. Drew Wissler, a record-holding *Ocarina of Time* player, not only assisted Verner with his project but also began to perform blindfolded speedruns of his own. Facing away from the screen, with a green pillowcase over his head, on March 7, 2008 Wissler videotaped himself navigating the virtual space without visual feedback (see Figure 3.15). Unlike Verner, Wissler relied on his memory and spatial intuition in conjunction with the sound cues and scripts he had helped Verner produce. The result is not a blind run but a *blind-folded* run. And Wissler is the first to admit that he and Verner are not playing the same game. When blind and blindfolded play are compared, the difference is obvious. Verner's YouTube videos appear choreographed, meticulously performed and obviously practiced in advance through a careful reading of *MasterScript.txt.* As Link constantly vaults backward, the camera angle is inconsequential to his backflips and side hops through Hyrule. On the other hand, Wissler's live attempts to navigate appear sloppy and ad hoc, based on muscle and visual memory, stereo sound cues, and frequent slashes on obstacles with Link's sword *cum* cane. Here, Link stumbles around drunkenly, slamming into walls and getting stuck in corners for hours—a debacle that earned Runnerguy the nickname "Cornerguy."

Figure 3.15. Jordan Verner (top) and Drew Wissler (bottom) metagame *The Legend of Zelda: Ocarina of Time* without the use of vision.

In *Optics* (1637), Descartes famously uses the metaphor of the blind man's cane to conceptualize vision. For Descartes, the blind man taps the field to build an image, a mental map of the world through a tactile prosthetic. Georgina Kleege (2006b, 392) has challenged Descartes' analogy for the way it reinforces an ocularcentric perspective by assuming the cane operates as a kind of haptic eyeball deployed for the purposes of mental imaging:

> The stick serves merely to announce the presence of an obstacle, not to determine if it is a rock or a tree root, though there are sound cues—a tap versus a thud—that might help make this distinction. In many situations, the cane is more of an auditory than a tactile tool. It seems that in Descartes' desire to describe vision as an extension of or hypersensitive form of touch, he recreates the blind man in his own image, where the eye must correspond to the hand extended by one or perhaps two sticks.

This distinction between the two models of a cane also illustrates the difference between Verner's and Wissler's play. Although, in both cases, the sword is tapped as an auditory tool, much of Wissler's struggle is produced through the disconnect between the auditory information revealed by the cane and his mental map—a virtual visuality—of the space developed through years of sighted play. By contrast, Verner is not using the sword to build a mental map of the space in its totality, but to check and avoid obstacles he knows are coming. It is no coincidence that Verner transformed *The Legend of Zelda* a text-based adventure game by translating the actions into a series of textual commands.

Jeremy Parish (2012) once described the starting screen of the original *The Legend of Zelda* in terms of Will Crowther and Don Wood's *Colossal Cave Adventure* (1975–76) writing: "You are standing in a clearing, surrounded by high rock walls on all sides. The cliff behind you to the south rises too steeply to be scaled. Winding dirt paths lead through the stone to the west, the north, and the east. Just ahead, the mouth of a deep, dark cave yawns from the rock to the north. What will you do? >_" (see Figure 3.16). More than ten years before *The Legend of Zelda* was released in 1986, Crowther's original *Colossal Cave Adventure* made its way across PDP mainframes in 1975, eventually appearing at Stanford where it was updated and popularized by Don Woods before circulating as *Adventure* or *ADVENT* in 1976 (Jerz 2007). While *Adventure* inspired Infocom to make their own text-based game, *Zork,* for PDP-10s in 1979,

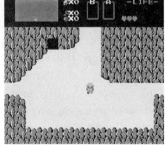

Figure 3.16. As Jeremy Parish points out, the branching paths at the beginning of both Will Crowther and Don Woods' *Colossal Cave Adventure* (left) and Nintendo's *The Legend of Zelda* (right) are structurally reminiscent of one another.

Warren Robinett began tinkering on his own graphical version of the game published for the Atari 2600 the same year. As Nick Montfort and Ian Bogost (2009, 45) note in *Racing the Beam,* "The development of the text-adventure genre, on the one hand, and the action-adventure genre, on the other, forked off from Crowther and Woods's *Adventure* at a very early point, long before the general public even knew that *Adventure* existed."[40] After Robinett's *Adventure,* Nintendo refined the action-adventure genre into one of their most famous franchises: *The Legend of Zelda.*

Although Shigeru Miyamoto's apocryphal story of childhood spelunking in the rural town of Sonobe has become, as Nick Paumgarten (2010) writes, "a misty but indispensable part of his legend . . . what the cherry tree was to George Washington, or what LSD is to Steve Jobs," the graphic convention of using single screens to represent rooms, the pixelwise motion of a player-controlled character, and the collision of that character with objects and enemies had perhaps more precedent in Robinett's game than in the caves of Kyoto. Quoting Montfort and Bogost again, although "games have moved to 3D and programmers have become more concerned with polygons than pixels . . . movement and collision detection remain the primary building blocks of [action-]adventure games, and, indeed, of most video games." But just because movement and collision detection function as the primary grammar of action-adventure games doesn't mean that these mechanics don't break down into discrete, textlike components.

Standing in a clearing, surrounded by high rock walls at the beginning of *The Legend of Zelda,* it appears as though Link has only four options. Whereas the dark green cliff faces block character movement due to nested rings of single-pixel collision detection embedded within each stony tile, the beige dirt paths lead left, right, and upward while the black mouth of the cave offers something to explore immediately upon starting a game. However, there is another way forward, or, more precisely, backward, due to the confluence between (1) the process by which Link's smooth, single-pixel movement gravitates toward an underlying 8 x 8-pixel grid upon direction change (in order to avoid getting snagged on rocks or blocks), and (2) the single-pixel collision detection routine responsible for scrolling the screen to the next location on the map. Given these two intersecting processes, if the green-clad hero is first positioned exactly five pixels away from the pixel responsible for scrolling the screen, and then receives a single frame of input from a direction perpendicular to his current orientation, something unexpected will happen. Link will move toward the sub-grid, bypassing the single-pixel collider and allowing the hero to continue forward without triggering the scrolling screen. Upon wandering off the right side of the screen, Link will wrap from one side of the level to the other as his horizontal position rolls over from 255 to 0 (see Figure 3.17). Unlike the infinitely looping Lost Woods or Lost Hills that simply reload the same location over and over again, in this case, Link never leaves the starting screen, looping from dirt path to dirt path via a pixel-perfect and frame-perfect exploit—a single, discrete, grammatized gesture that reduces the movement mechanics

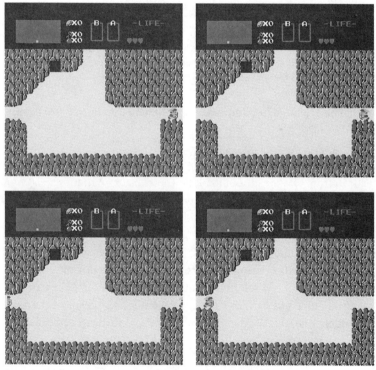

Figure 3.17. By first lining Link up with the single-pixel collider responsible for scrolling screen to screen (top left), then tapping a perpendicular directional input, in this case up or down, for a single frame (top right), Link will snap to the≈sub-grid undergirding his movement, allowing him to skip over the collider, wrap from one side of the screen to the other (bottom left), and continue walking (bottom right)—an action converging on textlike levels of grammatization.

of action-adventure games back to the text-based inputs of *Colossal Cave Adventure*'s "N," "S," "E," and "W" commands. Speedrunning the original *Legend of Zelda* begins by using this trick to skip through walls and quickly scuttle into the third dungeon after only three screens, and, as seen in the distinct play styles of Wright and Verner, the discrete effects of motion and collision transform into texts when read the right way.

As much as speedrunners rely on the eye to navigate videogames, their success depends on scripts, routes, and instructions that reconfigure the granularity of action-based gameplay in terms of metric sequences. As Narcissa Wright may have written for Verner,

> Side hop right 5 times. Hear Link fall off the edge and climb up the edge. Z-Target. Roll forward-left 3 times. Side hop left 4 times. Roll forward-left. Side hop left 4 times. Roll forward-left. Side hop left, side hop left, roll forward-left, roll forward-left. Side hop left. Backflip. Backflip. Use a bomb. Instant shield drop. Roll forward and backflip. Roll forward. Press backward. Now "Mega Backflip" across the canyon in Gerudo Valley.

Welcome to a blind or blindfolded, text-based action-adventure game.

[SCENE:] Disability and Games

Fade in from black. Fade out to black. Cut to black. While *The Phantom Pain* and *The Helen Keller Simulator* represent the extents of the visual economy of games (and each, in their own way, disable play), Jordan Verner and Drew Wissler's practices shift the conversation from cinematic excesses and minimal mechanics to the embodied performances of and the social contexts of play—from disability as an impediment or impairment to disability as a cultural identity and critical concept. The term *disability*, as numerous scholars have noted, is not a fixed category, but a moving target. Rosemarie Garland-Thomson (1997, 6) challenges essentialized distinctions between "able-bodiedness" and "disability," stressing that both categories are the product of "legal, medical, political, cultural, and literary narratives that comprise an exclusionary discourse." Lennard Davis (2006, 3) emphasizes "the 'problem' is not the person with disabilities; the problem is the way that normalcy is constructed to create the 'problem' of the disabled person." Disability expands from a self-evident medical condition to be cured or a personal problem to be overcome to a social construction rooted in historical contexts, inaccessible architectures, discriminatory policy, and ableist ideologies that only normalize some bodies. So although it may seem, at first glance, that Verner and Wissler are playing the same game, there is a difference between playing *The Legend of Zelda* blind and playing *The Legend of Zelda* blindfolded. Even though the mechanics may be the same, they are different metagames.

In *The Philosophy of Sport,* Steven Connor (2011, 18) challenges this distinction between able-bodied and disabled sports by arguing,

> The objects and instruments of sport are the means both of imposing and surpassing disability, of imposing disability in order for it to be possible partially to overcome it. It is for this reason that there is no real difference between able-bodied and disabled sports, since all sports are means towards the exertion of freedoms through the imposition of impediment.... Sport is not possible without the assumption of disability, which means that disabled sports are *the only kind there are.* (Emphasis original)

Connor's theory of sport echoes the definition of game and play that Bernard Suits (2005, 55) proposes in *The Grasshopper: Games, Life, and Utopia* in which "playing a game is a voluntary attempt to overcome unnecessary obstacles." For Suits and Connor, players are not merely choosing to play games fast or without the use of vision but a time constraint or blindfold makes it a game in the first place. The act of applying an unnecessary obstacle or self-imposed limitation *is* the game. However, not every impediment is self-imposed and simply reframing a disability as an unnecessary obstacle to be overcome within the magic circle of a game does not change how disability is historically, politically, practically, or phenomenologically constructed. It also doesn't change how a disability might affect the experience of everyday life.

Although temporarily donning a blindfold in order to learn about the realities of living with visual impairments has been a common occurrence at disability awareness events, Alison Kafer (2014, 4) notes that there are limits to running "disability simulation exercises." Apart from the fact that these exercises "focus on the alleged failures and hardships of disabled bodies," Kafer (2014, 4–5) argues they are also ineffective because "there is no accounting for how a disabled person's response to impairments shifts over time or by context. . . . Wearing a blindfold to 'experience blindness' is going to do little to teach someone about ableism, for example, and suggests that the only thing there is to learn about blindness is what it feels like to move around in the dark." Tobin Siebers (2008, 29) makes a similar case when he suggests that rather than blindfolding students, a more fruitful exercise would be to send them off wearing sunglasses and wielding a cane so that they might "observe firsthand the spectacle of discrimination against blind people as passersby avoid and gawk at them, clerks refuse to wait on them or condescend to ask the friend what the student is looking for, and waiters request, usually at the top of their lungs and very slowly (since blind people must also be deaf and cognitively disabled), what the student would like to eat." Clearly there is a difference between between blind and blindfolded play.

Although Connor's (2011, 18) claim that "there is no real difference between able-bodied and disabled sports" and that "disabled sports are the only kind there are" could be seen as a democratizing gesture (perhaps recalling the sentiment that disability activists and scholars such as Joseph Shapiro [1993, 7] have expressed that disability "is the one minority that anyone can join at any time"), the conflation of involuntary disabilities with voluntary impairments elides the very real differences in the embodied conditions of play that are always in operation, both in and outside the magic circle. Metagames, on the other hand, acknowledge the fact that some obstacles are always necessary and some pursuits are always involuntary. In this sense, videogames function as a particularly useful media for thinking about disability by means of the contrast between embodied feedback generated between player and game and the ideology of control, mastery, and escapism that attend videogames as a medium (features that make these technologies particularly valuable in physical and psychiatric rehabilitation). And although videogames always operate as open platforms and elastic equipment for making so many metagames, their screens, interfaces, and protocols can be inaccessible and disabling for many players. As seen in this chapter, however, disabling acts can become enabling acts. By considering the possibilities of videogames with too much video, videogames without video, and the nonvisual games we constantly play, from *The Phantom Pain* to *The Helen Keller Simulator* and from Wright's speedruns to Verner and Wissler's collaborative text-based action adventure games, metagaming uncovers blind spots in the scopic regime of digital media and looks toward new horizons of play.

Metagame 3

It Is Pitch Black

Inspired by Will Crowther's inaugural text-based adventure game, *Colossal Cave Adventure* (1975–76), Nintendo's graphical action-adventure, *The Legend of Zelda* (1986), and Mark Z. Danielewski's transmedial novel, *House of Leaves* (2000), *It Is Pitch Black* is an original "text-based action-adventure" game combining the text parsers of interactive fiction with the polygonal collision of 3D navigable space. *It Is Pitch Black* features a nonvisual environment illuminated not by lamp, but by the quickly scrolling debugger log of recombinant poetry (see Figure 3.18). The speed and scale of output are directly proportional to the speed of the computer running the game and, as such, index each of the game's discrete states while representing the streams of consciousness of two women: Patricia Wilcox, an avid caver married to Will Crowther in the 1970s, and Karen Green, Will Navidson's long-suffering partner in *House of Leaves*. In *It Is Pitch Black,* both Patricia's and Karen's journeys through the dark are narrated through the footnotes of "Will," the conflated author-figure. To download *It Is Pitch Black,* go to http://manifold.umn.edu/pitchblack.

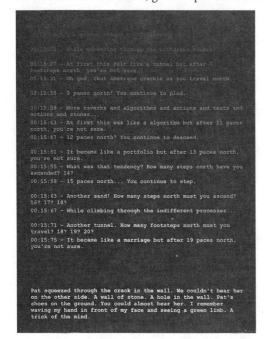

Figure 3.18. *It Is Pitch Black* is an original metagame that consists of a scrolling text log of recombinant poetry that indexes an unseen, navigable 3D space.

FOUR

Hundred Thousand Billion Fingers

Serial Histories of Super Mario Bros.

> Thank you Mario! But our princess is in another castle.
> —Nintendo, *Super Mario Bros.*

> At each moment of the playthrough there's a lot of different
> things Mario could have done, and almost all of them lead to
> horrible death. The anthropic principle, in the form of the
> emulator's save/restore feature, postselects for the possibili-
> ties where Mario actually survives and ensures that
> although a lot of possible paths have to get discarded, the
> camera remains fixed on the one path where after one
> minute and fifty-six seconds some observer still exists.
> —Andi McClure, "Super Mario World vs. the Many-Worlds
> Interpretation of Quantum Physics"

Over the past thirty years, thousands of thumbs have piloted herds of Marios over Goombas and green pipes before sending the plumbers to their collective doom down the first pit of *Super Mario Bros.* (1985). Clouds of blurred bodies dodge and weave in red-capped flocking patterns above while great masses of Marios ebb and flow like crowd simulations below. Yet, despite these dynamics, not a single footprint or fingerprint is preserved within World 1-1 of the Mushroom Kingdom.[1] Mario's fleeting movements, along with the manual gestures driving them, remain distinct from one another, isolated in the homes of countless players.[2] Upon game over or reset, the histories of in-game actions are effaced and the Sisyphean task of rescuing Princess Toadstool begins anew. From 3 to 2 to 1, the eight-bit font of the submenu's scoreboard ticks down as even the convention of multiple lives built into games like *Super Mario Bros.* reinforces the mass repetition of videogames. Whereas the individual experience of play arises from a unique and irreducible assemblage of technological, physiological, psychological, and material phenomena, players also participate in a vast network of composite actions that make up the aggregate histories of digital media. The princesses are always in other castles, there are always second quests, and hundreds of thousands of fingers continue to direct parallel processes in digital landscapes.

In 1961, the co-founder of the Ouvroir de littérature potentielle (Oulipo) Raymond Queneau produced *Hundred Thousand Billion Poems*. The Oulipo's experimental practice of incorporating mathematical systems with literary production, writing under constraints, and making use of recombinatory poetics is now widely regarded as a precursor to the aesthetic strategies commonly seen in digital media production.[3] Decades before digital poets produced permutations on desktops, laptops, smartphones, and even virtual reality goggles (though not before Theo Lutz programmed a Zuse Z22 to recombine chapter titles and subjects from Kafka's *The Castle* [1929]), Queneau's sonnet generator was already generating 10^{14} unique poems (Funkhouser 2008, 37). Although *Hundred Thousand Billion Poems* is only ten pages long with fourteen lines per cut-up page, it is impossible for a single individual (or even a million individuals) to read every iteration of Queneau's printed program (see Figure 4.1). In this work, Queneau created a highly constrained text with a reading potential that far exceeds the time and scale of legibility.[4]

While *Hundred Thousand Billion Poems* foregrounds the impossibility of ever accessing the totality of these many reading paths, videogames such as *Super Mario Bros.* limit the player to one isolated, incomplete perspective among an enormous (but finite) set of possible playthroughs emerging from interactions with an eight button controller. Whether reading Queneau's book or playing a videogame, the constraints of poem and program produce repetitions. Due to the technical processes through which videogames interpret input and generate output, the diverse practices, material nuances, and temporal infelicities of play are reduced to a finite and deterministic set of outcomes on screen.[5] Over time, individual engagements with these processes show signs of syncing, slipping, bleeding, and repeating as readers and players alike mash through a billion remixes of predetermined combinations of input and output. There is a key difference, however, between a hundred thousand billion poems and a hundred thousand billion twitching fingers.

Figure 4.1. Massin's book design for Raymond Queneau's *Hundred Thousand Billion Poems* recombines into more poems than could be read in a lifetime. Photographs by Patrick LeMieux, 2016.

Whereas Queneau's work directly juxtaposes each individual reading path with the immensity of possibilities, the gameplay of *Super Mario Bros.* obfuscates this potential. Players do not experience the multiplicity, but rather the singularity of each engagement as past playthroughs vanish, disappearing in time.

But what happens when the reset button is removed? When serial systems begin to feedback upon themselves to become sensible? What happens when in-game actions are not only recorded and analyzed, but also reorganized into new forms of play? Given a discrete set of inputs and outputs, how can we reroute the logic of control to metagame the seriality of twenty-first century play? This chapter will primarily examine two categories of metagames that expand and condense the serial logics of *Super Mario Bros.* The first way to play features systems that translate one player's actions onto multiple platforms or contexts: *single input, multiple output*. These practices include multigame tool-assisted speedruns (TAS), in which one controller is used to operate multiple games simultaneously, as well as videogame mashups that collage game mechanics appropriated from multiple sources. The second category of serial play reverses this relation to focus on games that produce a proliferation of player actions within a single setting: *multiple input, single output*. Some of these strategies yield games that enable the recording and playback of player performances, scripted artificial intelligences that parse all the available options for traversing a given level, and mass bots or AI swarms whose agents behave according to the rules of the game and resemble crowd simulations or fluid dynamics when composited together.

Of course there are many other ways to play. When a single sequence of button presses is applied to a single instance of a game, specific and often predictable patterns emerge as the result: *single input, single output*. As exemplified by the realtime attacks (RTA) or speedruns already addressed in chapters 1 and 3, the process of optimizing a playthrough according to the fastest route through a game tends toward a single series of inputs that articulates both the technical constraints of a given videogame and the physical limits of their most ardent players.[6] On the other hand, multiple instances of play are already occurring across multiple contexts, as is the case with the manifold practices taking place in, on, around, and through videogames: *multiple input, multiple output*. Within this final multiplicity, the metagame most often takes the form of the unstated rules and assumptions of those players who cooperate and compete with one another in multiplayer e-sports events examined in chapter 5.

Single input to single output, multiple input to multiple output: seriality structures the way we play digital games. In their essay "Digital Seriality," Shane Denson and Andreas Jahn-Sudmann (2013, 1) consider the seriality *between* games in a franchise, the seriality of repetitive levels *within* games, and the seriality of transmedial adaptations *about* games.[7] But beyond never-ending sequels, core gameplay loops, and rapid fire button presses, a more granular form of seriality organizes videogame play: the serial forms of information processing that makes communication between controller and console, client and host, as well as computer and server possible in the first place. Single input to multiple output, multiple input to single output, the metagames discussed in this chapter expose the serial structure of digital media by mixing and matching, modding and mashing, multiplying, manipulating, morphing, and metagaming Super Mario.

From Newspapers to Nintendo

From the industrial production of newspapers, comics, photographs, and film to the digital duplication of computational media and networked information, the term *seriality* is generally used to mean objects that are arranged in a series, whether temporal or spatial, diachronic or synchronic. In literature and popular media, seriality can refer to stories or publications that are released in intervals over a period of time or constructed with forced pauses incorporated into the diachronic reception of the work like a book series, serial television, or a series of videogames. Alternately, the seriality associated with the literary genre of the *nouveau roman* and authors such as Alain Robbe-Grillet or the minimal art of Donald Judd and Sol LeWitt (or even Ad Reinhardt) generally implies a synchronicity based on the discontinuity and repetition of multiple objects at the same time like the hundred metal boxes standing in Marfa, Texas, or the hundred black paintings once hanging in the Jewish Museum in New York. In computing, serial communication is a technical term for information protocols that transfer discrete numerical values one bit at a time (such as the way in which a controller sends data to a Nintendo Entertainment System). Some serial data transfers may seem synchronic, like when Mario appears to jump at the precise moment the A button is pressed, but at microtemporal speeds and scales videogames also move 0s and 1s in diachronic patterns, one after another. What binds these competing forms of philosophical and technical seriality, endemic to popular media, fine art, and computer science, is their relationship to industrial culture.[8] Modes of mass production, distribution, consumption, and organization rely heavily on serial logics. And videogames like *Super Mario Bros.* subsume these multiple and sometimes contradictory uses of seriality under their regime of operation.

Jean-Paul Sartre deployed the concept of seriality to model an individual subject's relationship to the aggregated group formations of the whole in *Critique of Dialectical Reason* (1960). For Sartre, seriality is the condition of modernity that results in individual disempowerment and alienation. This serial theory of social networks argues that urban and industrial life simultaneously isolates individual actors and arranges them into repetitive structures. The act of reading the newspaper while waiting for the bus was Sartre's principal example. In his *Critique,* Sartre paints a portrait of the man in the gray flannel suit who waits for the bus every day with his fellow commuters. "Their acts of waiting are not a communal fact," Sartre (2004, 262) insists, "but are lived separately as identical instances of the same act." The implication of representational or mimetic similarity between commuters is only the sensible effect of the larger serial processes of capitalism that manufacture desire, fashion, posture, behavior, and consumption. Despite the similarity of the overarching behavioral patterns, each actor's experience of waiting is not perceived as part of a series. The first step toward collective empowerment is to become aware of these larger systems of organization. The serial condition, however, emerges only when these simultaneous instances are "lived separately" and when the individual is generally unaware of how her actions are part of a serial system. With this model of culture, Sartre critiques the way in which modern life becomes serialized. The phenomenal impossibility of ever grasping the relation between larger forms of systemic organization and the individual's position as an othered object is how, for Sartre, seriality produces urban alienation.

The kind of anomistic repetition Sartre saw as a defining element of modernity can be compared with certain forms of gameplay. Videogames operate as an ideal medium for expressing as well as critiquing the serial structures that define both the digital repetitions of software and the quotidian repetitions that conduct the rhythm of daily life. In the twenty-first century, the figure of the man in a gray flannel suit, holding a newspaper while waiting for the bus or train, has been at least partially replaced by the contemporary commuter fiddling with a laptop, smartphone, e-reader, or handheld videogame console. And although the number of Apple earbuds seen on the New York subway far outnumber the folded newspapers, the effect remains much the same. Just as Sartre identified the irony of reading a newspaper—a medium designed to foster collectivity and participation within the imagined community of the nation—as a means to both create a mental and material barrier from fellow commuters, there is a palpable irony in the public operation of so-called social media. Sartre (2004, 257–58) writes, "These are often operations for making the transition from one group to another (from the intimacy of the family to the public life of the office)" and "to isolate oneself by reading the paper is to make use of the national collectivity and, ultimately, the totality of living human beings . . . in order to separate oneself from the hundred people who are waiting for or using the same vehicle." Writing in an era prior to the emergence of digital communications networks, Sartre grasped the paradox of serial processes and their capacity to simultaneously assure a subject's segregation in the very moment of feeding her into a network.

Sartre's critique of seriality resonates with some contemporary theories of networked technology that stress the alienation and separation of networks as much as their capacity to connect. In the second half of *Alone Together: Why We Expect More from Technology and Less from Each Other*, Sherry Turkle (2011) argues that computer-mediated social interactions threaten to supplant rather than enhance community engagement. Steven Shaviro (2003, 29) echoes Turkle's criticism of networks, writing, "Indeed, our being each alone, rigidly separated from one another, is a necessary condition for our being able to log on to the same network." Similar to Sartre's newspapers, portable and networked electronics perform the contradictory operations of both connecting their users to one another while isolating them from their local context, but on a scale that goes well beyond technology as a means of avoiding the eye contact of adjacent commuters. The legacy of Sartre's search for ways to escape the serial conditions of industrial life reverberates throughout media theory and is echoed in the search for methods of dispelling network anxiety and solve the problem of being "alone together." The sudden realization that one's circumstances are part of an ineffable network in which countless others participate disrupts the serialized isolation on which games like *Super Mario Bros.* depend for their escapist pleasures.[9] From the minor jolt of arriving at a party to find another guest wearing the same dress to the major shock of the Pacific Trash Vortex, these moments of recognition provide networked antidotes to serial stupor.[10]

Within the private, domestic spaces of the home, game consoles made by companies like Magnavox, Coleco, Fairchild, Atari, Nintendo, Sega, Sony, and Microsoft since the early 1970s reinforce serialized isolation. Each moment of domestic play, in Sartre's (2004, 262) words, is "lived separately as identical instances of the same act." The work of game designers, however, often obscures the explicitly repetitive aspects of computational media. The careful rearrangement of both graphic and procedural elements via clever level designs and the addition of mechanical constraints like time limits, collectibles, and other obstacles keep repeat playthroughs fresh. Whereas a culture of play and unique metagaming practices can form *around* environments like Level 1–1 from *Super Mario Bros.,* there is no evidence of past plays recorded *within* the gamespace itself.

Even the ways in which videogames save progress or relay passwords are ahistorical. Punching "A1, B5, C3, C4, D5, E1, E2, E3, E4" into *Mega Man 2's* (1988) password screen does not call up a transcription of a unique playthrough, but generates a new gamestate according to a small set of parameters (e.g., bosses defeated and energy tanks collected) that resembles past play. In *Mega Man 2* there is no record of the twists and turns the player took to get there. Instead, the save state or password is a generality, standing in as a placeholder for the totality of all actual and possible plays that led up to a particular point. In this respect, videogames model a history without causality, as in-game inscriptions are nothing more than indices that unlock preprogrammed parameters fatalistically encoded before any hand clasps the controller. Like *Hundred Thousand Billion Poems,* there is nothing truly generative about these works. Queneau's book does not write poems, but allows for recombinations of prewritten strings, determined long before a reader ever selected a particular arrangement.

Contrasting the preset histories of passcodes, the communal and social aspects of play cannot be reduced to (only influenced by) serial processes. In arcades, scoring systems and the physical proximity of cabinets suggest the possibility of much larger group formations that transcend individual instances of play. Inscription technologies like VHS recordings, mail-order fan clubs, and even Nintendo's famous tip hotline offer traces of a social history that are not necessarily rendered within the rules of any one videogame. Nevertheless, some parts of arcade culture have been emulated and encoded for individual consumption by Valve's Steam (2003), Microsoft's Xbox Live Arcade (2004), Nintendo's Virtual Console (2006), and Sony's PlayStation Store (2006). Within these systems, networked play, public score boards, community achievements, and sales statistics account for some serial phenomena by collecting and visualizing player data. Following the creation of these networked platforms, game development and gaming practices have begun, by necessity, to metagame the serial structures of videogames. And many of these experiments begin with Mario.

Whither Mario?

Red cap, blue overalls, brown mustache: Super Mario not only stands in for Nintendo's corporate identity and game design philosophy, but videogames in general. Since at least the release of *Super Mario Bros.* in 1985, the Mario series has served as Nintendo's flagship franchise, making the plumber one of the most iconic figures associated with videogames. Mario is so widely known that a director at Nintendo once famously claimed the character to be more recognizable than Mickey Mouse among American school children (Iwabuchi 2004, 30). The *Super Mario Bros.* games are often marketed as launch titles or bundled with hardware to demonstrate the technical capabilities of Nintendo's latest console, recycling the story of a plumber who rescues a princess from the clutches of an evil turtle. This formulaic abduction cycle is often the framework for displaying Nintendo's vanguard technology. Fueled by both nostalgia and Nintendo's impeccable game designs, the *Super Mario Bros.* series has also become a popular vehicle for metagaming practices.

Alongside the original *Super Mario Bros.* trilogy[11] on the Nintendo Entertainment System (NES) and the ever-unfolding *Super Mario Land, World, Sunshine,* and *Galaxy* titles on later consoles,[12] there are also hosts of player-created variations that expand the Mushroom Kingdom into multiple timelines, parallel dimensions, and folded spaces. Beyond simply building modifications, or "mods," by rearranging read only memory (ROM) data in classic Mario cartridges or completing Mario games in record times in the form of speedrunning, metagames stretch Mario to his limits. There are Mario quadruns, in which the first four Super Mario titles are played simultaneously, and Mario mashups starring Mario in other 8-bit–era videogames. There are brain- and mouth-controlled NES interfaces made to pilot Mario without the use of hands,[13] while *Infinite Mario Bros.* (2006), a Java application by Marcus "Notch" Perssons, features randomly generated levels stretching out as far as the thumb can play. Dozens of automatic Mario sequencers convert custom *Super Mario World* levels into J-pop beat machines,[14] automatically propelling Mario across each level like the proverbial bouncing ball set to synthesized music, while "Asshole Mario" hacks make it difficult for the player to do anything at all. Exploring multiple dimensions of Mario, Andi McClure's emulator extension plays with the Everett–Wheeler "Many-Worlds Interpretation" of quantum physics; and Mario AI competitions have been held at the Ph.D. level since 2009 in many computer science departments. Playing and programming converge when Allan "DwangoAC" Cecil and Peter "Micro500" Greenwood (with the help of Masterjun and p4plus2) prepare hardware interfaces like TASbot to play *Super Mario Bros.* inside *Super Mario World;* and Seth Bling deploys the TAS community's research to inject assembly code bit by bit to transform Mario in realtime. Even Cory Arcangel's *Super Mario Clouds* (2002, 2009), one of the first videogames exhibited in the Whitney Museum of American Art, imagines a *Super Mario Bros.* evacuated of all content except the blue, monochromatic sky and a few blocky, leftward-floating cloud-forms.[15] From remakes of ROM hacks to speedruns of sequencers, Mario has been manipulated, duplicated, generated, appropriated, and aggregated across dozens of unique practices and diverse material platforms as players grow bored with the standard challenges and begin to game the limits of the software itself. Here Mario is no longer just a videogame, but a medium for making metagames.

Single Input, Multiple Output

While wall jumping, clipping through bricks, wrong warping, and careening through the Mushroom Kingdom, real-time attacks (RTA) depend on the disciplined practice regiments and virtuosic live performances of human players, the competitions between community members on both live races and leaderboards, the public presentation in the form of livestreaming or marathons, and, of course, the correlation between serial input and output. Tool-assisted speedrunning (TAS), on the other hand, transforms twitch-based platform games like *Super Mario Bros.* into turn-based puzzle games through the affordances of various videogame console emulators.[16] From slow motion, save states, and instant replays to interfaces for composing frame-by-frame button presses, cutting and pasting data, and building complex macros, tool-assisted speedrunning is related to realtime attacks, but takes a vastly different approach to metagaming the serial interfaces of videogames. TASVideos.org (2016), the primary forum and clearing house for tool-assisted speedrunners, announces

> The emulators we use allow for undoing mistakes, slow-motion gameplay, and even in some cases utilizing robots to do our bidding. Using these tools, we overcome human limitations to complete games with extremely high precision, entertaining our viewers as our players tear through games at seemingly impossible speeds. The end result of this process is simply a series of key-presses which may be performed on the original hardware.

While "impossible speeds" still seem to be the primary objective, the TAS community's interest in "entertaining" stretches well beyond the typical categories like Any%, 100%, and Low% discussed in chapter 1. Prolific *Super Mario Bros.* TASer HappyLee's collection of world records extends from standard categories like "warps" and "warpless" to "walkathon," "warpless walkathon," "maximum coins," "lowest score," "-3 stage ending," to even speedruns of ROM hacks like *Extra Mario Bros.* (2005) and *Hard Relay Mario* (2004)—games that cannot be played without the use of tools. Nevertheless, in each of these cases, the end result remains "simply a series of key-presses."

Beyond the categories in which HappyLee achieved his myriad *Mario* records, in December 2004, the TAS community played a game to "see who can find the highest score made by a movie file" by running discrete sets of inputs within Nintendo's *Pinball* (1984) (FODA 2004). The result was a direct translation of jumping over a pit in *Mario*, swinging a sword in *Zelda*, or rotating a block in *Tetris* to twitching the paddles in *Pinball* that, in turn, produced different scores. Forum members then

competed with one another, not by playing *Pinball,* but by trying to figure out which previous speedruns produced the highest score when used
as input in another game (flagitous 2005). At the time, the world record
TAS of *Blaster Master* (1988), for example, scored a whopping 37,960
while input from *The Krion Conquest* (1990) only scored 1,780.

Following these serial experiments, in May 2005, the concept of a
multigame TAS or "Bigame Movie" originated from the idea of executing the same bit of code in both Perl and PostScript computer languages—a code pun not unlike John Cayley's poem *Pressing the "Reveal
Code" Key* (1996), which can be read as both natural language and exe-
cutable code. Given how well a tool-assisted speedrun of *Blaster Master*
performed in *Pinball,* would it be possible to complete goals in two
different games using the same input? As a way of adding further constraints and increasing the challenge (as well as the entertainment value)
of tool-assisted speedruns, these examples of multigame TAS illustrate
how a single series of button presses can serve as the input for successfully progressing through multiple games at the same time.

These single input, multiple output playthroughs were pioneered by
Sean "DeHackEd" P., Lennart "Baxter" W., Yashar "AngerFist" Nasirian,
and agwawaf at TASVideos in the mid- to late 2000s. Inspired by
DeHackEd's dual-boxing mashup in 2005 in which he navigated *Mega
Man X* (1993) and *Mega Man X2* (1994) simultaneously, Baxter and
AngerFist produced a quadrun in 2007 that featured *Mega Man 3* (1990),
Mega Man 4 (1991), *Mega Man 5* (1992), and *Mega Man 6* (1993) being
executed at the same time. AngerFist went on to successfully multigame
a single level of the first six Mega Man titles in 2010, the first documented
"hexrun," and, as of 2016, is working sequencing nine Mega Man games—a
"nonrun" that is not the negation of speedrunning but an expression of
the serial communication organizing all games.

The history of speedrunning and tool-assisted speedrunning (along
with other metagames) often feature Mario at their experimental origins. After agwawaf released a "trirun" of *Mega Man X, Mega Man X2,*
and *Mega Man X3* (1995), it didn't take long for a quadrun, in which
Super Mario Bros. 1, 2, 3, and *Super Mario Bros.: Lost Levels* (1986) were
played concurrently using one controller, to emerge in 2011 (see Figure 4.2).
Submitted to TASVideos after almost two years of production, agwawaf's
Mario multigame begins with an arcade-like explosion of parallel videos and polyphonic sound. After acclimating to the visual and sonic

chaos of watching four seemingly different videogames at once, these quadruns, hexruns, and nonruns reveal the repeating patterns of running to the right and jumping up and down. Although each videogame was originally created for an audience of anxious, twitching fingers in order to test coordination and reflexes, when played simultaneously the games morph into elaborate, interlocking puzzles in which any wrong move results in not one, but many game overs. Here, discrete gestures, whether manual or programmatic, must account for not only the current on-screen action, but the ramifications of each command within parallel worlds—play as a pun operating in multiple contexts at once.

While, from one perspective, multigame TASs are simply an example of virtuosic play, the practice of playing multiple games with a single string of inputs also functions as a critique of videogame seriality. Such playthroughs demonstrate the skill of the player or programmer while

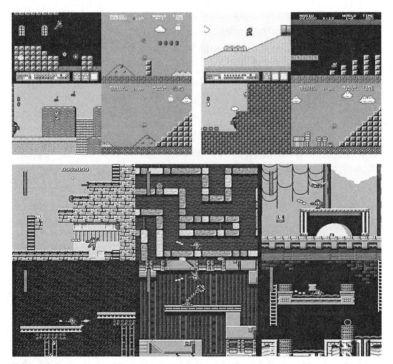

Figure 4.2. A quadrun of four *Super Mario Bros.* games by agwawaf (top) and a "hexrun" of six *Mega Man* games by Yashar Nasirian (bottom).

exposing the interchangeability between games. As the editors at TAS-Videos (2007) state, "Baxter and AngerFist prove that Capcom really has been making the same game over and over again by playing *Mega Man 3, 4, 5,* and *6* using the same input." The serialization of *Mega Man* is a product of both corporate franchising and recycled code. For example, the geometry and physics of *Mega Man*'s basic mechanics—run, jump, and shoot—have not changed in the ten iterations of the classic series built between 1987 and 2010.[17] The game engine shared by the Mega Man games released on the Nintendo Entertainment System as well as the embodied memory required to succeed in challenges tuned to the franchise's mechanics are dependent on modularity and repetition. And although Mario's mechanics have certainly morphed over the course of the series, these multigame TAS videos not only showcase machinic precision, but also reveal the serial patterns that migrate from game to game. By expressing the fundamental similarity between these videogames, the tool-assisted speedruns and multigame mashups demonstrate how there is more than a conceptual or aesthetic resemblance: there is also a structural correspondence that exists on the level of platform, engine, and code. Despite the similarities, only a limited number of games have been completed simultaneously. These multigame TAS might evolve, however, to include larger numbers of games and perhaps more disparate types of gameplay. Like the fabled "theory of everything" in popular physics, there could exist input sequences that successfully complete every videogame ever made (and ever will be made) simultaneously.[18]

Still operating within a category of metagames that distribute single input across multiple outputs, numerous mixups and mashups have been programmed that collage and conflate one or more previously discrete videogames. Although these mashups do not explicitly allow players to control many games at once as with multigame TASs or multiboxing MMOs,[19] the recombinations of familiar game mechanics inspire strategies that resemble the cognitive multitasking prompted by DeHackEd, Baxter, Angerfist, and agwawaf's tool-assisted speedruns. Rather than allowing players to control *Pac-Man* (1980) and *Donkey Kong* (1981) at the same time, these metagames make *Pac-Man* a playable character *within Donkey Kong.* Mashed-up, mixed-up, and memefied games participate in an aesthetic of sampling that Shaviro (2003, 64) suggests "is the best way, and perhaps the only way for art to come to terms with a world of brand names, corporate logos, and simulacra." In some instances, corporations have attempted to capitalize on sampling as a marketing gimmick by promoting crossovers between videogame franchises,[20] but within fan communities, amateur programmers produce far more complex forms of recombination that remix not only visual and auditory cues, but metagame mechanics themselves.

Not surprisingly, Mario is one of the most appropriated characters in player-designed mashups. Software such as *Grand Unified Game* (2002) by Andy Weir,[21] *ROM CHECK FAIL* (2008) by Jarrad "Farbs" Woods, *Tuper Tario Tros.* (2009) by French game development studio Swing Swing Submarine,[22] and *Mari0* (2012) by Maurice Guégan[23] place Mario within the context of other arcade classics. The premise of *ROM CHECK FAIL,* for example, is that the read-only memory of a dozen 8-bit videogames has been corrupted, causing a sequence of unpredictable mashups with the graphics, mechanics, and levels of games like *Space Invaders* (1978) and *Asteroids* (1979), *Defender* (1981) and *Spy Hunter* (1983), *Qix* (1981) and *Pang* (1989), as well as *The Legend of Zelda* (1986) and *Super Mario Bros.* (see Figure 4.3). Farbs's game challenges players to micromanage the properties of multiple franchises by preemptively positioning characters not only according to the current recombination present on the screen but also an imagined totality of all the other arcade games. As *Play This Thing!* editor Patrick Dugan (2011) notes, "You'll find yourself metagaming, you know that as the *Defender* jet, you can merc those rainbow cascade things pretty well, but in the process of getting over there, there is a good chance they'll turn into Goombas, and you'll get hit. Or maybe you'll hesitate, as Link, to walk up that hallway, because you could become the *Space Invaders* turret, unable to move vertically, and get caught by pursuing *Gauntlet* ghosts."

More recently, in his carefully constructed Flash game *Super Mario Bros. Crossover* (2010), Jay Pavlina satisfies the desire to navigate *Super Mario Bros.* with a wide array of 8-bit videogame protagonists complete with their native graphics, sound effects, and mechanics (see Figure 4.4). In Pavlina's game the selection of visiting characters includes Samus from *Metroid* (1986), Bill Rizer from *Contra* (1987), Ryu Hayabusa from *Ninja Gaiden* (1988), Sophia the 3rd from *Blaster Master* (1988), Simon Belmont from *Castlevania 2: Simon's Quest* (1990), Bass from *Mega Man 10* (2010), Mega Man from *Mega Man 4*, Link from *The Legend*

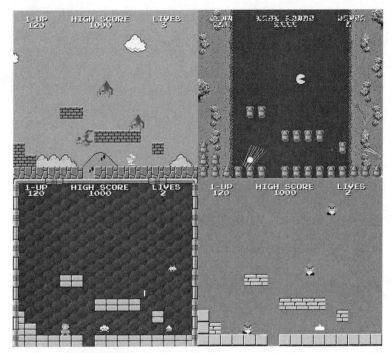

Figure 4.3. Jarrad "Farbs" Wood's *ROM CHECK FAIL* mashes up the graphics, mechanics, and music from dozens of 8-bit and 16-bit videogames into a glitchy metagame about games.

of Zelda, Luigi from *Super Mario Bros.: The Lost Levels* (1986), and, as a default, Mario himself. Selecting Mario simply produces a Flash approximation of the original *Super Mario Bros.* carefully re-crafted level for level in order to simulate the Mushroom Kingdom—a tabula rasa ready to compare different colors of paint. Considering these crossovers, blogger Henry Gilbert (2011) gushes, "Why stomp a Goomba when you can hit him with a Mega Buster or boomerang? Why break bricks with a jump when you can throw an axe and destroy them all? It all works so well even though it really shouldn't." Like Masahiro Sakurai's design philosophy for both the *Kirby* and *Super Smash Bros.* series, explored in chapter 1, *Super Mario Bros. Crossover* challenges the user to micromanage the mechanics of many diverse franchises, rewarding those players

Figure 4.4. The title screen and first levels of *Super Mario Bros.* feature characters like Mega Man, Link, and Simon Belmont in *Super Mario Bros. Crossover* by Jay Pavlina.

who match the strengths of other games' protagonists with specific level design in *Super Mario Bros.*

Whereas Sartre's seriality corresponds to mechanized forms of repetition and industrial production and Denson and Jahn-Sudmann's digital seriality articulates the transmedia adaptations, narrative franchises, and level design of videogames, Marc Steinberg proposes yet another concept: *new seriality.* Steinberg's (2003, 96) new seriality "corresponds to the information capitalist model," which "has no origin and proliferates through metamorphosis and translation." Steinberg adds that this form of new seriality leads to "a mode of consumption which is itself serial: a character is consumed in its many object forms, as pieces of a constantly expanding universe" (2003, 100). Mario's corporate branding follows this logic of repetition. In the single input, multiple output metagames discussed in this section, Nintendo's mustachioed mascot is an infinitely renewable resource whose potency lies not in scarcity, but in its multiplication and cross-pollination in numerous projects and media experiments. Integral to this process are not only Mario's sequels, articulated by agwawaf's multigames, but also the mashups exemplified by *Super Mario Bros. Crossover.* The mutations, modulations, and manipulations that occur by placing these series in relation to each other only further activates Mario's proliferation and brand power.

Multiple Input, Single Output

Rearranging blocks, tempting the player into traps, building impossible architectures, and distributing new games built on old platforms, ROM hacking is the process of changing or altering read-only memory data, a practice usually associated with videogames.[24] Working in conjunction with the debugger, trace loggers, memory watchers, hexadecimal editors, and various viewers now packaged with emulators like FCEUX, this community metagame can take the form of researching how games work, building ROM and RAM maps, hacking hex data, or even writing new assembly routines into old videogames—a difficult process that must account for the material platforms and programming idioms of past forms of play. As the central community hub at ROMhacking.net (2005) puts it,

> Comprising both the analysis and manipulation of data, hacking can appeal to the spirit of exploration, creative problem solving, engineering, and creativity. Thanks to the subject's breadth and its propagation through the Internet, ROM hacking has become an art form of sorts.

Like the tool-assisted speedrunning discussed in the last section, ROM hacking is made possible by the extended functionality of videogame emulators and, as a practice, enables new forms of play operating in the idiom of game design and leveraging the data from games like *Super Mario Bros.*

In his press kit for *ROM CHECK FAIL,* Farbs (2008) notes that the seven avatars, seven enemies, seven chipsets, thirty-four audio tracks, thirty-one end screens are an "authentic re-implementation" of arcade and home console classics. What kind of reverse engineering and reconstruction is necessary to simulate *Super Mario Bros.*, a game so intensely wed to the affordances and constraints of its technical platform? It's immediately clear from the open source Python code Farbs released as *ROM CHECK YOURSELF* (2011)[25] that *ROM CHECK FAIL* simulates the graphics and mechanics of *Super Mario Bros.* but aside from these resemblances is in no way the same as Nintendo's game. On the other hand, ROM hacks like ATA's *Mario vs. Airman* (2008) attempt to more directly combine *Super Mario Bros.* code and assets with other well-known NES-era titles. Based on (and including a chiptunes remake) of a Japanese dōjin video called *Air Man ga Taosenai* or *Can't Beat Air Man* (2007),[26] in *Mario vs. Airman* the player guides Mario or Luigi, complete with the familiar control scheme and jump physics of *Super Mario Bros.*, to navigate Air Man's famous level from *Mega Man 2*. After hosting a download of the game on her blog, anna anthropy (2008) argues, "Mashups like this illuminate design trends between games. Mario and megaman [*sic*] share 'jump' as a primary verb, which is why it's possible to complete this hack at all." Another example is Bennett Foddy and AP Thompson's *Multibowl* (2016), a gamified combination of both the MAME and MESS emulators that boot up save states and subsequently track scores over 230 arcade and console games. The result: a kaleidoscopic sampling of competitive, two-player action from the expanded history of videogames. Through careful curation and custom emulation, *Multibowl* imagines every videogame as a minigame within its *WarioWare*-like metaverse.

Mashups like *Mario vs. Airman* and *Multibowl* are not the only metagames made possible by ROM hacking. From Mario's many worlds to Mario artificial intelligences to Mario crowd simulations, the design philosophies that evolve alongside the increased functionalities of emulators like FCEUX lead to game designs that assume players will use slow motion and save states to complete even the most complex challenges by grinding each serial instant over and over. Discussed in chapter 1, the result of this ROM hacking metagame is the emergence of a whole genre of intensely difficult games that Douglas Wilson and Miguel Sicart (2010, 40) call "abusive games." From tool-assisted input patterns designed to play multiple games simultaneously to mechanics mashups programmed to mix and match multiple titles, tenacious players have found ways to explore the seriality of both videogame sequels and videogame platforms through multigame metagaming of quadruns and mashups. But considering ROM hacks are designed to be played over and over with tools, how do multiple inputs produce a single output?

In a *Popular Science* article titled "The Super Mario Multiverse," Abby Seiff (2011) gives a lesson in basic quantum theory using a video created with Andi McClure's[27] *Many Worlds Emulator* in which "134 overlaid playthroughs represent the manifold possibilities Mario encounters as he progresses through his world." The *Many Worlds Emulator* was published in response to video documentation of players attempting to complete the unreasonably difficult *Kaizo Mario World*, which roughly translates to *Hack Mario World*. According to McClure (2008), "*Kaizo Mario World* is one of a series of ROM hacks people created in special level editors that let you take *Super Mario World* and rearrange all the blocks; the point of *Kaizo* appears to have been *to create the most evil Super Mario World hack ever*" (emphasis original). Given the absurd difficulty of this particular ROM hack, affectionately referred to as "Asshole Mario," most playthroughs of *Kaizo Mario World* rely on an emulator's ability to save and load game states in order to redo a single section until it is properly executed.[28] In order to complete the game each second must be replayed over and over "Steve Reich style" (McClure 2008).

To make the *Many Worlds Emulator,* McClure adapted the SNES9X emulator to composite the replays rather than erase them when the player rewinds. As opposed to a flawless playthrough with all of the failed attempts scrubbed out, her emulator incorporates these blunders into a final video render (see Figure 4.5). As McClure writes, "what makes *Kaizo* great is watching someone fail over and over and over again until they finally get it right." Since the release of *Super Mario Maker* (2015) for Wii U, a game through which Nintendo attempts to enclose the ROM hacking practices that birthed *Kaizo Mario,* these near impossible level designs that test player's patience and skill as well as their physical and mental health have transformed from a niche practice to a thriving scene. Clearly, there is a masochistic audience for these sadistic level designs as perverse hacks become a spectator sport in which hundreds of Marios fall in pits, run into spikes, and get stomped by Goombas.

Another manifestation of quantum Mario appears in Sergey Karakovskiy and Julian Togelius' Mario AI competitions, hosted annually at various computer science conferences including EvoStar, World Congress on Computational Intelligence (WCCI), and the Institute of Electrical and Electronics Engineers Conference on Computational Intelligence

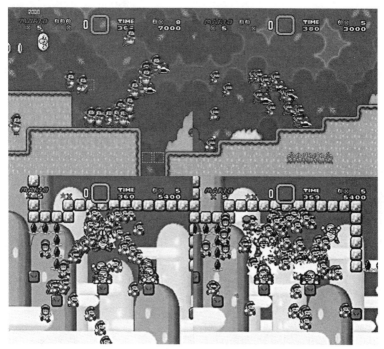

Figure 4.5. Andi McClure's *Many Worlds Emulator* visualizes multiple playthroughs of *Super Mario World* (top) and the *Kaizo Mario World* ROM hack (bottom).

in Games (IEEE-CIG). Using Notch's *Infinite Mario Bros.* (2006), a Java application that procedurally generates random levels based on the gameplay mechanics of *Super Mario Bros. 3* with the sprite-based graphics of *Super Mario World*, Karakovskiy and Togelius invited ROM hackers and AI researchers alike to compete by programming Mario to traverse Persson's infinite terrain.[29] In 2009, Robin Baumgarten[30] achieved minor celebrity with his elegant solution based on the A* Algorithm, a pathfinding heuristic using the best-first search.[31] Alongside a zipping, seemingly infallible Mario, Baumgarten's algorithm renders webs of red pixel vectors—tendrilized feelers shooting out in front of the plumber, cataloging every possible path from second to second (see Figure 4.6).

Finally, the massive artificial intelligence or mass AI is a common player-produced rendering technique that collects the individual performances of human players or automated bots and overlays or composites them into one game environment. Rather than suggest the invariant

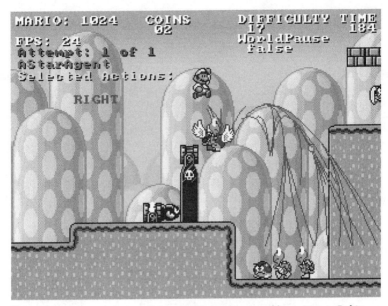

Figure 4.6. Red vectors are traced from Mario to every possible position in Robin Baumgarten's winning entry from the Mario AI Competition in 2009.

singularity of digital data, videos produced with games like *Team Fortress 2* (2007) and *Trackmania* (2003) use mass AI to create crowds of thousands of bots executing a multitude of actions in-game to reveal the geometric limits of level design through the physics of automated avatars. Like Maurice Guégan's visualizations of a thousand Marios cascading through a custom *Mari0* level at Gamescon in 2015, these crowd simulations range from the surreal layering of hundreds of moving images, to domino-like chain events, to granular fluid dynamics (see Figure 4.7). By collaging thousands of mechanically mediated playthroughs, rendering experiments like mass AI or crowd simulations implicitly invoke the serial conditions under which all games are played. The once-anomistic, individualized activities are collectively visualized.

Instead of executing the game in a discrete, sequential order, these three examples convert the player's labor (be they human or nonhuman) into a visual cacophony as hundreds of Marios simultaneously follow all possible paths as they traverse a level. McClure sees this "Mario cloud" as an emblem for the multiplicity of potential action suggested by the many-worlds interpretation of quantum mechanics. In the *Many Worlds*

Figure 4.7. Mass AI resembles fluid dynamics in Blackshark and Amraphent's "The 1K Project II," made in *Trackmania* (top) and reveals geometric patterns in the USK Clan's "USK Mass Bots," made with *Team Fortress 2* (middle) whereas a thousand human players pilot Mario through Maurice Guégan's custom *Mari0* level (bottom).

Emulator, the struggles of one hundred playthroughs are collaged within the same frame. These renderings produce a cubist-like overlaying of temporalities as the real and the possible converge and invite the player to imagine how their own actions fit into a pattern of wave–particle duality—their individual choices represented as both unique events and part of a larger system of relations. Whereas Sartrean seriality describes the relationship of individuals to groups, this pop-physics example of the many-worlds interpretation frames a self in relationship not to other selves, but to a cloud of all possible, parallel versions of selves.

The seriality of a player's performance, both imaginary and actual, has also been incorporated into new forms of gameplay that posit button presses as probabilities within a much larger set of aggregate actions. For example, an emerging genre of self-cooperative gameplay involves recording a player's actions for a limited time and then simulates a multiplayer environment by replaying the combined actions of a limited number of previous playthroughs. These multiple recordings—or past lives—do not function simply as ghosts visualizing past plays but perform realtime actions necessary for further exploration of the game (e.g., holding a door open for future navigation). Self-cooperative gameplay was popularized by Yoshio Ishii's *Cursor*10* from Nekogames and has proliferated in other Flash applications like *A Good Hunch* (2007–8), *Timebot* (2007), and *Chronotron* (2008), as well as in games for more advanced platforms including *Braid* (2008), *Onore no Shinzuru Michi wo Yuke* (2009), *Time Donkey* (2009), *Ratchet and Clank: A Crack in Time* (2009), *The Misadventures of P. B. Winterbottom* (2010), *Super Time Force* (2014), and *Echoshift* (2009)—a sequel to the *Echo* series discussed in chapter 2. Alternatively, this mechanic is sometimes used self-competitively rather than self-cooperatively, as seen in *The Road Less Taken* (2007) and *DefeatMe* (2009).[32] While many videogames require multiple playthroughs either as punishment for mistakes or to elongate playtime, in self-cooperative games both graphic and ludic layering rely on cumulative results that arise from the interactions between prerecorded playthroughs as space and time are layered with multiple inputs but only a single output. While playing within a crowd of past actions and producing new input with future outcomes in mind, players must navigate the strange effects of their own stacked and serialized aggregations.

Incorporating Metagames

Since at least the release of the Nintendo Entertainment System in 1985, Nintendo has been notably cautious when it comes to protecting their proprietary technologies, intellectual properties, and global brand. Starting with the star-shaped security screws holding together cartridges, the NES10 lockout chips that attempt to verify only licensed software, and even the gold Official Seal of Quality marking the company's curated games, Nintendo hoped to carefully control their corporate console and avoid the fate that befell Atari's considerably more open platform during the North American videogame crash of 1983 (signified by the *E.T. the Extra-Terrestrial* [1982] cartridges dumped in Alamogordo, New Mexico, mentioned in chapter 2). These early forms of digital rights management both camouflage the serial structures of the standard metagame and inspire the multigamic, mashed-up, many-worlded, and mass metagames discussed throughout this chapter (as well as a few ingenious piracy techniques).[33] However, when indie games, digital storefronts, persistent user names, and online chats transform videogames from platforms for private play to social networks in the twenty-first century, apparently Nintendo's closed systems leave something to be desired.

In an effort to expand their corporate control beyond individual instances of domestic play, Nintendo has begun to recapture and capitalize on those games occurring in, on, around, and through Super Mario. For the first time, at the Electronic Entertainment Expo (E3) in 2014, Nintendo invited players to compete with one another on stage at the Super Smash Brothers Wii U Invitational Tournament. Whereas Sakurai added luck-based mechanics to *Super Smash Bros. Brawl* (2008) in order to explicitly stymie the competitive metagame, *Super Smash Bros. Wii U* (2014) seemed open to the possibility of competitive play that culminated in the grand finals between Gonzalo "ZeRo" Barrios and Juan "Hungrybox" Debiedma (the latter of whom, coincidentally, was piloting Sakurai's favorite pink puffball, Kirby). Then, at E3 in 2015, Nintendo held *Ultimate NES Remix* (2014) competitions in eight locations across the United States before flying the eight winners alongside eight invited players to the L.A. Convention Center to compete in the Nintendo World Championships. After playing through a number of minigames reminiscent of the original Nintendo World Championships in 1990, the grand finals featured none other than Narcissa Wright facing off against John Goldberg (AKA John Numbers) in Nintendo's new *Super Mario Maker* (2015)—a *Mario Paint*–like program for designing, testing, sharing, and playing custom levels created from the assets and mechanics featured across Nintendo's entire Mario franchise.[34] Beyond their late entry into hosting competitive tournaments Nintendo worked to absorb and appropriate many forms of metagaming back into the Mario series itself culminating in videogames like *Super Mario Maker*.

From smashing and speedrunning to multigames, mash-ups, many-worlds, and mass AI, in the 2010s Nintendo is starting to expropriate the Mario metagames played with emulators since the early 2000s (see Figure 4.8). For example, redeploying the cherries that first appeared as bonus items in *Super Mario Bros. 2*, the "Double Cherry" power-up first featured in *Super Mario 3D World* (2013) and then again in its spinoff,

Captain Toad Treasure Tracker (2014), multiplies the number of player-controlled characters jogging around seafoam cliffs, pink hills, and bolted boxes of Double Cherry Pass. Directed by a single set of controller input, groups of two, three, four, or five Marios, Luigis, Princesses, and Toads articulate the parallel processes of videogames and operate according to the same logic as the quadruns, hexruns, and nonruns considered at the beginning of this chapter. Apparently, whether it's Baxter, DeHackEd, AngerFist, and agwawaf's multigame tool-assisted speedrun or the Double Cherry, playing many games with one controller is no longer outside Nintendo's gloved grip.

Beyond the way the *Super Smash Bros.* series remixes Nintendo's popular franchises and corporate branding, games like *NES Remix* (2013) and *NES Remix 2* (2014) explicitly recombine discrete pieces of old software into new forms of gameplay. Unlike Farbs's *ROM CHECK FAIL* and Jay Pavlina's *Super Mario Crossover* and following the strategies of ROM hacks like ATA's *Mario vs. Airman* and gamified frameworks like Bennett Foddy and AP Thompson's *Multibowl, NES Remix* begins with emulation. Building metagames around the instruction sets and algorithmic processes of original Nintendo ROMs, *NES Remix* cleverly isolates and re-presents critical moments of games such as *Super Mario Bros., The Legend of Zelda, Donkey Kong, Metroid,* and *Kirby* (among twenty-three others). These short tutorials evolve from simply loading a game state and tracking player progress to more complex ROM hacked recombinations: Mario as a single-switch infinite runner where only the A button matters, Samus from *Metroid* breaking blocks in the sewers of the Mushroom Kingdom, a swordless Link climbing ladders to avoid barrels in *Donkey Kong,* and ghastly Boos from *Mario* chasing down Kirby in the Whispy Woods. As Nathan Altice (2014, 330) argues in the conclusion of *I AM ERROR,* "Nintendo is not simply re-presenting their own legacy, but directly competing with the emulation ecosystem that has thrived for decades, generating their own Famicom hacks and remixes. Nintendo is redefining its platform in its own emulated image."

Beyond the duplicities of the Double Cherry and the mashups of *NES Remix,* some of Nintendo's software shows a different form of seriality: the replays and recordings left behind when we play videogames. Following instances of enemy AI that simply mirrors player movement such as the rat-like Goriya in *The Legend of Zelda: Link to the Past* (1991) or the Mario double in the Sunken Ship of *Super Mario RPG: Legend of the Seven Stars* (1996), in *Super Mario Galaxy 2* (2009) and *Super Mario 3D World,* Mario's in-game actions are sometimes replicated by "Cosmic Clones" that proliferate endlessly and force the player to navigate the level while avoiding an array of temporally delayed doppelgängers trailing behind. Across the galaxies, hoards of maroon Marios propagate along paths originally pioneered by the player, becoming a record of past play as well as obstacle to overcome. Like Andi McClure's *Many Worlds Emulator* or the self-cooperative and self-competitive games explored earlier, the recording and playback in Nintendo's games historicize play itself as their games mark, if only fleetingly, traces of player movement.

Although the mirror movements of Nintendo's simple AIs are not as complex as Robin Baumgarten's all-knowing Mario, automation has become central to Nintendo's game design—especially in the case of modulating difficulty and teaching players through bots. Starting in both *New Super Mario Bros. Wii* (2009) and *Super Mario Galaxy 2* (2009), the company has included a "Super Guide" in the form of an automatic Luigi who can run through levels without player intervention. If the player fails enough times on any given level, an option appears to activate the Super Guide after which Luigi will expertly work his way through the bothersome level. Like a tool-assisted speedrun or Baumgarten's Mario AI, Luigi dances across the digital landscape, ducking and dodging enemies while both teaching the player new tricks and furthering his or her progress throughout the game. However, rather than generating every possible path, the Super Guide operates more like a demo in which Nintendo's employees have recorded specific instances of pedagogical play reminiscent of the looping attract screens of arcade games and the original *Super Mario Bros.*[35]

It is no coincidence that many of the metagames discussed in this chapter are conflated in Nintendo's *Super Mario Maker* (see Figure 4.9). From the rotating characters and tilesets of Mario mashups to playthroughs of multiple Mario games at once and from the community practices of ROM hacking to the time trials of realtime attacks, *Super Mario Maker* is the company's attempt to incorporate the metagame. The game allows players to build and share levels, but only to other players who have the game and only through Nintendo's network. Beyond the limitations of the interface, there is no way to alter the source code, archive level data, or burn the game onto original hardware. This incorporation is perhaps best indicated by the cease and desist letters designed

Figure 4.8. In Nintendo's *Super Mario 3D World* (top left), *NES Remix* (top right), *Super Mario Galaxy 2* (bottom left), and *New Super Mario Bros. Wii* (bottom right), previously ignored metagaming practices are incorporated into the Super Mario series.

to funnel those player practices produced on open platforms back into Nintendo's corporate ecosystem. Sent to YouTube channels from the Nintendo Anti-Piracy Team in the days and weeks preceding the release of *Super Mario Maker,* the company states in no uncertain terms "please note that this Code of Conduct prohibits you, among other things, from posting any content using unauthorized software or copies of games. This includes videos featuring tool-assisted speedruns, which require making a copy of a game's ROM file, and running the copied ROM

through an emulator" (Hernandez 2015). So *Super Mario Maker* both attempts to enclose metagaming while simultaneously disenfranchising metagamers.

The following chapter tracks this behavior in the context of the modding communities and pro gamers that made *Defense of the Ancients* (2003–) and Valve, a company that extends these forms of incorporation by building a business plan based on colonizing (rather than policing) the metagame. Whereas Nintendo has been reluctant to expand its platform into online marketplaces, downloadable content, cosmetic markets, competitive gaming, live streaming, and modding, Valve has embraced this as their core game design (and managerial) philosophy. And while the time

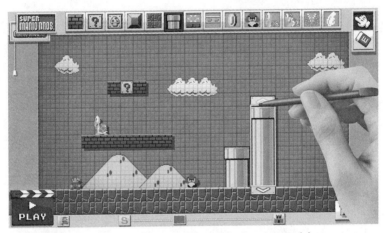

Figure 4.9. In some ways, *Super Mario Maker* encapsulates Nintendo's strategy to enclose the work of ROM hackers, speedrunners, and other metagamers by building corporate platforms for what was, historically, community labor.

represented by videogames as the ideological avatar of play is often coded as off the clock, outside of work, or a waste of time, suddenly all that time spent playing serial games like *Super Mario Bros.* does not seem nearly as ineffable. A hundred thousand billion fingers, and a hundred thousand billion years of working with our hands, have ultimately emerged as a valuable commodity as play becomes a form of production.

Hundred Thousand Billion Years

How much time do we play? How much play do we time? Serial games encourage the partitioning of smooth durations into individuated units of empty homogenous time—exchangeable, measurable time. Jane McGonigal's *Reality is Broken: Why Games Make Us Better and How They Can Change the World* (2011) begins with a manifesto-like celebration of the serial effects of networked culture. In a frequently cited passage of the book, McGonigal (2011, 52) claims that "if you add up all the hours that gamers across the globe have spent playing *World of Warcraft* since the massively multiplayer online (MMO) roleplaying game (RPG) first launched in 2004, you get a grand total of just over 50 billion collective hours—or 5.93 million years." Although these numbers may be awe inspiring—there are no doubt hundreds of thousands of millions of hours invested in gaming platforms like *World of Warcraft*—the rhetorical potency of McGonigal's figures relies on a misrepresentation of seriality. Why characterize years of collective action involving millions of players as a singular, linear duration instead of, for example, a rate like twenty hours a week per player? When compared to the finite life of the reader, McGonigal's 5.93 million years appear sublime and beyond measure, but relative to the serial processes of collective life, the statistic falls flat. Using the same logic McGonigal applies to *World of Warcraft*, one could say that the 7 billion people on Earth collectively live 19 million years every day (and that is certainly not counting for those automatic or automated forms of labor and leisure).

Further compounding this confusion, McGonigal proposes a homology between time spent playing *World of Warcraft* and the process of human evolution. "5.93 million years ago is almost exactly the moment in history that our earliest human ancestors first stood upright," she writes, and "by that measure, we've spent as much time playing *World of Warcraft* as we've spent evolving as a species" (2011, 52). In order to demonstrate the power of network phenomena and render these operations legible, McGonigal treats human evolution as an unbroken and linear flow of time and translates the synchronic actions of the multitude onto a diachronic timescale. But evolution is not a single-player game. If one were to make an equivalency comparing the total playing time in *World of Warcraft* to the total time humans have spent living on Earth, McGonigal's original 5.93-million-year timeline would have to be multiplied by the average size of the human population at each instant of that timeline, producing a number that far exceeds all but a mathematical understanding of scale.

There is another assumption implicit in McGonigal's suggestion that somehow "evolving" from level one to eighty-five is co-terminous with the progress from bipedalism to the present. Her analogy is underwritten by a fixed concept of "the human" and the assumption that agency is the dominant contributing factor in the evolution of a species. But there is no singular, unbroken lineage that can be traced back to the Paleolithic Period. Evolution is the product of a complex interweaving of genetic and environmental factors (including the playing of *World of Warcraft*) that contribute not to the flow of species, but to what Manuel DeLanda (1997, 259) might describe as a serial "flow of biomass through foodwebs as well as the flow of genes through generations" over a thousand years of nonlinear history. The desire for a monolithic and totalizing metaphor for network activity is constantly thwarted by the units within the network model itself—the combinations of mechanical, electrical, and computational processes that can never be fully reduced to the time-space of an individual human subject. This bitwise approach is echoed by Ian Bogost (2006, 8) when he writes in *Unit Operations*, "The Internet, the brain, human genetics, and social fads are examples of complex, unit-driven networks."

In "Cybernetics and Ghosts," Italo Calvino (1986, 8–9) notes the similarities among *Hundred Thousand Billion Poems,* the game of chess, and the "electronic brain": "Just as no chess player will ever live long enough to exhaust all the combinations of possible moves for the thirty-two pieces on the chessboard, so we know (given the fact that our minds are chessboards with hundreds of billions of pieces) that not even in a lifetime lasting as long as the universe would one ever manage to make all possible plays." Encountering every poetic, programmatic, or neural combination is impossible, and yet it is exactly those hidden patterns and unconscious repetitions that serial games explore. Thus, like readers, computer game enthusiasts engage in vast networks of patterns that make up the aggregate histories of virtual worlds. But rather than remaining subject to the mechanisms of control as defined by the rules of the game, the Mario modifications, alternative practices, and digital histories explored in this chapter successfully metagame the serial constructs players are working within and against to model the movements of a hundred thousand billion fingers.

Metagame 4

99 Exercises in Style

Based on the constrained writing of the Ouvroir de littérature potentielle, and specifically Raymond Queneau's *Exercises de style* (1947), as well as the serial experiments of Lars von Trier and Jørgen Leth's *Five Obstructions* (2003) and Matt Madden's *99 Ways to Tell a Story* (2005), *99 Exercises in Play* features World 1–1 from the original *Super Mario Bros.* (1985) as a constraint for producing ninety-nine different metagames. An "Oujeupo" project that engages the serial history of a single level, in *99 Exercises in Play*, Mario finds himself stretched, squashed, duplicated, displaced, slowed down, sped up, zoomed in, or zoomed out in order to reveal the kinds of metagames that constantly occurs outside any individual's experience of the Mushroom Kingdom (see Figure 4.10). To download *99 Exercises in Play*, go to http://manifold.umn.edu/99exercises.

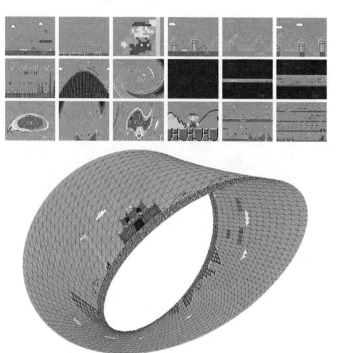

Figure 4.10. *99 Exercises in Play* is an original metagame by Patrick LeMieux and Stephanie Boluk featuring ninety-nine variations of World 1–1 of *Super Mario Bros.*

FIVE

The Turn of the Tide

International E-Sports and the Undercurrency in Dota 2

And tell me Mr. Waugh, what do both baseball and
business need? Someone to keep the books.
            —Robert Coover, *The Universal Baseball Association, Inc.,*
                                                J. Henry Waugh, Prop.

I realize I am not only watching the game differently but
am watching a different game. . . . I'm watching the whole
game, and responding the way an ordinary fan responds. . . .
They're watching fragments—not the game itself but
derivatives of the game—and responding, so far as I can
tell, not at all.
    —Michael Lewis, *Moneyball: The Art of Winning an Unfair Game*

Well before the TAT-8 fiber optic cable was dragged across the
bottom of the Atlantic Ocean in 1988, the deep sea had already been
bisected by American and British business. Even a hundred years before
the TAT-1 telephone line was engineered in 1956, the first transatlantic
telegraph cables were already descending to the depths of the ocean.[1] The
infrastructure and ideology supporting these kinds of bit torrents is not
new. Since the Age of Sail, the Earth's oceans have operated as a technology for trade. According to the logic of combat and capital in the six-
teenth century, current and currency have been wed to each other for
hundreds of years. Earth is not a desert planet, but a water world whose
surface is traced by trade winds and shipping lanes—ecological phenomena labeled according to their geopolitical role, rather than the
relation of atmosphere to lithosphere. Whereas the topographies of trade
and travel mapped the movements of Empire on a continental territory,
the smooth surface of the sea was also dissected and differentiated by
capital.

If exchange is contingent on comparison and comparison requires the individuation of otherwise undifferentiated matter—the *cut* that differentiates quantitative measure from qualitative movement—then cutting characterizes capital. Capitalism cuts. The cut of competition, which sociologist and game theorist Roger Caillois (2001, 12) calls *"agon,"* also makes games possible. Videogames are not simply equipment for sequencing, serializing, and scoring the performance of various actors (both human and nonhuman alike), but in the process of measuring analog play in terms of digital rules they also enact a necessary comparison or competition. Numbers level the playing field and, in the process, reduce play to what can be measured, what can be cut. The precise character of this cut is what is at stake in the difference between videogame and metagame. Beginning with the history of statistical play—from the first German wargames in the eighteenth century to the tabletop encounters of *Warhammer* (1983–) to the real-time strategy of *Warcraft* (1994–) to the international competitions surrounding *Dota 2* (2013–)—this chapter investigates games that operate according to the agonistic logic of what Steven Connor and McKenzie Wark call "cutting." These games also mirror the agony of *grammatization,* a term originally used to describe the transformation of undifferentiated sounds into discrete words and a term with which Bernard Stiegler characterizes the relation between digital technology and labor in *For a New Critique of Political Economy* (2010). Like Claude Shannon's definition of information as the probability of a given signal within a field of noise, for these theorists both games and money produce statistical information and behave probabilistically. Whereas Connor and Wark focus on their own brand of economic game theory, the management strategies of Gabe Newell, the co-founder and general manager of Valve, puts the homology between digital games and finance capital into play.

Since founding the game development studio, digital distribution retailer, and increasingly multifaceted tech company in the late 1990s, Newell's moneygames have harnessed vectors of information to derive value not from gameplay as such, but from the metagames that operate outside the computer screen. From simply purchasing and playing videogames to modding software, selling virtual commodities, spectating live events, and predicting future markets, for the past decade metagaming has become synonymous with an untapped ocean of informatic and affective labor. The precarious labor of players is not a form of currency, but an *undercurrency* driving a deluge of vectoralist management strategies. The undercurrency carries with it the sedimentary traces of all forms of play. As play accretes within this digital undertow, different forms of metagaming are made exchangeable and flattened into one monolithic unit of measure: productivity. This chapter charts the undercurrency through an in-depth analysis of one of the most famous play in the history of *Dota 2,* a sea change in which the statistical play of two tide hunters transformed the metagame.

The Turn of the Tide

In the last weekend of August, in 2012, the audience assembled at Benaroya Hall were not enjoying the Seattle Philharmonic perform the *Pines of Rome* (1924). They had not gathered to watch an Indigo Girls concert or listen to Ira Glass reinvent the radio. Drawn forward as if automated, spines pneumatically straightening and hands moving to meet faces and mouths, the spectators in Seattle were caught up in The Turn of the Tide. Assembled on the stage, like some kind of *ballet mécanique,* stood two enormous glass boxes. Onlookers gazed beyond the wood-trimmed proscenium and oversized vitrines to an industrial spectacle of another sort: professional players packed behind computers, fingers clicking mechanical keyboards and multibutton mouses, faces lit by rows of LCD screens, and heads entombed in noise-cancelling headphones. Hanging above the booths, massive movie screens projected aggregate electronic performances alongside live commentary and statistical analysis in three languages. Rather than rioting, like the audiences attending Futurist concerts nearly a hundred years ago,[2] twenty-first-century spectators cheered from stuffed chairs, waving iPads in lieu of pennants as silk banners streamed from box seats, billowing in the air conditioning at The International: Valve Corporation's 1.6-million-dollar *Dota 2* tournament (see Figure 5.1).[3]

As its name implies, The International featured sixteen five-player teams from around the world digitally duking it out within Valve's then-forthcoming remake of *Defense of the Ancients* or *DotA* (2003–), a classic *Warcraft III* (2002) mod independently developed by a community of player-programmers since 2003. Hailing from Sweden, Germany, Ukraine, Russia, China, Malaysia, Singapore, Australia, and the United States, at The International pro gamers not only competed for what was

Figure 5.1. A panoramic photograph of The International at Benaroya Hall documents the crowded hall, box seats, and two teams competing at the heart of the event.

the largest cash prize in the history of electronic sports, or "e-sports"—an astounding million dollars to the winning team[4]—but also hoped to earn a living by playing a game that had not even been officially released to the public. Almost a century ago, Bertolt Brecht (2002, 183) derisively joked, "There seems to be nothing to stop the theatre having its own form of 'sport.' If only someone could take those buildings designed for theatrical purposes . . . and treat them as more or less empty spaces for the successful pursuit of 'sport,' then they would be used in a way that might mean something to a contemporary public that earns real contemporary money and eats real contemporary beef." With *Dota 2* and The International, Valve is producing an electronic sport for a new kind of spectator and in the process has revealed a corporate metagame in which "real contemporary money" has found new ways to imbricate itself within the industry, software, culture, spectatorship, and play of videogames.

Out of the hundreds of hours of tournament proceedings, seventeen seconds stand out. During the winner's bracket semifinals, the Ukrainian team Natus Vincere (Na`Vi) and their star player Danil "Dendi" Ishutin competed against Invictus Gaming (iG), a Chinese team with an intimidating track record led by Wong Hock Chuan (see Figure 5.2).

Figure 5.2. From left to right, in 2012 Na`Vi included Sergey "ARS-ART" Revin, Danil "Dendi" Ishutin, captain Clement "Puppey" Ivanov, Alexander "XBOCT" Dashkevich, and Dmitry "LighTofHeaveN" Kupriyanov (top), while iG includes Luo "Ferrari 430" Feichi, Zeng "Faith" Hongda, Chen "Zhou" Yao, Jiang "YYF" Cen, and captain Wong Hock "ChuaN" Chuan (bottom).

Na`Vi were the clear fan favorites. The beloved Ukrainians were defending champions, Internet celebrities, and rags-to-riches "*Dota* millionaires" after winning the first international tournament held at GamesCom in Cologne the previous year.[5] Whereas fans consider Estonian captain Clement "Puppey" Ivanov a tactical genius and refer to power-player Alexander "XBOCT" Dashkevich as a suicidal killing machine, Dendi is hailed as "the face of *Dota*" and a digital trickster likened to the "Lvivian *batiar* . . . a class of urban mischief maker" native to his home-town in Ukraine (riptide and McEntegart, 2012). Given the influx of utterly dominant teams from China at the second International, the Ukrainian champions had been recast as underdogs and the "last for-eign hope" after all European and North American teams had been defeated.[6] In the prelims the five Chinese teams seemed unbeatable, and in the tournament brackets not much had changed.[7] After the first match with iG, a sixteen-minute-and-fifteen-second stomp and the shortest game at The International, Na`Vi's teetering trajectory through the ranks of Chinese teams seemed all but over.[8]

Interpreted in terms of Na`Vi's failure rather than iG's success, shout-casters and statisticians alike felt robbed by the anticlimactic first game. Throughout The International, and in *Dota 2* more generally, Western teams are often described in terms of risky, aggressive play styles that result in thrilling, high octane spectacles loaded with the exceptional achievements of individual athletes. On the contrary, the rhetoric at The International characterized Chinese and East Asian teams as passive, patient, and predictable; their players were portrayed as anonymous agents of some Red machine grinding away behind the "Great Firewall." Fans felt as though they "weren't watching Na`Vi play against iG; [but] were watching Dendi, Puppey, XBOCT, ARS-ART, and LighTofHeaveN versus *China*" (emphasis original), five superheroes fighting an undif-ferentiated enemy on the battlefield of *Dota 2* (riptide 2013).[9]

Racialized rhetoric is not uncommon in e-sports and, with the origi-nal *Defense of the Ancients'* intense popularity and relative insularity in China and other parts of East and Southeast Asia, terms like "farm-ing" and "ricing" have become common ways to describe long-term, economy-driven strategies in contrast to the micromanagement of team fighting (see Figure 5.3).[10] During iG's victory over Na`Vi in game one, commentator David "Luminous" Zhang joked, "The Chinese [have] about two thousand years of farming experience so they have to be

Figure 5.3. Around the time of The International, more than one racist meme emerged online depicting Chinese players (top) or Anti-Mage (bottom) (a powerful hero with a long experience curve) as rice farmers.

leading here" (Valve 2012b). As commentators attempted to generate compelling frame narratives on the fly, the often inscrutable and intensely complex teamwork taking place on the screen was reduced to common cultural stereotypes for the sake of spectacle. Lisa Naka-mura (2009, 151) has argued that "early journalistic and academic accounts of the Internet stressed its utopian, democratic potential for erasing (or at least hiding) race and creating a 'level playing field,'" but The International made it patently evident that there was nothing post-racial about Dota 2.

Popular narratives in which Western teams perform audience-friendly feats of daring and heroic individualism while Chinese teams opt for cal-culated collective wins at the expense of visual spectacle reveal how nationalism and race are still at play in digital games and how stereo-types function to reduce both the skill and, at the time, the winning strat-egies of East Asian players to racist tropes. In another essay on World of Warcraft (2004), Nakamura (2013, 189) discusses the ways in which certain play styles are portrayed online, arguing that "specific forms of gamic labor, such as goldfarming and selling, as well as specific styles of play, have become racialized as Chinese, producing new forms of networked racism that are particularly easy for players to disavow."[11] Dis-avowal is contingent on the cognitive dissonance between, on one hand, the leisure activity of playing (and watching) games and, on the other hand, the labor associated with making money from those same activi-ties. In the particular case of e-sports, it is with equal fanaticism that the right hand evangelizes the encroachment of global capital in the form of professionalization and monetization while the left casts out the value-seeking behaviors of so-called "farmers" that are coded (in both massively multiplayer online games and Dota 2 alike) as specifically Chinese. Alexander Galloway (2011, 120) flattens these differences by declaring that "we are the gold farmers" in a post-Fordist economy in which all forms of play and work, productive and nonproductive labor, are "impossible to differentiate." The perception of two distinct play styles emerging at the second International not only reveals how racial difference is produced and negotiated within online digital communi-ties (and the Orientalist image economies in which the Western com-mentators traffic), but also demonstrates the difference between the production of e-sports as a spectator sport and as a numbers-driven pursuit of wins in order to turn a profit (to the tune of 2.6 million dollars, no less). So despite the perceived tediousness of "Chinese *Dota*," iG's economic strategies, both inside and outside the game, seemed to be working.

When Na`Vi and iG logged in to the second game, so did over half a million people from around the world (Valve 2012g). More than two hundred thousand sleep-deprived Chinese fans pulled all-nighters on Sunday to watch the end of the tournament. The International was broadcasted with live commentary in English, Russian, and Chinese on at least two streaming video providers and, importantly, within the *Dota 2* client itself.[12] Spectators were encouraged to download *Dota 2* for free through Steam, Valve's online store and digital distribution service, in order to watch the game *in the game*.[13] Within the software client, viewing *Dota* and playing *Dota* occur through the same actions. Audiences were invited to watch The International in real-time through the same technical apparatus and graphic interface as those players competing live. Rather than relying on the skilled hand and eye of an "observer" (a category of digital cameraman and real-time editor made popular in televised e-sports such as *StarCraft* [1998][14]), telematic spectators at The International became their own digital director, choosing the perspective from which to view the game and even spying on the precise mouse movements and interface manipulation of individual players half a world away. Beyond manipulating the perspective oneself or following the gestures of a live observer or professional player, Valve also implemented an artificially intelligent camera that exploited the delay between action and broadcast to algorithmically select and prematurely pan to those locations with the highest density of incoming information. Within this holistic software client, viewers selected their unique vantage point among a vast, in-game audience while, at the click of a button, they could jump from spectating to playing into their own 5 vs. 5 pickup games. In *Dota 2*, watching sports and playing sports are no longer easily separated. Even analytics gathered within each individual viewer's Steam profile (e.g., total time played) do not distinguish between playing *Dota* and watching *Dota*.[15]

To this end, it is crucial that the company does not simply distribute free software, but requires users to first install Steam. Once the hurdles of installing the storefront (and hooking up a credit card) are overcome, the convenience of the digital marketplace, viral consumption within social networks, and impulse purchases (usually at extreme discount) far exceed the potential profit from the sale of a single title. For example, Valve's multiplayer shooter, *Team Fortress 2* (2007), made twelve times as much money as a free-to-play game with its booming cosmetics market[16] than it did while packaged in *The Orange Box* (2007) and sold on Steam (Miller 2012). Contrary to their label, *free-to-play* games are not the altruistic offerings of the game companies, but rather the giftlike distribution of software in order to combat piracy and create a temporary credit economy that, after a momentary delay or deferral, will generate greater profits through in-game advertising, cosmetic markets, and player-to-player evangelization. For *Dota 2* and e-sports in general, videogame software ceases to operate simply as a game and transforms into service platforms, social networks, and online marketplaces for another type of play: a massive, million-dollar moneygame, in which *free-to-play* is actually a code word for *free-to-pay.*

Beneath the surface of spectatorship software, amidst the currents of international currency, and caught up in the undertow of tacit racism, the tide was about to turn in game two of the winner's bracket semifinals at The International. Back at Benaroya Hall, the crowd's response moved from agitation to elation. After their flawless victory in the first game, the hunters became the hunted as Na'Vi sprang an elaborate trap preying on iG's predictable, economic strategies and that summer's metagame, the in-game decisions and team configurations that were fashionable in 2012. The Ukrainians were able to invert what seemed like a perfectly executed ambush into a "reverse all-kill" that left the Chinese team gasping for air. This seventeen-second sea change became the breaking point of both The International 2012 and the strategic metagame that had governed much of the gameplay that summer. The English transcript for what has come to be known simply as "The Play" has since become the stuff of legends:

> DAVID "LUMINOUS" ZHANG: [Invictus Gaming is] coming to the left, smoking up, and here we go!
> DAVID "LD" GORMAN: Oh man, big wrap-around gank is going to be the name of the game for iG. Who leads the way? I believe it should be Zhou. They're going to cut for the shorter path. They storm up the river. Patience from Zhou, waiting in the wake. Na'Vi is about to be caught. Oh, there's the sleep! The surge! He catches everyone! Oh, this could be a total disaster! Vacuum in! Ravage on everyone! The black hole as well!

LighTofHeaveN turns it around! Ravage as well, stolen by Dendi! Are you kidding me? They turn it around! Four heroes dead for iG!
DAVID "LUMINOUS" ZHANG: Five heroes dead! Chuan trying to survive. Chuan's going to go down. Puppey talked about the Naga counter. It's LighTofHeaveN, with his BKB! They turn it around. I don't even know how they can do it! Standing ovation from the crowd! The last tower will be going down and I think they sense blood in the water! (Valve 2012c)

As Chuan's onscreen avatar burned in effigy, Dendi leapt from his seat, spitting expletives in Russian as the packed hall began to rhythmically chant "Na`Vi! Na`Vi! Na`Vi! Na`Vi!" Awash in emotion, Russian shoutcaster Vitalii "V1lat" Volochai lost his voice completely, breaking into choked sobs as he watched his team turn it around. Whereas the English and Russian commentators worked themselves into a frenzy, the three Chinese commentators observed the reverse all-kill in a stunned radio silence, dead air hanging over their drowned team.

Despite the differing emotional responses based on obvious allegiances, the question still remains: *What exactly happened here?* These remediated, real-time narratives of the commentators do not adequately account for what is at play beneath the phenomenal surface of The International. There is an immense and incommensurable gulf between the human experience of The Turn of the Tide and the ultrafast electrical undercurrents governing the computational processes and network protocols that make up the mechanics of *Dota 2*. The spectacle of The Turn of the Tide dramatizes the phenomenological problem that Mark Hansen frames in *Feed-Forward: On the "Future" of 21st Century Media* (2015). First discussed in the introduction of this volume, in *Feed-Forward* Hansen (2015, 27) acknowledges the shifting status of human experience in an age of vast, ubiquitous, ultrafast, atmospheric media, and determines that the central question of twenty-first-century media is "How can consciousness continue to matter in a world where events no longer need it to occur, and, indeed, where they occur long before they manifest as contents of consciousness?" Videogames are one such media ecology in which players sink, swim, and surf the statistical undercurrents that exist beyond not only the horizon of consciousness but also the horizon of embodied sensation and perception. Rather than manipulating these currents directly, pro gamers and publishers alike rely on inductive techniques not to control, but to predict the atmospheric operations that exist along the vanishing point of human experience.

Beyond the mechanics of the game itself, Valve's desire to redevelop and redistribute a decade-old modification of another company's game is due to a different kind of undercurrent: that of an untapped attention economy in China. The original *Defense of the Ancients* has been popular in East Asia for a decade and, in 2010, boasted around 10 million suspected Chinese players.[17] By releasing a regularly updated, standalone version of the game for free (not to mention offering unparalleled access into a carefully cultivated competitive scene) on the condition that customers first download Steam, Valve hopes to exploit a previously inaccessible consumer (and prosumer) base—a leviathan of potential profit in China.[18] Selling the Steam service rather than a single piece of software is one endgame of *Dota 2.* Through Steam, Valve converts metagames into moneygames by investing in the productivity of their player base. From community-designed cosmetics to the spectacle produced by live spectators to player-programmed mods, Valve seeks out historically undervalued metagames and capitalizes on the undercurrent of player production, the undercurrency at work in The Turn of the Tide.

From Wargames to *Warhammer* to *Warcraft*

Over two hundred years ago, in the late eighteenth century, ripples of The Turn of the Tide were beginning to gather in the most unlikely places: in the classrooms and parlors of Johann Christian Ludwig Hellwig, the German professor of mathematics and natural science credited for inventing the wargame, or *kriegsspiel.* In his marvelous seven-hundred-page tome, *Playing at the World: A History of Simulating Wars, People and Fantastic Adventures from Chess to Role-Playing Games* (2012), Jon Peterson documents the first wargamers and their attempts to build miniature models of combat for recreation and research. Starting in 1780, Hellwig expanded and instrumentalized the rules of chess in an attempt to more faithfully represent the terrain and tactics of large-scale military combat for pedagogical purposes. Divorced from the consequences of battle and based on a familiar game, the first *kriegsspiel* was designed with the dual function of entertaining and educating Hellwig's students, "the pages of Braunschweig . . . bound for military service"

(Peterson 2012, 213). Although in principle his skeuomorphic design was accessible to anyone familiar with the rules of chess, Hellwig's wargame expanded the chessboard from a manageable yet complex 8 by 8 grid to an enormous 49 by 33 and added thousands of movable, multicolor cells to designate different types of terrain. Under careful instruction, players began each game with over a hundred pieces adapted from pawns, knights, bishops, rooks, and queens to represent contemporary infantry, cavalry, and artillery with which they captured fortresses instead of slowly moving kings (see Figure 5.4).[19] Encouraged by the game's modest success among military enthusiasts, Hellwig would continue to expand and modify his *kriegspiel* for the next twenty years, adding more pieces but retaining the basic mechanics of chess. Whether or not the wars of the eighteenth century could be reduced to a series of discrete commands corresponding to clearly demarcated rules of engagement (or were simply romanticized as such within the historical imaginary of Enlightenment Europe), Hellwig's war was born on the chessboard and

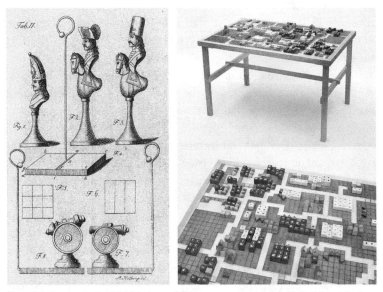

Figure 5.4. As seen in Rolf F. Nohr's careful reconstruction (right), Hellwig's original *kriegspiel* attempted to convert both the board and pieces of chess into a game of military strategy while retaining their original logic (left). Photographs by Ralf Wegemann, 2010, reproduced with permission from Rolf F. Nohr.

embraced the turn-based strategy and abstract topography of that grid-locked game.

Despite Hellwig's attempts to transform chess into a historically accurate model of combat, the earliest wargames delighted in the visualization of the battlefield as an idealized, Cartesian space and reduced the complex movements of troops to the orders of their commanding officers. "The invention of wargames," Peterson (2012, 218) explains, "depended on recent improvements to maps, which were, a century before Hellwig, only loosely anchored to the grid of longitude and latitude." With their predictive powers, eighteenth-century mapping technologies became an "intense interest to the various military powers of Europe" (Peterson 2012, 218). In *The Right to Look* Nicholas Mirzoeff (2011, 475) also acknowledges that "visualizing was . . . the hallmark of the modern general from the late eighteenth century onward, as the battlefield became too extensive and complex for any one person to physically see." As such, visualization became a technology for "classifying, separating, and aesthetizing" warfare, business, and, one might add, games (Mirzoeff 2011, 3). The term *visuality* itself, Mirzoeff (2011, 474) notes, was first coined in 1840 by Scottish historian Thomas Carlyle and was used not to refer to visual perception, but to an imaginative strategy of "making the processes of history perceptible to visual authority." From the origin of the term, visualization has been an act of harnessing "information, images, and ideas" to assert the power by making legible acts that exist beyond the visible that were previously "too substantial for any one person to see" (Mirzoeff 2011, 474).

Along with the growth of mapping technologies as well as the mathematization and abstraction of vision at the turn of the nineteenth century, new disciplines like statistics and probability became of interest to governmental, economic, and military powers. Although ancient gamblers rolled astragalus bones for play, profit, and prophecy, Ian Hacking (2006, 11) designates the period around 1660 as the moment when contemporary Western concepts of probability emerged throughout Europe. As a result of these scientific developments, "society became statistical" in the nineteenth century and "a new type of law came into being, analogous to the laws of nature, but pertaining to people. These new laws were expressed in terms of probability" (Hacking 1990, 1). Whereas the desire for a more mimetic wargaming simulation established many of the genre's conventions, it was the design innovations of the Reiswitz family, specifically Georg Leopold von Reiswitz and his son Georg Heinrich Rudolf von Reiswitz, in the 1820s that, according to Jon Peterson (2012, 205), "freed [wargaming] from the abstractions of boards and figurines, as well as primitive conflict resolution mechanisms. . . . These gave way to mathematical principles of probability that decides game events." The development of wargaming was predicated on the reconfigured relationship to both image and number that was emerging out of contemporary scientific, economic, and military culture.

Whereas Hellwig's *kriegspiel* was designed such that "nothing depend[ed] on chance," the Reiswitzes' emendations introduced dice and luck-based mechanics as a way of reflecting the indeterminacy of the battlefield (Peterson 2012, 231). And although the Reiswitzes shared Hellwig's goal of maximizing the verisimilitude of military scenarios, Peterson (2012, 220) speculates that "with a consistent scale, a game ceases to be an abstraction like the game of chess, and begins to evolve towards something entirely novel: a simulation." The ability to simulate historical events occurred through the application of probabilistic models based on empirical data gathered from studies such as Gerhard von Scharnhorst's "On the Effects of Firearms" (1813). Von Scharnhorst's work collated the data produced by firing weapons multiple times packed with differing amounts of gunpowder and ammunition in order to determine the odds of hitting a target. Although the results derived from statistical studies benefited military leaders, it was "less the conclusions than the data itself that would inspire the Reiswitz family" (Peterson 2012, 234). The Reiswitzes imported statistical models and interfaces into their wargames. Peterson (2012, 237) emphasizes that these innovations in simulation and wargaming are not to be underestimated, as the act of "combining empirical probability with implements of chance has no obvious precedent in intellectual history, and represents a paradigm shift that underlies a great deal of the science of simulation that followed in the twentieth century."

What ties these historical developments in statistics, cartography, and gaming together is the reliance on numerical abstraction—the conversion and compartmentalization of otherwise undifferentiated material phenomenon into discrete quantities to be compared, exchanged, and procedurally operated upon. Following Steven Connor's (2011, 151) *A Philosophy of Sport* (last mentioned in chapter 3), all games involve numbers in the form of scoring, and "scoring involves a conflict and convergence between two entirely incommensurable orders, the qualitative syntax of bodily motions and actions (*kinesis*), and the qualitative calculus of number (*ratio*)." It is no coincidence, therefore, that statistical forms of organizing space, time, and bodies pioneered in the eighteenth century translate effectively into gamelike simulations. From gridded topographies and mathematical probabilities, the history of wargaming negotiates the ontological tension between measurement and measured. In the twentieth century, tabletop games would further dissociate themselves from military simulation, displacing their historical diegesis with a newly popularized form of literary abstraction: the high fantasy of *Dungeons & Dragons* (1974).

Beyond their function as a leisure activity for aristocrats and training exercises for military students, wargames found a new audience and narrative storyworld in the twentieth century. Peterson (2012, 109) considers that "the study of wargaming in the late 1960s is the study of a conservative youth movement, a bastion of early post-war values preserved in middle-class suburban America." As disillusionment with Vietnam steadily increased (particularly within a draftable player base) along with the growth of countercultural movements in America, wargaming received a makeover with the adoption of J. R. R. Tolkien–inspired fantasy settings.[20] Rather than reenacting the theater of World War I or II, orcs and elves replaced American GIs in the games played on tabletops around the world. An early pioneer of fantasy roleplaying, Gary Gygax co-developed *Dungeons & Dragons (D&D)* with Dave Arneson in 1974. A tabletop game that retained many of the mechanics of the wargame, *D&D* replaced the historical military context with a fantasy world more palatable to players seeking not to embrace but to escape the realities of contemporary warfare.

D&D is often cited as the first roleplaying game and added elements of storytelling and improvisational theater to the tabletop formula dating back to the eighteenth century. Matthew Kirschenbaum (2011) notes that in the nineteenth century wargames split into "rigid" and "free" *kriegsspiel* with the "elaborate rules and calculations of the von Reiswitz game" replaced by new mechanics: a human "umpire" (anticipating *D&D*'s Dungeon Master) who "made decisions about combat, intelligence, and other aspects of the battlefield." In the twentieth century, not all wargames would become loregames, and, in addition to popular roleplaying games, there were plenty of fantasy-themed *roll*playing games developed in the 1970s and 80s. One such example that would be of particular historical significance to the development of *Dota 2* was *Warhammer: The Game of Fantasy Battles.* First published in 1983 by Bryan Ansell, Richard Halliwell, Graham Eckel, and Rick Priestley, *Warhammer* adapted the miniature tabletop combat of wargaming to the fantasy genre. Small, painstakingly detailed lead statuettes of wizards and warriors replaced traditional infantry and artillery. Although the roleplaying aspect was limited, *Warhammer* capitalized on a unique visual style that inspired blockbuster videogames like Blizzard Entertainment's *Warcraft: Orcs & Humans* (1994), one of the most popular real-time strategy (RTS) computer games in the 1990s.

The RTS genre of videogames adapts elements of the classic wargame to a computational environment. Miniature figures are still positioned around a modular battlefield with the intention of simulating large-scale combat, but many of the gameplay elements are automated and, as such, are far more granular than most tabletop games in terms of space and speed. Instead of placing hand-painted figurines on massive, foam-core topologies, RTS games automate dice rolls, unit positions, and even the passage of time. Henry Lowood (2009, 410) stresses that "in contrast to the turn-based game . . . the states of the [RTS] game occur at specific times in a continuous stream—time flows in an uninterrupted (generally) and synchronous way for both players." Borrowing many now-common features from *Dune II* (1992)—one of the earliest examples of modern RTS, often cited as the progenitor of the genre[21]—Blizzard's first *Warcraft* title further calcified gameplay around the production and manipulation of military units without the down time or alternating turns in which players could patiently consider each command (see Figure 5.5).

In RTS games, combat takes the form of mouse clicks and relies on manual dexterity to direct troops, expand territory, defeat enemies, and complete missions from an isometric, bird's- or god's-eye perspective. In a retrospective article, Patrick Wyatt (2012a), the producer and lead programmer for *Warcraft: Orcs & Humans,* recalls that the inspiration for the graphic user interface and game controls were based on his experiences with "low-end 'Computer Assisted Design' (CAD) programs like MacDraw and MacDraft . . . so it seemed natural to use the 'click &

Figure 5.5. Blizzard's original *Warcraft* (bottom) borrowed many elements from *Dune II* (top), including its graphic user interface, point-and-click controls, and real-time combat.

drag' rectangle-selection metaphor to round up a group of units to command." Starting slowly with a focus on basic subsistence and resource management, in *Warcraft*, players manipulate common metaphors of desktop computing as the main interface for scrolling over a large, multiscreen map while directing peasants to mine mountains and mill trees in order to build a digital fief. The game's simplified macroeconomics are tailored to support the steady production of military units which, in turn, must be strategically micromanaged against enemy elves or orcs controlled by either human or AI opponents.

The built structures in the *Warcraft* series range from the familiar to the fantastic with farmhouses, barracks, and blacksmiths sharing the same geographic space with goblin apothecaries, gryphon aviaries, and gnomish ateliers. In his postmortem account, Wyatt (2012a) admitted that "*Warhammer* was a huge inspiration for the art-style of *Warcraft,* but a combination of factors, including a lack of traction on business terms and a fervent desire on the part of virtually everyone else on the development team (myself included) to control our own universe nixed any potential for a [licensing] deal." Even Blizzard's 1998 follow-up to the *Warcraft* series, *StarCraft,* closely mirrored the narrative themes and visual styles of *Warhammer 40,000* (1987), the dystopian science fiction game in which miniature models of space marines, noble aliens, and big bugs engage in tabletop combat.[22] From wargaming to *Warhammer* to *Warcraft,* the homology between the abstract rules of chess and historical combat in the first *kriegspiel* evolved through the incorporation of statistics and the application of fantasy in a way that would eventually lead to the procedural operations and RTS of a new genre of digital games like *Defense of the Ancients* and, eventually, to The Turn of the Tide.

Whereas military strategy and stochastic combat are the ostensible thematics of wargaming (anticipating the emphasis on competitive violence that has come to define both board games and computer games in the following centuries) the abstractions on which these games are based inaugurate what both Steven Connor and McKenzie Wark see as a more primary form of violence or "cut." As Wark (2007, 023) explains in *Gamer Theory,* "the real violence of gamespace is its dicing of everything analog into the digital, cutting continuums into bits. That games present the digital in its most pure form are reason enough to embrace them, for here *violence is at its most extreme—and its most harmless*" (emphasis added).[23] Even the production of oppositional categories like "digital" and "analog" is a binary logic that enacts a discursive, digital violence. Like Wark, in *A Philosophy of Sport* Connor (2011, 154, 151) argues that "the most general and abstract kind of *agon* [competition], which characterizes all sports, is that between number and motion, score and play" noting "['score'] has as its primary signification, from Old Teutonic *sker-*, the act of cutting . . . [and] the etymology of the word 'decision', from Latin *caedere*, to cut." It is not the diegetic or representational violence of mortal combat, grand theft auto, or modern warfare that produces the agony of videogames, but the transformation of continuous play—of mind, motion, materiality, and matter—into "cut" abstractions.

Confronted with the formal and mathematical mechanisms driving these virtual battlefields, human play tarries with the number, the statistic, and the score that Connor calls *ratio*. *Ratio* renders otherwise irreducible material components, spatial gestures, or temporal events abstract and exchangeable. The urge to compare scores, to reduce unique moments of play and make them fungible with one another, is also the motor driving what Roger Caillois (2001, 12) calls *agon*, or competition. *Agon* lies at the heart of the most ancient games and, not coincidentally, the heart of capital. Following Marx's distinction between use value and exchange value, Bernard Stiegler's concept of *grammatization* applies the philosophical cut between quality and quantity to characterize the operations of both technical media and capitalist economies. As discussed later, the fantasy of a level playing field represented by both fair games and the free market are conflated within Valve Corporation's "flatland" in which production and play are linked through a quantifying impulse.

With the drama and agony of competition, it is easy to forget that actions and events of both games and commodities must, at some point, be abstracted, or grammatized, into number. In the process, play becomes precisely the act of negotiating the discontinuity between phenomenal experience (or, on the other hand, material substance) and the abstract rules of the game (or market). If all games are constituted in terms of their formal rules, then, as McKenzie Wark (2007, 79) boldly determines, "all games are digital." "Without exception," Wark continues, "[games] all come down to a strict decision: out or in, foul or fair, goal or no goal. Anything else is just 'play.'" Connor (2011, 149) reiterates the distinction between game and play when he writes that "sporting rules and scores always in a sense limit or finitize the infinite possibilities of play." Whereas play is theorized as a voluntary and unnecessary activity that can never be wholly predicted, measured, or even known, games offer the chance for uncertainty, the units to measure play, and the conditions for *unknowing* in the form of rules.

If, as Bernard Suits (2005, 55) writes in *The Grasshopper*, play is the "voluntary pursuit of unnecessary obstacles," then the player must freely submit to an absolute set of rules and play for the sake of play alone. When play for play's sake occurs within rules occurring in and of themselves, the game transforms into an aesthetic object and play must be, in a Kantian sense, disinterested in results obtaining outside its magic circle. Both play and game, in this cut up form, entail utopian horizons— two divergent lines of flight propelling human desire. This dream of an immersive, escapist, autonomous, and fantastic gamespace structures consumption and production within the videogame industry. More than merely selling entertainment products, the games industry sells an ideology. As the term *game* becomes codified and calcified in the form of fetishized commodity, videogames become this ideology's avatar. Here the practical possibilities of play are expropriated into yet another form of statistical labor, an affective economy privatized within an industry designed from the ground up to capture and mobilize desire.

However, despite these utopian fantasies, play and game do not stand absolutely apart, nor do they precisely correlate. There has never been a game that is absolutely unnecessary, immaterial, and ahistorical. There has never been a player able to resist involuntary action like the process of metabolism or the Earth's gravity. Since the Reiswitz family, the material and historical friction that has always existed between rules and play has been expressed and allegorized through the inclusion of probabilistic or chance-based mechanics. Connor (2011, 171) writes, "Just as probability can neither be distinguished from nor wholly identified with number, so number can neither be extricated from nor entirely exhaust play. Probability is the play of number that number itself makes possible." Probabilistic games are, in part, structured around this form of playful unknowing. From wargames to *Warhammer* to *Warcraft*, it is probability that most closely resembles the deeply commingled, historical relation between game and play—and the primary operation driving The Turn of the Tide.

After the emergence of wargaming in the eighteenth century, Connor (2011, 150) states, "the nineteenth century was the most decisive era in the formalization of rules, which is to say, the development of explicit codes, standing abstractly apart from the play, and obtaining in all circumstances" and notes that "as the rules became more abstracted from the playing of the game, the regulative role of the official, as the mediator between rule and play, became more important." Following this trajectory, in the mechanical, electrical, and computational games of the twentieth century the rules of the game cease to behave like social contracts that can be officiated over by an umpire and agreed upon by players and instead are replaced by mechanics. In pinball cabinets, electric toys, and videogames physical forces like gravity, momentum, friction, acceleration, and electricity—along with the infelicities of MacDraw- and MacDraft-style interfaces—replace the rules of the game (sometimes skeuomorphically simulating the rules of analog games, sometimes disavowing rules altogether). In digital games rules become mechanized; in analog games mechanics are often ignored. Whereas the official rulebook of Major League Baseball details the composition of each team, methods for scoring, and the precise geometry of the field, it does not include the gravity of the Earth (see Figure 5.6).[24]

Whereas videogames attempt to reduce all player actions and social rules to their mechanics, exposing the ideological drive to conflate the game with play, metagaming entails the material, historical, and experiential complexities that videogames that the ideological avatar of play rule out. How disabled players negotiate standardized control schemes, how siblings take turns according to house rules, how partygoers drink for each digital death, and even how probabilities predict play are all metagames. Metagaming accounts for those external rules or social customs built in, on, around, and through videogames. The strategies of speedrunners, preferences of pro gamers, and even the tendencies of conspicuous consumers are not what is packaged and sold in stores, distributed on digital networks, or produced by hardworking programmers. Whereas the videogame can be reduced to an abstract set of binary numerals or algorithmic instructions that nevertheless structure the way we play, metagaming constitutes the material histories exceeding the algorithm. And one of the most intricate and influential metagames evolved (and continues to evolve) within *Warcraft III* is a mod called *The Defense of the Ancients*.

The Evolution of *Dota*

When Zheng "Faith" Hongda logged in to the second game of the winner's bracket semifinals, he could not predict exactly what would happen,

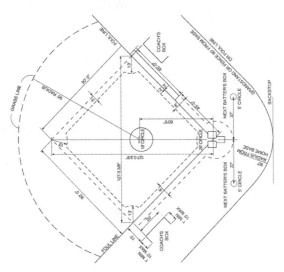

Figure 5.6. Like *Dota 2*'s map (right), Diagram No. 1 from the *Official Baseball Rules* (left) defines a field of play in terms of absolute, geometric coordinates. Unlike *Dota 2*'s polygonal geometry, however, a physical baseball stadium can never precisely correlate to the abstract diagram (Major League Baseball 2013).

only what would probably happen. Although Faith could not know what hero he would be assigned, what lane he would be playing, or which Na`Vi players he would be matched against, Invictus Gaming's de facto "support" player understood what professional players and e-sports enthusiasts call the metagame. The personal preferences and quirks of individual players coupled with the coevolution of common strategies and patch updates is the metagame of *Dota 2*. Just as with *StarCraft, Counter-Strike,* and other multiplayer e-sports, *Dota 2* competitions are based not simply on the game's mechanics but on the psychological and probabilistic metagame with which teams wage war against one another: strategy, counterstrategy, counter-counterstrategy, and maybe back to square one to surprise or confuse an opponent.[25] *Dota 2*'s metagame is perhaps most evident in the draft phase of the game. In the draft, each team's captain begins the game by banning and picking not players, but characters from the game's massive roster.[26] At the time of The International in 2012, there were ninety-two heroes, each with diverse attributes (from physical size and movement speed to stats like agility, strength, and intelligence) and, importantly, at least four special abilities. Ninety-two heroes with about four abilities each who can use one hundred and thirty-eight items offer an almost inconceivable range of statistical variation (not to mention the specific strategies executed in real time within a match) (see Figure 5.7). With the draft, *Dota 2* offloads game design decisions like the balance between various hero combinations to the players, as they collectively design—via the ever evolving metagame—what kind of *Dota 2* they will play.

Before The Turn of the Tide, iG planned to follow that summer's dominant metagame in which Naga Siren and Dark Seer were regarded as an overpowered pair able to unleash a game-winning "wombo combo" by combining their particular abilities (Valve 2012c). The Siren-Seer metagame is all too evident in the statistics for The International. Out of ninety-two possible heroes, the top three banned and picked throughout the entire tournament were Dark Seer at 155 times and Naga Siren (tied with Rubick) at 152.[27] It is not a coincidence that these heroes saw the most action during the draft phase of The International in 2012. Captains used their limited number of picks and bans to prevent the competition from lining up overpowered combinations of heroes. Knowing all this, it must have looked odd when Na`Vi, seemingly unfazed by the loss of Game 1, did not pick or ban either Naga Siren or Dark Seer. Clearly

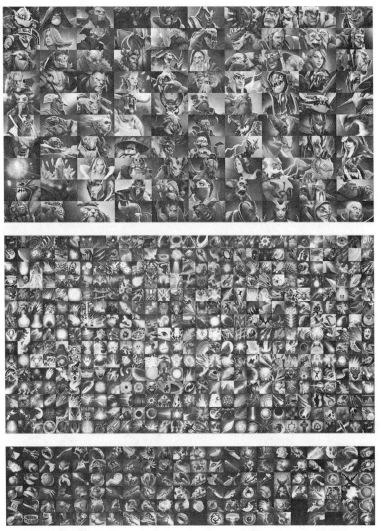

Figure 5.7. As *Dota*'s heroes (top) gain experience and gold throughout a game, they can learn a host of spells (middle) and purchase a plethora of items (bottom). Images by sweetlikepete, 2013 (top); BnJx, 2013 (middle); and Patrick LeMieux, 2016 (bottom).

disappointed at the moment iG drafts both heroes, English commentator "LD" Gorman explains:

> For anybody who doesn't know Naga's Song of the Siren obviously puts
> everyone to sleep. You can then Vacuum them in [with Dark Seer] while
> they're asleep, drop [Dark Seer's Wall of Replica], unleash the pain train. . . .
> Oh god, if they give up the Tidehunter. How do you take a fight? You don't
> take a fight. (Valve 2012c)

Considering their swift defeat in game one, Na`Vi's picks looked sui-
cidal. Yet, the footage of the team gathered together in their glass box
shows the Ukrainians grinning ear-to-ear and giggling mischievously.
LighTofHeaveN and XBOCT crowd around their captain's computer as
Puppey picks the Juggernaut, an unconventional hero who was banned
and picked a mere ten times during the entire tournament. With Na`Vi's
third pick out of the way, there was only one option for Faith, iG's support player: the Tidehunter.

Evolved from the polygonal Sea Giant Hunter in Blizzard's *Warcraft
III,* Valve's version of the Tidehunter is a bipedal fish that carries a fish
(see Figure 5.8). While not the strongest or fastest hero in *Dota 2*, in 2012,

Figure 5.8. When compared to the original Tidehunter (aka Leviathan) from
Warcraft III (left), Valve's version (right) sports a graphic overhaul while retaining
the exact same abilities: Gush, Kraken Shell, Anchor Smash, and Tidehunter's
ultimate ability, Ravage.

Tidehunter was a very defensive pick who could be used to support fragile teammates and buy them time to level up and get some gold. Beyond his early game utility, Tidehunter also has a powerful ultimate ability called Ravage that can stun a whole team if they are clustered together and is often used to initiate large 5 vs. 5 battles called team fights. Having seized the opportunity to select an unbanned Naga Siren and Dark Seer, Faith's fate seemed inevitable. In this tournament, in this series, in this match against this team, and with this specific metagame, how could picking Tidehunter go wrong?

Whereas iG picked Tidehunter in accordance with the strategic metagame in the summer of 2012, *Dota 2* itself is also a game *about* another game—a mod originally designed within and disseminated through Blizzard's *Warcraft III*. Beyond appropriating content and components from *Warcraft III* (a fan-made way to play with Blizzard's IP), *Dota*[28] also represents a hybrid videogame genre that recontextualized and reinvented RTS game mechanics within the ecology of multiplayer online games in the early 2000s. Like *Counter-Strike* (1999), *Team Fortress* (1996), and *Day of Defeat* (2003) before it, Valve has built a business on converting player-produced metagames into service platforms that flatten leisure activities alongside other forms of labor. Whether playing matches, competing in tournaments, talking on forums, analyzing statistics, authoring tutorials, designing cosmetics, debugging beta software, modding new mechanics, or even working as an employee at Valve, *Dota's* users operate according to a decade-long metagame whose origins are notoriously difficult to identify. As Nicholas Werner's documentary series *All Your History* aptly puts it, *Dota*

> came from nowhere with no corporate backing, no advertising campaign, and no business model. It's worth millions of dollars yet only a handful of studios have done any work with it. It's a genre, except it's a game, except there are dozens of them, except it's just a mod. It's a brand new word, except it's an acronym that is trying to be trademarked by its founder, except there is no founder. It's been called MOBA, it's been called ARTS but to the millions of players around the world who play it, it's just *Dota*. (Werner 2012)[29]

In *All Your History,* and in games journalism more broadly, *Dota* is presented as a historical anomaly, a mutant mod with evolutionary origins outside the umbrella of the games industry. The industry—a complex ecosystem of corporate stockholders, development studios, trade shows, global distribution companies, retail vendors, and both independent and completely dependent journalists—attempts to subsume much of the history of videogames (and games in general) within its sphere of influence.

But if "all your history belong"[30] to a linear model of production based on the rigid schedules, intellectual property rights, sales figures, and numerical ratings surrounding discrete pieces of software, *Dota 2* arrives on the scene as an outsider, its historical origins obfuscated by its genesis from the seabed of collective play rather than corporate pay. It is no surprise that most major videogame journals, magazines, and blogs did not cover *Dota*'s longer history as a popular mod, a competitive sport, or even its public beta, preferring instead to write articles only after its "official" release by Valve on July 9, 2013 (Valve 2013b). Although *Dota is* a mutant, it did not spontaneously emerge. From wargaming the statistical and probabilistic mathematics of the eighteenth century to restaging tabletop combat according to the logic of fantasy literature to automating the complex calculations of role- (and roll-) playing games with digital computers, *Dota*'s evolution can be traced back through time though it has only recently been absorbed within the videogame industry proper. As such, *Dota* represents a remarkably disruptive and deconstructive entry in the history of games, upsetting the stable, smooth, and simply chronological timeline so often deployed by videogame companies to further the ideological avatar of play—what Erkki Huhtamo (2005, 4) calls the "chronicle era" of videogame history.

Based on the records of software revisions and the firsthand accounts of fans, *Dota*'s ancient ancestors first crawled up onto land from the primordial ooze of the RTS genre in the early 2000s.[31] Life didn't spring from the software itself, but from player-designed games made within *Warcraft* and *StarCraft*. These early metagames were distributed in the form of unit mods and map packs uploaded to online forums or shared across peer-to-peer networks like Blizzard Entertainment's Battle.net.[32] One such custom map, *Aeon of Strife* (*AoS*) by Aeon64, was produced with StarEdit, a standalone interface for building levels and designing new campaigns shipped with *StarCraft* and its expansion, *StarCraft: Broodwar* (1998).[33] Instead of echoing *StarCraft*'s standard gameplay by focusing on the real-time production and deployment of a large military force, *AoS* featured four individually controlled "heroes" protecting defensive structures or "towers" against endless waves of artificially

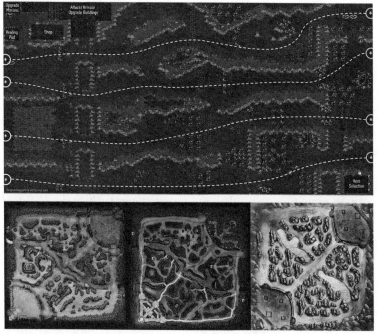

Figure 5.9. Compared to an early four-lane tower defense map like *Aeon of Strife* (top), the onscreen mini-maps from *Dota 2* (left), *Heroes of Newerth* (middle), and *League of Legends* (right) reveal a very similar, symmetric design for team versus team gameplay. Image by Softmints at https://lanepushinggames.com/, 2013 (top).

intelligent enemies or "creeps" that traveled down four "lanes" connecting the two opposing bases (CtChocula 2011) (see Figure 5.9). Featuring a seemingly counterintuitive mixture of gameplay borrowed from RTS, action adventure, roleplaying, and tower defense games, *AoS* instituted many of the defining (albeit nascent) features of *Dota*: the map, the mechanics, and the mission.[34] A game of *AoS* would end when the players were able to offset the balance between the otherwise equally matched AI units and destroy the opposing team's base. Yet the mod was underplayed. The bizarre mixture of mechanics would not prove viable until remade in another game engine: the Warcraft III World Editor (2002).

Warcraft III: Reign of Chaos (2002) continued Blizzard's trend of releasing limited versions of their in-house development tools for fanbased game design. Like StarEdit before it, Blizzard's Warcraft III World

Editor included tools for modifying terrain, objects, and triggers as well as an Import Manager which allowed players to import their own art assets like sounds, textures, and 3D models (Feak and Mescon 2009). Furthermore, the World Editor's triggers made use of JASS, "just another scripting syntax," which afforded users the flexibility to both choose their development environment and dabble with more complex aspects of game design than was possible with the utilities released with *Warcraft II* and *StarCraft*.[35] Fans recall that "in 2003, the game changed. . . . Blizzard released *Warcraft III*, along with its editing tools, and modders went crazy. . . . [Use Map Settings] had become prolific and fun, with games like *Lurker Defense* and *Zone Control*" (Dimirti 2013). In 2003, around same time that other *AoS*-inspired games (like *The Valley of Descent* by Karukef) were being produced, a modder named Eul remade *Aeon of Strife* in *Warcraft III*'s more powerful engine.

Titled *Defense of the Ancients,* or *DotA,* Eul's mod expanded *AoS*'s basic formula, adding more players and more mechanics, some inspired by *Warcraft III* itself. Blizzard's game featured RPG-inspired "hero units" which gain experience, level up, and collect items alongside mass produced, disposable troops spawned from production facilities and controlled within a typical RTS setting. Importantly, the original *DotA* focused more on player-versus-player (PvP) competition than *AoS* by allowing two teams of five players aided by AI rather than a single set of players working together against a computerized opponent. The goal of the game remained the same: to upset the balance of the incessantly marching creeps, exploit tactical advantages to overtake towers, and destroy the opposing team's "Ancient," the largest structure at the heart of the enemy base. In Eul's mod, teams of five players sparred against one another for experience, earned gold by "last hitting" enemies, purchased items to boost their abilities, and engaged in team fights. With these basic elements added to *AoS, DotA* began to gain steam. The mod became so popular that Eul's follow-up project, *DotA: Thirst for Gamma,* could not even compete with remakes of his previous game within Blizzard's *Warcraft III: The Frozen Throne* (2003) expansion. Soon after *The Frozen Throne* was released on July 1, 2003, Eul retired from the modding community but not before publishing the JASS code for the original *WCIII DotA,* code that would inspire an explosion of *DotA* games like the *DotA DX Series, DotA Unforgiven, DotA Mercenaries,* and *DotA Outland* (CtChocula 2011).

With *The Frozen Throne* expansion and Eul's open source code, *DotA* began to multiply. In 2003, there were dozens of *DotA*s and *AoSe*s as well as *DotA*-clones, *DotA*-likes, *DotA*-based, and *DotA*-esques. With the growing popularity of the World Editor and the number of players selecting "use map setting," Battle.net served as the Cambrian sea, incubating more and more versions of *DotA* with new heroes, spells, items, and maps. With so many tweaks and changes being tested out within this ad hoc, player-driven development community, compilations emerged over time featuring the most popular mechanics and hero units borrowed from dozens of different games. Some of the earliest attempts to build the ur-*DotA* were Meian and Ragn0r's various *Allstars* titles in 2003 that compiled popular heroes from across the *DotA*-verse into one downloadable map launched on February 3, 2004 (CtChocula 2011). Following these mods, Stephen "Guinsoo" Feak began to work on *DotA Allstars* 2.0 in February, and released 3.0 in March that year. More than simply building a clearinghouse for favorite heroes, items, and abilities, Feak took on the mercurial task of consolidating, tweaking, balancing, and debugging the game with a loose team of modders who designed many of the features that have come to define the genre.[36]

Between 2004 and 2005, Feak oversaw the development of more than fifty heroes and over fifty items, a system for item creation and combination based on recipes, the randomly appearing "runes" that temporarily alter hero abilities, "super creeps" that spawned after the destruction of all barracks, a large and centrally located neutral creep named "Roshan,"[37] and the addition of booming "kill streak" voiceovers borrowed from Epic's *Unreal Tournament 99* and *2004* (e.g., "FIRST BLOOD," "OWN-AGE," "M-M-M-M-MONSTER KILL," etc.), signature sound effects that still exist in Valve's version to this day (Feak and Mescon 2009). Beyond these now familiar features, Feak's most important contribution was guiding the team of amateur developers to balance heroes for competitive player-versus-player competition rather than focusing strictly on tower defense and lane pushing against AI opponents. As Feak and Steve "Pendragon" Mescon (2009) explain in their postmortem account of *DotA All-stars*, "balance was tuned each version, and the only way for [Feak] to know if he got it right was to see if the players stopped complaining." To further organize the player base, Mescon built a set of forums that "became the main medium of communication between Feak and the community, and contained everything from player guides to player-created hero and item suggestions, and the organizations of the first real *DotA* tournaments" (Dimirti 2013). Feak worked on *DotA Allstars* until version 6.0 when he left the *Warcraft III* modding scene, it is rumored, to focus on playing Blizzard's new blockbuster, *World of Warcraft.*

In many ways, *DotA* could be figured not only as an evolutionary mutant but also a missing link between two distinct species of game represented in Blizzard's *Warcraft* franchise: RTS games like *Warcraft III* and massively multiplayer online (MMO) games like *World of Warcraft.*[38] Between these two major bookends of the *Warcraft* series, *DotA* wrested *Warcraft III*'s mechanics and point-and-click interface away from the macroeconomics and micromanagement of the RTS genre to create a different kind of collaborative and competitive online play. But rather than building a game around leveling a single unit for cooperative player versus environment (PvE) challenges like *World of Warcraft*, *DotA* focused on manipulating individual units in a team-based, PvP setting.[39] For a number of reasons, the historical origins and evolutionary influences of *DotA* have been obfuscated—within corporate-, industry-, and even the player-created histories surrounding Blizzard's franchises. Because the game emerged from a community of modders rather than the games industry proper, for many years *DotA* was undervalued in terms of both economic and cultural capital. In an era of MMOs dominated by games like *World of Warcraft*, *DotA* continued to flourish, particularly in non–North American contexts. After the newfound euphoria for the MMO and a rocky shift of power, Neichus picked up where Feak left off before handing *Allstars* over to IceFrog, who continued to labor in relative obscurity (and without pay) to maintain *DotA.*

Not much is known about IceFrog, the elusive and longest-serving developer of *DotA* who began modding the game with Feak and Neichus in October 2004. The first new hero shipped with IceFrog's input in *Allstars* 5.74 that year was none other than the Tidehunter. According to Michael Walbridge (2008), he "may be named Jeremy . . . may be from Boston and . . . may study at UCLA" and may have been born in 1983. IceFrog may be many things, but to the *DotA* community he is a mysterious and "almost spiritual figurehead," responsible not only for coding and distributing the game but for organizing a team of beta testers in order to playtest and adjust the most arcane and nuanced aspects of the game (Walbridge 2008). Like Tarn "Toady One" Adams, Marcus "Notch" Persson, and Dean "Rocket" Hall, IceFrog belongs to a class of game developers who operate as virtual landlords responsible for maintaining games such as *Dwarf Fortress (2006–)*, *Minecraft (2009–)*, *DayZ (2013–)*, and, of course, *DotA* for digital renters who pay with their attention, time, and money as the game is developed. Whereas Eul propagated the explosion of experiments with his JASS source code and, following the first *Allstars* mods, Feak carefully selected features which would come to define *DotA*, IceFrog introduced a half-decade-long, glacial age in which the mod stabilized and hardened around a centralized director, a unified design philosophy, and an international scope. The long evolution of *DotA* as a species of software slowed as player productivity migrated from the creation of ever-multiplying mods to the culture of competitive play. While Neichus co-authored a few versions of the map starting with 6.0, version 6.1 ushered in the era of IceFrog as the game began "to take large leaps toward competitiveness" (CtChocula 2009).[40] This moment in *DotA*'s history also marks the introduction of China to the competitive scene as another modder, Heintje, translated the game into Chinese for the first time.

With a stable, international version of *DotA Allstars* available in 2005, version 5.83B appeared in the Malaysian and Singaporean World Cyber Games while 6.12B was featured as a side event at the World Cyber Games championships in the Suntec City convention center in Singapore alongside corporate titles like *Warcraft III: The Frozen Throne* and *StarCraft: Broodwar*. In 2005, international teams were beginning to treat *DotA* like a sport and with its aging technical requirements the mod could be played on almost any personal computer, from the newest gaming laptops to the beige towers and CRT screens of the late nineties. It was relatively easy to find (or pirate) a cheap copy of *Warcraft III* in the mid-2000s, and at this point *DotA*'s gameplay was so diverse that the recombinatory potential of the game far outpaced any one player or team. In 2009, Ice-Frog estimated between five and eight million new downloads, especially in Asia and South America, and by 2010 "it [was] roughly estimated . . . that the Chinese *DotA* audience is about 40–50 percent of the world-wide audience. Not counting China, the player base is estimated to be somewhere between 7–11 million" (IceFrog 2009a, 2010). With a thriving community and informal global economy, it was only a matter of time before *DotA* moved from the realm of play to that of profit.

In the late 2000s, while *DotA* was emerging as "arguably one of the most popular game mods of all time," the corporate game industry began co-opting the map, mechanics, interface, and even specific statistics of each hero in order to simulate the original mod (Feak and Mescon 2009).[41] Whereas Feak and Mescon were hired by Riot Games to design *League of Legends* (2009), IceFrog assisted S2 Games during the development of *Heroes of Newerth* (2010) before he and Eul, the original creator of *Defense of the Ancients*, were recruited by Valve. Rather than design a new game with original characters, edited map, and different items (like *League of Legends*) or attempt a faithful remake of the *Warcraft III* mod with similar frame rates and polygon counts (like *Heroes of Newerth*), Valve tasked IceFrog and Eul with translating *DotA* to their Source Engine. With *Dota 2*, vestigial features that arose due to the eccentricities of the Warcraft III World Editor become deliberate game design choices. As Chris Thursten (2013, 44) notes in the first formal announcement of *Dota 2*, "several unintentional side-effects of Dota's design have become fullblown features" and "bizarre behaviour" like creep stacking, pulling, and juking that developed based on the limitations of the original mod have become defining mechanics of a whole genre.[42] Even in 2015, IceFrog continued to develop *Dota 2* within the Warcraft III World Editor before translating game design decisions into Source. And although IceFrog's identity remains a mystery, it is now believed that he may be living in Seattle, may have turned 30 in 2013, is still stewarding *DotA Allstars* (version 6.83d was released on September 6, 2015), and is employed at a games and digital distribution company known for its experimental and unorthodox approach to game design, economics, and labor organization.

At the end of *Defense of the Ancient*'s long evolution, Valve filed a trademark application for the name *Dota* in 2009. What resulted was a series of countersuits initiated by Riot Games and Blizzard Entertainment—corporations made up of ex-modders with vested interests in the future of the game. Under the aegis of their old company, Dota Allstars, Riot employees Feak and Mescon filed for the *Defense of the Ancients* trademark in order to "protect the work that dozens of authors have invested to create the game and on behalf of the millions of *DotA* players all over the world" (Augustine, 2010). Blizzard, on the other hand, argued that "by attempting to register the mark *DotA*, Valve seeks to appropriate the more than seven years of goodwill that Blizzard has developed in the mark *DotA* and in its *Warcraft III* computer game and take for itself a name that has come to signify the product of years of time and energy expended by Blizzard and by fans of *Warcraft III*" (Plunkett, 2012). Whereas both Riot and Blizzard appealed to the rights of the community of modders and players, each planned to protect the name of the game for its own interests.[43] In the end, though, Valve settled out of court and agreed to forgo both *Defense of the Ancients* and *DotA,* instead trademarking *Dota 2*—a sequel to a *Dota 1* that never existed. The land grab that took place between 2010 and 2012 in the form of these trademark lawsuits demonstrates one way that corporations enclose the metagame. It was not until Valve's attempt to trademark the name *Dota* that those companies directly responsible for the evolution of the mod began to value the longer history of community play and production in, on, around, and through their games.

Following Valve's settlement with Blizzard Entertainment, the corporate struggle shifted from the name of the game to the name of the *genre.* Despite its generality, Riot promoted the acronym MOBA (multiplayer online battle arena) as a way to distance their product, *League of Legends,* from *Dota* after Valve acquired the proprietary eponym. In opposition to Riot's acronym Valve offers ARTS, a slightly more descriptive if less common term because, as Gabe Newell (Nutt 2011) states, "action RTS seems to make a lot of sense to customers. If you say that, they have a pretty good idea what you're talking about. I don't even know what MOBA stands for." The debate over nomenclature and lack of consensus on how to define this genre of 5 vs. 5, lane pushing games stands in as a metonym not only for the growing pains of *DotA* and its ilk, but the difficulty of institutionalizing and branding a mod. Even the transition from the acronym *DotA* to the word *Dota* reified the game as a commodity and relocated the metagame from early communities of play built on the exchange of unique designs to a service platform for cosmetic markets, e-sports, and emerging forms of spectatorship.

The technical evolution of *Dota* began in the antediluvian wake of RTS games and, after surfacing as one of the most successful mods of all time, generated an entire genre of competitive play. From a mutant mod to the genesis of a genre to a spectator sport and international marketing tool and cottage industry of user-generated content, *Dota 2*'s evolution outside the industry extends the horizon of videogaming as a medium, encapsulating previously undervalued ways to play and converting them into organs of productivity and profitability. *Dota*'s evolution grinds to a halt precisely at the point at which the game's design is at its most general and most open to divergent possibilities defined not by what is materially present in the software, but by the diverse play made possible by its noisy, entropic systems. Under the management of IceFrog and newly funded by Valve, *Dota 2* is less a sequel and more of a service platform, expropriating the metagaming practices that have long supported the game as a global sport. In biology, the term *sport* refers to organisms that have undergone dramatic mutations, and in the early years of *Dota*, many "sports" erupted out of the recombinatory potential of early network culture. Yet, the calcification of the play into a professional sport—specifically what has come to be known as e-sports— marks a moment when the evolution of *Dota* stabilizes and moves away from the production of software to culture.

From Sports to E-Sports

Well beyond the evolution of *Dota* and its recent acquisition by Valve, the origins of e-sports stretch back to the development of the earliest electronic games. In *Raising the Stakes: E-Sports and the Professionalization of Computer Gaming* (2012) T. L. Taylor offers a rich history of competitive videogaming and documents a half-century of attempts to position computer games within the arena of spectator sport. In one respect, games have always engaged *agon*, the cut between *ratio* and *kinesis*. The technical operations of digital media automate this kind of cutting as switches, transistors, and semiconductors cleave binary bits of data from otherwise analog pulses of electricity. Even at the beginning, videogames conflated these two related forms of agony, allegorizing their digital processes of grammatization, individuation, and quantification via the cut of competition. *Tennis for Two* (1958) was, of course, for two players, and *Spacewar!* (1962) inspired the "*Spacewar* Olympics," a four-hour tournament at the Stanford Artificial Intelligence Laboratory (SAIL) sponsored by *Rolling Stone* magazine in 1972—perhaps the first e-sport event.[44] Later, single-player games continued to incorporate player-versus-player competition like *Sea Wolf* (1976), an early arcade game with the first persistent scoreboard. Although individual players played early videogames games serially, scoreboards added a social component, a historical record that could be competed and compared with over an extended time period. As Taylor (2012, 4–5) recounts, in the early eighties there were televised game shows in which players competed against each other, such as *Star-*

cade (1982–84), that stand as further attempts to convert videogames into a spectator sport. These two traditions manifest in two distinct types of sport: the player-versus-player competitions of the strategy, fighting, and first-person shooter communities and the player-versus-records of the speedrunning, high-scoring, and some MMO communities.[45]

According to Taylor (2012, 36), "long-standing debates about what constitutes a 'real' sport intersect deeply held notions about masculinity (and femininity), class, and culture . . . Only the most naive and ahistorical would suggest the coveted legitimacy of sport is bestowed objectively, outside of any deep cultural values about what constitutes meaningful human and social action." Rather than engage in a semantic discussion of sport versus game, Taylor observes the way in which computer gaming communities have created a competitive architecture that follows many of the same patterns as professional sports: the emphasis on athleticism and the embodied actions of the player, the importance of standardized equipment, the negotiation of both written and unwritten game rules, the development of professional tournament rules (what Steven Connor [2011, 150] calls "metarules"), gambling and betting on the outcomes of matches, and even the proliferation of scandals in which e-sports players collude to throw important games for profit.[46] From the growth of corporate sponsorship to the broadcasts on television stations like TBS and ESPN to the U.S. government issuing "professional athlete" visas when players compete abroad, the perception of videogames as a sport is less of a philosophical question than a social, legal, and political issue with the most important factor contributing to the changing perceptions of competitive videogaming being the realization of its profitability.

From another angle, all sports are e-sports. Taylor (2012, 40) emphasizes that "the sporting body has always been tied up with technology," but, more importantly, that the precondition for sports is the digitization of analog action—the conversion of continuous motion into discrete metrics for scoring and judging.[47] Based on the primacy of this relationship between *kinesis* and *ratio*, the homology between sports and e-sports can be inverted: rather than seeking to legitimize videogames as sport, it is important to recognize the computational kernel driving all sporting competitions.[48] "From the start," Wark (2007, 079) suggests, all "games were . . . proto-computer—machines assembled out of human motion, inanimate materials, and the occasional dubious call by the referee." As

much as videogames may be sport, all sports are also videogames. Undifferentiated and irreducible physical fields, material equipment, human
bodies, and other forms of play are reduced to a calculation, a score, a
cut. Moreover, this form of abstraction that marks one player a winner
and the other a loser could be said to go by another name: capital.

As evidenced by The International in 2012, the burgeoning movement
of electronic sports models itself closely on the culture and business of
professional sports. Major League Gaming (MLG) adopts the branding
idioms and iconography of other national leagues such as Major League
Baseball (MLB), the National Football League (NFL), the National Basketball Association (NBA), and the National Hockey League (NHL) (see
Figure 5.10). Games like *Dota 2* inspire international tournaments, lav-
ish prize pools, diverse media coverage, lucrative sponsorship deals, live
commentary in dozens of languages, and communities of fans who tune
in weekly not to play, but to *watch* their favorite videogames. The discourse undergirding the administration, advertising, and dissemination
of e-sports co-opts myths of human exceptionalism, the pleasure of
visual spectacle, and the monetization strategies of professional sports
in order to orient audiences toward alternative forms of play based
on watching computer games.[49] On the other hand, contemporary
sports like football, basketball, and baseball have adopted digital technologies for broadcasting, officiating, and otherwise abstracting the
movements of players into exchangeable numbers for transmission,
consumption, analysis, and prediction. The mathematical probabilities
governing play within MLB, for example, extend well beyond the dia-
mond and the dugout to include marketing, management, and, most of

MAJOR LEAGUE BASEBALL   MAJOR LEAGUE GAMING

Figure 5.10. Mirroring Jerry Dior's red and blue Major League Baseball logo (left),
Major League Gaming (right) has added a curved, skeuomorphic highlight
popularized by Apple's Aqua interface in the late 2000s. The subtitle uses a square
sans serif font, connoting the pixelated graphics of videogames. These small
changes adapt the iconography of national sports to a digital medium.

all, money. The more money saturates the culture of videogaming, the more sportslike it becomes. After all, money is the ultimate referee and one of the first digital medium.

When IceFrog (2009b) announced his collaboration with Valve to port *Defense of the Ancients* from Warcraft III World Editor to the Source Engine in 2009, he reassured the game's global fan base that the "goal and top priority in the future is to solve the surrounding issues that affect the *DotA experience* in order to allow it to reach new heights" (emphasis added). While "gameplay, mechanics, and in-game feel" were still important to the developer, Valve offered IceFrog a once-in-a-lifetime opportunity to change not the way *Dota* was played but how it was distributed, spectated, networked, and monetized in relation to the larger Steam marketplace. By treating *Dota 2* as a platform, Valve has not only developed experimental forms of biometric and statistical analysis that expropriate attention and create new ways of "seeing," but has also built spectatorship into the game as a form of play. With *Dota 2*, spectatorship is no longer a superfluous byproduct of gaming, but a productive part of a much broader ecology in which all player activities are measured and funneled back into the development of the game.

In a report titled "Gamers on YouTube," Google researchers James Getomer, Michael Okimoto, and Brad Johnsmeyer undertook an analysis of the company's video sharing service to demonstrate how watching footage of videogames has become a market in and of itself. Their study shows how YouTubers watch games as much as play them and that the "growth rate of time spent viewing gaming videos was greater than YouTube's overall growth in the U.S." (Getomer et al., 2013, 2). What is striking about "Gamers on YouTube" is its resolute focus on one specific model of value derived from the relationship of view count to game sales. Rather than valuing individual views as such, view count serves as an index of the indirect monetary benefit derived from the viewer's attention. Turning toward mainstream videogames, Google reports that "82% of game console sales occur in first 4 months" and the top ten best-selling console games represented "49% of 2012 total console game revenue" (Getomer et al. 2013; 6, 7). Focusing on these games, when Getomer, Okimoto, and Johnsmeyer (2013, 7) "compared all pre-launch video views . . . for the top 2012 games to their sales in the first four months and a compelling correlation of 0.99 emerged." This marketing study suggests that YouTube serves as an accurate forecasting device, predicting the "correlation between views and sales" of videogames (Getomer et al. 2013, 7). However, Google's analysts fail to see the more complex relationship between consumption, production, and attention at stake in the widespread transformation of spectatorship online.

Watching is not merely an index of revenue (or of play) but a form of capital accumulation based on attention. As Christian Fuchs (2012, 704) writes, "On Facebook, YouTube, Twitter, etc., all consumption time is commodity production time." Although selling consumption itself is the primary condition of social media and user-generated content in general, nowhere is the attempt to capture previously undefined sources of value and productivity more evident than in Valve. The reconfiguration of modes of spectatorship in games like *Dota 2* is just a small part of a much larger project of redefining the systems of value that circulate around gaming and recasting play as a form of productivity within a flattened corporate gamespace. Whereas the Google study focuses only on how viewing videogames correlates to future sales, Valve's model of valorization and evaluation assumes that spectatorship and, more generally, all forms of play are, in themselves, valuable commodities. The problem is how to capture these forms of undervalued production.

With *Dota 2*, Valve has invented increasingly complex and compelling ways to augment, gamify, track, and play with spectatorship. E-sports flourishes in a complex media ecology designed around converged modes of playing, laboring, and watching. In "The Cinema of Attraction," Tom Gunning (1986, 70) observes that "every change in film history implies a change in its address to the spectator, and each change constructs its spectator in a new way." Even at the first International tournament in 2011, a publicity stunt in which Valve unveiled *Dota 2* by inviting teams to first learn then compete for a million dollars in a game they had never played, commentators (and viewers at home) were treated to a suite of in-game analytic tools that were far more advanced and centralized within the game's client than those offered in other e-sport platforms or streaming services such as Twitch.tv. From simple gold and experience graphs to visualizations of galvanic skin response units hooked up to competing players, reviewer Chris Thursten (2013, 41) remembers this shift from individual virtuosity to statistical inevitability as "commentators [were] just as likely to get excited about a character pulling ahead on a graph as they are a particularly skillful play."

In 2012, Valve introduced further means to quantify and gamify watching by offering 99-cent "digital pennants" that fans flew in hopes of both increasing the viewer count for their favorite team—a metric clearly visible to competing players in-game—and increasing the odds of winning cosmetic items and other digital commodities distributed to random viewers with each "FIRST BLOOD" or "ULTRA KILL" achieved by their respective teams (shouted by the familiar voices of *Unreal Tournament*). These light gambling mechanics were extended outward to social media platforms and video streaming providers that, if synced with a player's *Dota 2* account, will also reward that player with in-game giveaways outside the game. Beyond the virtual pennants, 2013's *Interactive Compendium* was initially conceived as an up-to-the-minute digital almanac that aggregated statistical information about the players, teams, and matches of the third International (Valve 2013a). Described as a "living document" and "virtual passport," the *Compendium* allowed viewers to assemble automated fantasy leagues, collect virtual trading cards of their favorite *Dota 2* players, enter into lotteries for exclusive items, and even vote on two dream teams that would compete face-to-face in a local exhibition match. Whereas part of each 99-cent digital pennant sale went to each respective team, 25 percent of each ten-dollar *Interactive Compendium* was added to the tournament's prize pool—a sum crowdsourced from $1.6 million to over $2.8 million after fans bought 509,752 copies of the e-book. This number exponentially increased in the following years, expanding Valve's $1,600,000 prizepool to $10,931,105 in 2014, $18,429,613 in 2015, and $20,770,460 in 2016. Beyond the hype of these astronomical figures and despite myriad analytical tools, players and spectators alike had trouble decoding The Turn of the Tide.

Seventeen Seconds of *Dota 2*

Returning to Benaroya Hall and the second match of the winner's bracket semifinals at The International in 2012, a question still lingers: *What exactly happened here?* After the glow of particle effects, the standing ovation from the Seattle crowd, the stunned silence of the Chinese commentators, and Na'Vi's improbable solution to that summer's metagame, spectators new to *Dota 2*, e-sports, or LAN tournaments must have wondered how iG's winning strategy failed and what mechanics Na'Vi had exploited to turn it around. Did the virtuosic play of pro gamers reverse the outcome of the match, or did the deterministic, microtemporal processes of technical media overshadow their agency? And how do these seventeen seconds play into Valve's corporate interests in China? Of course, the answer is in the metagame. Along with narrative explanations and MS Paint schematics scattered across various online forums, two alternative forms of spectatorship surfaced in the months following The Turn of the Tide: a one-thousand-frame-per-second (FPS) slow motion replay and a 'pataphysical performance of strange statistics.

Shortly after videos of The Turn of the Tide made waves across the Internet in August 2012, Michael Krukar typed "host_timescale 0.001, host_framerate 1000" into the *Dota 2* command line interface before replaying the .DEM or "demo file" of Na'Vi and IG's historic match.[50] Instead of a real-time record of the second game of the winner's bracket semifinals, what resulted was a microtemporal version of The Turn of the Tide. Like high-speed film appears in slow motion when played back at thirty or sixty frames per second, Krukar rendered the sub-second record of mouse clicks and key presses in *Dota 2* at a thousand frames per second. Whereas the commentators at The International could not cope with the density of pixels, polygons, and particle effects erupting for the seventeen seconds the two teams collided, the glacial images of Krukar's decelerated replay tell a different story. Krukar's one thousand FPS animation obfuscates the ecstatic narratives produced in the heat of The International in favor of the aesthetic genre associated with slow motion cinematography. Accompanied by the French electronic music group M83's ostentatiously titled "Lower Your Eyelids to Die with the Sun," the sequence channels the majestic and melodramatic images of Ron Fricke's cinematography and the repetitive sonic landscapes of Phillip Glass's minimalist compositions in *Koyaanisqatsi* (1982), a film in which techniques like slow motion and time lapse cinematography are used to signal temporal events operating outside the range of human sensation. The statistical information stored in *Dota*'s .DEM files begin to tell a different story as the procedural rhythms of Valve's Source Engine appear from beneath the visual spectacle in Benaroya Hall. Instead of illegible explosions of frenetic energy, the mouse movements and button mashing of professional players are organized according to the serial mechanisms and statistical record of The Turn of the Tide. As avatars float calmly from coordinate to coordinate, The Turn of the Tide drifts in and out according to the pull of the *Dota*'s probabilistic mechanics as much as the pull of human will.

Krukar's evocative animation points to a deeper source of information: the record of inputs within *Dota 2's* .DEM. Using a tool produced by Bruno "Statsman" Carlucci, these files may be mined for the statistical data and textual description of any given *Dota 2* match. With 17,463 lines of logged combat events, the spectacular narrative of Ukrainian underdogs facing the impenetrable wall of Chinese *Dota* may be replaced by an exact set of serial events. Returning to the postplay confusion surrounding The Turn of the Tide, the textual inscriptions reveal a discrete sequence of recorded events from the moment iG's Chen "Zhou" Yao initiates the team fight to the moment Na`Vi's Dendi turns the tide:

29:06 (17:35). Juggernaut loses the
    modifier_naga_siren_song_of_the_siren.
29:06 (17:35). Shadow Shaman loses the
    modifier_naga_siren_song_of_the_siren.
29:06 (17:35). Rubick loses the modifier_naga_siren_song_of_the_siren.
29:06 (17:35). Enigma loses the modifier_naga_siren_song_of_the_siren.
29:06 (17:35). Enigma gets the Black King Bar Immunity.
29:06 (17:35). Enchantress loses the
    modifier_naga_siren_song_of_the_siren.
29:06 (17:35). Juggernaut gets the Blade Fury Buff.
29:06 (17:35). Rubick gets the Force Staff Push.
29:06 (17:35). Rubick loses the Force Staff Push.
29:06 (17:36). Shadow Shaman gets the Ravage Debuff.
29:06 (17:36). Enchantress gets the Ravage Debuff.
29:07 (17:36). Tidehunter deals 187 damage to
    Shadow Shaman using Ravage.
29:07 (17:36). Tidehunter deals 178 damage to Enchantress using Ravage.
29:07 (17:36). Juggernaut deals 21 damage to Naga Siren using Bladefury.
29:07 (17:36). Juggernaut deals 21 damage to Dark Seer using Bladefury.
29:07 (17:36). Juggernaut deals 21 damage to Tidehunter using Bladefury.
29:07 (17:37). Lina gets the modifier_rubick_telekinesis.
29:07 (17:37). Naga Siren gets the modifier_enigma_black_hole_pull.
29:07 (17:37). Dark Seer gets the modifier_enigma_black_hole_pull.
29:07 (17:37). Tidehunter gets the modifier_enigma_black_hole_pull.
29:08 (17:37). Puck gets the modifier_enigma_black_hole_pull.
29:08 (17:38). Shadow Shaman loses the Ravage Debuff.
29:08 (17:38). Enchantress loses the Ravage Debuff.
29:08 (17:38). Enigma deals 45 damage to Naga Siren using Black hole.
29:08 (17:38). Enigma deals 22 damage to Tidehunter using Black hole.
29:08 (17:38). Enigma deals 45 damage to Dark Seer using Black hole.

29:09 (17:38). Enigma deals 45 damage to Puck using Black hole.
29:09 (17:38). Rubick gets the modifier_rubick_spell_steal.
29:10 (17:39). Lina loses the modifier_rubick_telekinesis.
29:10 (17:39). Lina gets the Ravage Debuff.
29:10 (17:39). Naga Siren gets the Ravage Debuff.
29:10 (17:39). Dark Seer gets the Ravage Debuff.
29:10 (17:39). Puck gets the Ravage Debuff.
29:10 (17:39). Tidehunter gets the Ravage Debuff.

These timestamps dredge up the precise sequence of events after iG "cut for the shorter path . . . [and] storm up the river" and unleash the "wombo combo" that defined the metagame in the summer of 2012 (Valve 2012c). Following these numeric footsteps, the play begins when the Chinese team's "big wrap-around gank" takes the form of an incognito, five-man blitz that hopes to take Na`Vi from the rear and pinch the Ukrainians between the incoming team and iG's second tier of towers (see Figure 5.11). Zhou initiates the aquatic ambush with Naga Siren's ultimate ability: a powerful "Song of the Siren" that locks the enemy team into an invulnerable slumber. While incapacitated, Na`Vi are immobilized but, importantly, physically immune from taking damage. At this point, YYF's Dark Seer uses "Vacuum" to suck Na`Vi into one centralized position. Everything is ready, but Naga Siren must stop singing before IG can enact their *coup de grâce* and win the team fight (and, inevitably, the game). Due to the time scale of human reflexes and the delay of team coordination, a window emerges for another probability. Between Song of the Siren and iG's next important move, the Tidehunter's 2.77-second, area-of-effect stun and damage ability called "Ravage," there is a small yet critical window. Between Zhou cancelling the Song and Faith initiating Ravage, Na`Vi have a chance to change the metagame. Crucially, these two moves cannot overlap or Na`Vi will still be invulnerable and the Tidehunter's ultimate ability will go wasted. Operating with as much temporal efficiency as possible, it took Zhou and Faith 0.46 seconds to stop one spell and cast another. But a half second was all Na`Vi needed to mount their counterattack.

From the moment Puppey gave away Seer and Siren in the draft phase, Na`Vi had engaged in a gamble. Knowing iG would select the popular heroes, Na`Vi also bet they would attempt to use them in a predictable way: first singing, then stunning. While under the effects of Siren's song,

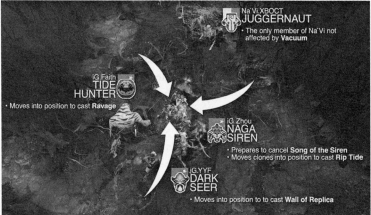

Figure 5.11. Under the cover of the Smoke of Deceit, iG ambushes Na`Vi with Naga Siren's ultimate ability (top), putting them to sleep while Dark Seer Vacuums them together (bottom).

Na`Vi engage in another gamble. Although they have no way of knowing exactly when Zhou's spell will end, they hope to exploit the brief window between the syncopated, serial execution of Song of the Siren and Ravage. Rather than relying on a gut reaction, Na`Vi address the probability of play by *becoming machine*. While their avatars are immobilized by the sleep spell, each member frantically mashes buttons. The Ukrainians wager that they can tap faster than Zhou and Faith can coordinate their spells. Even if a tap lands a single frame before Song of the Siren ends, the next rote tap should theoretically occur before Faith can coordinate his single button press. By contrast, Faith cannot engage in the same frenzied button mashing but must deliver a single button press at microtemporal scales of precision, what photographers call the "decisive moment."

Na'Vi's prediction is correct and exactly 0.46 seconds after the Naga Siren ceases her five-second song, as the Tidehunter's tentacles begin to spread across the screen, they *break the metagame*.[51] The series of actions that follow have not only brought celebrity status to Na'Vi but serve as one of the most memorable moments to date in the history of e-sports (see Figure 5.12). First, the Grand Magus, Rubick, piloted by Dendi, deploys a force staff to fly outside of the reach of Tidehunter's Ravage, avoiding the 2.77-second stun. Within the same fourteen-frame window, XBOTC's Juggernaut activates his invulnerable "Blade Fury" and LightofHeaven's Enigma, standing in the center of the screen, uses an item called a "Black King Bar" in order to evade the Tidehunter's ultimate ability as it stretches across the field. The result of these carefully coordinated countermaneuvers is that only two of the five heroes, Puppey's Enchantress and Ars-Art's Shadow Shaman, are stunlocked by the Tidehunter's Ravage. As if the result of Na'Vi's clever counter picks, in-game preparation, and quick button clicks is not enough, at this moment Faith makes a critical mistake.

Beyond the metagame of popular picks and bans at The International in 2012, Rubick, the Grand Magus, represents a kind of metagame in and of himself. Rubick's ultimate ability, "Spell Steal," allows the player to capture the last ability used by any hero in the game. Thus, like Masahiro Sakurai's pink puffball, Kirby (discussed in chapter 1), Rubick is a kind of meta-hero who represents the recombinatorial possibility space generated by the almost 400 spells in *Dota 2* that summer.[52] The only way to guard against Rubick's Spell Steal is for an opponent to immediately follow any powerful or game-changing spell with something inconsequential. The tighter the window, the lower the chance a skilled Rubick can steal the coveted spell. Faith understood this. Yet instead of adopting Na'Vi's frantic and mechanistic mashing to prevent Dendi from stealing the Tidehunter's Ravage skill, Faith waits just over a full second—an eternity in this time scale—before attempting to block the Spell Steal. Whereas Faith hesitates for 1.33 seconds while repositioning,

Figure 5.12. As the Tidehunter's ultimate ability, Ravage, begins to cross the field, Na'Vi springs their countermaneuver (top) so that only two of their five heroes are affected by the area-of-effect stun (bottom).

Dendi does not waste this narrow window of opportunity. After dodging Ravage with his force staff, Dendi turns around, disables Chuan with "Telekinesis," and then steals Tidehunter's ultimate ability before Faith can use "Anchor Smash."[53] At this point the tide finally turns (see Figure 5.13).

LightofHeaven's Enigma initiates his ultimate ability, "Black Hole," to gather and stun the entire iG team. Next, Dendi turns the purloined Ravage against iG by letting loose his stolen spell on the tightly clustered

Figure 5.13. With iG engulfed by the Enigma's Black Hole, Dendi is able to steal the Tidehunter's Ravage (top) and turn it against the Chinese team (bottom), resulting in a teamkill that wins the match.

team. With the Chinese team disabled and damaged, Na`Vi operate in unison to swiftly deliver the kill. The 0.46- and 1.33-second windows of opportunity are the decisive moments that reverse the course of the game. From that point they easily go on to win the match and the winner's bracket semifinals. Here The Turn of the Tide ceases to correlate to the human experience of seeing the drama unfold at The International or even playing *Dota 2*, but signals a different turn altogether. Na`Vi does not deliver an act of athletic beauty as much as they execute a statistical exploit. By first picking heroes with abilities that specifically counter the metagame, then spamming their spells in order to rebuff the "wombo combo," Na`Vi gives Dendi room to cast out and hook the machinic undercurrent to reverse the flow of the game.

As a way of establishing more robust play, anticipating probable outcomes, and tracking the metagame, a cottage industry of statistical aggregation and analysis has flourished around competitive *Dota 2.* Lacking the institutionalization of large databases available to more established professional sports, websites like Dota-Academy.com have developed their own datasets produced by particularly inventive and industrious players. Representing the first archive of *Dota 2* statistics, Dota Academy was designed by two South Americans, Bruno "Statsman" Carlucci from Argentina and Bruno "Shostakovich" Tomaz from Brazil. The duo began collecting data the hard way, Carlucci (2013) explains, first by simply "watching the [video-on-demand (VOD) or] replays and entering the info by hand" before he "decided to finish [his] early parser in order to start using it on [Dota Academy]." By developing software to analyze Valve's .DEM files and scrape game statistics, Carlucci (2013) realized "that there was *lots* more info to extract than [he] initially thought" (emphasis original). As Steven Connor explains, "we are seeing the statistical ecstasis of sport" in the sense that statistics operate both *within* and *around* the game. In the case of the game statistics surrounding *Dota 2,* they have taken on a life of their own and become a metagame in their own right. As with Krukar's one thousand FPS animation, Dota-Academy.com images *Dota* differently and opens up alternative avenues for spectatorship. In addition to Dota Academy and the Dota 2 Replay Parser, Carlucci produced the first *Dota 2* Fantasy League [54] and found himself, after a stroke of luck, extemporaneously commentating The International in 2012.

Affectionately nicknamed "Bruno the Statsman," Carlucci's presentation of statistics is as playful as it is productive. Making his first official appearance as a live commenter during The International in 2012, Carlucci donned a diverse array of flamboyant leisure suits (with unbuttoned collared shirts that reveal both chest hair and a silver *Dota 2* medallion). Bruno's performance of nerd-inflected machismo operates not only in contrast to his more homogenous North American and European colleagues on the commentary desk (almost universally dressed in uniform-like hoodies and plaid button ups that year), but also offers another example of how racial difference operates within the culture of *Dota 2* apart from the narrative of China versus the world. At The International, Carlucci leveraged his outsider status and nationality to play the part of the court jester and eventually appeared, for example, in an Orientalized fortuneteller outfit and even as *Star Wars'* C-3PO in later tournaments (see Figure 5.14). Beyond wearing fluorescent costumes and adopting colorful affectations, the statistics Bruno presents while broadcasting are not particularly useful, or at least not useful in a traditional, positivist sense. Whereas Dota Academy, the Replay Parser, and the Fantasy League represent rigorous investigations into the untapped potential of data analytics in *Dota 2,* during The International the Statsman worked behind the scenes to produce statistical information while simultaneously undermining the authority of statistics.

Although Carlucci's performances can be read simply as quirky jokes or a defense mechanism against the inevitability of failed predictions, they also challenge the naive correlation between probabilistic projection and how the tournament actually unfolded. For example, at times Carlucci argued for statistics founded on elementary arithmetic errors: "You pick an Anti-Mage who has a 50% chance of winning. You pick a Lycan who has a 65% chance of winning. That makes . . . a 115% chance of winning. There's no way to lose!" (Valve 2012d). In another instance, statistics are culled from seemingly irrelevant correlations with racist punchlines: "Tobi, whenever he casts, he's 5–3 on China team's winning. Lumi is 5–5. But Ayesee whenever he casts he's 7–2 for China teams winning. So it's confirmed. Ayesee is secretly a Chinaman" (Valve 2012e). (As discussed earlier in the chapter, Chinese stereotypes and racism saturated The International.) Finally, Carlucci drew attention to the absurd specificity of certain statistical anomalies as a means of questioning the very possibility of generalizable or comparable actions and events. After a match between Evil Geniuses and TongFu the Statsman jokingly observed that "the problem with EG was a surplus of legs. Look at TongFu's lineup: Naga, no legs; Venomancer, no legs; Morphling, no legs; Enigma, no legs; Lina has two legs but she's flying so she doesn't use it. That's the strat right there" (Valve 2012f). Just as Rosencrantz and Guildenstern's coin landing on heads ninety-two times in a row is *improbable* but not *impossible,* Carlucci's deeply ironic and skeptical statistics suggest that anything is

Figure 5.14. A colorful character, Carlucci has performed as a fortuneteller, as *Star Wars'* C-3PO droid, in fan-made memes that edit his appearance to make him look like the Riddler from *Batman,* and also replaced Mark Zuckerberg's portrait in parodies of the poster from *The Social Network.*

possible, everything is equally meaningful, and nothing is exchangeable despite the projected probabilities.

Carlucci's statistics parody the supposed generality and predictive potential of quantitative data by suggesting that any given statistical record is absolutely specific to a given historical moment. Like Borges' cartographic critique of "exactitude in science," Bruno has conflated the statistical map with the historical territory. This kind of statistician is no longer interested in the probability of signal to noise, but in the significance of all noises. Following a "science of the exception" rather than that of the common denominator, the Statsman offers an example of 'pataphysical play in which the probability of an event is absolutely contingent with the event itself. Alfred Jarry (1911, 21–22), best known for his shocking and much-reviled play *Ubu Roi* (1896), defines 'pataphysics as

the science of the particular, despite the common opinion that the only science is that of the general. Pataphysics will examine the laws governing the exceptions . . . since the laws that are supposed to have been discovered in

the traditional universe are also correlations of exceptions, albeit more frequent ones, but in any case accidental data which, reduced to the status of
unexceptional exceptions, possess no longer even the virtue of originality.

In the tradition of Jarry's turn-of-the-century satire, Carlucci's jokes
speak to the impossibility of generality in physics and critique the Enlightenment dream of finally resolving the relation between reason and reality.
In this way they caution the viewer against the narrative potential of
numbers by a surrealist statsman. Carlucci's buffoonery constantly footnotes the tenuous relation between math and matter, *ratio* and *kinesis*. The
agony (and augury) of the statsman is the constant, nagging knowledge of
this philosophical tension. If, as Jarry (1911, 21) writes, 'pataphysics "is the
science of that which is superinduced upon metaphysics . . . extending as
far beyond metaphysics as the latter extends beyond physics," then where
are the 'patagames that extend beyond metagames?

Back in IG's booth, although Zheng "Faith" Hongda knew what *probably* should have happened in the second game of the winner's bracket
semifinals, he could not have predicted how Dendi's Rubick would turn
the Tidehunter against him and his team. In the end, although Na`Vi's
twenty-second victory has been lionized on forums and archived on
video sharing websites, their success in the second and third games of the
winner's bracket was ultimately a pyrrhic one. What *probably* should have
happened in the match *actually* happened across the greater *Dota* tournament. iG would go on to dominate the loser's bracket finals and return to
rematch Na`Vi for the grand prize. With very little fanfare and lots of safe,
highly calculated plays, iG won The International and a million dollars in
2012. And, in retrospect, Dendi's Turn of the Tide figured more as statistical anomaly in the face of a long, macro strategy that ultimately outpaced
the mechanical, micro movements of the Ukrainian team. Na`Vi won
the seventeen-second battle but iG won the million-dollar war. The far
less crowd-pleasing but overall more effective method of playing to the
numbers rather than to the audience or even to individual games is what
would ultimately take the million-dollar prize—and this result suited
Valve just fine. Beyond The International tournament, there was another
international game the company was winning.

Since the turn of the millennium, the Chinese Ministry of Culture has
enacted a ban "forbidding any company or individual to produce and

sell electronic game equipment and accessories to China" (Ashcroft 2010). Discussed in relation to Narcissa Wright's speedrunning practices in chapter 1 and 3, part an act of censorship (to "protect the mental and physical development of the nation's youth") and part protectionist economic strategy, the "console ban" deeply affected Chinese gaming in the 2000s, producing a profitable gray market of international goods, a host of alternative and after-market consoles,[55] a culture of both software and hardware piracy, and a boom in PC gaming (Clark 2013). With over a hundred million PC gamers in China—worth a whopping 6.8 billion dollars of the twenty-billion-dollar global market—both domestic and international publishers of MMO games and free-to-play web games were quick to capitalize on the fastest-growing market for PC games over the last decade (McNew 2014, DeCarlo 2013). Furthermore, freely downloadable mods like the original *DotA* were able to run on almost any PC given the age, popularity, and piracy of *Warcraft III*. As stated earlier, at its height in 2010 IceFrog (2010) estimated around 10 million Chinese *DotA* players (IceFrog 2010).

Thus, hiring IceFrog, rebuilding *DotA* as *Dota 2* in 2010, and then inviting five Chinese teams to compete in (and eventually win) The International in 2012 was not simply a way to generate enthusiasm among the Chinese players but was an important part of Valve's global strategy to expand their digital distribution platform, Steam, into China as a means to tap the country's PC gaming (and piracy) market. It is already estimated that 75 percent of *all* videogame purchases take place through Steam, but Valve has taken up the challenge of converting pirated games to purchased games in Russia and China through their "frictionless" marketplace (Edwards 2013).[56] Only a few months after iG won The International, Valve contracted East Asian publishers Perfect World and Nexon to publish and distribute *Dota 2* in China and Korea respectively. Though Valve cannot simply release Steam in China due to the country's stringent economic regulations, Perfect World's *Dota 2* client is driven, nonetheless, by the Steam backend. The undercurrency at the heart of The International is not the ebb and flow of Na`Vi's mechanical Turn of the Tide, nor is it the explosion of sales on the other side of the world—no, The Turn of the Tide is nothing less than the redefinition of the videogame from a leisure activity (a waste of time) to productivity (labor time). And the undercurrency in which Valve traffics is not fame, not profit, not entertainment, not fun (though these can be shored up), but productivity.

Welcome to Flatland

Before their incorporation in 2003 and well before their release of *Dota 2* a decade later, Valve was in the business of managing metagames. In 1996, Gabe Newell and Mike Harrington left their jobs at Microsoft to found a new company based on three undervalued business strategies. In their next venture, the two "Microsoft millionaires" planned to (1) invest in the exponentially decreasing costs of communicating with customers, (2) acquire and retain the most expensive employees instead of outsourcing, and, eventually, (3) capture player productivity through videogames—a genre of productivity software not entirely different from the Windows operating systems that Newell and Harrington worked on at Microsoft (Newell 2013). The duo's counterintuitive business plan arose after they noticed something astounding: even with an install base of thirty million PCs in the mid-1990s, Windows 3.0 was only the *second* most used piece of software in America. Towering above the operating system was the shareware release of *Doom* (1993), the early first-person shooter developed by id software. Although most remember *Doom*'s brutal 3D graphics and blazingly fast gameplay, Newell (2013) still marvels at the illogical idea that "somehow the largest software company in the world was being out-distributed by a twelve-person company in Mesquite, Texas. . . . *Doom* [had] a completely different approach to connecting users with value." If a company like id could stand on even footing with Microsoft, suddenly the world seemed pretty flat.

Following in the footsteps of Michael Abrash, who left Microsoft in 1995 to work on id's next game, *Quake* (1996), in 1996 Newell and Harrington quit their jobs and licensed the Quake Engine to begin building what would become the Valve's first game: *Half-Life* (1998). As anticipated in chapter 2, *Half-Life* is not just a first-person shooter operating according to the same gameplay idioms as "Quake and Doom"; it is also a metagame made *within Quake* and *about Doom*—or at least *Doom's* distribution model. Through its dissemination via a not-quite-frictionless, early version of Steam released first in 2003, *Half-Life* functioned like a sequel to *Doom* not only in terms of its genre conventions, but because it attempted to emulate *Doom*'s ubiquitous dissemination and id's flattened approach to "connecting users with value." In the late nineties, Valve sought to become an economic sequel to id and *Half-Life* would be their *Doom*, a vector connecting the company directly to their customers and a major platform for generating productive play in the form of metagames.

By actively courting customers *cum* content producers and mining the productivity of their player base, Valve's history of products coincides with the acquisition not only of popular mods, but the players responsible for making them. *Team Fortress 2* is a class-based multiplayer deathmatch mod originally released in 2007 as part of Valve's *The Orange Box* collection, but was only released after the company hired John Cook, Robin Walker, and Ian Caughley, the original team that made the *Team Fortress* mod for *Quake* in 1996. *Counter-Strike*, the globally popular competitive shooter, began as a *Half-Life* mod by Minh "Gooseman" Le and Jess "Cliffe" Cliffe in 1999 before Valve hired the pair of programmers to institutionalize their work at the company in 2000. *Portal*'s (2007) revolutionary mechanics started as a student project at DigiPen Institute in Seattle titled *Narbacular Drop* (2005) before Valve hired the whole team along with writers Erik Wolpaw and Chet Faliszek,[57] who worked to adapt the gameplay to both the company's proprietary Source Engine and the *Half-Life* universe. And *Dota 2*, of course, had an extensive history within Blizzard's *Warcraft III* before Valve hired IceFrog and Eul to remake it hero by hero in Source. Very few of Valve's innovations center around the creation of original, in-house IP; instead, they have developed a business model based on colonizing, expropriating, and assimilating metagames into a framework of benevolent capitalism.[58] The company typifies the post-Fordist corporation designed not around the creation of new products *ex nihilo*, but the organization of a social factory that extends beyond the labor of employees to the leisure of customers. As Gabe Newell (2013) is fond of saying, "the only company we've ever met that kicks our ass is our customers. We'll go up against Bungie, or Blizzard, or anybody but we won't try to compete with our own user base, because we already know we're going to lose." Why compete with the work of metagamers when you can organize their communities, analyze their practices, absorb their modifications, and profit from it?

For McKenzie Wark, the locus of power no longer rests with those who control the mode of production, but lies instead in the management of the vectors, connections, and networks organizing information—from the financial instruments responsible for high frequency trading to the social media platforms that collect user-generated content. In an information economy, the bourgeois capitalist has been replaced by a new ruling order that Wark (2004, 21) calls the "vectoral class." After first introducing the term in *A Hacker Manifesto*, in *Telesthesia* Wark (2012, 72) asks,

> What if the ruling class of our time were not exactly capitalist any more, but more properly vectoralist? What if a fraction of that ruling class acquired its political-economic power through the ownership and control of vectors along which financial information flows, and with it the flows of that information, not to mention stocks of these weird para-things, these instruments of a purely digital private property, with somewhat attenuated relations back to referents in other natures, other worlds.

The vectoral class represents a new species of managers who do not simply control the mode of production, but crucially, mediate connection, dissemination, and access to information. In an era in which production and consumption frequently take place in the same act, in which Marx's use value and exchange value are no longer mutually dependent antinomies, companies like Valve generate profit not only by making and selling games but through the capture, steering, and control of information flows. Whether appropriating metagames by hiring successful modders, building economic infrastructures to cultivate an international e-sport, or mining Steam stats to predict future sales, Valve's business model is based on locating those practices that exist outside the market and monetizing relations that previously were regarded as having no value (even though this extra-market activity operates as the precondition for exchange in the first place).[59] As Wark (2013) states "the new stage of commodification is less about extracting surplus value from labor as extracting surplus information from play. It extracts value by offering information for free, but extracting more information in return—surplus information." The vectoral class does not traffic in fixed capital, but instead profits from continuous and promiscuous exchange within a flattened economy. And nowhere is this flat world better represented than in Valve's business model and corporate culture.

"Welcome to Flatland." Valve's (2012, 37) official *Handbook for New Employees* opens with an invitation to join a company without higher-ups, corporate ladders, or corner offices. Like Gilles Deleuze and Félix Guattarri's (1987, 5) declaration in *A Thousand Plateaus*, Valve decided they were "tired of trees" and "stop[ped] believing in trees, roots, and . . . all of arborescent culture." Instead, Valve attempts to operate rhizomatically, starting with their office space (see Figure 5.15). In terms of a flat, physical space, the company's headquarters in Bellevue, Washington is famous for its open floor plan and reconfigurable desks on wheels that represent the effervescent flexibility of affective, informatic, creative knowledge work and the dream of a job that is not work.[60] In the *Handbook*, Valve (2012) suggests new employees "think of those wheels as a symbolic reminder that you should always be considering where you could move yourself to be more valuable." The flat office space symbolizes Valve's flattened corporate hierarchy. Valve has no management, no quality assurance, no marketing department, and no job titles. Newell (2013) argues that much like offices, "titles are actually [Valve's] enemy rather than something that makes them more productive," and the *Handbook* confirms, "we don't have any management" (Valve 2012h). Following the company motto, "boss-free since 1996," every employee determines for herself how to be productive and generate value (Valve 2012h).[61]

Valve's spatial and hierarchical flatness, expressed by their wheel-friendly workplace and advertised in their *Handbook*, is a tool for attracting, acquiring, generating, and retaining valuable employees. When Newell and Harrington organized the company in the mid-1990s, they not only hoped to exploit the exponentially decreasing friction between producer and consumer (implicitly understanding that their player base was ultimately the more significant substrate of outsourced labor), but began investing, counterintuitively, in the most valuable employees instead of outsourcing cheap labor. In 1996, the two "became convinced . . . that everybody was going in the wrong direction [by outsourcing their employees] for the lowest cost English language speakers in the world" (Newell 2013). So Valve decided to buy "the most expensive talent that was out there . . . [because] those were the people that were least correctly valued" (Newell 2013). Newell (2013) clarifies, "By talent, which is a word I hate, I just mean the ability to be productive." Valve's model of value flattens all activity and energy into a single, dereferentialized and abstracted metric: not money, but productivity.

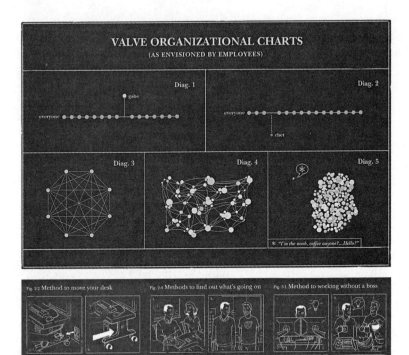

Figure 5.15. Where Figure 1-3 from Valve's *Handbook for New Employees* does away with vertical hierarchy, Figures 2-2, 2-4, and 3-1 offer 1950s-inflected illustrations of the company's fattened management philosophy.

For Valve, productivity is measured in two ways. First, the pure volume of output is quantified. For example, "in IBM in the 1980s, typical productivity would be 1000 debugged, shipped lines of code per year. . . . Whereas when [Valve] was shipping *Half-Life 1*, one employee, Yahn Bernier, was shipping 4k lines of code per day" (Newell 2013). Beyond lines of code, Newell notes, "Even though it's easy to see there is huge variation [of productivity] in software programmers, there was probably that same variation in a lot of other roles." So, second, on an internal level, productivity is peer reviewed to assess employee contributions and award bonuses based on four main categories:

1. Skill Level/Technical Ability: How difficult and valuable are the kinds of problems you solve?
2. Productivity/Output: How much shippable (not necessarily shipped to outside customers), valuable, finished work did you get done?
3. Group Contribution: How much do you contribute to studio process, hiring, integrating people into the team, improving workflow, amplifying your colleagues, or writing tools used by others?
4. Product Contribution: How much do you contribute at a larger scope than your core skill? (Valve 2012h, 30–32)

Although the *Handbook* introduces new employees to the company's culture and philosophy, Valve's assessment of value ideologically extends beyond the Flatland located in Bellevue, Washington. There are about 330 employees at Valve, but the productivity and value of the players is as significant as the contributions of those on salary. One could imagine a fifth category added to Valve's "Stack Ranking" to account for play.

Valve's nonhierarchic, flattened philosophy not only applies to the architecture of their office and corporate hierarchy at Bellevue, but also informs the company's approach to game design.[62] The salutation "Welcome to Flatland" applies just as much to its community of players as to the employees. Few of Valve's games originate in-house but they do not outsource. In the case of *Dota*, they chose to *insource* a preexistent development team, flattening play into a form of productivity that could then be measured in terms of the work logs of any Valve employee. In an article in *PC Gamer*, Erik Johnson (Thursten 2013, 40) outlines Valve's relationship to the *Dota* players: "We look at every single person in the game as creating user-generated content. . . . A person who just plays the game is generating some value for the other nine people playing." The line between Valve's data-driven game design philosophy and data-driven economics is porous. Players are no longer thought of simply as customers for whom the company must deliver, but as fellow producers within a gamespace of global capital who voluntarily generate surplus. By offering three thousand unique applications to over 75 million active users, generating more Internet traffic than most countries as one of the largest bandwidth consumers in the world, and growing about 50 percent a year since 1996, for Valve play is not only a byproduct, but a valuable resource.

Whereas *Dota*'s producers see play as an undercurrency of flattened productivity, in turn many players see the ability to financialize play is one of the appealing aspects of the *Dota 2*:

> *Dota 2* is built around these transactions, beginning at the individual player level, passing through the Workshop—where user-created cosmetic items begin their journey to the in-game store, earning six-figure sums for some—all the way to the competitive scene, dispersed among dozens of tournament showrunners who sell tickets and merchandise through the game client. These surrounding systems are a vital part of *Dota 2*'s identity—they're game mechanics too, in a sense. (Thursten 2013, 41)

With the cosmetic markets associated with *Team Fortress 2, Counter-Strike: Global Offensive,* and *Dota 2,* Valve has created an economic system that flourishes through the contributions of both local employees in Bellevue and remote players on Steam. In 2013, for example, Stephanie "Anuxi" Everett was able to quit her job and make a living modeling original *Dota 2* cosmetic items while collector PAADA sold a rare "Ethereal Flame Pink War Dog Courier" for $38,000 within the same market (Cameron 2013; PAADA 2013). With Valve taking a cut of the tens of thousands of dollars circulating between individual players (not to mention twenty million dollar collective prize pools), it would appear the metagame is quite profitable.

Whether working at Valve or playing *Dota 2,* "money needs to flow as a signaling tool. . . . In order for people to really assess that what they're doing is valuable or not you need currency" (Newell 2013). Rather than treat money as the ultimate product, it has become an integral part of a generative, productive process. Newell (2013) tempers any claims of success with a simple question: "But is [Valve] interesting beyond being another company that makes a bunch of money?" Money is not merely an outcome, but has become a core aspect of Valve's game design philosophy. No longer simply a medium of exchange, money is the equipment with which both the company and its customers play.[63] The mechanics of money, the informatics of money, and the communicability of money is meaningful to Valve. Beyond the flattening of an office space, the flattening of a corporate hierarchy, the flattening of software design, and the flattening of play, Valve is also flattening one videogame to another as a means of building a metaverse in which money can flow to the most valuable parts of the network.

Most games exist independent of one another, as magic software circles or secret Internet enclaves whose forms of production (virtual currency or otherwise) are often imagined as incommensurable with one another. As anyone moving from one MMO to another or switching e-sports knows, exchanging content or migrating production between two games is the equivalent of trying to mail a postcard to Mars—content is returned to sender to waste away within an abandoned virtual world. In the absence of a flattened gamespace, videogames are designed with what Newell (2013) describes as a "whimsical notion of property rights," because the labor time invested and value generated in a game easily obsolesces and cannot be translated between platforms. Steam is designed to "plumb [the] notion of both ownership and authorship throughout the entire system. So [a player will] be able to create something in one game and exchange it for value with somebody else" (Newell 2013). Rather than attempt to create a "game of games" in the form of a universal game engine—a totalizing metaverse[64] representing the sum of all games (although Steam certainly aspires to this standardization), money has become the general equivalent. Money is the code through which Valve is building its metagame of metagames.

The act of making money is also tied to the generation of alternative forms of currency. Considering the markets surrounding the *Team Fortress 2* hats and *Dota* cosmetics dropped randomly in-game, bundled with other purchases, or available for limited times in their online store, Newell (2013) ponders some of the ethical and practical issues surrounding the production of money and markets in Valve's games:

> We started to see things like inflation. We started to see deflation. We started to see users creating their own versions of currencies, mediums of exchange. Countries started to create regulatory structures so in Korea you actually have to create the equivalent of a W-4 form for your players to account for the virtual income they get in playing your game. . . . Should we increase the drop rate for those customers to offset the implicit sales or income tax that they're having? And what do we do about purchase price parity? Should we adjust drop rates to provide welfare to people who are playing in lower incomes or do we drop the value of their drops to reflect the fact that they can trade their hats for cheeseburgers?

Once players begin to create value and that value can be translated between different domains, there is nothing to stop the equivalency of in-game object to real-world goods and services. So, what at first seemed to be a game design problem becomes a moral, ethical, and political problem within Valve's economic Flatland. As Steam continues to extend its functions to grammatize material platforms and capture attention through biometric devices like the Steam Controller, console-like hardware platforms like Steam Machines, Linux-based operating systems like Steam OS, crowdsourcing spaces for developing new games like Steam Greenlight, and even player-driven prediction markets like Steam Curators, Flatland becomes Flatworld—something akin to what McKenzie Wark (2007, 1) labels the "gamespace"—the smooth topology of global capital in which everything is different *in the same way* and abstract exchange proliferates without the friction of play.

Much like Anuxi, PAATA, Carlucci, or IceFrog himself produce value through the way they play *Dota 2,* one of the three featured players in Valve's 2014 documentary *Free to Play,* Na`Vi's Dendi is described by Gabe Newell as one of the most high-value *Dota* players not only for his virtuosity, but for the value he adds to e-sports as an entertaining personality. According to Newell (2013), "being a really good player is a super valuable thing for the community. And the challenge isn't that you created value, the challenge is coming up with the monetization method." So rather than selling YouTube ads, hawking Twitch subscriptions, or establishing a PayPal tip jar (though Dendi invests in these forms of monetization as well), Valve's pennants and tournaments offer a possibility for financialized play within the Flatland. Dendi's hobby has become a way of life, a metagame that turned into a moneygame once his value had been abstracted and broken down into discrete units and made profitable within the world of Steam.

Similarly, Valve's employees have claimed that *Dota 2* originated as "a post-work diversion" (Thursten 2013, 37). Gabe Newell himself, who confessed to playing *Dota* around twenty hours a week during its development, has experienced the same kind of flattened productivity throughout his life. Newell has been described as "brilliant and wildly productive" and former colleagues recall him "doing 30 products a year" (Barret, 2005). At the end of a 2013 lecture at the University of Texas, Newell briefly turned to a discussion of his own hobbies, sheepishly admitting that even his play tends to eventually become work. Newell (2013) explains,

> I have a million dollar CNC [milling machine]. . . . [At first] I thought, oh good, I'm going to have a hobby, it's going to have nothing to do with my

day job. Well, the reality is all the problems related to machining are software problems. They're problems of how do you have engagement angles that look a lot like rendering problems. The difference between carving something out of aluminum and drawing something in 3D space are astonishingly similar. And the way that you keep this thing busy is you standardize a lot of stuff and create a network interface so jobs can flow through this thing. And this hobby of mine ends up looking like *Counter-Strike* in terms of the sets of decisions you would make to improve it.

Recalling his work on Windows at Microsoft and Steam at Valve, Newell perversely finds himself confronting non-standardized interfaces and attempting to maximize the efficiency of industrial processes in his spare time. Newell's attempt to escape the circuits of productivity ultimately falls flat.

In 1961, Roger Caillois (2001, 32) argued that "industrial civilization has given birth to a special form of *ludus,* the hobby, a secondary and gratuitous activity, undertaken and pursued for pleasure." For Caillois (2001, 32), the hobby is "a compensation for the injury to personality caused by bondage to work" and "the hobby of the worker-turned-artisan readily takes the form of constructing complete scale models of the machines in the fabrication" in which the worker ultimately "avenges himself upon reality, but in a positive and creative way." This homeopathic act of reproduction as revenge against labor within a distinct sphere of leisure (that simultaneously serves to reinforce and reconstitute the system) no longer applies. Under a vectoral regime there is no hobby. There is no fun, there is no work: only productivity for player, laborer, and even millionaire manager alike.

Two Tide Hunters

From wargaming to *Warhammer* to *Warcraft,* the tension between *ratio* (e.g., digital quantity, numeral, abstraction) and *kinesis* (e.g., analog quality, motion, materiality) operates in all games and is activated and allegorized through the informatic play of real-time strategy games. Steven Connor (2011, 171) reminds us, "Just as probability can neither be distinguished from nor wholly identified with number, so number can neither be extricated from nor entirely exhaust play. Probability is the play of number that number itself makes possible." If, according to Claude Shannon, information can be defined by the probability of signal to noise, *Dota 2*'s game design is extremely noisy, information rich, and constantly tending toward states of stability. Instead of entropically evolving more explicit genre conventions or mechanical specializations (like, perhaps, Riot's *League of Legends* or the multitude of contemporary *Dota*-likes and even *Dota*-like-likes), IceFrog's approach to game design is glacial in the sense that *Dota*'s evolution has stalled at the cusp of a phase change—between genres—where the immense possibility space offers a wealth of signals that the player must pick out of the noise. The homeostasis of *Dota*'s *adaptability,* rather than any one specific adaptation, is what allows so many metagames to proliferate as different players explore the possibilities of a noisy game.

Despite the human experience of these freely chosen signals—the material, historical, and phenomenal instance of play—videogames like *Dota* and sports like baseball still cut. Like capital, digital games grammatize quality into digital quantities so particulate (in terms of time, space, and scale) that, on some level, the statistical relation between game and play escapes human experience entirely. Bernard Stiegler calls this form of proletarianization "systemic stupidity" as players no longer know what game they are playing. Similarly, Mark Hansen (2015, 55) argues that "in the face of contemporary data capitalism, time itself becomes an agent of surplus value extraction that operates within a system structurally dedicated to exploiting the imbalance between microtemporal, machinic sensibility and human consciousness." Both Stiegler and Hansen clarify the philosophical stakes of Newell's managerial strategies that cut human consciousness out of the loop to better serve the production of quantitative information and accelerate the rate at which labor time is turned into abstract productivity. The metagame, while continuing to function as a human history, no longer seems to matter as human activity itself is flattened by an ever more granular statistical average operating beneath the surface of experience.

In response, different aesthetic practices have been adopted to counteract the explosion of information and the precarity of human subjectivity within digital game spaces. Michael Krukar's one thousand FPS video applies traditional narrative and hermeneutic forms of knowledge to numeric figures, naively correlating consciousness and cutting. Bruno Carlucci's commentary, on the other hand, attempts to resist a narrative or conscious conception of numeral as a disruptive, aesthetic form of spectatorship that articulates the disconnect between experience and abstraction. Despite these approaches to spectatorship, Valve generates value from every interaction within their flatworld. Like *Dota*, Steam is designed around a radical generality and homeostatic adaptability. The scale of each grammatizing function within Valve's network is so small that rather than conventional, corporate modes of productivity, Valve produces not only *Dota*-like games, but a *Dota*-like *economy*.

Rather than specialize, Valve's "*Dota* economics" generalizes and becomes not merely a metonymy for but operates as a fractalized symbiote with the wider circulatory system of Steam. In the same way that steam is invisible and cannot be seen, Valve functions as the valve that controls the flow of productivity and profit, of both currency and the much larger undercurrents that take the form of player labor time, server space, and bandwidth. Within this digital flatworld, play has been cut up and the immaterial labor of thousands of players has been quantified. The sweat of players' brows within this emergent ecology precipitates into Steam's atmospheric media. This computational vapor becomes the primary energy source powering a distributed global machine, a world system designed around a ludic mode of production. Within this steam-powered ideology, Valve and value are synonymous.

Hearkening back to medieval moments in history prior to the emergence of industrial capitalism in European culture, when the "v" and the "u" had yet to be divided into distinct linguistic operations, Valve has created a system of neofeudalism in which the distinctions between work and play, leisure and labor, no longer hold water. Indifferent to such Protestant moralizing that compartmentalizes life into different categories, Valve oversees an agnostic economic system in which player-tenants are not farming for gold or money or even for fun, but to be productive despite themselves—a form of data capitalism that captures player attention and productivity on both macro- and microtemporal scales. In a world where the ability to manipulate an avatar can turn you into a millionaire and millionaires find themselves thinking about steel fabrication in terms of first-person shooters, Valve embodies the new value-form.

Within the undercurrency of untapped productivity, managers like Gabe Newell and players like Dendi are tide hunters. Each hunts, speculatively, for a certain kind of undercurrent. The undercurrent cannot be seen, felt, or experienced because each tide hunter is, in their own way, adrift in a sea of data. The undercurrent they seek, though fluid, is not aqueous. Not an undercurrent, but an undercurrency, a deep-seated form of finance capital at the heart of each of their respective games. The undercurrency moves the tide hunter. It rises and falls, yet its influence seems as distant as that of the moon. The waxing and waning of these abstract liquidities is beyond the horizon of human experience as we, humanity, are marooned at sea.

Metagame 5

Tide Hunter

Tide Hunter is a data visualization application designed to process statistical output from Bruno "Statsman" Carlucci's *Dota 2* (2013) replay parser. To produce *Tide Hunter,* data was collected during "The Turn of the Tide," a seventeen-second upset that has since been regarded as one of the most important plays in the history of *Dota 2.* Within the visualization, this information is repurposed to drive alternative representations of e-sports and dive beneath the spectacular surface of Valve's software. Set within an aqueous landscape in which the eponymous Tidehunter's abilities were famously turned against him in just seventeen seconds, the game offers players a navigable interface for exploring the micro-temporal operations that took place during the match between Natus Vincere and Invictus at The International in 2012 (see Figure 5.16). To download *Tide Hunter,* go to http://manifold.umn.edu/tidehunter.

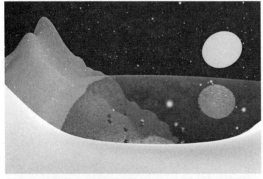

Figure 5.16. *Tide Hunter* is an original metagame by Patrick LeMieux and Stephanie Boluk that visualizes The Turn of the Tide as an aqueous landscape for the Tidehunter to explore.

SIX

Breaking the Metagame

Feminist Spoilsports and Magic Circle Jerks

In the game of patriarchy, women are not the opposing
team, they are the ball.

—Anita Sarkeesian, Twitter

The figure of the spoil-sport is most apparent in boys'
games. The little community does not enquire whether the
spoil-sport is guilty of defection because he dares not enter
into the game or because he is not allowed to. Rather it
does not recognize "not being allowed" and calls it "not
daring."

—Johan Huizinga, *Homo Ludens*

Standing in front of a packed audience at the Sydney Opera House
on March 8, International Women's Day 2015,[1] feminist media critic
Anita Sarkeesian (2015) admitted

What I couldn't say is "fuck you." To the thousands of men who turned their
misogyny into a game, in which gendered slurs, death and rape threats are
weapons used to take down the big bad villain (which in this case is me).
My life is not a game. I've been harassed and threatened for going on three
years with no end in sight. And all because I dared to question the obvious,
self-evident sexism running rampant in the games industry.

The game Sarkeesian referenced didn't come in a box. It wasn't on sale at
some electronics superstore or available for download on digital distribution services. Her harassment wasn't protected by any intellectual
property laws, end user license agreements, or digital rights management. Witch hunting, vote brigading, forum raiding, email spamming,
Internet stalking, and threats of violence cannot be easily reduced to an
advertising campaign, a packaged product, or packets of program data.

Although the metagame never precisely aligns with or completely reduces to the mechanisms of digital media, all videogames are surrounded by and saturated with metagames. The social, political, and economic metagame that Sarkeesian referenced in Sydney determines much of how we play videogames, make videogames, and break videogames. Her words are a sobering reminder that not all metagames are good, and that many are downright toxic. As Sarkeesian (Kolhatkar 2014) testifies,

> Harassment is the background radiation of my life. . . . It is a factor in every decision I make. Any time I tweet something, or make a post, I'm always thinking about it. When I post our videos, it's a consideration. It affects where I go, and how I behave, and how I feel walking down the street every day.

From trash talking to verbal abuse in arcades; griefing to cyberbullying in online games; trolling to hate speech on web forums; and from pizza bombing to DDoSing,[2] doxxing,[3] swatting,[4] and stalking through locative, biometric, and other forms of identifying media, the metagames that both emerge from and envelop videogames contain varying amounts of toxicity, sometimes reaching pH levels so high that they become uninhabitable. If media, as Mark Hansen (2006a, 297) writes, constitute an "environment for life" and metagames function as an environment for games, what happens when the environment becomes unlivable? How did Sarkeesian find herself in such an acidic ecology, playing a toxic metagame that toyed with her life?

Two years earlier, on May 17, 2012, Sarkeesian (2012a) launched a crowd-funding campaign on Kickstarter requesting donations to finance a series of YouTube videos intended to "explore, analyze and deconstruct some of the most common tropes and stereotypes of female characters in games." Following her original *Tropes vs. Women* (2011) videos, which analyzed conventional plot devices and recurring narrative representations of women in film and television such as "The Manic Pixie Dream Girl," "Women in Refrigerators," "The Smurfette Principle," and "The Mystical Pregnancy" among others, Sarkeesian hoped to raise enough money to increase her production quality and get paid to shoot a second series called *Tropes vs. Women in Video Games* (2013–) aimed explicitly at the gendered and sexist storytelling conceits common to videogames such as the "Damsel in Distress," "Ms. Male Character," "The Fighting Fuck Toy," and "The Sexy Sidekick," to name a few.

The first episode of the series, released on March 17, 2013, defines the damsel in distress as a "plot device in which a female character is placed in a perilous situation from which she cannot escape on her own and must be rescued by a male character, usually providing a core incentive or motivation for the protagonist's quest" (Sarkeesian and McIntosh 2013). Whereas the video documents individual instances of the trope in over sixty games, Sarkeesian's *Bits of Tropes vs. Women in Video Games* Tumblr image blog demonstrates the scale and ubiquity of damsels in distress by archiving an additional five hundred examples (including many of the videogames discussed in this book such as *Donkey Kong, Super Mario Bros., The Legend of Zelda, Metal Gear Solid, StarCraft II, and Super Meat Boy*). The apparent thoughtlessness and obvious frequency with which this trope is deployed highlight the default subject position through which many videogames are both produced and consumed, a standard way of playing that tolerates clichéd depictions of women and throwaway plotlines. Although Sarkeesian's definitions, diagnosis, and documentation are not particularly controversial and her modest $6,000 funding goal was quietly met within the first twenty-four hours of the Kickstarter, the backlash was extreme.

Before the campaign ever finished and before the first video was released, on June 7, 2012, Sarkeesian (2012b) posted a grim update on her Kickstarter's project page:

> As some of you may be aware, this project has recently been subject to a coordinated online harassment effort waged by various online video game forums vowing to "take me down." I always expect a certain level of harassment when discussing gender issues online. This time however, it's a more organized and sustained effort than I've experienced before. The intimidation and harassment effort has included a torrent of misogyny and hate speech on my YouTube video, repeated vandalizing of the Wikipedia page about me, organized efforts to flag my YouTube videos as "terrorism," as well as many threatening messages sent through Twitter, Facebook, Kickstarter, email and my own website. These messages and comments have included everything from the typical sandwich and kitchen "jokes" to threats of violence, death, sexual assault and rape. All that plus an organized attempt to report this project to Kickstarter and get it banned or defunded.

Rather than lose funding, over the course of a week the number of sup-porters and total donations to *Tropes vs. Women in Videogames* increased tenfold in solidarity with Sarkeesian. The Kickstarter soared from 648 to 5,545 backers and from $17,171 to $158,922—figures that further gal-vanized and radicalized the campaign's opponents. From bomb threats at the fourteenth annual Game Developers Choice Awards when Sar-keesian won the Ambassador Award in March 2014[5] to anonymous threats that included not only her home address but also her parents' address in August the same year, the torrent of abuse only intensified as the project progressed over the years.

One of the most disturbing incidents occurred on October 14, 2014 when multiple faculty and staff of University of Utah, including Ann Austin, the director of the Center for Women and Gender Studies, received an email threatening that a "Montreal Massacre style attack" would take place if Sarkeesian was permitted to speak on campus. The email was signed "Marc Lépine" and describes the man who murdered fourteen women at École Polytechnique de Montréal on December 6, 1989 as a "hero to men everywhere for standing up to the toxic influence of feminism on Western masculinity" (Cimaron 2014). This citation of Lépine references not only one of the deadliest school shootings, but a mass murderer who specifically targeted women studying technology and enrolled in an engineering school.[6] The fact that Sarkeesian is Cana-dian and produced the *Tropes vs. Women* series of videos at York Uni-versity in Toronto was apparently not lost on her harassers. A month before he was elected prime minister, even Justin Trudeau (2015) went so far as to identify "video game misogyny in popular culture" as an urgent social issue for Canada.[7] When threats of violence are made on social media and sent to game developers and critics, when social secu-rity numbers and banking information are released online, when uni-versities must install metal detectors for public talks, and when world leaders are addressing the ongoing violence occurring in, on, around, and through videogames, the metagame doesn't seem like a game anymore.

Just as the term *metagame* has been deployed to describe a large and diffuse category of play occurring alongside videogames, it has also been used as a label for Sarkeesian's videos and public outspokenness as well as a shorthand for the ongoing harassment campaign surrounding her work. Some players doubt the relevance of criticism and claim the metagame is a distraction from the games themselves: "Neither side actually cares about gameplay. Every fuck involved in this conflict of interest only seems to care about the meta game and calling other people out" (McJobless 2014). Others are in denial about the toxicity of the community and incredulous that the metagame of harassment is worth reporting: "It seems like every month someone has to shout 'OMG SOMEONE SENT ME A MEAN LETTER!' [sic] . . . and then we have to go right back to playing the meta game" (Pring 2015). In an article for *Ars Technica,* Casey Johnston (2014) laments the similarity between Sarkeesian's plight and the tropes she critiques: "It is, on a sad meta level, a real-life version of what Sarkeesian discusses in 'Women as Background Decoration Part 2': women being treated as less-than, harassed and harangued out of the conversation, in service to a different, 'bigger' problem. And every time it happens, it advances the goals of the most poisonous 'gamers.'" Games researcher Megan Condis (2014) also noticed that the harassment itself is a gendered game: "The trolls see these campaigns as skirmishes in a grand metagame, one that pervades every social circle in which gamers can be found. This game serves as an on-going test of worthiness for those who want to identify as 'gamers' and it, too, is profoundly gendered."[8]

Apart from using the term *metagame* as a label for the broader debate about sexism in the videogame industry as well as Sarkeesian's continued harassment, in the aftermath of the Kickstarter campaign original software was also produced featuring her likeness. One abhorrent example, *Beat Up Anita Sarkeesian* (2012) by Benjamin Daniel, features a slideshow in which Photoshopped portraits of Sarkeesian are progressively battered and bloodied with each mouse click. By contrast, Matt Thorson's *TowerFall: The Dark World* (2013)[9] celebrates the critic's contributions to the games industry by including an alternate design for the Blue Archer which sports Sarkeesian's signature plaid shirt and hoop earrings (see Figure 6.1). Whereas these examples explicitly invoke the concept of metagaming—either through the direct use of the term or by producing games about Sarkeesian's battle against sexism—there is also an often unstated, implicit metagame that governs the play of ideology in, on, around, and through videogames.

The implied, default, or standard metagame (first discussed in chapter 2) not only trains players to consume software in particular, often narrowly defined ways but also conflates how we play videogames with videogames as a black box and commodity fetish. Like the magic circle, these concepts reduce complex material, historical, economic, and political

Figure 6.1. Although numerous attempts have been made to smear Sarkeesian's image online, the alternate Blue Archer design in *TowerFall* (right) celebrates *Tropes vs. Women in Videogames* by referencing her signature hoop earrings and plaid shirt (left). Image courtesy of Matt Thorson, 2015 (right).

realities to idealized, serialized, exchangeable, and easily consumable products. As such, the rules of the standard metagame—often suggested by the design and dissemination of digital technologies—take the form of cultural conventions and unspoken assumptions about how to engage videogames. We play the standard metagame any time we pre-order, purchase, and progress through a piece of software. It's the metagame we play when we don't think we are playing a metagame. Guided by technical conventions and conspicuous consumption, the standard metagame assumes that videogames should be executed on approved hardware platforms; displayed at certain specified frame rates in accordance with video standards; interfaced with through official and unmodified controllers; experienced by a normative binocular, bidextrous, bipedal body performing freely and without distraction; enjoyed for their own sake and without recourse to outside elements; and completed according to their intended design.[10]

Of course purchasing and playing a videogame is never this frictionless a process. There is always some kind of metagame at work in even the most common gaming activities. Not all metagames disrupt the operations or radically change the rules of the game. Yet the standard metagame continues to obfuscate all manner of practical play, conflating voluntary choice with involuntary mechanics. As a result, twiddling dual thumbsticks with two thumbs; viewing the display straight on from a certain distance; and even progressing in the game by scrolling left to right, accumulating points, unlocking content, and reaching the credits are voluntary choices but have become tacitly understood as the "normal" or "correct" way to play. These standard forms of play not only disavow their status as a metagame, but, in doing so, inhibit the production of more diverse forms of play. The standard metagame is an *anti-metagaming metagame*. The way in which this standard play conforms to and is rewarded by the ergonomic interfaces, authored design, advertising campaigns, and commodity form of videogames as a mass medium while disavowing their own existence is precisely how software encloses play as a cultural practice to become its ideological avatar.

When operating as the ideological avatar of play (formulated in chapter 1), videogames privatize and obfuscate the metagame by enclosing it within mechanical equipment, electronic appliances, software packages, and legal documents. Entangled with videogames as a mass medium and as a digital technology, play's avatar incorporates the fantasies and fallacies of the twenty-first-century technical imaginary. As a result, the standard metagame reinforces the techno-utopian belief in the progressivist and teleological upgrade path, the escapist fantasy of sensory and cognitive immersion within virtual realities, the ideal of a magic circle that levels the playing field and guarantees fair competition, the postgender and postracial hope that in the game all players are equal and can be quantitatively compared, the authority of an implied author whose creative choices are autonomous from historical or political contexts, the libertarian dream that the market is not only free but just and that "voting with your wallet" is democratic, and the nostalgia for a collective identity based on consuming videogames (rather than making metagames). Taken together, this suite of beliefs both structure and are structured by the "right" way to play and could be called the *ideology of the ideological avatar of play*. Not unlike other forms of power, this standard metagame disavows its own existence. In the same way male privilege (as well as white privilege, heteronormativity, ableism, etc.) has historically been produced largely through its ability to circulate as an unstated default subject position, so too does the standard metagame draw its power from the fact that it is easy to take for granted and easy to forget that it is only one metagame among many. As argued at the beginning of this book, bringing the practice of play into alignment with the technological black box and commodified mass medium is the greatest trick the videogame industry ever pulled—a magic trick that makes the magic circle materialize.

When we began writing *Metagaming* we thought that a naive or orthodox belief in this kind of magic circle was a straw man—that no player could be so dogmatically utopian in their approach to videogames. In a frequently cited passage from *Homo Ludens,* Johan Huizinga (1949, 10, 12) suggests that "all play moves and has its being within a playground marked off beforehand either materially or ideally . . . within which special rules obtain" and that "inside the circle of the game the laws and customs of ordinary life no longer count."[11] The magic circle is a useful heuristic for differentiating leisure from labor, play from practice, and games from life, but it is also fairly easy to challenge. Countless game theorists have critiqued this popular concept by arguing that the magic circle is porous, that "we cannot say that games are magic circles, where the ordinary rules of life do not apply" and "there is a gap in the magic circle through which players carry subjectivity in and out of the game space. If the magic circle were really some kind of isolated antithesis to the world, it would never be possible to access it at all" (Consalvo 2009, 416; Bogost 2006, 135). As one of the authors responsible for popularizing Huizinga's theory in *Rules of Play* (2003), Eric Zimmerman (2012) has gone so far as to suggest that the belief in the magic circle is one of the most pervasive "straw men" in game studies and that debunking the concept has become a "rite of passage" for many scholars even though no such "magic circle jerk" exists. Zimmerman (2012) writes,

> I have made a harsh caricature of the magic circle jerk—as a silly superstructuralist that dogmatically believes in the truth of a hard-edged magic circle. Perhaps I have replaced the myth of the magic circle with a myth of my own—the impossibly idiotic magic circle jerk. But is it possible that the ghost of the jerk remains somewhere, as a tendency, as a predilection, as a potential that can still poison game studies?

Given the force of such critiques, we too wondered if there are players who actually believe in the magic circle, who unthinkingly abide by the logic of the standard metagame, who promote the anti-metagaming metagame as the "right" way to play, and who identify with the ideology of the ideological avatar of play. Is there a magic circle jerk or some kind of idiotic avatar of play arguing for videogames as a magic circle?

Metagaming begins by arguing against this phantom, claiming that all games are enclosed in a messy circle structured not by ideal rules but by the material practices and community histories of players who make metagames games using videogames as equipment. At first it wasn't clear if this specter had any substance, but the response to *Tropes vs. Women in Videogames* revealed that the magic circle jerk did indeed appear to still be haunting videogames. Along with unwarranted outrage, systematic abuse, hate speech, and general misogyny, Sarkeesian's harassers responded by circling their wagons in order to protect the standard metagame. Aside from ad hominem attacks (which number in the hundreds of thousands), recurring comments continue to be published ad nauseam across all manner of social media platforms that work to reinforce and police the border of the magic circle of videogames. Repeated over and over on YouTube, Facebook, Twitter, Reddit, and 4chan, the magic circle jerk posted "who cares?" "they are just games," "leave us alone," "stop talking," "fuck off," "make your own game," "she is not a gamer," "she doesn't care about games," "she is only in it for the money," "we are gamers," "we love games."[12] These disavowals and dismissals of Sarkeesian's work are underwritten by the standard metagame, a magic circle that she was perceived not only as commenting upon or critiquing, but actively spoiling.

Although *Tropes vs. Women in Video Games* expressed common critiques of gender representation, Sarkeesian found herself in the unfortunate position of what Sara Ahmed (2010) calls the "feminist killjoy" or the figure who intervenes to critique "how happiness is used to justify social norms as social goods" (and in the process is blamed for the problem). As Ahmed (2010) argues, the perverse result of this displacement is that "situations of conflict, violence, and power are read as *about* the unhappiness of feminists, rather than being what feminists are unhappy *about*" (emphasis original). So, for her harassers, Sarkeesian represents the cynical and defeatist killjoy whose critique is coded as sexist because it discusses gender, coded as racist because it discusses diversity, coded as elitist because it discusses class, or coded as partisan because it discusses politics. But, as Ahmed (2010) observes, "To be unseated by the table of happiness might be to threaten not simply that table, but what gathers around it, what gathers on it," and, for some, Sarkeesian's cultural criticism seemed so powerful (and the standard metagame so fragile) that to bring conversations about gender to the table would bring the whole meal crashing to the ground.

In the case of *Tropes vs. Women in Videogames,* the feminist killjoy threatens the integrity of the magic circle and in doing so begins to resemble another maligned figure who refuses to accept the rules of the game: the spoilsport. In *Homo Ludens,* Huizinga (1949, 11) outlines,

> The player who trespasses against the rules or ignores them is a "spoil-sport." The spoil-sport is not the same as the false player, the cheat; for the latter pretends to be playing the game and, on the face of it, still acknowledges the magic circle. It is curious to note how much more lenient society is to the cheat than to the spoil-sport. This is because the spoil-sport shatters the play-world itself.[13]

If hackers and modders, speedrunners and pro gamers, traders and farmers are sometimes considered cheats because they engage the machinations of videogames well beyond the standard ways of play, their tweaks and changes, exploits and expertise, gambling and grinding are nevertheless granted some leniency. These kinds of metagames do not stray too far from the central tenants of the ideological avatar of play. They don't disrupt the social order of videogaming even as they test the boundaries of the rules, experiment with unintended mechanics, and expropriate the virtual economies of videogames. Forms of play that stray further from the standard are not as easily tolerated. When the metagame is no fun, it begins to expose the ideological avatar of play as just that, an avatar. By performing a critique of happiness that also punctures the magic circle, Sarkeesian is cast not only as a feminist killjoy but as a *feminist spoilsport.* And indeed, as Huizinga predicted over seventy years ago, no mercy is granted to the spoilsport.

He writes, almost prophetically,

> The figure of the spoil-sport is most apparent in boys' games. The little community does not enquire whether the spoil-sport is guilty of defection because he dares not enter into the game or because he is not allowed to. Rather [the community] does not recognize "not being allowed" and calls it "not daring." (Huizinga 1949, 1)

Despite the fact that the magic circle has been widely dismissed as fiction, the shocking, strident, and ongoing vilification of Sarkeesian suggests that the desire for the magic circle wields far more power than many want to admit. Haunted by a toxic game that doesn't know it's a game, living with the background radiation of harassment, and surrounded by magic circle jerks and idiotic avatars of play, if the metagame is a way of life then it can also be a way to make life hell.

The Ends of *Metagaming*

If you can make a metagame, can you break a metagame? Do metagames have an endgame? How do metagames come to an end and what is the endgame of *Metagaming*? Difficult to control, impossible to predict, the metagame is always moving. Recalling Catherine Malabou's radical notion of neural plasticity, metagames are plastic; they are explosive, but are also surprisingly resilient to change. Metagames have a way of surviving well beyond the sale of original software and outside the purview of the corporations that initiate them as well as the communities that develop them. Metagames can lie dormant for years only to spontaneously re-emerge into new contexts of play and spread swiftly at the most unexpected moments. They can impact the private play of single players as well as the massively multiplayer games of networked communities. Metagames are viral; they are infectious, and are often rendered invisible even as they structure how we play games. Like viruses, they are both dead and alive depending on their environment (and, like viruses they can kill you).[14] As such, the metagame thrives in the relationship between game and play, between involuntary operations and voluntary experience. Without relationality, in the absence of aboutness, withoutness, withinness, and aroundness, there can be no metagame. And the endgame of *Metagaming* is to at least imagine such an end.

At the ends of perspectival rendering, when embodied vision finally aligns with high-resolution screens or virtual reality goggles, there can be no game *about* games. When mimesis is no longer a myth and simulation becomes simulacrum, *aboutness* itself ends. While working at id Software before taking a position at Oculus, John Carmack (McCormick 2011) imagined perspectival rendering "converging at the limits of our biological systems." With the release of head-mounted displays such as the Oculus Rift, HTC Vive, PlayStation VR, Samsung Gear, Microsoft HoloLens, and even Google Cardboard (a smartphone-holding headset literally made out of cardboard) in 2015 and 2016, it is clear that the dream of immersive virtual reality is alive and well in the twenty-first century. As advertised on their 2012 Kickstarter campaign and on Oculus's (2015) website, "Whether you're stepping into your favorite game, watching an immersive VR movie, jumping to a destination on the other side of the world, or just spending time with friends in VR, you'll feel like you're really there." If being "really there" merges realism with reality and conflates likeness with living, then the metagame of mimesis must end (and with it human subjectivity). If, as Richard Garfield argues, "a game without a metagame is like an idealized object in physics," then the Platonic ideal of *aboutnessless* that VR headsets promise would ultimately be too bright for any cave dweller. Perhaps it's best to continue playing in the shadows.

When a videogame (or VR headset) finally sees the light of day after months, years, or even decades of sneak peeks, crowdfunding campaigns, beta testing, theory crafting, and other forms of expectant metagaming, the game *without* a game must end. Without *withoutness*, the anticipatory fun and financial speculation played in, on, around, and through fundraising platforms like Kickstarter, Indiegogo, Greenlight, and even Patreon comes to an end. Following Oculus's lead just a few months after the Rift was fully backed, on October 18, 2012, Cloud Imperium Games (CIG), a development company spearheaded by Chris Roberts, the creator of *Wing Commander* (1990) and *Freelancer* (2003), launched a Kickstarter for their massively multiplayer space simulator *Star Citizen* (forthcoming). The pitch included a series of "ship commercials" that were not simply advertisements for the game itself, but advertisements for in-game vehicles like the 2944 Aurora, the MISC Freelancer, the Anvil Aerospace Hornet, and the Origin 300 Series, to name a few. Mimicking the rhetoric and affect of various car commercials—from Ford and Chevy to BMW and Volkswagen—*Star Citizen*'s ads sold players on virtual vehicles with four-digit price tags (not to mention monthly insurance policies at premium rates so players could protect their investments before they even had access to the hangers and launchpads CIG promised).[15] Paying is a form of playing, and by 2016 *Star Citizen* had raised over 100 million dollars—leagues beyond the prize pools of *Dota 2*. Preproduction, prerelease, preordering, preloading, and pregaming: the videogame industry cultivates games of speculation (financial and otherwise) long before any product is packaged up and dropped onto store shelves. *Star Citizen* is not a work of science fiction because it takes place in the distant future and in a galaxy far, far away; it is a science fiction because it cultivates an anticipatory economy of affect and attention, allowing players to actively speculate on a future that does not yet exist.[16] When the game finally comes out, these games of *withoutnessless* will end. Until then, *Star Citizen*'s metagames will continue to orbit the black hole of withoutnessless, siphoning the money and attention of its star-struck players.

From withoutness to *withinness*, the end of the metagame veers away from the event horizon of a financial black hole toward the inner workings of mechanical black boxes and the entropic ends of the game *within the game*. Pixel by pixel, frame by frame, speedrunners inch closer and closer to the technical limitations of measured time. Once a videogame's mechanics are reverse engineered and once an optimized route through a game is agreed upon, record-holding speedrunners from Narcissa Wright to Andrew Gardikis, Blubbler, Kosmicd12, and Darbian reduce videogames like *Super Mario Bros.* to mere numerals. First 4:57.693, then 4:57.627, 4:57.427, 4:57.260, 4:57.244, 4:57.194, until, for the first time, 4:56.878.[17] How low can the metagame go? When a human player has achieved the fastest possible real-time attack and once the complex inner workings of a videogame are reduced to one historical, embodied performance of play, then the game within the game ends. The metagame of withinness, however, guarantees that the mechanical, electrical, computational processes of technical media are black boxed, siloed away from conscious awareness and sensory perception. If any player could pierce the materiality of a given game, then that game would cease to offer possibility for play. Speedrunning ends when the game ceases to operate in terms of human agency and transitions from a game of skill supported by a community metagame of research and invention into a game of chance: a grind, a gamble, a random number generator. 4:56.878, then, represents the end of withinness, a *withinnessless* that without recourse to new techniques or alternate routes, would leave nothing left to do. And with nothing left to do, speedrunners migrate to other metagames, abandoning their microtemporal endgames and finish lines.

Beyond flickering frames and ticking timers, embodied habits and muscle memory, crowdfunding platforms and advertising campaigns, there are still games *around* these games that continue to elude their ends, games that take place across a wide range of media—from chain letters, scavenger hunts, geocaches, dead drops, public performances, and other forms of locative media to web rings, spectrographic imagery, datamoshed images, SSTV transmissions, and hundreds of cryptographic codes to disguise and disseminate their gameplay. Whether called pervasive games, immersive games, transmedia games, or alternate reality games (ARGs), these games around games "are not contained to any single medium, hardware system, or interface . . . [and] use the real world as both a platform and medium, even as they complicate the concept of realism in a digital era" (Hayles, Jagoda, LeMieux 220). Given their diverse materiality, diffuse proliferation, patchwork aesthetic, transmedia narratives, ephemeral temporality, and collective play, how could the *aroundness* of alternate reality games end?[18] In the strange riddles strewn about race tracks within *Trials Evolution* (2012), in the series of two-digit codes scribbled on desk notes within *Surgeon Simulator* (2013), in the alphabetic language found in the tetromino towns within *Fez* (2012), in the random radio chatter that suddenly appears throughout the test chambers within *Portal* (2007), in the conceptual possibilities that may never cohere into a *Frog Fractions 2* (forthcoming),[19] and even in the gamified sales events that occasionally appear within the Steam store,[20] ARGs are increasingly enclosed within videogames. Whereas ARGs thrive in the atmosphere around games, when the air is sucked out from around them, they return to their original function as advertising in the vacuum of *aroundnessless*.

Aboutnessless, withoutnessless, withinnessless, and aroundnessless are the ends of metagaming—or at least signify the ways in which the relationship between videogames as technical media and the human experience of play mutates, morphs, modulates, and multiplies through metagaming. Conceptualizing this game of relationality, a *meta-metagame* that projects the possibility space of all metagames, is one of the purposes of this volume. And of course, *Metagaming* itself is also a metagame. This book is our attempt to both account for and play with the phenomenal experiences, material practices, community histories, economic markets, and technical ecologies of videogames—playing, competing, spectating, cheating, trading, making, and breaking videogames. Videogames are not only black-boxed technologies or consumable commodities or escapist fantasies or even allegories of control. Instead, they stand in for media generally because they highlight our assumptions about the larger technical circuits that operate in excess of (and often at the expense of) human consciousness. From text messaging to ATM machines to ultrafast algorithmic trading to predictive search algorithms, the goal of this volume is not only to consider the way we play videogames, but to become conscious of the ways in which we are constantly playing with (and being played by) technical media. And this book is no exception. Reading this text, writing in the margins, dog-earing pages, and bending the spine or annotating online, sharing across servers, printing out passages, or loading on e-readers are ways of metagaming *Metagaming*. It won't always be a smooth, frictionless, or fun game to play, and cheating, trifling, and even spoiling these pages is expected, but the odds are, whether you want to or not, you are already playing a metagame.

How do you stop *Metagaming*? We'll start: □.

Acknowledgments

Metagaming began, like so many metagames, as a way to play—a way to extend the life of software, continue to engage after game over, recover the histories of player communities, invent new methods for exploring media ecologies, design our own videogames, and, ultimately, investigate and intervene on the ways in which we play and are played by the autonomous operations of technical media. After all is said and done, *Metagaming* continues to be one of the best games we've ever played and one we hope to keep playing indefinitely. After all, metagaming is not just an environment for games, but an environment for life.

Having lived with this project for the past five years, it's hard to trace all of its various influences and inspirations, but it's clear that *Metagaming* was never a single-player game. Among the many people we have to thank, this book would not exist without the mentorship, confidence, and direction of N. Katherine Hayles and the foresight, trust, and patience of Doug Armato. We are also grateful for the careful guidance of our readers at the University of Minnesota Press as well as the assistance of Danielle Kasprzak, Erin Warholm-Wohlenhaus, Jen McIntyre, Kimberly Giambattisto, Jason Begy, Terence Smyre, Cast Iron Coding, and the whole Manifold team.

Well before we started working with the University of Minnesota Press, *Metagaming* began in Gainesville thanks to the early encouragement of Don Ault, Richard Burt, Sid Dobrin, Katerie Gladdys, Terry Harpold, Jack Stenner, Gregory Ulmer, and Phil Wegner at the University of Florida. The project was further developed in Durham thanks to continued conversations with Mark B. N. Hansen, Timothy Lenoir, Eric Monson, Mark Olson, Bill Seaman, Victoria Szabo, and Claire Woods at Duke University.

We are thankful for the continued support of our colleagues from Vassar College, Pratt Institute, and University of California, Davis; our cohorts at University of Florida's English department and Art and Technology Program as well as Duke University's Department of Art, Art History, and Visual Studies and Media Arts + Sciences Program; our collaborators in the Digital Assembly Working Group, the s-1: Speculative Sensation Lab, the Greater Than Games Lab, the Game Changer Lab, the Mod Lab, GameCamp!, Center for 21st Century Studies, and Babycastles Gallery; our many co-presenters and co-players at the annual meetings of the Society for Literature, Science, and the Arts, the Electronic Literature Organization, Utopian Studies, and Awesome Games Done Quick; and our students in Montreal, Gainesville, Durham, Poughkeepsie, Brooklyn, and Davis.

We would like to personally thank Zach Whalen and Laurie Taylor for inspiring us to begin early; Mark Bernstein and Stacey Mason for blogging about our early work; Peter Waites and Danuta Fjellestad for inviting us out; Melissa Bianchi and Kyle Bohunicky for inviting us back; Luke Caldwell and James Hodge for reading along; Craig Gordon and Jack Sapperstein for playing along; Jacob Gaboury, Laine Nooney, David Parisi, and Carlin Wing for slacking off; Kris Cohen and Peter McDonald for responding; Mac and Izzy for being there the whole time; and everyone that we (almost certainly) left out. Finally, we would like to especially thank Patrick Jagoda, Ian Bogost, Colin Milburn, and Anil Venkatesh for their close readings, thoughtful critique, and continued encouragement throughout this lengthy process. And, most of all, *Metagaming* would not have been possible without the love and support of Jean Boluk, Eileen LeMieux, Vince LeMieux, Steven LeMieux, Jacob LeMieux, Kellie Miner, and our entire immediate and extended families for putting up with us as we wrote through breaks, vacations, and holidays in Lampasas and Sherbrooke.

Notes

Introduction

1. Although the algorithmic operations of computational media appear digitally discrete, zeros and ones emerge from analog mechanisms like switches, transistors, and capacitors. Taking a page from the work of N. Katherine Hayles and Johanna Drucker, Matthew Kirschenbaum (2008, 10) distinguishes between digital and analog materiality in *Mechanisms: New Media and the Forensic Imagination*. For Kirschenbaum, whereas *formal materiality* leverages formal or symbolic logic for "the simulation or modeling of materiality via programmed software processes," *forensic materiality* "rests upon the potential for individualization inherent to matter" (Kirschenbaum 2008, 9, 11). In other words, formal materiality expresses difference through symbolic abstraction, while forensic materiality functions in terms of the irreducibility and individuation of matter. Noting this distinction between the symbolic operations of formal materiality and the physicality of forensic materiality, in *How We Think: Digital Media and Contemporary Technogenesis* Hayles (2012, 91) suggests that both formal and forensic "materiality [come] into existence . . . when attention fuses with physicality to identify and isolate some particular attribute (or attributes) of interest." Importantly, "attention" and "interest" are not necessarily human attributes. A wide variety of nonhuman mechanisms can observe, identify, and isolate patterns (e.g., regulatory systems, electrical sensors, recursive algorithms, etc.). The term *materiality*, then, labels those emergent processes by which the physical, mechanical, and electrical attributes of videogames are *made* digital by various players (be they human or nonhuman). As Hayles (2002, 33) summarizes in her earlier work, *Writing Machines*, "materiality emerges from the dynamic interplay between the richness of a physically robust world and human intelligence as it crafts this physicality to create meaning." In this sense, *Metagaming* is an attempt to account for the play of materiality.

2. The desire for a knowable state, and the failure of the player's expectations to ever account for the material operations of technical media, is precisely how play manifests in, on, around, and through videogames. Ideological assumptions about

what constitutes input and output, analog and digital, or what is or isn't a game often overwrite the human experience of computational, electrical, and mechanical processes even as the physical attributes of matter underwrite the random chances, unpredictable consequences, and other unknowable operations of so many of the games we play. The intractable and irreducible physicality of a game's mechanics is always in excess of conscious experience as the play of materiality far outpaces not only the rules of the game but also the rulings of the players. Whereas a formal approach to games assumes full knowledge of the rules, the concept of metagaming is premised on the fact that some parts of games will never cohere within human consciousness. This is not to say that we aren't always playing with and against and through the micro and macro times and scales of videogames, only that we do not know it.

3. Discussed later in this chapter, the Prisoner's Dilemma is the canonical thought experiment in the mathematical and economic field of game theory. In the Dilemma, two people are charged with the same crime, incarcerated separately, and are given the choice of betraying each other with various positive and negative outcomes. The choice to confess or not confess is typically based on assumptions about an opponent.

4. This call to collectively and concurrently play, think, and make is an attempt to account for the material complexity of all media—from digital games to print manuscripts. As such, our game design philosophy integrates making and critique in the hopes of adequately theorizing the complexities of technical media while experimenting with new forms of creative practice. As N. Katherine Hayles and Jessica Pressman (2013, xvii) argue in *Comparative Textual Media,* "without theorizing, practice can be reduced to technical skills and seamless interpolation into capitalist regimes; without practice, theorizing is deprived of the hands-on experience to guide it and develop robust intuitions about the implications of digital technologies." The very concept of metagaming decenters and reconceptualizes the production of both hardware and software within the videogame industry as well as scholarly research within the academy. As Hayles and Pressman (2013, xix) suggest, this comingled form theory and practice "explores the possibilities for cultural, social, economic, and theoretical transformation not only by tearing down but also by building up, thereby opening new horizons of understanding and alternative practices." In the academy, the hope is to "catalyze new kinds of research questions, attract students, reconceptualize curricula, and energize faculty," whereas the industry should benefit from a deeper engagement with the phenomenology, history, and materiality of play (Hayles and Pressman 2013, xxi).

5. In *Gaming: Essays on Algorithmic Culture,* Alexander Galloway (2006, 109) applies the term *countergaming* to the work of artists like Cory Arcangel, Tom Betts, Brody Condon, Joan Heemskerk, and Dirk Paesmans (Jodi), Joan Leandre (retroYou), Anne-Marie Schleiner, and Eddo Stern. In the same way that French countercinema contrasted Hollywood narrative, countergames "conflict violently with the mainstream gaming industry's expectations for how games should be designed . . . [and] often defy the industry's design style point-for-point, with the goal of disrupting the intuitive flow of gameplay" (Galloway 2006, 108). Despite the strength of Galloway's (2006, 125) examples, he is dissatisfied with what he characterizes as primarily visual modifications and continues to call for "a critique of gameplay itself. . . . [that redefines] play itself and thereby realiz[es] its true potential as a political and cultural avant-garde." He admits that countergaming is thus far an "unrealized project" which "has yet to flourish" (Galloway 2006, 125).

6. In *Gamer Theory* McKenzie Wark (2007, 023) argues "gamespace needs theorists—but also a new kind of practice. One that can break down the line that divides gamer from designer, to redeploy the digital so that it makes this very distinction arbitrary." In the tradition of the Guy Debord's *dérive* and Walter Benjamin's *flâneur,* Wark's (2007, 021, 022, 225) gamer theorist is a "trifler" or "archaeologist" who is "not out to break the game" but "wants to hack or 'mod' the game . . . to play even more intimately within it" and "make the now rather familiar world of the digital game strange again." Like Galloway, Wark (2007, 023) resists incorporating those practices already exploring the psychogeography of virtual games and instead frames the gamer theorist as a nascent category.

7. Inspired by the aesthetic experiments of twentieth century artists, in *Critical Play: Radical Game Design* Mary Flanagan (2009, 6, 261) makes the case for "a careful examination of social, cultural, political, or even personal themes that function as alternates to popular play spaces" and imagines the future of this kind of play as "a new discipline of theory and practice" and "a tool for future game makers, game designers, and scholars" that would "instill the ability to think critically during and after play." Flanagan's (2007, 261–62) book concludes with a chapter called "Designing for Critical Play" in which she urges game designers to "unplay, reskin, and rewrite the hidden transcripts so tenaciously rooted in the systems of our world" in order to "manifest a different future" through "interventions at the level of popular culture."

8. Dyer-Witheford and de Peuter (2009, xv) borrow Michael Hardt and Antonio Negri's theory of the multitude in order to characterize videogames as their *"paradigmatic media of Empire"* (emphasis original). Embedded firmly within the dialectical processes of capitalism, Dyer-Witheford and de Peuter (2009, 213) see the potential for videogames to offer resistance through a diverse array of activities they label "counterplay, dissonant development, tactical games, polity simulators, self-organized worlds, and software commons." These ludic practices comprise what they term "games of multitude," yet "the play of the multitude still remains locked inside games of Empire" (Dyer-Witheford and de Peuter 2009, 213). For Dyer-Witheford and de Peuter, the videogame industry exemplifies the capacity of informatic capitalism to appropriate "so many apparently iconoclastic and utopian ideas" such as "team production, modding, machinima artists, MMO populations, digital distributions, and peer-to-peer networks." Despite their avowed skepticism, Dyer-Witheford and de Peuter (2009, 228) remain hopeful that "in this process of cooptation, Empire cultivates capacities that might exceed its grasp."

9. Eleanor Maguire's research on navigation-related structural change within the hippocampi of taxi drivers as compared to various control groups including London bus drivers (whose working conditions mirror those of London's cabbies but who follow fixed routes) continues to explore brain plasticity in relation to the actions and experiences of individual people.

10. Plasticity is commonly used to refer to the brain's ability to model neuronal connections while in development (i.e., morphogenic plasticity), to modify those connections throughout life (i.e., modulational plasticity), and to self-repair in the case of post-lesion or post-stroke rehabilitation (i.e., reparative plasticity) (Malabou 2008, 5). The term originates from the Greek *plassein,* meaning to mold, but the word *plasticity* has come to mean the dual capacity to *receive form* and the capacity to *give form* (Malabou 2008, 5).

11. In his work on "Games without Play," David Golumbia (2009, 180) points out that Derrida's use of the term *jeu* (a common French word meaning both "game" and

"play") was initially translated as "freeplay," leading to mistaken assumptions that Derrida's play meant an infinitely pliable substitution of signs.

12. For Malabou (2008, 13), flexibility is an accessible, "vague notion, without tradition and without history." Flexibility operates under the guise of plasticity, which she sees as form of "neuronal liberation" in which consciousness of the brain itself becomes a vehicle for "producing the conditions of possibility for a new world of questioning" (Malabou 2008, 13). Whereas the term *plasticity* has a long history rooted in neuroscience as well as Hegelian philosophy, Malabou notes how the concept of flexibility is subject to its own dehistoricizing forces. Form and content align in this infinitely adaptive, reactive, and delocalized concept as even the word *flexibility* is a victim of its own cultural amnesia.

13. A term originally coined by Johan Huizinga (1949, 10) in *Homo Ludens,* the "magic circle" is the "consecrated spot" or "play-ground" that is "marked off beforehand either materially or ideally, deliberately or as a matter of course . . . [and] dedicated to the performance of an act apart." The magic circle separates the logic of play from the realities of quotidian life and, although easy to dismiss as impossible, continues to inform the production and consumption of videogames.

14. From Aristotle and Archimedes to Galileo and Kepler, the term *mechanics* historically designates those philosophical, scientific, mathematical, and practical disciplines concerned with the description of physical bodies in motion. First published in 1687, the Laws of Motion in Newton's *Philosophiæ Naturalis Principia Mathematica* are the foundation of classical mechanics, a subset of the field focusing on the movements of large, macroscopic objects at sub-light speeds. Quantum mechanics, on the other hand, is a twentieth century discipline working through the physics of small, atomic and subatomic objects at high speeds. Although, in traditional sports, the word *mechanics* can be used to describe the basic skills necessary to play a game (e.g., dribbling a ball in soccer and basketball or the follow-through of a swing in baseball or golf), based on the historical use of the term, *game mechanics* (and especially *videogame mechanics*) typically refer to the involuntary processes of a game (or game engine) not freely chosen by the player. The Earth's gravity, the material composition of a baseball bat, the display rate of a CRT screen, and the conditional logic of a videogame are game mechanics native to the given field, equipment, platform, or code and cannot be altered at will. The term *rules,* on the other hand, refers to voluntary constraints or social contracts that can be broken by a player. Whereas mechanics are implicit parts of a game and operate with or without a player, the decision to either follow the rules or break the rules is a conscious choice determined by each player.

15. As Mia Consalvo (2009, 114) writes in *Cheating: Gaining Advantage in Videogames,* "exploits don't involve a player actively changing code in a game or deceiving other players; instead, they are 'found' actions or items that accelerate or improve a player's skills, actions, or abilities in some way that the designer did not originally intend, yet in a manner that does not actively change code or involve deceiving others."

16. Douglas Hofstadter's *Gödel, Escher, Bach: An Eternal Golden Braid* (1979) popularized the slippage between an understanding of *meta* as self-reflexive and *meta* as recursive. Hofstadter braids descriptions of Bach's endlessly rising canon and other "metamusical offerings," Escher's recursive artworks like *Metamorphosis* (1939–40), and Gödel's paradoxical incompleteness theorem based on "metamathematics" or "metalogic" in order to build his "metabook" around the concept of the

"strange loop" (Hofstadter 1999, viii, 15, 23, 10). A strange loop is a recursive "phenomenon [that] occurs whenever, by moving upwards (or downwards) through the levels of some hierarchical system, we unexpectedly find ourselves right back where we started" (Hofstadter 1999, 10). Recursion, however, is not entirely commensurate with self-reflexivity. Whereas a self-reflexive film about film such as Dziga Vertov's *Man with a Movie Camera* (1929) may include references to itself and its medium, the feedback produced when a camera pointed at a screen produces recursive instances *ad infinitum*.

17. The conflation of *meta-* with second-order concepts and a notion of the beyond can be attributed to a misconception surrounding the title of Aristotle's *Metaphysics*. While the content of *Metaphysics* may describe an ontology "beyond" the physical, the original meaning of the title *Metaphysics* simply signified the order of a series of books. As Peter van Inwagen notes, "an editor of his works . . . entitled those fourteen books *'Ta meta ta phusika'*—'the after the physicals' or 'the ones after the physical ones'—the 'physical ones' being the books contained in what we now call Aristotle's *Physics*" (van Inwagen 2013).

18. In game theory the term *game* refers to a "situation in which two or more decision-makers (called 'players') each has two or more alternative decisions (called 'strategies'), and for each player the result he will experience depends on the decisions of all the players" (Howard 1971, 8–9).

19. The RAND Corporation, short for Research and Development, is a nonprofit military research group and global think tank founded by the Douglas Aircraft Company in 1948 and funded by the U.S. government among other sources.

20. Morgenstern and von Neumann called these kinds of meta-formulations "majorant" and "minorant" games (Morgenstern and von Neumann 1944, 100).

21. Although various metagaming practices necessarily conflate game theory, game studies, and game design, in this book each field is differentiated according to their common use. Therefore, the term *game theory* refers to the mathematical and economic study of rational decision making founded by von Neumann and Morgenstern in 1944; the term *game studies* refers to the nascent academic discipline that critically engages the history, culture, and materiality of games as a mass medium and cultural commodity; and the term *game design* refers to either the process of producing a game or the specific elements that compose a game.

22. Salen Tekinbaş and Zimmerman recognize the importance of the metagame in *Rules of Play* (2004). Examining the metagame from a design perspective, they argue that "game design is a second-order design problem. . . . [M]ost of any given game's metagame is beyond the reach of the game designer, for it emerges from play communities and their larger social worlds" (Salen Tekinbaş and Zimmerman 2004, 484). Considering the ways in which the metagame impacts play, Stewart Woods also deploys Garfield's concept throughout his study of tabletop gaming culture in *Eurogames* (2012), including lengthy descriptions and responses to surveys he conducted regarding the metagame. Finally, Garfield's own coauthored book, *Characteristics of Games* (2012), includes a chapter that schematizes and compares various metagames according to six general categories: "status, money, socialization, achievement, knowledge, and fantasy" (Elias et al. 2012, 209–10).

Although Salen Tekinbaş has continued to explore the metagame through studies on the videogame culture surrounding e-sports like *StarCraft II* (2010), Zimmerman has approached the concept less as a descriptive tool and more as part of his game design philosophy (Kow et al. 2014). In 2006, Zimmerman and Frank Lantz developed a prototype of *The Metagame* (2011), a board-based trivia game about videogames originally planned for Will Wright's "game issue" of *Wired Magazine* (Zimmerman 2011). Eventually redesigned with the help of Colleen Macklin and John Sharp in 2011, *The Metagame* evolved into a collectible card game, a clever reference to both *Magic* and Richard Garfield's theories while still functioning literally as a game about games.

23. Garfield (1995, 87) writes that the metagame "breathes life into the experience of game-playing" and "[inducts players] into a larger game community." He stresses "there is something magical, even infectious, that happens in the metagame" and "metagames tend to have application and meaning beyond the game itself; often, they seep into real life" (Garfield 1995, 87).

24. Following Marshall McLuhan's definition of media as the extensions of man and Bernard Stiegler's concept of epiphylogenesis, in his essay "Media Theory," Hansen argues that "my interrogation ultimately conceptualizes the medium as an environment for life: by giving concrete form to 'epiphylogenesis' (the exteriorization of human evolution), concrete media find their most 'originary' function not as artifacts but through their participation in human technogenesis (i.e., our co-evolution with technics)" (2006, 297). Similarly, one might argue that games do not function as autonomous objects or abstract rules but require participation by players (be they human or nonhuman).

25. As Ian Bogost (2009) contends in "Videogames are a Mess," whether defined as "kilobytes [of data]," "a flow of RF modulations," "a mask ROM," "a molded plastic cartridge," "a consumer good," "a system of rules," "an experience," "a unit of intellectual property," "a collectible," or "a sign," videogames, and in this case metagames, are a mess.

26. Videogames, in this context, refer to all mechanical, electrical, and computational games in which rules are automated, especially those industrial products, consumer goods, and mass media "created and played on arcade machines, personal computers, and home consoles" (Bogost 2006, xiii). Acknowledging the relationship between metagames and videogames both requires that one distinguish the physical attributes of the game from the voluntary choices adopted by players and reveals that videogames are not simply an entertainment to consume but platforms for producing games.

27. Discussed further in chapter 2, in "Rules in Computer Games Compared to Rules in Traditional Games" Chris DeLeon (2013, 7) deconstructs what could be called the standard or default metagame that "players have the ability [to] ignore or deliberate[ly] violate these rules, and doing so might lead their achievement in a game to be regarded as illegitimate by peers." This metagame includes implicit cultural and social rules like interacting with only standard controllers on legitimate hardware, being individually responsible and unencumbered for your actions, and playing a legitimate copy of the game as released by the developer (DeLeon 2013, 7–8).

1. About, Within, Around, Without

1. Connotations of the Gulf War in *Magic: The Gathering* are as much a reference to Neil Gaiman's comic book series *The Sandman* (1989–96) as to 1990s American geopolitics. A significant influence on the production of *Arabian Nights,* cards such as "City in a Bottle" explicitly cite issue 50 of the comic *Distant Mirrors: Ramadan,* in which mythical Baghdad is framed as a story within the story of a beggar in war-torn Iraq (Garfield 2002; Gaiman 1993, 31).

2. Garfield titled the card based on the Persian transliteration *Shahrázád* rather than *Scheherazade.*

3. An increasingly common practice, all three games featured in *Indie Game: The Movie* include music from third parties. Instead of hiring a composer to produce an original soundtrack, Jonathan Blow licensed *Braid*'s music from a variety of artists including Jami Sieber, Shira Kammen, and Cheryl Ann Fulton. On the other hand, Team Meat hired Danny Baranowsky to produce the soundtrack for *Super Meat Boy,* while Rich Vreeland, aka Disasterpeace, produced *Fez*'s music.

4. Maria B. Garda and Paweł Grabarczyk (2016) distinguish between the concept of *independent game* and *indie game.* They argue that as popular (and often interchangeable) as these two terms are, their meaning is also "exceptionally elusive." Garda and Grabarczyk undertake an overview of how these two terms have been applied, suggesting that while financial, creative, and publishing independence are characteristic of independent games and can be applied to a much broader history of games, the term *indie game* is largely restricted to "a specific kind of independent game that has emerged around mid-2000s in the Western world" (i.e., the types of games documented in *Indie Game: The Movie*).

5. By more closely examining and expanding the time-based mechanics of previous games such as *Max Payne* (2001), *Blinx: The Time Sweeper* (2002), and (most notably) *Prince of Persia: The Sands of Time* (2003) while undertaking more extensive time manipulation only recently possible due to technical innovations, *Braid* has become the preeminent example of chronocentric gameplay in the videogame industry.

6. *Braid* deploys the tropes of *Super Mario Bros.* (1985) and platforming games in order to allegorize the Proustian consciousness of a young boy whose "remembrance of things past" must be slowly pieced together according to the logic of a puzzle game. Tim is not simply the Mario-like avatar indexing the player's actions, but a complex figure that allegorically braids together a critique of multiple forms of obsessive desire and linear progress—from the ludic challenges of 1980s platformers, their depiction as the quest for an unattainable princess, the unquestioned scientific pursuit of increasingly powerful technology, and the philosophical concept of time. Through this interweaving of concepts, *Braid* tells a cautionary tale about formal abstraction, abusive relationships, and the atomic bomb. *Braid*'s system of referentiality calls into question not only the status of videogames, but also the formal operations of games and their longer history rooted in the military–entertainment complex and Cold War nuclear anxiety. Moving from metafiction to metagames, *Braid* explores the entangled relationship between the techniques of self-reflexivity and nuclear anxiety as the shattered, psychic fragments of the game's narrative are slowly pieced together to reveal a nonlinear story of a nuclear scientist who worked on the Manhattan Project. The hyperreferentiality and multilinear hypertext in *Braid* invokes not only a history of videogames, but a larger history of simulation and digital media that serves as the condition of possibility for videogames. Moreover, the obsessive, masculine gamer that is critiqued in *Braid* further allegorizes the constant drive and model of progress in science. Working with Jacques Derrida's theory of language as "fabulously textual" from the essay "No Apocalypse, Not Now," Patrick Jagoda (2013) further explores the relationship between *Braid* and Cold War ideology in his essay "Fabulously Procedural."

7. *Super Meat Boy* is the sequel to *Meat Boy* (2008), a short prototype developed in Adobe Flash by McMillen and Jonathan McEntee and released on Newgrounds, a well-known Flash portal. McMillen released dozens of games on Newgrounds and would even develop his next major release, the *Zelda*-inspired *The Binding of Isaac* (2011) in Flash with Florian Himsl.

8. *Super Meat Boy* would surely stand up alongside some of Swink's (2009, 7) best examples of "true game feel": *Super Mario 64* (1996) and *Half-Life* (1998).

9. While Team Meat (2011) and Polytron Corporation (2013) proudly announced when their titles surpassed a million sales (each in under two years), Jonathan Blow has been guarded about publicly releasing sales data. After interviewing Blow for his book *Extra Life,* Tom Bissell (2010, 95–96) jokes that the game "made him wealthy enough that when I asked for some ballpark idea of how well the game had done he requested that I turn off my tape recorder."

10. Baio's taxonomy of metagames includes "abusive games" like *I Wanna Be the Guy* (2007) and *Tetris HD* (2009), "minimalist games" like *Don't Shoot the Puppy* (2006) and *You Have to Burn the Rope* (2008), "game mechanics gone wild" like *Achievement Unlocked* (2008) and *Upgrade Complete* (2009), "violent games" like *Super Columbine Massacre RPG!* (2005) and *Close Range* (2009), and "gaming culture" like *Segagaga* (2001) and *Game Dev Story* (2010) (Baio 2011).

11. Some of the bonus characters featured in *Super Meat Boy* function as citations meant to credit previously released independent games that inspired Meat Boy's mechanics (e.g., the ninja from Raigan Burns and Mare Sheppard's famous Flash game *N* [2005]). The roster also includes shoutouts to other successful independently produced games by including characters like the eponymous alien from Behemoth's *Alien Hominid* (2002), one of the first Flash games released on a home console in 2004; the pink knight from Behemoth's follow-up XBLA hit, *Castle Crashers* (2008); a "goo ball" from Kyle Gabler and Ron Carmel's early WiiWare title, *World of Goo* (2008); Commander Video from the *Bit.Trip* (2009–) series by Santa Cruz–based Gaijin Games; Derek Yu's explorer from *Spelunky* (2009); Captain Viridian from Terry Cavanagh's *VVVVVV* (2010); and even Steve from Marcus Persson's runaway hit, *Minecraft* (2011). Aside from the head crab monster from Valve's *Half-Life* franchise and the ubiquitous, boxy avatar from *Minecraft*, Meat Boy's sixteen other unlockable characters are all from independently produced 2D platformers from the late 2000s.

12. Like *Super Meat Boy,* games like *I Wanna Be the Guy* and *Syobon Action* (2007) not only explicitly reference the look and feel of early platformers (lifting graphics directly from *Super Mario Bros.,* for example), but they deploy those familiar references in order to subvert player expectations. Greg Costikyan (2013, 103) calls this kind of metagame "a form of ludic self-referentiality" and explains, "It's a game commenting on a game, but it's the cultural meaning of *Mario*'s tropes that make *Syobon* interesting (and infuriating, and hilarious) to experienced platformer players." Whereas Ian Bogost (2011, 42) thinks the genius of the parodic Japanese platformer *Syobon Action* "is that of a well-honed, methodically planned prank: it systematically disrupts every expected convention of 2-D platform gameplay," Anna Anthropy adopts the language of BDSM to describe the player's voluntarily submission to the relentless difficulty of "masocore" games like *Super Meat Boy.* Anthropy's own game, *Mighty Jill Off* (2008), is a BDSM-themed follow-up to Tecmo's arcade-era masocore, *Mighty Bomb Jack* (1986)—a game of unrelenting difficulty due to its peculiar control scheme in which the player must furiously mash the jump button to control each of Jack's gliding descents. Anthropy borrows the game's masturbatory mechanics and pixelated aesthetics, replacing Jack with Jill, a similarly caped and horny-helmeted hero decked out in (pixelated) leather or latex. In Anthropy's game, Jill, a submissive "boot licker," must scale her dominatrix queen's castle of demanding dungeons via Bomb Jack's masochistic jump mechanic. The perversity of platforming and the pleasure of pain are made evident in *Mighty Jill Off,* in which

an empowered Queen, not a kidnapped princess, produces a Sisyphean economy of desire. This libidinal logic is narratively submerged within McMillen and Refenes' more traditional and normalized hero quest of a boy rescuing a girl. While it is difficult to ignore the reproductive subtext in which an anthropomorphic piece of meat pursues an Oedipal fetus that has kidnapped a woman made of bandages, this ironic reenactment of the hero quest does not necessarily avoid its pitfalls. Whereas *Super Meat Boy* clearly acknowledges its debt to *Mighty Jill Off* by including Anthropy's original character and contains a goldmine of Freudian nuggets, it is telling that *Super Meat Boy* and not *Mighty Jill Off* is canonized as one of the most emblematic examples of indie games.

13. The apparent preference for Nintendo's 1985 console correlates not only to the ages of these independent developers, but their audience in the late 2000s. As both game makers and their players grow younger (and as indie games begin to include the aesthetic preferences of older games and gamers as well), the metagame will change. For example, many speedrunners and stream viewers grew up in the nineties and, as such, prefer to make metagames on the Nintendo 64 and GameCube. Alongside consoles by Atari, Sega, Sony, and Microsoft, Nintendo's well-known properties and strong brand identity continue to operate as a popular touchstone for many metagamers.

14. Apart from the indie game, the concept of the art game emerged around the same period (and was met with similar controversy, inciting hundreds of entropic forum debates). Despite the fact that experimental, minimalist games such as Jason Rohrer's *Passage* (2007) and Rod Humble's *The Marriage* (2007) as well as hits like *Braid* questioned the arbitrary challenges of most videogames and deployed interactivity as a metaphor for control or power, these games did little to challenge industry norms. Not only were the games still mostly produced by men, but these art games that Ian Bogost calls "proceduralist" depict extremely conservative gender relations (with the exception of the more subtle representations in *Braid*). In *The Marriage,* the player must balance pink and blue squares whose asymmetrical operations re-inscribe naive assumptions about gender and marital relations. Owing to the abstract nature of the game, which is composed of geometric, monochromatic squares, it is possible to disavow certain meanings even if one can assign fairly obvious interpretations of the pink and blue squares that portray a 1950s model of marriage through the game mechanics. Pink needs blue for survival and blue needs to regularly escape pink in order to refuel. In *Passage,* a white, blond, blue-eyed sprite travels through stages of life, while his female companion (should one choose to bond with her) physically takes up space to get in the way of the protagonist's exploratory desires. While Humble and Rohrer have expressed that these games are autobiographical, it is striking that they portray their unique and contingent subject positions as an ideological universal—the avatars in each game are framed as default representations rather than specific portraits of their authors. Compare *Passage* and *The Marriage* to something like Anna Anthropy's *dys4ia* (2012), which also conveys autobiographical material but in a way that explicitly situates itself in the personal, historical, embodied experience of its designer. In Anthropy's *dys4ia* (featuring music by Liz Ryerson), the disconnect between body and identity is mirrored in the phenomenological disconnect between player and software. Anthropy explicitly resists any attempts to universalize the depiction of quotidian life and the experience of her body as represented in *dys4ia,* whereas Rohrer and Humble present autobiographical material in such an abstract and uncontextualized way that the games generalize the experience of their designers.

15. As James Mielke (2013), the organizer of the Japanese independent game development festival Bit Summit, notes, even though Daisuke "Pixel" Amaya's *Cave Story* (2004) is considered by many to be the quintessential indie game, "the term 'indie' . . . is not favored in Japan—although 'independent' is fine . . . because the term 'indie,' in Japan, usually comes across negatively, as 'amateur.'"

16. In 1981, Gunpei Yokoi's dual-screen *Donkey Kong Game & Watch* was the first in his series of early handheld videogames to support a D-pad. One of the early examples of directional input on the left and precision timing input on the right, both the interface and aesthetic of *Donkey Kong Game & Watch* influenced Yokoi's industrial design for the original Famicom home console, which sported the same layout, metallic decals, and colorful plastic (though maroon instead of orange). Yokoi, one of Nintendo's longest employees who began at the company as a toy maker before assisting the inventor of the Game Boy and inaugural director of Nintendo's Research and Design 1 (R&D1) division, would work at Nintendo until 1996, when he retired and began his own company which was contracted to make the Bandai WonderSwan. The proximity of his death and the failure of his last major project at Nintendo, 1995's Virtual Boy, make his death all the more tragic.

17. Ken Yankelevitz is almost singlehandedly responsible for "sustain[ing] quadriplegic game controllers for 30 years" (Dockery 2011). The retired aerospace engineer is famous for designing a sip-and-puff controller that uses the movements of the tongue and breath as input that allows for over a dozen different actions to be performed. Following in Yankelevitz's footsteps, in April 2014 Fred Davison launched a successful Kickstarter campaign for the "Quadstick," a mouth-operated joystick that can be used on multiple computers and consoles. With these devices quadriplegic players are not simply granted access to some normative notion of games and gaming, but they radically reinvent videogames according to an alternative logic of not manual, but oral dexterity.

18. An open source collaboration between members of Free Art and Technology (FAT), OpenFrameworks and the Graffiti Research Lab (including Zachary Lieberman, Evan Roth, James Powderly, Theo Watson, and Chris Sugrue), the *EyeWriter* (2010) is an open source interface and application suite for producing art through eye tracking built for Tony "Tempt1" Quan. The design for the *EyeWriter* appropriates Sony's PlayStation Eye, a spherical webcam originally designed for tracking and inserting bodily gestures into the typically sedentary console gaming of the living room. But instead of tracking moving bodies, the *EyeWriter* tracks polarized pupils, interpreting both eye movement and angle in order to activate a cursor in various applications with which Quan continues his work as a Los Angeles graffiti artist despite his ALS.

19. In micha cárdenas and Elle Mehrmand's series of live performances titled *technésexual* (2009–2010), the artists engaged in erotic play while outfitted with wearable biometric devices that tracked their heart rate and temperature. Data from the performers was accessed from an Arduino microcontroller, manipulated in the visual scripting language Pure Data, and then indexed to avatars in Linden Labs' *Second Life* (2003), a massively multiplayer game in which players model the architecture and script the behaviors of their shared virtual world. Projected on top of the two performers, both live and virtual audience commingled in the sensual play set to a soundtrack of heartbeats amplified in both first and second life.

20. In 2001, Sega released *Rez*, an on-rails shooter set to electronic music. Based on the idea of synesthesia, a Japanese-only version of *Rez* for the PlayStation 2 was shipped with the "Trance Vibrator," a peripheral that rhythmically vibrated to the

music. Jane Pinckard (2002) famously documented how the Trance Vibrator (unlike rumble packs, which do not vibrate at a consistent pace) could be effectively repurposed as a sex toy for extending the game's synesthesia into the realm of erotic pleasure.

21. In *Super Mario World* (1990), for example, the two bytes of data stored at RAM addresses $7E:0015 and $7E:0017 are updated on each frame according to the buttons pressed on the controller. Since a byte stores eight bits, then, rather than using the byte as a whole, each binary digit represents a single on–off value where 1 equals pressed and 0 equals not pressed. For most Super Nintendo games, the eight values at $7E:0015 represent B, Y, Select, Start, Up, Down, Left, and Right, while $7E:0017 stores values for A, X, L, and R—a total of twelve possible inputs. So, for *Super Mario World* it does not matter what kind of controller is used. Whether pressing A on a standard North American SNES controller or circuitbending the RAM on the SNES motherboard, as soon as the first bit of $7E:0017 changes from 0 to 1, Mario will jump.

22. In the late 2000s, around the same time as the "indie games" craze, many women-only spaces opened across North America and Europe including (but certainly not limited to) Girl Develop It (est. 2010), Rails Girls (est. 2010), Black Girls Code (est. 2011), PyLadies (est. 2011), Ladies Learning Code (est. 2011), Tech Girlz (est. 2012), and LadyHacks (est. 2013).

23. Jasbir Puar's (2010, 165) "Prognosis time: Towards a geopolitics of affect, debility, and capacity" cites Julie Livingston's sobering observation that "while four-fifths of the world's disabled persons live in developing countries, there is a relative dearth of humanities and social science scholarship exploring disability in non-Western contexts." Videogames are luxury items and much of mainstream videogame design is built around fantasies of intellectual and physical virtuosity that neglect bodily difference. This *which* reinforces not only the ideological categories of able bodies, but also the larger systems of global capital, production, and consumption, and the military–industrial entertainment complex out of which videogames emerge.

24. The Jakks Pacific 10-in-1 joystick features versions of *Adventure* (1980), *Asteroids* (1979), *Breakout* (1978), *Centipede* (1981), *Circus Atari* (1980), *Gravitar* (1983), *Missile Command* (1980), *Pong* (1972), *RealSports Volleyball* (1982), and *Yar's Revenge* (1981). The Atari Flashback, on the other hand, is a full-size plug-and-play console that shipped in 2004 with twenty games originally developed for both the Atari 2600 and 7800 consoles.

25. An unmodded Atari 2600 uses a radio frequency (RF) cable to transmit video and audio to the television. Many CRTs and most LCD televisions are not designed to accept input from RF, so Atari players must either bootstrap their retro consoles to peripherals like VCRs or mod their systems to output AV (a relatively simple process).

26. In order for Flanagan's *[giantJoystick]* to easily play a variety of Atari 2600 games in an exhibition setting without cartridges, RF adapters, and idiosyncrasies of 1980s hardware, *they cannot be Atari 2600 games.* Even though the Jakks Pacific attempts to emulate the Atari 2600 there are some significant differences. For example, in the Jakks Pacific version of *Adventure* Warren Robinette's signature easter egg is replaced with the word "TEXT" (Kohler 2006). As evidenced by these changes, even so-called digital games are not so easily reduced to the binary digits of ROM files but always operate according to the electrical capacities and material specificity of a given hardware platform.

27. While plenty of platforms perform faster than the Nintendo 64, the iQue's status as an "official" Nintendo product made the platform an accepted, if controversial, option for competing within the speedrunning community despite its distinct technical operations. In her blog post "Ocarina of Time—speedrunning & version differences," Wright (2013a) argues for the viability of the iQue platform based on a survey of *seventeen* officially released (and presumably widely accessible) versions of Nintendo's software.

28. After Miyamoto's success designing the original *Donkey Kong* arcade game with Gunpei Yakoi in 1981, and with Nintendo's transition from a card and novelty company to a toy company focusing on electronic games, Research & Design 4 (R&D4) was founded in 1983. Under the influence of Nintendo's "golden triangle" of game designers Miyamoto, Tezuka, and Nakago, and with music and sound effects composed by Kondo, R&D4 would produce two of Nintendo's most beloved and enduring brands: *Super Mario Bros.* and *The Legend of Zelda*. After attracting young talent with these successes, R&D4 was expanded into Nintendo Entertainment Analysis & Development (EAD) in 1993 and continued to reinvent and release critically acclaimed sequels to their foundational brands. With designers from past *Zelda* entries like Yoichi Yamada and Yoshiaki Koizumi, as well as new team members like Eiji Aonuma, *The Legend of Zelda: Ocarina of Time* would become the best-selling *Zelda* game of its time.

29. Beyond Any%, hundreds of categories have been invented as historical and regional communities branch out and explore different options for speedrunning their favorite games. Completing 100% of a game may take longer, but in some cases like *Super Mario 64* may also show off more of the game, take more skill, or be more entertaining for the community. Collecting as few in-game items as possible, known as Low%, can be slower, but is usually much more challenging, as is the case when beating *The Legend of Zelda* with only three hearts. Of course, these major categories also overlap. Low% *is* the fastest way to complete *Mega Man X* (1993), while collecting (almost) 100% of the items to unlock a powerful endgame attack turns out to be the fastest way to complete *Mega Man X2* (1994). When a game does not have clear percentages, other metrics such as "96 Exits" in *Super Mario World* stand in. There are also plenty of arbitrary categories that may seem absurd but explore the manifold, underexamined possibilities of play, such as "Reverse Boss Order" (RBA), "One Player, Two Controllers" (1p2c), and even physical constraints like playing one-handed or blindfolded. Finally, there may be categories banning the use of certain techniques in games where the specific use of exploits changes the gameplay radically or regionally. In the case of *The Legend of Zelda: A Link to the Past,* going out of bounds (OoB) by exploiting the "Exploration Glitch" (EG) allows players to beat the game in under two minutes. Any% may be fast, but is not very fun. Since the *Link to the Past* Any% metagame cannot sustain a community, new categories proliferate to limit specific kinds of play and recover parts of the original software valuable to speedrunners. The most played (and most renamed) category of *Link to the Past* is (currently) "All Dungeons," aka no EG, no OoB, no S&Q, and no YBA or "Yuzuhara's Bottle Adventure" (an exploit whose name references both the runner who discovered the "Dark World Flute" glitch in April 2014 and the classic Bottle Adventure Glitch from *Ocarina of Time*).

30. In "Dwarven Epitaphs: Procedural Histories in *Dwarf Fortress*," we discuss Tarn and Zach Adams' *Dwarf Fortress* (2006–) as a strange IDE, an unconventional platform "for playing with programming and programming play" in which players

create in-game computers like "Dwarven Computer, Dwarven Calculators, and even a Dwarven Game of Life based on John Horton Conway's classic example of emergence" (Boluk and LeMieux 2012; 152, 142).

31. Alongside multiple versions for Nintendo 64, *Ocarina of Time* was rereleased for the GameCube in 2002, the iQue in 2003, and the Wii Virtual Console in 2007, and was remade for Nintendo's handheld 3DS in 2011.

32. Pioneered by *Ocarina of Time* and adopted by many third-person 3D videogames which require realtime combat, "Z Targeting" is a control scheme in which players can modify their directional input by "locking on" to an enemy unit (with the Z button). While a player is Z Targeting, radial movement in relation to the given enemy or object temporarily replaces Cartesian navigation in relation to the larger world map. When the player is facing the target, left and right directional inputs circle the enemy or object, while up and down decrease and increase the distance from that central point.

33. This calibration exploit was popularized in _Peaches' *Doom 64* speedruns.

34. Just as Andrew Gardikis' longstanding world record for *Super Mario Bros.* was finally beaten by Blubbler's 4:57.693 on June 6, 2014 and then again by Darbian's 4:57.627 on October 18, 2015, Joel "Jodenstone" Ekman rang in the new year by beating Wright's *Ocarina of Time* record by three seconds on January 1, 2015. Ekman improved his run from 18:07 to 18:05 to 17:55 in March 2015 before skater82297 achieved a 17:47 on May 7, 2015 using the new "Get Item Manipulation" to divine a bottle in the basement of the Deku Tree instead of collecting Cuccos in Kakariko Village.

35. In the late nineties, an e-sports bubble emerged in which millions of dollars were funneled into competitions and teams. Just as quickly as e-sports grew, the metagame crashed when companies suddenly halted the cash flow, bidding a hasty exodus from, rather than to, the virtual world. The recent development of livestreaming has created a more sustainable model including live spectatorship and, along with the immense amount of community-based, crowd-sourced funding, corporate sponsorship of e-sports is once again returning to the scene transforming the metagame into a thriving moneygame.

36. When Machinima Inc. approached Wright with funding to produce a speedrunning competition with weekly races and a small prize for the winner, the outpouring of community resistance led to the immediate cancellation of the production. This backlash against professionalization runs counter to the general trend of e-sports in which fans are more likely to embrace outside funding into their community metagame.

37. Whereas AGDQ 2013 raised $448,425.27, at AGDQ 2014 the community cracked the one-million-dollar ceiling for the first time, reporting a total of $1,031,665.50 raised. This figure climbed to $1,576,085.00 at AGDQ 2015.

38. Paolo Pedercini (2014) critiques speedrunning as the hobbyist manifestation of the accelerated pace and quantification of life under late capitalism. However, within the progressivist logic of world records and the competitive framework that grows the metagame, there are ways in which the speedrunning community functions against the market forces in which any practice based around consumer products is necessarily enmeshed. Although much of speedrunning operates through the accelerationist logic of the market, it also represents the play of a leisure class that self-selects its economic bracket. Since it is a relatively cheap and infinitely renewable hobby, many speedrunners are satisfied to subsist in the aftermarket economy

outside the upgrade path. Rather than simply playing the standard metagame and moving from game to game and console to console, speedrunners design the conditions of their own play.

39. Although the very act of measuring play and boiling down material and embodied processes to an abstract number necessarily produces competition, speedrunners constantly collaborate on new times and organize around community charity marathons. While there are individual rivalries and community-based teams, and while international differences still exist in speedrunning, in contrast to the corporate and competitive culture surrounding e-sports like *StarCraft* and *Dota 2*, by and large speedrunners consider their metagame a hobby and leisure activity in contrast to their life and work.

40. The name HAL, like the sentient computer in Stanley Kubrick and Arthur C. Clarke's *2001: A Space Odyssey* (1968), is one (alphabetic) step ahead of IBM.

41. From the "Fire Power" of *Super Mario Bros.* (1985) to the "Frog Suit," "Tanooki Suit," and "Hammer Bros. Suit" of *Super Mario Bros. 3* (1988), to the "Wing Cap," "Metal Cap" and "Vanish Cap" of *Super Mario 64* (1996), Mario's wardrobe expands with a diverse collection of in-game abilities.

42. Nintendo's *NES Remix 2* (2014) showcases the plasticity of Kirby's game mechanics in a challenge in which a level from *Kirby's Adventure* must be completed without directional input or the A button by simply spamming the "Fireball" ability. Because Kirby ascends slightly when Fireball is interrupted by terrain collision, the B button alone is adequate to overcome some of Sakurai's level design.

43. For example, speedrunning *Kirby's Adventure* becomes a strategy game in which the diversity of abilities is prioritized according to the time it would take to attain a given ability versus how much time each ability saves in a given level.

44. Although Nintendo games like *Super Mario Kart* (1992) feature an ensemble cast, they do not typically include characters from outside the *Super Mario Bros.* franchise.

45. Aside from Mario sports titles like *Super Mario Kart* (1992), which features the denizens of the Mushroom Kingdom, Nintendo's other franchises cross diegetic boundaries to appear outside their gameworlds as either oblique references (e.g., Mario as a referee in *Mike Tyson's Punch out!* [1987] and Mario-like side characters in *The Legend of Zelda: Ocarina of Time*) or Easter eggs (e.g., Link and Samus' brief appearances in *Super Mario RPG: Legend of the Seven Stars* [1996]). The worlds of Hyrule, Planet Zebes, and Dream Land would not explicitly collide until *Super Smash Bros.*

46. Fabiszak is one of many "smashers": others include his sparring partner and teammate Kevin "Husband" Dassing and fellow community members, competitors, and commentators like Lilian "milktea" Chen, Juan "Hungrybox" Debiedma, Antoine "Wes" Hall, Kashan "Chillin" Khan, and Wynton "Prog" Smith, not to mention Beauchamp's "seven greatest competitors of all time": Christopher "Azen" McMullen, Ken Hoang, Joel "Isai" Alvarado, Christopher "PC Chris" Szygiel, Daniel "Korean DJ" Jung, Jason "Mew2King" Zimmerman, and Joseph "Mango" Marquez. Beauchamp recently completed fundraising for a full-length feature follow-up to *The Smash Brothers* starring the Swedish champ Adam "Armada" Lindgren.

47. First known in the speedrunning community as KirbySSB, Wright started her gaming career as a smasher in the "Central Wisconsin Crew."

48. It appears that as of 2014, Nintendo has slightly shifted its approach regarding competitive *Super Smash Bros.* and has made some tentative steps toward facilitating the metagame within their marketing campaigns and corporate philosophy. To cele-

brate the release of *Super Smash Bros.* for Wii U in 2014, during E3 that year Nintendo invited sixteen players to share the Nokia theater stage and compete in a tournament in front of three thousand people in the venue as well as an online audience on Twitch.

49. Coincidentally, one of Narcissa Wright's earliest screen names and *Smash Bros.* handles was KirbySSB.

50. The *Smash* community emerged in an era prior to the ubiquity of YouTube and Twitch (platforms that facilitate the exchange and archiving of the collectively created metagame in the form of video documentation). Although, in the early 2000s, *Smash* players were not entirely disconnected, sharing videos locally or through peer-to-peer software like the "Napster-esque program called the DC++ hub" was "awkward and unreliable" (Terrell 2011). The decentralized circulation of a game designed for home consoles made it impossible for a universal metagame to emerge. The history of the highly regional metagame, in the form of scattered footage from camcorders and extended conversations on forums, has not been well preserved.

51. On December 1, 2015, the Project M Dev Team announced that they had not only ceased development on the "homebrew" and "hackless" versions of their popular mod, but that they had also removed the links to each download. Luckily, a poetically titled website, "Project Mirror," popped up almost instantly, offering players access to the entire history of *Project M* downloads.

52. Explicitly referencing the dolls at the start of *Super Smash Bros.* that return as trophies in *Super Smash Bros. Melee,* Nintendo has released a line of figurines called Amiibos that double as real-life Smash Bros. Each plastic statue uses near field communication to send and receive data to and from Nintendo's Wii U. The result is augmented-reality trophies that all manner of Master Hands can literally plop into the arenas of *Super Smash Bros. for Wii U.*

53. Borrowing from the tradition of vaudevillian sideshows and stage magic, J. Stuart Blackton's *The Enchanted Drawing* (1900) and *Humorous Phases of Funny Faces* (1906), Émile Cohl's *Fantasmagorie* (1908), and Winsor McCay's *Little Nemo* (1911) and *Gertie the Dinosaur* (1914) each feature the animator's hand (and sleight of hand) as the metaleptic link between maker and made, process and product, storyteller and story. These early animations each begin with a demonstration. Whether on oversized drawing pad, chalkboard, loose leaf, or film screen, the animations first reveal the laborious process of producing a single frame of animation. The brief, pedagogical introductions in early animations represent a fictionalized production process to both educate *and* misdirect turn-of-the-century audiences. In Blackton and Cohl's work, for example, the hand of the animator appears to trouble the ontological status of drawings by reaching into the frame to pull out physical objects like a bottle of champagne and a cigar or directly manipulate the drawing itself as if it were an object (a clever trick in which both Blackton and Cohl's chalkboard drawings are secretly replaced with chalk-outlined black paper cutouts). Whereas Blackton helps himself to cartoon refreshments and erases half of a clown whose remaining (secretly) paper parts continue to move, Cohl screws the circular head back onto his clowning mischief-maker using a similar technique of interchanging stop-motion and drawn animation. These early traditions persist throughout the history of animation, from Winsor McCay's self-reflexive and vaudevillian animations to variations like Chuck Jones' *Duck Amuck* (1953), in which Looney Tunes regular Daffy Duck plays patsy to the fickle and perverse hand of an animator eventually revealed as not one of the denizens of "termite terrace" on the Warner Bros. lot, but their

avatar, Bugs Bunny. In each of these examples, the hand of the animator metaleptically upsets the diegetic storyworld of each animation while, of course, becoming animated itself. Whether through stop motion or clever editing, the hand of the animator is the figure that represents what is both within and without animation, blurring the distinctions between different narrative orders.

54. Blizzard's Electronic Entertainment Expo (E3) exhibition in 1996 was a month-old prototype of *StarCraft* which, at the time, consisted of a heavily modded *Warcraft II* (1995) engine that Patrick Wyatt (2012b) remembers was "derisively called 'orcs in space'" at the time.

55. Although Nintendo appears to slowly be relaxing its approach toward competitive gaming, the differences between Nintendo's and Blizzard's business philosophies concerning e-sports and metagaming in general may be attributed to both the cultural and technical differences between the two companies. Even at time of writing in 2017, Nintendo, a Japanese corporation invested in the console market since the mid-1980s, was just warming up to digital distribution, persistent screen names, and the social media of online gaming; whereas Blizzard, with their focus on PC gaming since the mid-1990s, had their online service Battle.net up by the end of 1996—almost 20 years before Nintendo's Miiverse. While these different approaches to networked connectivity are not directly responsible for all metagaming (*Super Smash Bros. Melee,* after all, had a strong competitive scene in the early 2000s), the differences are indicative of the larger business strategy that each company follows in relation to nurturing or ignoring the metagame around the game.

56. Stewart Brand (1972) may be the first e-sports commentator, since he was the reporter for the four-hour tournament at the Stanford Artificial Intelligence Laboratory sponsored by *Rolling Stone* magazine in 1972. Apart from the free beer, first prize was a year-long subscription to *Rolling Stone* and the opportunity to be photographed by Annie Leibovitz. Later, single-player games continued to incorporate player-versus-player competition. For example, *Sea Wolf* (1976), an early arcade game with the first persistent scoreboard allowed for asynchronous competition. Though these games were played serially by many single players, scoreboards added a social component, serving as a historical record that could be competed and compared with over an extended time period. In the 1980s, televised game shows such as *Starcade* (1982–84) were produced in which players competed against each other; this is one example of an early effort to convert videogames into a spectator sport (Taylor 2012, 4). These two traditions have led to the relatively recent emergence of two distinct types of electronic sport: the player-versus-player competitions at the center of the fighting, strategy, and first person shooter communities and the player-versus-game-records of the speedrunning and scoring community.

57. Dennis Jerz (2007), *Adventure's* unofficial historian, cites Tim Anderson's recollection that "it's estimated that *Adventure* set the entire computer industry back two weeks" due to the collective attention directed toward playing *Adventure,* which required both human labor as well as the time-shared processing power of the PDP-10. Although one person may have inputted the commands, the collective work and attention were distributed across multiple human and nonhuman bodies.

58. Whereas machinima leverages game engines and assets to create scripted, cinematic video sequences like Rooster Teeth's long-running *Red vs. Blue* (2003–) series of comedic, Beckettian conversations between *Halo* (2001) soldiers, Let's Plays document individual playthroughs of videogames as video or text and focus on the player's experience, reactions, and commentary alongside videogame play. For more

information, see Henry Lowood and Nichael Nitchsche's *The Machinima Reader* (2011).

59. In "Manifesto for Ludic Century," Eric Zimmerman (2013, 2) argues that although the twentieth century was dominated by the moving image, in the "ludic century, information has been put at play" and games will replace other media as the most prominent cultural form.

60. IRL, an acronym for "in real life," is commonly used to designate that which occurs outside the diegesis of a given game (e.g., "I'm also a soldier IRL"). Some players intentionally use AFK, "away from keyboard," instead of IRL in order to challenge the false distinction between real and virtual life.

61. A high-ranking ex-diplomat in Reddit's Test Alliance Please Ignore also admitted, "To be honest, I never really got hooked by the actual game play of Eve. I was hooked by the metagame and the politics. I had gotten to the very top of the Eve metagame, and outside of starting a massive coalition level war which wasn't possible at that time for various reasons, there was nothing left for me to aspire to" (Leodavinci 2014).

62. In a chapter of N. Katherine Hayles and Jessica Pressman's *Comparative Textual Media* (2014) on Tarn and Zach Adams' *Dwarf Fortress,* we call these player-made narrative accounts of computational processes "Dwarven Epitaphs" (Boluk and LeMieux 126, 2012).

63. Before Twitch playthroughs and YouTube tutorials were the norm, text-based, fan-made frequently asked questions (FAQs) were uploaded to websites like GameFAQs—an archive of metagaming practices that is still viewable to this day.

2. Stretched Skulls

1. Emerging from the subterranean burial site of New Mexico, Bogost uses the infamous example of Atari's *E.T. the Extra-Terrestrial* (1982) as one of his first examples of object-oriented criticism. In terms of an ontology in which "all things equally exist, yet they do not exist equally," Bogost (2012, 11, 17–18) defines *E.T.* as "8 kilobytes 6502 opcodes and operands," "a reformatted version of . . . assembly code," "a flow of RF modulations," "a mask ROM," "a molded plastic cartridge," "a consumer good," "a system of rules or mechanics," "an interactive experience," "a unit of intellectual property," "a collectible," or "a sign that depicts the circumstances surrounding the videogame crash of 1983, a market collapse partly blamed on low-quality shovelware (of which *E.T.* is often cited as the primary example)." In the same way the metagame replaces the magic circle of autonomous games with the "messy circle" of material reality, each of *E.T.*'s constitutive parts—from code to copyright to cultural history—occupies equal status and relevance within this flat ontology. In the case of *E.T.* and its burial in Alamogordo, the messy circle extends even beyond that game. In *Game After* (2014), for example, Raiford Guins documents his experience on the post-consumer archaeological dig in the local landfill in Alamogordo. Unearthing layers of dirt, dust, and concrete revealed not only the town's refuse, but the surprisingly well-preserved remains of Atari's corporate holdings when the company went bankrupt in the 1983. Among *Mrs. Pacmans* (1981) and *Defenders* (1981) are copies of Atari's much-maligned *E.T. the Extra-Terrestrial.*

2. Although the various schools of thought that make up the philosophical movement called Speculative Realism are radically distinct, each argue against the position that Quentin Meillassoux (2008, 5) first labeled "correlationism," or "the idea according to which we only ever have access to the correlation between

thinking and being, and never to either term considered apart from the other." If the fool sees only a finger when the wise man points at the moon, then what do we see when we look at a piece of New Mexico on Mars? And if, according to Harman (2009, 185), the correlationist can only ever see a moon made of fingers, then Mars may as well be New Mexico.

3. As discussed in chapter 6, in many ways, *Half-Life* is not just a first-person shooter in the vein of *Doom* and *Quake*, but is also a metagame made *within Quake* and *about Doom*. Built within a licensed and heavily modded version of the Quake Engine, *Half-Life* not only improved upon id Software's revolutionary real-time graphic technologies, but also attempted to replicate *Doom's* incredible distribution model. In the DOS universe of the mid-90s, id's game was more ubiquitous than Microsoft Windows. Beyond videogame engines and business models, *Half-Life* represents a turning point of the FPS genre: from frenetic and fast-paced action games to cinematic spaces for narrative storytelling.

4. In games like *Half-Life*, there is no correlation between the *image* of the gun represented on the screen and the *act* of shooting. The representation of the weapon onscreen is merely a vestigial, skeuomorphic interface. In a tradition going back to Étienne-Jules Marey's nineteenth-century camera gun, or even the "Smart Gun" assembled using the parts of a Steadicam that Private Vasquez wields in *Alien 2* (1986), photographic vision and violence are linked. Susan Sontag (1977, 15) labels the violence of photography a "soft murder," and in *Gaming: Essays on Algorithmic Culture* Alexander Galloway (2007, 40) traces the history of the FPS and its origins in cinema by looking at "subjective shots" in first-person films such as Robert Montgomery's *Lady in the Lake* (1947).

5. Xen, the dimension from which *Half-Life's* alien visitors emerge, is not only a take on the science fiction trope of "Dimension X" but a truncated version of the Greek word *xenos* (ξένος) which means "alien." In *Half-Life's* resource folder, the maps and textures used for Gordon Freeman's visit to Xen are labelled "xeno.wad."

6. As the processing speeds of computers have increased over the last twenty years, the loading times in *Half-Life* have decreased. At the time of the game's release, the tram ride could take over eight minutes.

7. Michel Foucault begins *The Order of Things* (1966) with a careful, close reading of Diego Velasquez's *Las Meninas* (1656). The painting conflates the point of view of the audience, the point of view of the painter, and the point of view of the subject to produce a paradoxical image that is not only a representation of the court of King Philippe IV but a representation of representation itself. In the sense of Foucault's "metapainting," these metagames are not just games about games, but they are games about *aboutness* itself.

8. Valve explicitly parodied the "Mac versus PC" commercials when advertising the release of Steam for Mac in 2010. Giving *Portal* away for free to every Mac user made intuitive sense seeing how the Aperture Science Handheld Portal Device references both the photographic aperture and the aesthetic sensibilities of Apple. Like the Nintendo Wii and DS or the iPod before it, the portal gun is white, rounded, glossy, and minimal. By deploying Apple's aesthetics, the portal gun invokes not only a particular formal design, but an entire corporate ideology of centralization as Apple has redirected its marketing away from specific technological products to the brand itself.

9. In "Eccentric Spaces and Filmic Traces: Portals in Aperture Science and New York City," we compare the "eccentric spaces" produced by the Aperture Science Handheld Portal Gun to the "filmic traces" of Dan Provost's augmented reality

mobile media app Trover. Whether editing the Aperture Science Enrichment Center or geolocating video in New York City, the palimpsest of perspectival play is evidence of a larger metagame surrounding vision and spatial storytelling (Boluk and LeMieux 2009).

10. Gordon Freeman embodies the classic videogame stereotype of the mute, masculine hero who saves the day. Literally the "Free Man" whose agency and freedom are under siege, his progress through Black Mesa is overseen by the mysterious G-Man, the quintessential man in black who appears to be controlling the situation behind the scenes. By contrast, both the protagonist and antagonist of *Portal* are gendered feminine. The Aperture Science Computer-Aided Enrichment Center building appears to be populated exclusively by Chell and the GLaDOS, an AI exquisitely voiced by Ellen McLain. Whereas Gordon Freeman stoically blasts his way through the corridors of Black Mesa (most likely at the discretion of the G-Man), Chell is much more explicitly under algorithmic servitude as she traverses from room to room at the will of GLaDOS, an increasingly unreliable narrator and guide. Like Gordon Freeman, Chell is the silent cipher who is similarly subject to a series of scripted corridors, but there is little illusion about the freedom contained within the panoptic surveillance system of Aperture Science's gamespace. Chell is a shell, an empty avatar wielding a yonic portal gun in direct contrast to Gordon Freeman's phallic crowbar.

11. Apart from Valve's sequel, *Portal 2* (2011), a short list of *Portal*-likes might include *Q.U.B.E.* (2011), *Quantum Conundrum* (2012), *The Unfinished Swan* (2012), *Perspective* (2012), *Antichamber* (2013), *Parallax* (2015), and a few still-forthcoming games like *Scale* (forthcoming) and *Museum of Simulation Technology* (forthcoming).

12. In Jay David Bolter and Richard Grusin's *Remediation* (1999), the concept of "immediacy" is treated as a powerful fantasy bound in a complex relationship with "hypermediacy." Immediacy is the desire for a completely transparent mode of communication through an interface that renders itself invisible to the user. Hypermediacy, on the other hand, draws attention to the multiple and interconnected layers of mediation at work in an object. As Bolter and Grusin (1999, 5) write, "Our culture wants both to multiply its media and to erase all traces of mediation: ideally, it wants to erase its media in the very act of multiplying them." This paradoxical, double logic has propagated within the popular imaginary throughout the history of Western art and continues to inform the development of image-making technologies from painting, photography, and film to computer-generated imagery, graphic user interfaces, and augmented reality and virtual reality. The desire for immediacy is expressed by the privileging of linear perspective which Bolter and Grusin (1999, 30) argue "is still regarded as having some claim to being natural . . . Meanwhile computer graphics experts, computer users, and the vast audiences for popular film and television continue to assume that unmediated presentation is the ultimate goal of visual representation and to believe that technological progress toward that goal is being made. When interactivity is combined with automaticity and the five-hundred-year-old perspective method, the result is one account of mediation that millions of viewers today find compelling."

13. In their careful, computer-aided reconstruction of *The Ambassadors*, Vaughan Hart and Joe Robson (1999, 5) argue for the primacy of this second, less conventional viewing angle—down and to the left (or "9.4 degrees from the picture plane, 250.5 degrees from the north")—based not on the way in which the skull resolves but on the formal and figural composition of the stretched and squashed *ambassadors*. When viewed below from this precise angle, the cocked shoulders of

the man on the left become horizontally level and his right leg vanishes into the shadows of the background. Perched there in cruciform, hovering above the unstretched skull, the ambassador mirrors the crucifix half-hidden behind the curtain on the upper left-hand corner of the painting. This metal crucifix is the most foregrounded element in the scene when viewed at this particular angle and Hart and Robson use this fact as a semiotic key for unlocking religious iconography of Holbein's painting. Based on the significance of this viewing angle, the authors further suggest that *The Ambassadors* was originally hung and lit at the top of a staircase and that glimpses of the skull could be caught upon approaching the painting from the bottom left.

14. Jacques Lacan (1998, 88) writes in the *Four Fundamental Concepts of Psychoanalysis* (1973) that the anamorphic distortion gives access to "a dimension that has nothing to do with vision as such—something symbolic of the function of the lack." Read psychoanalytically, Holbein's anamorphic skull is a "trap for the gaze" into which the subject disappears. Lacan (1998, 89) ultimately concludes his chapter not by distinguishing anamorphosis from traditional perspective, but by arguing that it demonstrates what is implicit in all image production (and by extension the concept of a stable Cartesian subject): "In any picture, it is precisely in seeking the gaze in each of its points that you will see it disappear."

15. We would like to thank Clare Woods for her assistance formulating the Latin construction of this term.

16. We would also like to thank Robert Lazzarini for his generous close reading, incisive commentary, and help correcting the technical details of our descriptions of *skulls*.

17. In *Tool-Being: Heidegger and the Metaphysics of Objects* (2002), Graham Harman reimagines Martin Heidegger's philosophy of objects and the distinction between "readiness-to-hand" and "presence-at-hand." The concept of "readiness-to-hand" is generally used to refer to the way in which objects are experienced not in themselves, but in terms of their relationship and utility to humans. Thus, the cup is not understood as an autonomous object, but defined instead based on its ability to hold liquid. When a cup breaks and becomes "presence-at-hand," an encounter with the pure presence of the cup as a being in and of itself occurs. The ontology of objects is defined in terms of their relevance (and nonrelevance) to human use and human users.

For his part, Harman (2002, 4) resists this reduction of objects to human phenomenology and proposes that "the famous tool-analysis holds good for all entities, no matter how useful or useless they might be. Beings themselves are caught up in a continual exchange between presence-at-hand and readiness-to-hand." According to Harman, Heidegger's idea of "presence-at-hand" and "readiness-to-hand" extend beyond human phenomenology to characterize an ontology of objects. Harman (2002, 1) constructs his "object-oriented ontology" around the concept of objects that "withdraw from human view into a dark subterranean reality that never becomes present to practical action any more than it does to theoretical awareness."

18. Hansen's term for this unsettling bodily awareness, the digital ASW, is based on Gilles Deleuze's (1986, 109) cinematic "any-space-whatever" (ASW) discussed in *Cinema 1: The Movement-Image*. Deleuze's ASW attempts to describe the empty, dislocated spaces of postwar cinema and distinguish them from the Hollywood logic of prewar film. What is highlighted in both Deleuze's and Hansen's version of the ASW is not the visual perception of this space, but the effects produced on the body. According to Hansen (2006b, 204), the key difference between the digital ASW and

Deleuze's theory is that "because it must be forged out of contact with a radically inhuman realm, the digital ASW lacks an originary contact with the space of human activity." As such, the digital ASW emerges within the body when the viewer comes in contact with the nonhuman logic and incommensurable perspectives of computational space.

19. The games mentioned here offer the player simulations of a poetic physics, or what Bill Seaman (2000, 41) has termed "e-phany physics" or "the code-based authoring of an artificial physics which is consistent within the virtual space, yet does not adhere to the laws of actual physics." Interestingly, Seaman also developed a definition of "metagames" for SIGGRAPH in 1993, around the same time Richard Garfield was developing *Magic: The Gathering*. For Seaman (1993, 1), "an 'Artificial Game' is a metagame. A Game of Games. An exploded territory in which one manoeuvres with sliding rules, open to the definition of their author and the interpretation of their participants. Play in this instance is an open category spinning off in different directions. The boundaries of these games have been blurred, become plastic, are floating."

20. Nintendo's transition from 2D to 3D games demonstrates the challenges of adjusting to these new spaces. Remembering the difficult launch of *Super Mario 64*, a release title for the Nintendo 64 in 1996, in a conversation with Nintendo's CEO Satoru Iwata (2011), Shigeru Miyamoto remarked that the reason why 3D action games were unpopular was because of how common it was for "people to get motion sickness" and that it was "easy to get lost in the playing field." Hansen likens the feeling of the digital ASW to motion sickness and, in the case of videogames, this is precisely the impairment a significant number of uninitiated players experienced upon first exposure to 3D graphics. Despite dramatic advancements in graphic processing technologies and the growth of audiences desiring to play in 3D virtual worlds, the difficulty of acclimatizing players to these spaces remains. Ten years later, particularly amongst Japanese consumers, Nintendo's 2D titles consistently outsell their 3D counterparts. Both *Super Mario Galaxy* (2007) and *New Super Mario Bros.* (2006), for example, were released around the same time and both were critically acclaimed; yet the side-scrolling platforming game sold two and a half times more copies than *Super Mario Galaxy*. *Super Mario Galaxy* was one of the first games to incorporate eccentric gravity and spherical levels into its design. In his interview with Miyamoto, Iwata (2011) comments, "At the time, I did not fully understand its benefits. I knew right away that visually [*Super Mario Galaxy*] would look great. But its true value was beyond what could be seen with the eyes, it was something that I hadn't realized." Both Miyamoto's remark on motion sickness and Iwata's observation on the way in which the effects of spherical space transcend visuality indicate an awareness of how the body functions while playing these games. The visual is only a small part in a much more comprehensive bodily engagement with digital space.

21. This generation included notable systems like the Sega Saturn (1994), the Sony PlayStation (1994), and the Nintendo 64 (1996), which ran at least 32-bit graphics processors in order to render the real-time polygonal meshes that make up the perspectival spaces of 3D games.

22. Although this chapter focuses on the increased visibility of anamorphic gameplay in the late 2000s, the tension between topological space and computational logic has been mapped by videogames since *Spacewar!* in 1962. Aside from the way in which a rectangular level or "board" may be mapped to the topology of a torus (as in late seventies and early eighties arcade games like *Asteroids* [1979] and

Pac-Man [1980]), videogames operating according to other graphic idioms also incorporated non-Cartesian cartography. Early text-based adventure games like Will Crowther and Don Wood's *Colossal Cave Adventure* or *ADVENT* (1975–76) included a "maze of twisty little passages" that repeats infinitely if the player does not input the correct sequence of navigational commands. These types of mazes that unhinge space from the flat, two-dimensional grid and embed it within an array of data continued to appear in graphical adventure games like *Adventure* (1978) on the Atari 2600 and *The Legend of Zelda* (1986) on the Nintendo Entertainment System.

Beyond this long lineage of spatial play within videogames, in the late 2000s many small or independently produced projects explicitly began to contrast the difference between three-dimensional spaces and the logic of the two-dimensional screen. Alongside the anamorphic games discussed in this chapter, games like Nintendo's *Super Paper Mario* (2007) for the Nintendo Wii, Kuju Entertainment's Zoë Mode's *Crush* (2007) for the PSP, DigiPen Institute of Technology's eagerly awaited student game, *Perspective* (2012), Ustwo's breakout mobile game *Monument Valley* (2014), and even Nintendo's *Captain Toad: Treasure Tracker* (2014) feature some degree of anamorphosis as a primary game mechanic. Unlike their predecessors, because these programs almost unequivocally feature anamorphosis as a puzzle to be solved, they subordinate anamorphosis within the regime of mathematical perspective, resolving the essential strangeness of subjective play into an abstract formation of levels and goals, problems and solutions.

23. Friedberg (2006, 12) suggests that Alberti's initial use of perspective as a "window" was not meant to treat the window (which during the Renaissance would have been composed of thick, opaque, and light-distorting panes of glass) as a "'transparent' 'window on the world,'" but as a framing device. As Friedberg (2006, 12) clarifies, "Alberti may have meant to use the window metaphor as an instructional device and not as a philosophical paradigm, and yet, as a metaphoric figure, it performs a coy slippage."

24. Terry Harpold also makes this observation in *Ex-foliations: Reading Machines and the Upgrade Path* (2009) when examining the default desktop wallpaper of Windows XP known as the "Bliss Screen," a vista composed of rolling grass and blue sky. Noting the uncanny connection between this pastoral imagery and Freud's description of an alpine meadow in his 1899 essay "Screen Memories," Harpold analyzes the advertising surrounding the release of the OS. One television commercial sets Madonna's "Ray of Light" against images of euphoric Microsoft users "diving" through the screen in order to soar through (indistinguishable) physical and virtual spaces, to the amazement of those looking on who have yet to test the GUI for themselves. The rhetoric of unmediated immersion and of a deep perspective, which the advertisement deploys in order to present the computer screen as a perspectival "window," renders invisible the complex and contradictory non-linear visual organization that truly comprises the Windows GUI (Harpold 2009, 238–41).

25. *The Ambassadors* also illustrates the tension between material surface and illusionistic depth. Applying the rhetoric of window and screen that Friedberg articulates, one can imagine viewing the two ambassadors as an act of looking through a virtual window. This fantasy is disrupted, however, through the presence of the smeared skull. The skull does not exist within the three-dimensional space of the painting, but instead appears as an object that is literally not of that world, or,

as Hansen (2006b, 202) writes, an "envoy from elsewhere." (Or, in the tradition of *Half-Life,* a visitor from Dimension Xen.) The fact that Holbein's skull does not inhabit the same virtual plane is reinforced by the fact that its shadows are not cast from the same light source. It is as if an imaginary pane of glass covers this "window" and the skull has been smeared over its transparent surface. There is an oscillation between figure and ground as the painting moves between drawing attention to itself as a window as well as a screen. This hypermediated effect of *The Ambassadors,* in which multiple lighting sources create layered windows into heterogeneous visual orders, is also at work in *Echochrome.*

26. The Sony Move is part of a generation of controllers released for consoles and competes with other motion-controlled sensors such as the Wii Remote and the hands-free Kinect for the Xbox 360. The Kinect is a human interface device that is able to track real-time 3D video using a grid of infrared laser beams. Not a graphic user interface (GUI) but a "natural user interface" (NUI), the Kinect attempts to read the physical gestures and voice commands of the player. These technologies are designed according to the same ideological conceits of the graphic user interface but call explicit attention to the player's body, situating them in a spatial relationship to the games being played. Unlike *The Ambassadors* and *skulls* that unsettle the human body through the tension produced between the virtual and the physical, however, these controllers attempt to suture the two realities together in a way that appears seamless and intuitive.

27. The flickering colors that Douglas Wilson (2016) lovingly terms a "single pixel screen" and the Sony Move's suit of accelerometers, magnetometers, and other digital sensors are utilized as a game in and of themselves in his hit non-video game *Johann Sebastian Joust* (2013)—a digital version of domestic balancing games.

28. Beyond the shadowy aesthetic of games like *Ico* (2001) or, more recently, *Limbo* (2010), there are a number of independently developed games that continue the minor tradition of "shadow play" showcased in *Echochrome II.* Games like *Lost in Shadow* (2010), *Closure* (2012), and *Contrast* (2013) each feature multidimensional puzzles represented by the difference between light and shadow. In their Flash-turned-console game *Closure,* for example, designers Jon Schubbe and Tyler Glaiel program onscreen objects that physically persist only if illuminated. A puzzle platformer following *Echochrome's* what-you-see-is-what-you-get logic, in the procedural architecture of *Closure* blackness *is* nothingness—any unlit object simply ceases to exist, allowing the childlike player-character to tiptoe through dimly lit walls and tumble through shadows cast on the floor. Recalling the aesthetic of Edward Gorey's *Gashlycrumb Tinies* (1963) and, like all the games mentioned above, following lone children through a kind of Purgatory, Schubbe and Glaiel present a child's-eye view of a world turned black and white, a world in which anamorphic light and shadow distort physical reality. Like the reader of *Gashlycrumb Tinies,* the player uncovers the many ways in which she can plunge into nothingness. In *Closure,* 3D space and the architecture therein do not exist without some form of anamorphic shading.

29. Although it may be trivial to define 4D, polygonal geometry as a series of four- rather of three-coordinate vertices, modeling and then animating these multidimensional shapes is another story all together. Every object and every angle of rotation within *Miegakure* is procedurally generated as ten Bosch had to write mathematical processes to both define the shapes and their motion.

3. Blind Spots

1. For many, formalism is the philosophy that defines mid-century modern art, but Reinhardt paradoxically resists a complete withdrawal from world history by peppering his public presentations with travel photos, writing about a universal aesthetic, and offering formalist works as part of a larger pedagogical program rather than as ends in and of themselves.

2. As fans were quick to point out on forums, the digital doctor in *The Phantom Pain* bears an uncanny resemblance to Sergio Canavero, the Italian neurosurgeon who made headlines in 2015 for speculating on the possibility of human head transplants.

3. In "*Journey* into the Techno-Primitive Desert," Irene Chien (forthcoming) considers Thatgamecompany's hit game *Journey* (2012) as both a sandbox for networked play and an allegory for how U.S. foreign policy transformed Iraq into a military playground. The same logic holds true for *Metal Gear Solid V*, as Snake bounds around from outpost to outpost, playing with the lives of Afghani, African, and Soviet soldiers. This fifth chapter of the series stands out from other *Metal Gear Solid* games because it is the first to attempt to combine "tactical espionage action" with the open world or sandbox style of level design. It is no coincidence that this dusty playground is mapped onto Afghanistan and an unnamed country in Central Africa (which holds more than a passing reference to the Angola–Zaire border during the Angolan Civil War). *Metal Gear Solid V* clearly follows in the tradition of the colonial sandbox games like *Far Cry 2*, which allegorize the complexity of war-torn nations (and their instrumentalization in the plots of those with power) via the production of procedural systems.

4. Following the basic formula of MTV's Music Awards, Spike TV's Video Game Awards (rebranded as VGX in its last year) were held annually from 2003 to 2013.

5. At GDC Kojima presented alongside CG art director Hideki Sansaki, technical director Junji Tago, and lighting artist Masayuki Suzuki with the help of translator Tom Sekine.

6. The most recent *Metal Gear* may well be Kojima's last. Despite quickly and quietly parting ways with Konami in 2015, it seems unlikely that Kojima's presence, or lack thereof, will ultimately influence the decision to keep producing *Metal Gear* games. That said, when Konami announced that they would be leveraging Metal Gear's beloved IP to skin "Big Boss" pachinko machines in 2016, fans of the series were outraged.

7. To show off the Fox Engine's graphic capabilities, Kojima also released computer-generated images of semi-translucent women's clothing (that was eventually modeled by the nurses in the game's prologue) and a very ornate bento box with food molded to look like *Metal Gear*'s protagonists (which unfortunately never appears in *Metal Gear Solid V*).

8. *Metal Gear Solid 2: Sons of Liberty* (2001) concludes with an encounter between Raiden, the unexpected protagonist of the game, and Solid Snake, the main character of Kojima's previous games. At the time, players were shocked and dismayed that Kojima had replaced the grizzled and battle-hardened Snake with the new, distinctly effeminate rookie. In keeping with the *Metal Gear* franchise's self-reflexive commentary on videogames (particularly in this second installment, notorious for pushing its metafictional aspects beyond the tolerance of many players), Snake remarks to a disillusioned Raiden at the conclusion of the game that "there is no such thing in the world as absolute reality. Most of what they call real is

fiction. What you think you see is only as real as your brain tells you it is." Perversely, both Raiden and the player are made to realize that they have both been playing a simulation within a simulation.

9. While Bolter and Grusin (2000, 30, 31) are careful to note "that the logic of transparent immediacy does not necessarily commit the viewer to an utterly naive or magical conviction that the representation is the same thing as what it represents," they admit that like the Immersive Fallacy: "This 'naive' view of immediacy is the expression of a historical desire."

10. It is also no coincidence that Kojima's last *Metal Gear* will be voiced and acted in English and then dubbed with Japanese, rather than the reverse, which was the practice for all previous games in the series. On the second *Kojima Productions Alert* podcast, host Sean Eyestone (2013) said, "This time, the facial performance that is being done by the English voice actor is what is driving the animation, what is driving the character. And actually, [Akio] Otsuka-san, who is the Japanese voice [for Snake], will be dubbing into that." The anglocentrism of this new version further situates the videogame series within the logic of Hollywood film.

11. Tim Lenoir's extensive research on the "military entertainment complex" (culminating in his 2016 book by the same name co-authored with Luke Caldwell) reveals this deeply entangled relationship between wargaming, military simulation, and the history of post–Cold War American military tactics. What is striking about *Metal Gear,* and distinct from other war games such as *Call of Duty* (2003–2014) and *Medal of Honor* (1999–2012) or even *America's Army* (2002–2013), is that it is not in fact a war game, but an *anti-war* game firmly rooted in Japan's anti-nuclear philosophy and deeply skeptical about American exceptionalism. Indeed, as Matthew Weise articulates in his extensive series of blog posts at *Outside Your Heaven*, "No other piece of popular entertainment at its level of budget and presentation disbelieves in America as much as it does, nor achieves its matter-of-fact pessimism about free-will. . . . It is the only anti-establishment military blockbuster, an Adam Curtis documentary masquerading as a Michael Bay explosion-fest (Weise 2010). *Metal Gear*'s conflation of photorealism with filmic realism ultimately serves as a commentary on the way in which contemporary infowar has turned the videogame simulation into not only a fictional, but a literal battleground.

12. Alongside *Metal Gear,* Kojima has also worked on the *Snatcher* series (1988–92), *Policenauts* (1994), the *Tokimeki Memorial* series (1997–9), the *Zone of Enders* series (2001–3), and the *Boktai* series (2003–6), among other, smaller projects.

13. In the seven years between *Metal Gear Solid 4* and *Metal Gear Solid V,* two comparatively smaller-scale titles were released within the series: *Metal Gear Solid: Peace Walker* (2010) by Kojima Productions and *Metal Gear Rising: Revengeance* (2013) by Platinum Games.

14. GRU is an abbreviation for Glavnoje Razvedyvatel'noje Upravlenije, Russia's primary military intelligence agency.

15. For example, 28.79% or 38 of 132 at *GameFAQs,* 29.01% or 121 of 417 at *Giant Bomb,* and 41.11% or 839 of 2041 at *NeoGAF* voted that Joakim Mogren was rendered in the Fox Engine (NaCl 2013, FluxWaveZ 2013, MormaPope 2013).

16. As N. Katherine Hayles, Patrick Jagoda, and Patrick LeMieux argue, in alternate reality games (ARGs), conspiracy theories and apophenia—the desire to uncover hidden patterns and secret meanings—inspire obsessive speculation that typically terminates in viral advertising. Hayles, Jagoda, and LeMieux (2014, 222) clarify, "As an emerging genre of digital games, ARGs navigate a number of contradictions that characterize convergence culture. On the one hand, these games

encourage open, participatory, and collective modes of play. On the other, the ARG form would not be possible without techniques such as gamification and viral marketing, as well as the convergence of media industries around specific reception platforms."

17. From the secret metachallenges that require collective, community effort to discover and complete in games such as *Braid* (2008) and *Fez* (2012) to full-fledged alternate reality games (ARGs) that take place inside games such as *Portal* (2007) and *Trials Evolution* (2012), many videogames have become platforms (even if just temporarily) for massively collaborative play in the form of online flash mobs, digital scavenger hunts, encrypted codes, multimedia riddles, and adaptations of other ludic happenings and folk games.

18. Although *Metal Gear Solid V: The Phantom Pain* features photorealistic graphics and complex artificial intelligence, it also sports the most robust cardboard boxes in the series. Since *Metal Gear* on the MSX, Solid Snake has been able to use cardboard boxes as both camouflage and transportation (in the case that the player hides in the back of a shipping vehicle or on a supply conveyor belt). In the latest entry of the series, however, Snake is also able to pop out of his box, run while wearing the box, slide down the hills of Afghanistan and Africa, and deploy life-size cardboard cutouts of military personnel and bikini models to trick enemy soldiers. The lush graphical realism of the game (and of the boxes themselves) contrasts with the surreal, cartoonish absurdity of the boxes' game mechanics—more Acme novelty than tactical espionage.

19. As a mainstream game, *Metal Gear* addresses issues of info war, drone warfare, and virtual simulations with surprising intelligence and sensitivity within its thirty-year melodramatic war opera. Such sensitivity is not displayed however, in its representations of race, gender, sexuality, and disability. One of the most recent installments, *Metal Gear Solid: Ground Zeroes,* depicts Paz, a non-playable character, getting raped and then murdered when multiple bombs are planted into her uterus and vagina. Rape is deployed as a cheap trick to showcase the villainy of the game's antagonist. As Ria Jenkins notes, Paz is made a victim "for the sake of the progression of another character; the scenes are careless, clumsy and childish." While this particular storyline is one of the most extreme examples of violence against women being enacted in order to service the story of the protagonist, *Metal Gear Solid: Ground Zeroes* is different in degree more than in kind from the supporting cast of women who are punished within the universe of *Metal Gear*—Eva, the Beauty and the Beast squad, Naomi Hunter, Emma Emmerich, Olga Gurlukovich and even "The Boss," a character Leigh Alexander (2012) suggested might even be "one of gaming's best female characters."

20. Another controversial figure in the series, a mute (and half nude) sniper who goes by the codename Quiet similarly exemplifies this platform specific concentration on videogame visuality. Like the Beauty and the Beast squad of female, cyborg antagonists who are all child survivors of war and suffering from PTSD in *Metal Gear Solid 4,* Quiet's inability to speak is linked to wartime trauma. Not only is Quiet mute, but her main skill is as a sniper—a weaponized form of vision. Impractically clad in a bikini, army boots, and torn stockings (a look that aesthetically follows the design choices of previous *Metal Gear Solid* heroines), both Quiet's abilities and disability allegorize the ocularcentric spectacle of videogames as the designers jettisoned Quiet's "unnecessary" features such as a voice in favor of producing the perfectly militarized eye (and eye candy).

21. At the end of 1997, following Nintendo's Rumble Pak controller peripheral by about six months, Sony released the DualShock, a PlayStation controller that featured force feedback vibrations. In the afterglow of these novelties in 1998, *Metal Gear Solid* featured more than a few explicit rumbles, which became campy reminders of platform exclusivity in future entries in the series.

22. *Metal Gear Solid V* is haunted by the phantom pain of a lost console war. Beginning with the images of a blood-smeared Sony Walkman—what could be considered the Japanese predecessor to the now ubiquitous Apple iPod—the game's 1984 storyline terminates with Punished Snake shifting a tape from the handheld music player to an MSX computer, the first machine Kojima produced games for and the videogaming platform that *Metal Gear* debuted on. Hissing and crackling with the sounds of data, the tape that plays at the end of *The Phantom Pain* is in fact a representation of the bitwise data of the original *Metal Gear* videogame first published for the MSX in 1983. Upon recording and decoding this information, players could boot a transmission of the first game in an emulator—another *Metal Gear* metagame that represents the phantom pain of a failing legacy of Japanese global electronics. This "console war" is further allegorized by setting the second half of *The Phantom Pain* in Zaire, indirectly referencing Sony's involvement (especially around the time of the PlayStation 2) in the conflict mineral wars occurring in the global south and specifically in the Congo. The metal in *Metal Gear* is coltan, the substance used to produce the microscopic capacitors that make up the on and off switches in computer processors like Sony's consoles or even the MSX.

23. Aside from her performance for "Snake Eater" in the *Metal Gear* series, Cynthia Harrell also sang "I am the Wind" for the *Castlevania: Symphony of the Night* credits in 1997.

24. The humor and absurdity of the ladder is enhanced by one of the song's most beloved lyrics: "Someday you go through the rain / And someday you feed on a tree frog."

25. CQC or close-quarters combat is the fighting style extensively discussed in *Metal Gear Solid 3* as a way to both tutorialize hand-to-hand encounters and promote the new analog buttons of the PlayStation 2 controller. Diegetically, CQC figures as both a unique fighting style that The Boss teaches Naked Snake and an allegory for their close but combative relationship.

26. Vivian Sobchack (2008, 251) describes the animated line as a "conceptual meta-object that has no existence other than as an idea or a graphic representation." She argues that "the line, indeed, is one of the sufficient conditions of animation for there are no lines inherent to the perceptible world of live-action, photoreal cinema," and that the single line in particular "foregrounds animation's own internal metaphysics and paradoxes, its own ontology" (2008, 252). *Super Paper Mario* is already self-conscious of its status as animation through its experiments with a hybrid world of 2D and 3D space, but the "World of Nothing" self-consciously reduces everything down to the horizontal line. If the player flips the perspective in order to move from a 2D platformer view to 3D vectoral space, the horizontal line transforms into an infinite vanishing point.

27. *Close Range* was preceded by *The Onion*'s other metagaming concepts: *Sousaphone Hero* (2007) and *World of World of Warcraft* (2008).

28. "Notgames" is a term coined by Auriea Harvey and Michaël Samyn, the two artists and game designers who founded the experimental videogame company *Tale of*

Tales. Five years after publishing their "Realtime Art Manifesto," Harvey and Samyn (2011) wrote "Not a Manifesto" as a challenges to obstacle- and rewards-driven videogame design: "Notgames is not a category. Notgames do not exist. There are no notgames. Notgames is not an art movement. Notgames is not a genre. Notgames is a project. Notgames is a challenge. Notgames is a question."

29. In 1960 Clement Greenberg (1990, 95) famously identified the characteristics of modernism as the ability to exhibit what is "unique and irreducible" about a particular medium. For Greenberg, "the task of self-criticism became to eliminate from the specific effects of each art any and every effect that might conceivably be borrowed from or by the medium of any other art." Although Greenberg's philosophy terminated with flatness in abstract, modernist painting, these games can be regarded as the product of a similar desire to generate medium-specific critical commentary through a process of negation. If art doesn't need to be representational, or have form, or have color, or have texture, or have contrast, then what does it need to be? The same questions could be asked of videogames.

30. Alongside *4 Minutes and 33 Seconds of Uniqueness,* there are numerous games that solely feature loading bars like *Progress Quest* (2002) or menu elements like *Do Not Push the Red Button* (2005). Perhaps where this micro-genre of metagames had the biggest impact was through the rise of incremental games like *Candy Box* (2013) and, subsequently, *Cookie Clicker* (2013) in 2013. What was once a largely unwanted and unintended byproduct of the hardware limitations of a particular platform's processing power (e.g., loading times) is converted into a core game mechanic. The most remarkable aspect of incremental games is not how they transform what was formerly a technical constraint on gameplay, but how surprisingly addictive they are. Without the random chance of roulette or slots, these games celebrate the predictable pleasures of progress in its purest form.

31. Some companies have gamified loading screens by including short animations or small "auxiliary games" to play while loading. Namco patented the latter technique in 1995, and still retain the sole right to "first [load] the smaller, auxiliary game program code into the games machine, before the main-game program code is loaded, then [load] the main-game program code while the auxiliary game is running" (Hayashi 1995).

32. Writing about the recent developments in immersive, virtual reality systems like the Oculus Rift, boyd speculates that these systems may fail to account for biological difference by designing systems that privilege male bodies. Citing from her previous research, boyd (2014) notes that "although there was variability across the board, biological men were significantly more likely to prioritize motion parallax" and "biological women relied more heavily on shape-from-shading." In other words, "men are more likely to use the cues that 3D virtual reality systems relied on" (boyd 2014). Although the evidence is inconclusive and more research is necessary, boyd wonders if the programming of Oculus Rift, even if unintentional, is right from the outset building in systems of gendered exclusion that would bar access to a technology with huge ambitions and potential use, from the creation of a Facebook "metaverse" to military and medical training simulations. Whereas the vertiginous effects of immersion software are hardly limited to women, the development of the Oculus Rift and other VR headsets demonstrate how a large category of the population might potentially be coded as disabled from the outset, barred from full participation in communities that arise from a specific technical milieu. This instrument of visual spectacle and cinematic excess conceals the gendered, racialized, and classed assumptions about what constitutes normative bodies. Wendy Chun (2004, 43) has

argued that "software and hardware are ideology machines," and the Oculus Rift is an example of how, in an attempt to produce an invisible and transparent interface, the ideological operations of the machine are rendered visible.

33. Siebers (2008, 3) writes that "The medical model defines disability as a property of the individual body that requires medical intervention" and "The social model opposes the medical model by defining disability relative to the social and built environment."

34. As Nicholas Mirzoeff notes in his essay "Blindness and Art," there is a long historical connection between the concept of blindness and insight, with gender often mediating this connection: The "visionary" artist uses a blind female muse as both subject matter and a path to knowledge. The way in which Helen Keller is taken up as the object of focus and subsequently denied agency in the *Simulator* reinscribes a gendered model of visuality in line with an art historical tradition from Butades's daughter to the minimalist artist Robert Morris's failed series *Blind Time II* (1976). In *Blind Time*, Morris recruited a blind woman, described only by the initials A. A., to assist in the production of his blind conceptual drawing. Mirzoeff (1997, 388) argues that Morris's work attempts to "recreate the origin of drawing in a woman whom he believed had no concept of visual representation" and "denied her the chance to formulate her own concepts of art practice and refused to let her establish any rules in her work."

35. Although in videogames random numbers are never truly random, speedrunners often refer to variables that they cannot control or account for as RNG. There are, however, many techniques runners employ to mitigate randomness by keeping as many variables as uniform as possible from one speedrun to the next. The veteran speedrunner Jeff Feasel, for example, predicts the location and composition of every random battle in *Final Fantasy* (1987) by walking the exact same number of steps at the exact same speed every time he plays the game. Feasel must, however, wait for the capacitors in the Nintendo Entertainment System to fully discharge before playing in order to reproduce one set of initial values—literally the control variables in this experiment. As long as the game boots with the same variables and Feasel maintains a degree of consistency, the game behaves predictably. None of this is part of the standard way of playing, and in order to invent this precise route Feasel played and planned for hundreds of hours in the summer of 2013, finally achieving a new world record on September 18 that year.

36. For example, Gardikis (2007) commented in Verner's thread "I never really noticed this topic because I was thinking it was the usual 'random speedrunner trying to get help with Oot.' . . . In the past I've made several attempts to beat super mario bros. without looking. . . . I have played through and beaten levels 1–1, 1–2, and 4–1 in a row. So I'm 3/8 of the way there. 4–2 probably wouldn't be a problem If I practiced it. . . . I don't think I will be able to beat any level in world 8. Maybe 8–3, because there aren't many gaps, but the end would sure be tough. . . . I wouldn't doubt that I could eventually beat the game blindfolded considering how many times I've played."

37. For example, Mario moves at different speeds in *Super Mario 64* based on when the next jump input is entered upon landing. Jumping immediately, on the first frame possible upon landing, produces a different result than jumping on the second, third, or fourth frame.

38. Unlike Verner's text-based playthrough, blind players like Terry "MegaTGarrett" Garrett, as well as blindfolded players like Drew "Runnerguy2489" Wissler, rely instead on stereo audio for spontaneous feedback while navigating the caves and castles of *Ocarina of Time*.

39. The hookshot automator is a small program written by Verner for *AutoIt,* HiddenSoft's open-source scripting language for automating Microsoft Windows. Without visual feedback, the first-person tilting and panning necessary to use the hookshot and bow in *Ocarina of Time* would be very difficult to time consistently. Verner's script translates keyboard buttons into millisecond-range joystick movements in the game, granularizing the Nintendo 64's analogue stick into a series of discrete degrees.

40. A third genre of adventure games, the graphic-adventure, was inaugurated by Roberta and Ken Williams' *Mystery House* (1980) before inspiring a generation of game developers at both Sierra On-Line and Lucas Arts in the 1980s and 1990s. For an excellent account of how Roberta Williams upsets the "patrilineal chronicle" of videogame history and offers "an alternative genealogy for gaming centered around relations of intimacy and labor in domestic space," see Laine Nooney's (2013) "A Pedestal, A Table, A Love Letter."

4. Hundred Thousand Billion Fingers

1. Of course there are always irreducible, material traces of play. Following Matthew Kirschenbaum's (2008, 10) theorization of "forensic materiality," the discharge patterns of capacitors, the warped pins of edge connectors, the oxidation rates of copper cartridges, and the literal fingerprints on controllers always mark a unique historical instance of play. However, much of the history of thumbprints on grey plastic, jelly or ketchup smears in controller seams, and the smell of cigarette smoke in insertion slots remain ineffable. Like the box of weathered "red fire buttons" that Raiford Guins (2014, 20) considers at the beginning of *Game After,* "Do these parts of game history remain locked away in some metal drawer within the rapid rise of game studies?" What is the history of the red fire button? The cigarette smell? The ketchup smear?

2. Since 1985 *Super Mario Bros.* has sold over 40 million copies worldwide. It is estimated that the *Super Mario* franchise as a whole has sold more than 500 million copies total ("List of Best Selling Videogames" 2016).

3. For further discussion of the relationship between the Oulipo and digital media, see Noah Wardrip-Fruin and Nick Montfort's (2003, 147–94) *New Media Reader.*

4. Even relatively simple recombinatory systems easily outpace the temporalities of human experience. Take for example Patrick LeMieux's (2014b) estimation that John Simon Jr.'s famous net artwork *Every Icon* (1997) "will take more than 5.85 billion years to reach the third line—sometime in a future beyond the death of the sun" and "enumeration of such a figure not only outpaces human consciousness but time and space."

5. The Nintendo Entertainment System polls input from the controller a finite number of times per second usually corresponding to the framerate of the platform. Thus, every button press is registered along a discrete and linear timeline that enables "build runs" and "speed demos" to be programmed sequentially, piece by piece, then executed reliably on both emulators and hardware.

6. In "From NES-4021 to moSMB3.wmv: Speedrunning the Serial Interface," Patrick LeMieux studies the serial structure of *Super Mario Bros.* as both a technical platform and medium for making metagames. LeMieux considers not only the serial repetitions required to progress through platforming games, but also the forms of serial communication that make the Nintendo Entertainment System controller and tool-assisted speedruns possible in the first place.

7. Denson and Jahn-Sudmann (2013, 11) develop three terms to differentiate their digital serialities: the *intra-ludic seriality* of "'levels' or 'worlds' of a game," the *inter-ludic seriality* of the "sequels, prequels, [and] remakes" of games, and the *para-ludic seriality* of the "transmedial narrativizations of game scenarios" such as "adaptations on film or television." Although they mention "the microtemporal scale of individual players' encounters with algorithmic computation processes (the speed of which escapes direct human perception and is measurable only by technological means)," they do not account for how the electrical pulses, crystal oscillations, and bit shift registers of serial communication might structure digital seriality as a whole.

8. Seriality was a foundational concept for Gilles Deleuze and Jean Baudrillard, who both elaborated on the concept in their dissertations, later published as *Difference and Repetition* (1968) and *The System of Objects* (1968), respectively. As Deleuze (1994, xix) notes in the preface to *Difference and Repetition*, "modern life is such that confronted with the most mechanical, the most stereotypical repetitions, we endlessly extract little differences, variations and modifications."

9. The phenomenology of serial play requires complicity on the part of the player in her own deception. In *Extra Lives*, Tom Bissell (2010, 4) describes his experience playing *Fallout 3* noting that "The pleasures of the open-world game are ample, complicated, and intensely private." The freedom to explore an open world or play around in software sandboxes is ultimately repetitive and, in this sense, Bissell's notion of privacy is a fragile form of serial bliss whose bubble is easily burst when multiple players' experiences of the same game are juxtaposed.

10. In *Network Aesthetics*, Patrick Jagoda examines *Journey* (2012), a game in which two players can collaborate to complete challenges using only in-game gestures to communicate. *Journey* dramatizes the networked intimacy of being "alone together" by both technically and diegetically modeling a form of networked and serial isolation. *Journey's* "uncertain relationality," as Jagoda (2016, 171) puts it, "calls the player's awareness, however subtly, to the affective dimensions of computer networks."

11. The second installment of the *Super Mario Bros.* trilogy differs depending on region. *Super Mario Bros. 2* (1986) did not appear in Europe and North America until its release on Wii's Virtual Console in 2007 (though it was remade with updated graphics as *Super Mario Bros.: The Lost Levels* as part of *Super Mario All-Stars* in 1993). Instead, another Miyamoto title, *Yume Kōjō: Doki Doki Panic* (1987), was re-skinned with Mario-themed graphics and released as *Super Mario Bros. 2* (1988) in Europe and North America in the late 1980s. In Japan, this title is known as *Super Mario USA*.

12. The plumber made his handheld debut as a launch title for Nintendo's Game Boy in *Super Mario Land* (1989). Shortly following that success, *Super Mario World* (1990) was packaged with the Super Nintendo Entertainment System (SNES). Although *Super Mario 64* did not conform to Nintendo's ever-expanding spheres of influence, *Super Mario Sunshine* (2002) continued this trend on Nintendo's Game-Cube, while *Super Mario Galaxy* (2007) and *Super Mario Galaxy 2* (2009) are two of the highest-selling titles on the Wii. With the possibility of a *Super Mario Universe* always on the horizon, it is becoming more and more difficult to imagine new territories for Mario to colonize. Perhaps the multiple dimensions discussed in this paper offer a temporary solution.

13. Specifically, Nintendo is one of the first companies to release an official interface designed with a sip-and-puff sensor for quadriplegic players in 1989: the NES Hands Free.

14. J-pop stands for Japanese Pop, a style of popular music produced in Japan that gained popularity in the 90s. Other Asian pop genres include K-Pop and C-Pop (produced in Korea and China, respectively).

15. Although many reviewers, critics, and theorists often parrot Arcangel's (2005) claim that *Super Mario Clouds* is "an old Mario Brothers cartridge which I modified to erase everything but the clouds," the game is more of a homebrew that uses the graphic data from Nintendo's famous game. In "The Art of Erasure," Nathan Altice clarifies that "*Super Mario Clouds* is merely a simulacrum of *Super Mario Bros.*, less alteration than visual reconfiguration, a game of magnetic poetry using common tiles but not common code. In other words, the processes driving game and artwork are wildly different. Inattention to the platform results in a partial understanding of either work."

16. In *I AM ERROR,* Nathan Altice argues, "The features built into NES emulators spawned new forms of play, performance, and videogame archiving. Suddenly players could record gameplay movies, save games at any point, play online, alter graphics, load translation patches, and more."

17. Even though *Mega Man 9* (2008) and *Mega Man 10* (2010), released on Virtual Console for the Nintendo Wii, are not demakes, ROM hacks, or homebrew produced in the aftermarket ecology of the Nintendo Entertainment System, their game design philosophy and 8-bit aesthetic function within the familiar idiom of the original Mega Man series.

18. The simplest solution to this equation of "everything" would be to string completed speedruns of every videogame in a linear order and allow this chain of button presses to function as the input for every game simultaneously. These concatenated speedruns would initially fail to complete those games they were not intended for. So, in order for the compilation to execute properly, this massive string would require buffers of button presses added between each original sequence in order to return each successive game to its null state (by achieving a game over). Though this equation would eventually complete every game ever made, it does not have the implied critique or entertainment value of the interwoven and threaded speedruns that the TAS community has created.

19. Another use of a single input on multiple operations is the practice of multiboxing in massive multiplayer online games (MMOs). In this metagame, a lone operator controls multiple instances of the same videogame either through a singular input or by juggling multiple controllers as a way to negotiate MMO environments balanced toward large group play. Multiboxers control anything from two to twenty games simultaneously, and in some of the largest documented cases, everything from an entire *World of Warcraft* guild of forty players a grand total of 107 has been operated at the same time by prepared WOW.

20. It is useful to distinguish between games that mash up mechanics (e.g., code) and games that mash up intellectual property (e.g., characters and storyworlds). Although this chapter focuses on examples that mash up gameplay by combining the mechanics of two or more previously discrete games, there is a large set of videogames that simply conflate the characters and settings of multiple franchises. Sports titles such as Nintendo's *Mario Kart* (1992), *Mario Tennis* (2000), and *Mario Golf* (1999) feature the likenesses of famous trademarked characters in new types of gameplay. Fighting games like Namco's *Soulcalibur* (1998) and Tecmo's *Dead or Alive* (1996), in addition to Nintendo's *Super Smash Brothers* (1998), investigated at length in chapter 2, license trademarks not only from other games but also from other forms of media (e.g., *Star Wars* characters in *Soulcalibur*) to produce a larger meta-

verse of intellectual property. The titles of Capcom's "vs." series makes this market-
ing strategy patent by incorporating the names of each participating corporation like
Marvel vs. Capcom (1998), *SNK vs. Capcom* (2000), and *Tatsunoko vs. Capcom* (2008).
Here the obligatory "vs." doubles as a signifier for one-on-one combat as well as the
marker of a temporary corporate merger (dramatizing the unease that accompa-
nies strategic business alliances). The Disney Corporation, in collaboration with
Square-Enix, created another unwieldy, character-driven mashup with *Kingdom
Hearts* (2002), an action role-playing game featuring both Disney and Square characters underwritten by Square-Enix game mechanics. Though these games might
be considered mashups on a thematic level, they typically do not mash up the
mechanics of multiple franchises.

21. As Andy Weir (2002) outlines on his website, *Grand Unified Game* (GUG) "is a
puzzle/platform game which puts Dig-Dug, Pac-Man, Mario, and the Jouster together
against all their old foes. Try to get these 8-bit buddies to the exit of the level without
any of them dying!" Featuring remediated mechanics from the aforementioned videogames, Weir's software compares and contrasts *Pac-Man* (1980), *Dig Dug* (1982),
Joust (1982), and *Super Mario Bros.* through level designs that require the player to
think about the affordances of all four pieces of software. In the same way the Grand
Unified Theory (GUT) attempts to model particle physics as a single, unified force,
GUG imagines the operations of digital media which make all games possible.

22. *Tuper Tario Tros.* combines Mario's platforming with *Tetris's* falling block
puzzles. In the French development team Swing Swing Submarine's Flash application, the screen continually scrolls to the right and pressing the spacebar shifts the
game from *Super Mario Bros.'s* platforming interface to a partitioned landscape for
playing *Tetris*. As bricks and blocks fall in the form of tetronimos, they add (and
subtract) from the physical environment Mario must traverse. The game begins with
a wall that the player must deconstruct by completing rows of bricks, then continues through an open area where bridges of blocks must be built, then concludes by
requiring the player to rebuild the castle while Goombas constantly fall from the sky.

23. After building physics-based versions of *Pac-Man* and *Tetris,* Maurice Guégan remade *Super Mario Bros.* in the Love2D game engine. His remake, however,
included one additional feature: the Aperture Science Handheld Portal Device from
Valve's *Portal* (2007). Titled *Mari0,* Guégan's game not only carefully simulated the
original *Super Mario Bros.,* but also lets players navigate the Mushroom Kingdom
via portals: "speedy thing goes in, speedy thing comes out." Given this framework
for Mario metagames, at Gamescon in 2013 Guégan invited one thousand guests to
navigate a time trial he designed. Carefully tracking the position values and animation states of each Mario, Guégan was able to visualize the movements of a thousand
Marios on their way through the Mushroom Kingdom, a spectacle reminiscent of
Andi McClure's *Many Worlds Emulator.*

24. Since emulators converged around the .NES file format that typically combines
the programming and graphics data found on ROM masks within cartridges, emulated games are often simply called *ROMs* (Altice 2015, 305). A notable exception is
the term ISO, which is a truncated version of ISO9660, a file standard designed for
optical discs like CDs.

25. Using *ROM CHECK YOURSELF* is Farbs' *ROM CHECK GO!,* a modified,
speedrunning version of *ROM CHECK FAIL* that automatically tracks player progress by communicating with the LiveSplit timer and allows the player to swap avatars at will. Run by a small community of players in August 2016, Farbs himself sits
at the top of the leaderboards with a final time of 1 minute 30 seconds.

26. *Mario vs. Airman* also includes an 8-bit arrangement of *Air Man ga Taosenai* as the game's background music. Like *Mario vs. Airman, Air Man ga Taosenai* is a fan-created music video featuring an exasperated-yet-determined Mega Man attempting to defeat Air Man, a particularly polarizing character who some Japanese fans insist is the most difficult robot master to defeat, while others argue the opposite.

27. Since creating the *Many Worlds Emulator,* Andi McClure has produced a smattering of small metagaming experiments: from the embedded worlds of *Jumpman* (2010) to playing pong with a thousand balls in *pongpongpongpongpongpongpongpong* (2012) to her collaboration with Michael Brough, *BECOME A GREAT ARTIST IN JUST 10 SECONDS* (2013) to the Emily programming language designed from the ground up to be simple and inclusive. McClure's experiments represent an alternative model of game design in which the goal is not selling software but making more metagames.

28. One notable exception is dram55's realtime attacks of the *Kaizo Mario World* ROM hacks. Playing the game in realtime on original hardware, dram55 patiently plays through each level, carefully executing each prepared trick in order to complete the games with minimal (and sometimes no) deaths.

29. Notch would go on to develop the wildly successful sandbox game *Minecraft* (2010), which features procedurally generated landscapes constructed out of Lego-like voxels able to be manipulated by the player. *Minecraft* was first distributed in a constantly updating alpha version. As a result of this serial format, players doubled as play testers and influenced the direction the development of the game took.

30. Since competing in the Mario AI competitions in 2009, Baumgarten has produced *Line Wobbler* (2014), a sculptural game leveraging a spring-based joystick, a flexible LED strip, and sin wave feedback to create a "one dimensional" dungeon crawler in which players traverse pointillistic environments and confront pixelated enemies by physically "wobbling" the controller.

31. Some contenders argue that Baumgarten ventured beyond the spirit of the rules by integrating the entirety of the *Infinite Mario Bros.* level generator into Mario's AI rather than using the much more limited default library of functions for addressing "vision." The result of this oversight (on the part of both the organizers and Baumgarten's AI) is that Baumgarten's Mario sees all from a godlike perspective when compared to the restricted viewpoints of the other bots—a meta-view encapsulating the entire game within its gaze.

32. Self-competitive games end up resembling MMOs like *Transformice* (2010). Developed in 2010 by Mélanie "Melibellule" Christin and Jean-Baptiste "Tigrounette" Lemarchand, *Transformice* is a networked, multiplayer platformer in which players are collectively loaded into a single simple level. The goal is that each player must acquire a brick of cheese and return to their mouse hole. Every player must work alongside dozens of others who, driven by the same desire, perform similar actions. Like Sartre's model of seriality that describes the processes by which individual actors fail to achieve awareness of how their actions function systemically, *Transformice* allegorizes the failure of individualism by revealing how the collective and cumulative result of individual actions work to produce the exact opposite of the intended effect. Unless the players learn to work together and sacrifice the immediate satisfaction of their needs, the mice will find themselves all tumbling—often hilariously—to their doom. *Transformice* follows the same ironic logic as the cascading effect of a bank run in which the reflexive rush to save oneself becomes, in the aggregate, the force that produces systemic financial failure.

33. From melting the tips of Bic pens to produce an impression of the security screws, to snipping the power pin of the lockout chip so that no verification needed to take place, to ignoring the corporation's software library and purchasing independently produced games, there were plenty of ways to circumvent Nintendo's structures of control to play in different ways in the 1980s and 1990s.

34. Beyond the various Marios who make an appearance from *Super Mario Bros.*, *Super Mario Bros. 3*, *Super Mario World*, and *New Super Mario Bros. U*, perhaps the most iconic image from *Super Mario Maker* is the white, slender, feminine hand holding a stylus meant to represent the player. This hand, cribbed from advertising materials surrounding the Wii U, is the default interface for building Mario levels. And although there is an option to change the hand's skin color to Photoshopped variations of darker and darker skin (or a dog's paw, a cat's claw, or even Mario's gloved hand), as argued in the context of Susan Kare's Macintosh icons in chapter 1, in Nintendo's attempt to make a seamless GUI, these skeuomorphic hand avatars reveal the way in which race is (and is not) represented in videogames.

35. Both the tool-assisted speedruns and the Mario AI show how far videogame "demos" have come since *Super Mario Bros.* was first released in 1985. In the original, if a player does not immediately "press start to begin," two demos of the game will loop in the form of an attract screen, depicting a computer-controlled Mario navigating Level 1-1. Phil Sandifer has conducted a close reading of the strange and illogical behavior that characterizes Mario's movements in the demo, suggesting that the failure to successfully move through the game indicates how undervalued this type of presentation was at the time: "The demo is not an essential part of learning to play. . . . The game needs an actual player to complete it in a functional and proper way." Sandifer describes the Mario in this video as "Player Epsilon." He argues that "the ε is the sign, within computer science, of the empty set—that set containing no members. Thus Player ε is the player without content—the player that is a player, but with none of the actual traits or aspects of the player. There is, in Player ε, only the consequences of the player—game and play—and no actual player. In one sense, then, Player ε represents the pure act of play—play without its attachment to the dyad." The development of AI that replaces the human hand with algorithms signals this shift from Mario's early history. If, as Sandifer suggests, the game once operated under the assumption that it held no value for the spectator in the absence of human interaction, the demo (and the machinic subjectivity that he characterizes as Player ε) has come to assume a more privileged place.

5. The Turn of the Tide

1. For an excellent material history and critical analysis of the subterranean network of undersea cables and their relationship to empire, colonialism, global capital, and both maritime and cyber warfare, see Nicole Starosielski's *The Undersea Network* (2015).

2. In 1914, Luigi Russalo's first noise recitals in Milan erupted into riots with "the futurists . . . fighting the public in the stalls" after the debut of industrial instruments like the exploder, the buzzer, the crackler, the whistler, the rumbler, and the screamer in a concert setting (Thorn 2002, 415).

3. The first International, hosted at GamesCom in Cologne, Germany, was nicely documented in Valve's first feature film, *Free to Play* (2014), which featured a mix of tournament footage and dramatized gameplay alongside the biographies of three up-and-coming players: Danil "Dendi" Ishutin, Benedict "hyhy" Lim, and Clinton "Fear" Loomis.

4. In 2012, The International boasted the largest purse in the history of e-sports. Each subsequent year has either met or broken the previous year's record with $1.6 million prize pools in 2011 and 2012 before the prize was crowdfunded in 2013. For the third International, Valve augmented the prize pool by contributing $2.50 or 25 percent of the profits from every sale of their *Interactive Compendium*, an electronic magazine built to track, analyze, and even play with The International. Two weeks before the tournament, fans had bought over 500,000 compendiums, increasing the original $1.6 million by an additional $1 million, easily the largest prize ever assembled for such an event (Spicer 2013). This trend exponentially increased from $2,874,380 in 2013 to $10,931,105 in 2014 to $18,429,613 in 2015 to $20,770,460 in 2016. The winningest *Dota* players are now taking home more money than professional athletes at the U.S. Masters or Wimbledon. Alongside these monetary increases, since 2014 The International has been held at Key Arena, a Seattle sports stadium that holds about seventeen thousand people. In 2015 the venue sold out in five minutes and garnered thirty million viewers on platforms like Twitch, YouTube, and even ESPN. With *Dota 2,* there are now more eyes are on the championships of competitive video games than Major League Baseball's world series or the NBA finals—each of which had about fifteen million viewers in 2015. E-sports are approaching World Cup numbers; not quite the Super Bowl, but good enough for the "Super Bowl of E-sports."

5. In 2013, Dendi, Puppey, and XBOCT, the three Na`Vi players who competed in the first three International tournaments, were are among the top ten highest earning professional gamers in e-sports history with around $435,000 of prize money earned per player (GGBeyond, 2014). Since then, players belonging to teams that have won the crowdfunded prize pools in 2014 and 2015 far outpace previous winners (as well as those players competing in other e-sport titles). In 2016, the top thirty winningest players in terms of cash prizes all play *Dota.*

6. Since much of the capital investment of e-sports—in terms of both tournament and league organization, sponsorship, and talent—is located in East Asia, players from Europe and the Americas are often referred to as foreigners, especially in Korean e-sports. This demographic homogeneity manifests through private, national tournaments (and network services) difficult for non-Koreans to access, as well as through the professionalization of players through exclusive contracts, institutionalized team houses, and practice regimes difficult to compete against without first moving to Korea and adopting these lifestyles.

7. In the preliminary matches held at Valve's Seattle headquarters a week before The International in 2012, the sixteen invited teams were divided into two groups of eight. Each team played two games against the other members of their group for a total of ninety-six grueling games. The top four teams from this "bootcamp" were seeded into the winner's bracket of The International while the others went into the single-elimination loser's bracket. Over the course of the preliminary matches, Invictus Gaming went 13–1, leading their group, while LGD's perfect 14–0 and DK's 11–3 topped the other half of the scorecard. Na`Vi placed fourth in iG's group, barely making it into the winner's bracket, which they would eventually win.

8. Though LGD Gaming, a Chinese team representing Guizhou Laogandie Food, had mopped the floor with the Moscow Five (M5) in sixteen minutes eleven seconds during the prelims, Na`Vi's loss to iG was the shortest game in the 2012 tournament proper. Given the sixty-nine games played in Seattle that week, the average time of any given game was about thirty-five minutes fifty seconds. The Chinese teams averaged higher overall, with a time of about thirty-seven minutes thirteen seconds, while the rest of the teams timed in at thirty-four minutes fifty-

four seconds per game. Although these statistics match the perception of the Chinese metagame at the time of The International in 2012, the strategies deployed within each game colored the crowd's perceptions more than the total time played.

9. Na`Vi capitalized on this heroic image, flying in-game banners depicting the team's crest and brand identity—a blue and gold logo in the shape of a fist, waving high among the polygonal leaves of digital trees and serving as a metonym not only for the team, but for their corporate sponsors like StealSeries, Alienware, Kingston, and Twitch.tv. All five Chinese teams invited to The International, however, were represented by one image: the national flag, as out of place within *Dota 2*'s fantasy landscape as the U.S. flag assembled on the moon.

10. In MMOs like *EverQuest* (1999) or *World of Warcraft* (2004), "farming" typically refers to the process of amassing virtual currency through repetitive actions that value in-game profit over other forms of ludic or diegetic play. Farming is especially popular in China where companies will hire players, dubbed "gold farmers" or use program bots to produce virtual wealth that is then sold on eBay or through other external services. "Ricing," on the other hand, is often used as a pejorative within the *Dota 2* community to describe strategies in which a single character's growth is prioritized over all else. Called "4 for 1 *Dota*" or sometimes "Chinese *Dota*," this type of long-term play attempts to give one team member the time and space to "eat," "get fed," or simply "rice" over the course of a single game.

11. Among many others, Lisa Nakamura studies the way in which virtual migrants like goldfarmers disrupt the pleasures of *World of Warcraft*'s more leisured inhabitants. In contrast to the activities of players who invest their spare time not in a fantasy game, but in the fantasy that play exists outside work, the practices of selling in-game currency for real-world money represent "the worst, most morally reprehensible form of cheating" (Nakamura 2013, 188). Goldfarming disrupts the autonomy of the gamespace as a moneyless utopia (recalling Thomas More's original *Utopia* [1516]) that stands apart from the worries and rigors of quotidian life. As Nakamura (2013, 190) argues, "While many players are fairly unaware that their computer hardware is born and dies, or is recycled, in China, they are *exceptionally* aware of the national, racial, and linguistic identities of gold farmers" (emphasis original). The figure of the specifically Chinese goldfarmer challenges the neoliberal notion that virtual space is a fair and democratic playing field by revealing the classed, gendered, and racialized ways in which certain forms of play are privileged over others. Although the goldfarmer has received a fair amount of analysis (especially in the scholarship surrounding massively multiplayer online games), less has been said about the pro gamer or e-athlete and the mode of production under which they too work. Whereas goldfarming is often frowned upon and regarded as a practice that spoils the carefree fun that games traditionally represent by incorporating real-world economies into the game, the financialization of e-sports has been enthusiastically celebrated as proof of the fairness of games, the virtuosic mastery of gamers, and the value of digital play in mainstream culture.

The vehemence with which goldfarming is perceived as breaking the magic circle—by indexing in-game processes with a virtual gold standard through the exchange of digital mining for real money—resembles the equally zealous evangelism that attends e-sports and its movement towards the professionalization and monetization of play. T. L. Taylor (2009, 189) attributes the fanaticism of some fans to the fact that e-sports is currently in "the teenager stage of development—full of emotion, passion, enthusiasm." Are not the training schedules, legal arguments, player salaries, sponsorship deals, and international relations of contemporary e-sports another side of the goldfarming coin? As with goldfarming in *World of Warcraft,* in *Dota 2* farming is strongly identified with the practices of "Chinese *Dota,*" which appear to place fun and winning in inverse relation to one another. Spectators may not derive much pleasure from watching players avoid direct combat in order to continue grinding away at endless waves of AI enemies, but, at the end of the day in this social factory there are only a few workers who will take home a paycheck, a wage ultimately independent from whether or not the spectator is treated to a high kill count or feats of bravado. The celebration of e-sports by an increasing number of players continues to reinforce the cognitive dissonance and contradictions that displace goldfarming on to an Eastern other while championing the increasing corporatization and professionalization of e-sports.

12. While, at the time, most live e-sports events would stream exclusively via Twitch, Own3D, or their own, proprietary service (e.g., GOMTV's media player), Valve streamed through as many providers as logistically possible.

13. *Dota 2's* client is not the first time a videogame has implemented broadcast technology directly within the software. Over a decade earlier, Valve released SourceTV, a similar feature in 1999's *Counter-Strike* (a fan-made mod of *Half-Life* [1998] that spawned a successful and long-lasting competitive scene). Yet, given the capabilities of contemporary network technology and the storage capacity of Valve's .DEM or demo files, *Dota 2's* spectator client is among the most robust platforms for in-game viewing (even when compared to other popular e-sports titles like Blizzard's *StarCraft II* [2010] or Riot Games' *League of Legends* [2009]).

14. In addition to the host on the floor, the analyst and color commentator in the booth, and maybe a statistician or media liaison checking in from off screen, most multiplayer e-sports tournaments also include the often invisible, yet crucial role of the observer. The observer is charged with piloting an in-game camera and presenting the game to not only the other commentators, but also the audience. Usually an ex-pro gamer or someone who has intimate technical knowledge of the game, the observer has the responsibility of not only fluidly navigating the interface, but also predicting and presenting the narrative throughline of a given match. From the perspective of the software, in many games the observer is actually considered to be just another player—watching is encoded as an equally important form of play. Using the tools provided by the game, the observer must extemporaneously produce the narrative by directing attention to the most dramatic and information-rich areas of the map—a task that is often not immediately self-evident in any given moment. They take the place of the entire editing booth at a live sports broadcast as they select the right angles, snap to the perspective of the correct players, and open up the proper maps, graphs, and charts. An effective observer is essential to watching e-sports and a bad observer can ruin the game.

15. The eighth generation of home videogame consoles like the Xbox One and PlayStation 4 have begun to explore the ludic potential of spectatorship, simplifying the process by which games can be streamed online in real time at the press of a button. While live streaming on Twitch does not allow viewers to control camera perspective and track player gestures as one can when viewing direct in the *Dota 2* client, play no longer ends in the living room. The result is that new software and hardware are increasingly supplemented with a complex participatory media ecology that leverages the expanded attention economy of videogames by expropriating surplus value not only from players, but from their viewers. These new strategies further intensify the ability of companies to colonize the gaze and attention of their users, turning both viewers and players into workers for companies who operate, as Matteo Pasquinelli (2009, 152) writes, as "rentiers of the common intellect."

16. Valve's cosmetics market begins with community-produced virtual commodities that are randomly distributed as prizes within *Dota 2*, sold online for a limited time, or packaged with other purchases like tickets to tournaments. Despite their digital status, these goods accrue value according to status and affinity within the community.

17. On April 30th, 2010, *Dota 2*'s main developer, IceFrog, reported, "I can only give estimates based on getdota.com usage, because I can't track ingame downloads or fansites or downloads from China. It is roughly estimated (based on the statistics from popular Chinese sites) that the Chinese DotA audience is about 40–50% the worldwide audience. Not counting China, the playerbase is estimated to be somewhere between 7–11 million" (IceFrog 2010).

18. While there is no lack of unofficial consoles and unlicensed software that have circulated throughout the country, it was only in July 2013 that China lifted its thirteen-year ban on consoles that began at the start of the millennium (Lobosco 2013).

19. In the 1780 edition, for example, each player began with "forty pawns, thirty knights, six queens, five 'jumping queens,' eight 'jumping bishops,' seven elephants, four rooks, and four bishops," and operated according to multiple win conditions (Peterson 2012, 215). The game was sold in sets of varying sizes with which Hellwig "encouraged experimentation and customization of the board to fit the needs of the players" and, as early as 1782, noticed his patrons beginning to reenact historic battles within the tabletop game (Peterson 2012, 214–15). Continuing to adjust, modify, and remake chess throughout his life, by 1803 Hellwig had completely replaced the standard pieces with grenadiers, cavalry, and cannon manned by infantry and developed a combat system based on the orientation and discharge of firearms.

20. Although the influence of Tolkien is undeniable, in *Twisty Little Passages* Nick Montfort (2003, 75) disputes "the extent to which *Dungeons & Dragons* is inspired by J. R. R. Tolkien's work," arguing, "Tolkien can sometimes seem like the single straw that those unfamiliar with fantasy and adventure writing grasp at when trying to understand where this game came from and how to situate it vis-a-vis literature." In response to rampant claims to the contrary from critics and fans alike, TSR, the makers of *Dungeons & Dragons*, insisted, "*D&D* was not written to recreate or in any collective way simulate Professor Tolkien's world or beings . . . This system works with the worlds of R.E. Howard, Fritz Leiber, and L.S. de Camp and Fletcher Pratt much better than that of Tolkien" (Kuntz in Montfort 2003, 75).

21. Patrick Wyatt (2012a) remembers, "We were inspired to create *Warcraft* after playing (and replaying and replaying) a game called *Dune 2*, by Westwood Studios. *Dune 2* was arguably the first modern real-time strategy (RTS) game; with a scrolling world map, real-time unit construction and movement, and individual unit combat. It isn't that much different in design than a modern RTS like *StarCraft II*, excepting perhaps a certain scale and graphics quality."

22. Not only was the first use of "space marine" to be found in the *40,000* series, but the three races of *StarCraft*—Terran (a direct citation of Robert A. Heinlein's *Starship Troopers* [1959]), Protoss, and Zerg—were unabashedly copies of the space marines, eldars, and tyrannids from *40,000* (Plunkett, 2010). Part of Blizzard's success with both the *Warcraft* and *StarCraft* series is due to appropriating the visual iconography of Game Studio's *Warhammer* and *40,000* as well as translating their wargaming tabletop mechanics to a 2D isometric computer game.

23. Perhaps the procedural undercurrent of digital violence, in contrast to representational violence, is not as "harmless" as Wark claims. The tie between videogames and war runs deeper than German war games. See, for example, Tim Lenoir's excellent genealogy of the military-entertainment complex in "All But War is Simulation"

(2000). Moreover, the threat of violent videogames has led to longstanding public debates and media panics when blamed for mass shootings. Alexander Galloway (2006, 72) labeled this correlation the "'Columbine theory' of realism" in which "games plus gore equals psychotic behavior." Apart from its manifestation within its paradigmatic expression form of the videogame, the logic of the digital has had a powerful transformative effect over culture. The biometrics of the border, the uncompromising categories of the census that reify identity categories, and overall dataveillance of human gesture and affect have become ways not of reflecting race, class, gender (e.g., social difference) but of *producing* difference via the mechanisms of algorithmic control and organization asserted over digitized, discretized, and differentialized bodies.

24. Just as no ball player can decide to lower the Earth's gravity for an instant, no gamer can change the rules governing a gamespace without reinventing (or reprogramming) the videogame—resulting in a different game. The fact that players can still cheat in baseball (e.g., through illicit use of steroids, corking the bat, throwing a game, or bribing the umpire) testifies to the fact that some rules are voluntarily chosen by those playing fairly. In a videogame, however, the player has no choice but to jump a certain height or move at a certain speed. There is no referee because the laws of physics cannot be broken. Even an exploit that breaks an intended gameplay sequence or shatters the story arc does not constitute a form of cheating but instead reveals how little is known about the field of possibility offered by each videogame. There is no cheating in *Mario*.

25. A surprising side effect of such a strict and studied metagame is that unskilled or unknown opponents can sometimes prove challenging as they do not follow (or at least do not seem to follow) the unspoken rules of a given community, introducing unoptimized timings or strange strategies into the game. For example, in Korean *Star-Craft* broadcaster GOMTV's variety show "Off the Record," professional players would occasionally have difficulty beating fans of the show because they were not playing the metagame. In another high-stakes competition with a robust metagame, thirteen-year-old Bobby Fischer famously exploited this weakness in the standard chess metagame, or "book," in 1956 when he surrendered his queen to checkmate Donald Byrne over twenty moves later in "The Game of the Century" (Radio Lab 2011).

26. The draft can be conceptualized as a zero-sum strategy game in and of itself. Drafts can win or lose a game despite the manual dexterity and coordination of a given team. There are whole websites dedicated to simulating, not *Dota 2*, but *Dota 2*'s draft. On http://dota2draft.the-cluster.org/, for example, players face off in a captain's draft and winners are determined based solely on statistics of the current metagame.

27. Though other characters like Leshrac (who was picked a whopping ninety-one times) may have been played much more than Naga Siren (who was picked only nineteen times) and Dark Seer (who was picked thirty-nine times), the number of bans to the two later heroes is a significant part of the *Dota 2* metagame in 2012. Only twenty-five of the ninety-two possible characters were not picked or banned at all at The International that summer.

28. From here on we will use *Dota 2* to refer to Valve's remake, *DotA* to refer to specific versions of the original mod, *DOTA* to refer to the broader genre, and, finally, *Dota* to refer to the larger phenomenon that includes all of the above—a multiplicity that exemplifies the problem of producing a history of this particular game.

29. Following Valve's trademark dispute over the name *Defense of the Ancients* with Riot Games in 2010 and their subsequent settlement with Blizzard Entertainment in 2012, the label for the genre *DotA* pioneered continues to be contested—

MOBA, ARTS, or even plain DOTA continue to circulate among the communities that play these games.

30. The name *All Your History* is a truncated version of the show's full title *All Your History are Belong to Us,* a reference to the popular "All Your Base are Belong to Us" or "AYBABTU" meme referencing the mistranslated cutscenes from the video-game *Zero Wing* (1991) for the Sega Mega Drive. The meme was popularized online in the form of a lengthy .GIF animation featuring the game's introduction in its entirety.

31. Although recorded instances of play dating back to the early days of *Dota* are few and far between, the fragmented fossil record exists in the folders and files on certain servers (as well as specific players' hard drives). YouTube was not available until 2005 and Twitch.tv only emerged in 2011, four years after Justin.tv was first launched. Beyond video recordings, resources like http://dotautilities-forums.net/Thread-Dota-map-archive-From-1st-beta-to-current-version unofficially archive change logs and even old releases, an archeology of play in the form of digital files. Beyond forensic evidence, a written record of human experience catalogued on forums and blogs provides insight into how people played in the past. Furthermore, *Dota 2* itself operates as an archive and index of this history, a homeostatic memorial of past play woven into the very fabric of the game's design. *Dota 2* would not be *Dota 2* were it not for its coevolution with the metagame.

32. Battle.net was launched in 1996 and was the first online gaming service players could access from within a game client. Battle.net continues to host Blizzard's games including *World of Warcraft* (2004), *StarCraft II* (2010), *Diablo III* (2012), *Hearthstone* (2014), *Heroes of the Storm* (2015), and *Overwatch* (2016).

33. Although previous mapping tools allowed players to customize level designs by arranging sets of predefined terrain tiles and placing units and structures for up to eight AI- or human-controlled players, StarEdit offered a comparatively complex, menu-driven scripting system built around "triggers" that executed events when specific conditions were met within the game. StarEdit's graphic user interface (GUI) limited what kind of code could be written to a set of preselected options but was more accessible than the modding environments offered by id Software's *Doom* (1993) and *Quake* (1996) engines (Dimirti 2013).

34. *AoS* featured the first appearance of *Dota*'s defining mechanics such as the single unit "heroes," ally and enemy "creeps," defensive "towers" protecting each team's major structures, the basic map bisected by a series of "lanes," and the "last hitting" mechanic, which rewarded players with gold not for simply killing a creep, but for getting the mortal blow or "last hit" on an enemy.

35. On Battle.net, *Warcraft III*'s World Editor is described as "much more advanced than the StarCraft editor" and Blizzard (2013) suggests "you can now replace any of the play-balance statistics. Also, whereas you were previously limited to scripting events through triggers that we provided, you can now create your own innovative behavior scripts and game events, using our extensive scripting language."

36. Early members of Feak's team included modders like Syl-la-ble and Zetta as well as personal friends turned beta testers, Mortred and About 11. Later, Feak worked with designers who would continue *Dota* after his tenure: Neichus and Ice-Frog (Feak and Mescon 2009).

37. Apparently Roshan was named after another piece of equipment for playing games: Feak's bowling ball (Feak and Mescon 2009).

38. Despite the history of the *Warcraft* series, with its deep links to both *Warhammer* and wargaming, *Warcraft III*'s innovative hero units strayed from the standard RTS formula of its historical predecessors. Rather than focus on the nameless

troops streaming out of modular production facilities, players embraced *Warcraft III*'s heavy narrative sequences and inclusion of named heroes on the battlefield like Thrall the Orcish Shaman and Prince Arthas Menethil who, throughout the missions of their respective campaigns, gained experience levels, unlocked abilities and skills, and accrued up to six items. Following the success of the game, *World of Warcraft* focused exclusively on these role-playing aspects of *Warcraft III*. Many of the story's playable heroes were converted into non-playable characters (often assuming the position of leaders in the various cities strewn throughout the game) and the RTS elements were removed. Algorithmically pathing peons were replaced with hundreds of players assembled on dozens of servers supporting a persistent, 3D virtual world: Azeroth.

39. *World of Warcraft*'s instanced "battlegrounds" approximate *Dota*'s gameplay, allowing teams of players to compete by controlling individual characters in head-to-head challenges like capture the flag. The first battlegrounds, Warsong Gulch and Alterac Valley, were released on June 7, 2005, after the establishment of *Dota* as a popular mod and competitive e-sport with multiple competitions taking place that summer.

40. Neichus's tenure started in October 2004 with *Allstars* 5.0 and lasted until 6.1 sometime in 2005. His contribution, which Feak and Mescon (2013) describe as "mostly . . . conceptual design and complex code implementation," also included the introduction of new heroes, "Earthshaker, Tiny, Chen 2.0, Stealth Assassin 2.0, Phantom Lancer, Enchantress, Enigma, Axe, Shadow Fiend, Visage 2.0, Nerubian Weaver, Bloodseeker and Dazzle" after Feak had left the project (CtChocula 2011). Despite all this, and recalling the lack of success Eul's *Thirst for Gamma*, an earlier version of *Allstars*, 5.84, continued to draw a significant player base until Heintje's Chinese translation of 6.12 and IceFrog's popular 6.20.

41. Beyond *League of Legends* (2009) and *Heroes of Newerth* (2010), there has been a resurgence of *DotA*-inspired games developed in the past few years across multiple platforms and incorporating different aspects of the original mod. Whereas games like *Demigod* (2009), *Awesomenauts* (2012), *Super Monday Night Combat* (2012), and *Smite* (2014) have been released by smaller developers, larger companies have jumped on the bandwagon with their own IP-injected games including Blizzard's *Heroes of the Storm* (2015), Monolith's *Guardians of Middle Earth* (2012) inspired by *Lord of the Rings,* and Warner Bros. Interactive's *Infinite Crisis* (2015) based on the DC Comics universe.

42. In addition to arcane mechanics like "denial" (in which players counterintuitively attempt to last hit their own units, buildings, and teammates to deny gold and experience to the enemy team), "pulling" and "stacking" are strategies based on how the Warcraft III World Editor instantiates new packs of neutral creeps in the various clearings and dens strewn throughout the "jungle" (those expanses of the map that do not coincide with the three main lanes or the river). First, pulling refers to the way that creeps will always follow the nearest hero unit, allowing heroes to control their positioning. Next, stacking depends on the fact that neutral packs nestled in the jungle respawn on the minute mark, but only if no entity (including creeps, heroes, and wards) has vision of the spawning location. What began as an ad hoc technique to curtail overspawning in the World Editor became a useful exploit. Support heroes like the Tidehunter can pull a group of neutral creeps away at the precise moment a new group is generated. The result is a stack of multiple monsters for a teammate who needs a gold or experience boost. These two strategies became so important to the balance of the game, that *Dota 2* was designed to simulate the

behavior. A technical eccentricity of the programming was transformed into a deliberate game design decision.

43. Riot distanced *League of Legends* from *Dota* via the term MOBA (multiplayer online battle arena), whereas Blizzard began development on a new game called *Blizzard DOTA* (eventually renamed *Blizzard All-Stars* and finally released as *Heroes of the Storm* in 2015).

44. Given the processing power of the PDP mainframes operating at the center of time-sharing labs in the 1960s and 1970s, the first computer games offloaded many processes to the player. Instead of navigating complex levels or battling artificially intelligent opponents, the first games pitted player against player within electrical environments determined not by self-selected and agreed-upon rules, but by circuits and switches. Without two players engaging one another, many early games would function like an empty ballpark with bats and balls strewn around the grass: equipment waiting to be played with. For example, US Games' *Sneak n' Peek* (1982) is a hide-and-seek simulator for the Atari 2600 in which two players take turns hiding and seeking within an array of low-resolution rooms within a small house. However, whether or not the other player closed their eyes or sneaked a peek while the other was hiding was in no way enforced within the mechanics of the videogame. Before contemporary game design standardized, decisions about how to play were offloaded to the players.

45. The upper echelon of raid guilds in *World of Warcraft*, for example, strive to get server firsts for newly released content, working together not only to assemble viable strategies for new boss encounters but also to beat every other guild in a race to the ever-expanding endgame.

46. Even discussions of performance-enhancing drugs have become common in the context of e-sports, as milliseconds mean the difference between a win and a loss. In 2015, for example, pro *Counter-Strike* player Kory "SEMPHIS" Friesen (Plunkett 2015) admitted, "We were all on Adderall."

47. Taylor invokes the category of *mediasport* to describe the practices surrounding e-sports. Working with a term coined by Lawrence Wenner, she suggests that *mediasport* reflects "the deep interrelation in e-sports between media, technology and sports. Whereas traditional athletics have morphed over decades into having decidedly transnational media components . . . e-sports has encoded in its very nature a deep rooting in both technology and media. There is no actual performance of e-sport outside of computation and media" (Taylor 2012, 210).

48. Although both sport and game are contingent on the abstraction of difference via the measurement of discrete information from some larger set of probabilities within an analog, material substrate, they are not the same. Steven Connor (2011, 15, 16), for example, insists that "a sport is a game involving physical exertion" and that "[if] games are subject to the first law of thermodynamics, which states that no energy can be created or lost, and therefore that time may be reversible, sports are subject to the second law, which states all exercise increases entropy, and that time is irreversible." Exhaustion, for Connor, separates sport from game and, in the case of e-sports, exhaustion extends from the reflexes, dexterity, coordination, and concentration of professional gamers to the entropy and energy consumption of the computer itself—the electrical and mechanical processes that enable computation generate heat. Whether through inefficiencies or overclocking, the entropy enacted by computer hardware is an often-overlooked form of exhaustion on the part of a different kind of electronic athlete.

49. In the last few years, online streaming providers have reported a surge in both videogame-related broadcasts and viewership. In their 2013 annual report, Twitch boasted "12,000,000,000 minutes watched per month; 45,000,000 unique viewers per month; 6,000,000 total videos broadcast per month; 900,000+ unique broadcasters per month; 5100+ partnered channels; 106 minutes watched per user per day" (numbers that have all nearly doubled since 2012). Targeting the millennial male demographic, Twitch's online broadcasts are besting both top cable networks like Syfy, MTV, TNT, and AMC, as well as other online video providers like Hulu and Vevo.

50. Not unfamiliar with the images of e-sports, Krukar directed and produced *Liquid Rising* (2013), a documentary featuring interviews with the professional *Star-Craft II* (2010, 2013) players representing Team Liquid.

51. "Break the Metagame" is the title of a series of lengthy metagame analysis by Aaron "Clairvoyance" Kim, published under the pseudonym cvx10210 on the *Dota 2* subreddit between December 18, 2012 and August 12, 2013.

52. One consequence of Rubick's ultimate ability, Spell Steal, is that the change-log for this hero can stand in for the evolution of the game as a whole since a change to any spell in the game also affects the Grand Magus.

53. Tidehunter's Anchor Smash is interrupted mid-animation due to LighTof-HeaveN's spell, Black Hole, which narrowly catches Faith out of position.

54. Rotisserie Baseball is one of the earliest examples of a fantasy league that "sought to simulate an actual baseball game . . . [by placing] players in the role of general manager of a team of real life baseball players" (Lewis 2004, 87). Invented by Dan Okrent, a *Sports Illustrated* writer, at Manhattan's La Rotisserie Française in 1980, Rotisserie Baseball put baseball statistician Bill James's sabermetrics at the center of a ludic experiment still ongoing in thousands, if not millions, of fantasy games today (Lewis 2004, 87). Whereas most fantasy baseball leagues draft a team from the roster of current major league players, competing with other fantasy teams through their aggregate statistics over a season, Carlucci's *Dota 2* fantasy league did the same for an international e-sport.

55. For example, in 2003 and well into the lifecycle of the Nintendo GameCube, Nintendo partnered with iQue, a Chinese electronics manufacturer, to release a cheap plug-and-play controller called the *Shén Yóu Ji,* or iQue Player, in mainland China. Labeling the device a "controller" and not a "console" allowed Nintendo to skirt China's regulations. Like the early Famicom Disk System in Japan, the iQue used external memory (a flash drive in this case) to transfer Nintendo 64 software like *Super Mario 64, Super Smash Bros.,* and *The Legend of Zelda: Ocarina of Time* from approved distribution machines to the home "not-console." Ironically, there has been a resurgence of interest around the iQue Player among *Ocarina of Time* speedrunners like Narcissa Wright (featured in chapters 1 and 3), whose 2013 and 2014 world record speedruns exploit the speed with which Chinese characters are animated in the game's various dialogue boxes.

56. Valve's success in Russia, another country in which piracy flourishes, was a proof of concept for how companies could compete against black markets by means of carrots rather than sticks. Newell has repeatedly argued that the issue is one of friction: "One thing that we have learned is that piracy is not a pricing issue. It's a service issue. The easiest way to stop piracy is not by putting antipiracy technology to work. It's by giving those people a service that's better than what they're receiving from the pirate" (Bishop 2011). Having cracked the code to mitigate piracy, Russia has become Valve's largest European market (Bishop 2011).

57. Like many of Valve's talent, Wolpaw and Faliszek were hired in 2005 to work on *Portal* and *Left 4 Dead* respectively, based on their highly acclaimed games criticism and humor website, *Old Man Murray*.

58. If companies like Zynga and EA are condemned as crass exploiters, conquering markets through irresponsible monetization methods and greedy DRM policies, Valve represents a seemingly benevolent and symbiotic model of computational capitalism. They are labeled as "the good guys" in a way that ominously recalls early perspectives toward Apple. Due to the scale and breadth of their in-game economic experiments and increasingly diverse markets, Valve has even gone so far as to hire an "economist in residence," Yanis Varoufakis. Varoufakis (2013) himself identifies as "an erratic Marxist" and embraced the company's ideology of participatory economies.

59. This paradigm recalls Silvia Federici's analysis of the "free" domestic labor of women. Domestic and affective labor does not exist outside the market even if not yet quantified or subsumed within the sphere of exchange. International labor movements like "Wages for Housework" in the early 1970s were not attempts to colonize women's work as an untapped site of production, but instead recognized that certain kinds of invisible work had *always* existed and were *already* colonized via their exclusion from wage. In the same way that women's reproductive and affective labor was regarded as a "natural, unavoidable, and even fulfilling activity," so too has the perceived intrinsic value of play been exploited as a means for working without a wage (Federici 2012, 16). These two forms of underappreciated labor converge in so-called "casual" games like Zynga's *FarmVille* (2009), one of many mobile or browser-based titles accused of "killing soaps" through asynchronous, ludic activity requiring neither manual dexterity nor undifferentiated attention—play, that for many, does not even register as play in the same way women's labor does not register as work.

60. As someone who believes in the management philosophy espoused in Tom DeMarco and Timothy Lister's 1987 book, *Peopleware*, Gabe Newell (2013) remembers abandoning the "one person, one office" model after "people kept sneaking into other people's offices and . . . started tearing doors down" and he realized that his "rigid adherence to 'one person, one office' was hurting . . . productivity."

61. While writing "A Workers' History of Videogaming," Nick Dyer-Witheford and Greig de Peuter recall Nolan Bushnell's promising yet problematic "flat" workspace with which Atari aimed to capture the counterculture of the student movement in 1976. Dyer-Witheford and de Peuter (2009, 12) write, "Atari paradoxically made [the] 'refusal of work' its key commercial success . . . [w]ith a 'work smart, not hard' philosophy, an Aquarian constitution ('a corporation is just people, banding together'), a legendary lack of bureaucracy, small development teams who 'bid' on games they wanted to design (and were rewarded by result), and parties awash in drugs and alcohol." In many ways Valve overcomes the management problems Dyer-Witheford and de Peuter attribute to Atari's decline in the early 1980s. After Bushnell sold the company to Warner Communications for $28 million in 1978, he was replaced as acting manager and "what followed was a clash between traditional management and immaterial labor, a civil war between 'suits' and 'ponytails'" (Dyer-Witheford and de Peuter 2009, 13). Almost four decades later, the desire to import play into work (and vice versa) is no longer a meaningful binary as companies like Valve flatten all activity into a single, abstract measure of value.

62. For a close reading of the feedback loop between Valve's economic model and the narrative storyworld and game design decisions in *Left 4 Dead,* see Stephanie Boluk's "Serial Death and the Zombie: The Networked Necronomics of *Left 4 Dead*" in *Birthing the Monster of Tomorrow: Unnatural Reproductions* (2014).

63. This is different from gambling in that money is not the only outcome, but is bound up within a more complex system of affect, affinities, and desires.

64. Michael Abrash (2012) has cited the model of the metaverse in Neal Stephenson's *Snow Crash* (1992) as a crucial influence on his work at id and Valve, going as far as to claim that "I wouldn't be at Valve doing this—in fact, Valve itself might not be here—if it weren't for *Snow Crash* diverting my career to id in the first place."

6. Breaking the Metagame

1. Anita Sarkeesian was invited to speak at All About Women 2015, an annual conference organized by the Sydney Opera House to commemorate International Women's Day.

2. DDoS is an acronym for "distributed denial of service" and refers to the attempt to slow or crash a website by continually requesting content from the given website's server (usually through automated means) such that the server cannot process the amount of traffic and becomes inaccessible to its intended users or goes offline all together.

3. Doxxing is slang for the unlawful dissemination of a victim's personal documents or "docs." This can include home addresses, phone numbers, tax information, and other personal or private documents of either the victim or their network of family, friends, employers, and even governments.

4. Swatting is the practice of prank calling a victim's local emergency services or law enforcement agencies with a false threat in order to dispatch a SWAT team to their residence. Coupled with doxxing, swatting is an extremely dangerous and highly criminal activity that is also difficult to prosecute given that the culprit is easily anonymized.

5. Sarkeesian was the first woman to win the Ambassador Award since it was instituted in 2008. Following her nomination in 2014, the Game Developers Choice Awards selected Brenda Romero for the award the next year.

6. Apart from Lépine's suicide note and paperwork bequeathing his fridge to his landlord found on his body, a third document was mailed to a friend which supposedly promised an explanation as to why he had committed a murder-suicide. Recalling her interview with "James," the anonymous source who allegedly investigated Lépine's apartment after receiving the letter, Lee Mellor (2013, 47) narrates:

> The turquoise lair was piled high with books on science and the Second World War, along with videocassettes of violent pay-TV movies and a plastic skull. As journalists hammered on the windows and doors, James began to explore, and spotted a sliver of paper lodged between the floorboards. "The author is the solution," it read. "If you have found this, it means you are already in the know." The note suggested looking on the shelf for a book by an author mentioned in the earlier letter. It turned out to be a biography of American pilot Chuck Yeager, who in 1947 became the first person to break the barrier of sound. Inside the pages, James discovered a second message: "If you have found this letter you are on the right track. It contains my last wishes. At the back of the room is a suitcase with a few things I would like to pass on." Given the context of this scavenger hunt, its contents were anticlimactic to say the least: hardware and computer games—hardly the secrets of Lépine's derangement.

From Montreal to Columbine, although the correlation of videogames with mass shootings certainly does not equal causation and is frequently deployed to scapegoat the medium and derail the discussion around larger social issues (e.g., gun control, mental health services, economic inequality, etc.), this unsettling story of a scavenger hunt and a trunk of videogames is both testament to the cultural ubiquity of videogames as a mass medium and makes the email sent to the University of Utah threatening Sarkeesian and the institution all the more chilling.

7. When asked about violence against women, Trudeau (2015) replied, "Yes, Yes. I am a feminist. Proud to be a feminist. My mom raised me to be a feminist. My father raised me, he was a different generation but he raised me to respect and defend everyone's rights, and I deeply grounded my own identity in that, and I am proud to say that I am a feminist."

8. Condis (2014) writes, "Those who refuse to 'take the bait' offered up by a troll demonstrate a cool-headed rationality, a mastery over the self that is associated with masculinity and are thus considered to be 'true' gamers. Those who engage with the troll, on the other hand, are imagined as overly earnest and emotional, too feminine to participate in online gaming."

9. *TowerFall: The Dark World* also included art by MiniBoss and music by Alec Holowka.

10. The standard metagame is what allows two players to believe that they are playing the *same* videogame despite the embodied, experiential, and material differences between multiple playthroughs (even by the same person). Because the standard metagame works to conflate the diversity of play with the industrial object and makes play comparable and exchangeable, much of the nostalgia around videogames is built on this fantasy. It's not uncommon for players to lament how metagames like speedrunning or pro-gaming "ruin" or "destroy" their childhood memories by showing that the software they supposedly mastered is always plastic and open to strange and unsettling metagames that may include sequence breaking, glitch hunting, and reverse engineering not approved by the standard practices of play.

11. First used by Johan Huizinga in *Homo Ludens,* the term *magic circle* has since become popularized in game studies, appearing in the work of many of the authors referenced in this book including Espen Aarseth, Ian Bogost, Mia Consalvo, Nick Dyer-Witheford and Greig de Peuter, Mary Flanagan, Jane McGonigal, Bernard Suits, Katie Salen Tekinbaş and Eric Zimmerman, and McKenzie Wark, among others.

12. Searching for any one of these phrases in conjunction with Sarkeesian's name yields thousands of results.

13. Katie Salen Tekinbaş and Eric Zimmerman (2003, 269) follow Huizinga's definition of the magic circle in *Rules of Play* when they argue that "this kind of game player is hardly a player at all. Unlike the cheat, the spoil-sport refuses to acknowledge the magic circle of the game and does not care about winning or about following the rules."

14. There is no shortage of lurid news stories reporting videogame-related deaths from gamers murdered during real-life altercations over in-game conflicts, crib deaths of infants at the hands of neglectful parents absorbed in an online game, and marathon sessions that exhaust the player to the extent that they drop dead (Parkin 2015).

15. As *Wired* reported, when two hundred Javelin spaceships went up for sale with an impressive price tag of $2,500 (despite not even being fully implemented in *Star Citizen*), they were scooped up in less than a minute. As Chris Baker (2015) suggests, these types of goods are "doubly virtual—they can only be used inside the gameworld, and the gameworld doesn't actually exist yet." In addition to the sale of

speculative ships, Cloud Imperium also offers an incredibly complex system of spaceship insurance that player-investors can purchase long before they have access to their virtual commodities.

16. Even the "in engine" footage of *Star Citizen*'s advertisements does not depict how the game will run on computers in 2012, but is based instead on the specifications of a computer in 2017 (when Cloud Imperium plans to finally launch the game).

17. After Darbian's 4:57.427 run of *Super Mario Bros.* on January 15, 2016, previous world record holder Blubbler calculated that the fastest possible speedrun of the game would be 4:57.07—a finish line that no one imagined ever crossing. At least until Chris "sockfolder" Milling invented a setup for executing the flagpole glitch in real time on September 18, 2016. After an intense competition between Kosmicd12 and Darbian, the record dropped to 4:56.878 on October 10 that year, the first *Super Mario Bros.* speedrun under 4:57.

18. While these forms of dispersed play are not new and "stretch back to diverse gaming practices such as nineteenth-century English letterboxing, the Polish tradition of podchody, the practice of invisible theater, the situationist art practice of *dérive*, scavenger hunts, assassination games, and live action role-playing games," their frequent enclosure within corporate advertising constitutes the formation of the ARG as a genre (Hayles, Jagoda, LeMieux 221). As Hayles, Jagoda, and LeMieux (222) surmise in their reflections on their ARG, *Speculation* (2012), "The corporate development of this experimental gaming practice constitutes, from the very start, an inherent context and historical possibility of the ARG form." The most famous examples of this type of gaming such as *I Love Bees* (2004), *The Beast* (2001), and *Year Zero* (2007) are almost always funded by corporations (such as Microsoft, Warner Bros., and Interscope respectively) and often function as elaborate viral marketing (for *Halo 2*, *A.I.*, and *Year Zero* respectively) in which the most diehard early adopters become the vectors for advertising.

19. Unlike *EVE Online*, in which the diplomatic metagame does not even require the game to be booted up, or *Star Citizen*, in which financial metagames thrive before a game is ever released, *Frog Fractions 2* appears to be composed of nothing but metagames to the extent that the entire world is now subsumed within Twin Beard's absurdist alternate reality game. In the same way that the original *Frog Fractions* expanded an educational math game to include courtroom dramas, text-based adventures, enormous undersea mazes, and a stock market simulation, the apophenic drive that is so common to ARGs is pushed to the limit with *Frog Fractions 2*. The refrain of "this is not a game" (TINAG) so common to most ARGs is replaced by "this is all a game." At the subreddit /r/isthisfrogfractions2, users ask "Is *Undertale Frog Fractions 2*?," "Is *Evoland 2 Frog Fractions 2*?," "Is this *Mario Maker* level *Frog Fractions 2*?," "Is this Twitter Adventure *Frog Fractions 2*?," "Is the *Kill Screen* website *Frog Fractions 2*?," "Is this sub[reddit] Frog Fractions 2?," and, finally, "Is *Frog Fractions Frog Fractions 2*?" Like *Star Citizen*, *Frog Fractions 2* is a metagame of speculation. By crowdfunding an alternate reality game and then specifically *not* producing it, the players are invited to design their own metagames that are circumscribed only by a willingness to ask "Is this *Frog Fractions 2*?"

20. On April 1, 2011, Valve's *Potato Fool's Day* alternate reality game began with codes showing up in thirteen indie games that were collected in the "Potato Sack Bundle" and offered to Steam users at a 75 percent discount. Including titles like *Super Meat Boy*, *Bit. Trip Beat*, *Audiosurf*, and *Amnesia: The Dark Descent*, the

Potato Sack bundle incentivized purchasing and playing the games to accelerate the release of the much-anticipated *Portal 2* (2011). By building a metaverse between multiple titles, Valve not only flattens a series of otherwise separate indie games into a single, monolithic genre, but also flattens alternate reality games to the pages of their online storefront, Steam.

Bibliography

Aarseth, Espen J. 1997. *Cybertext: Perspectives on Ergodic Literature*. Baltimore, Md.: Johns Hopkins University Press.

Abrash, Michael. 2012. "Valve: How I Got Here, What It's Like, and What I'm Doing." *Ramblings in Valve Time*. Apr. 13. http://blogs.valvesoftware.com/abrash/valve -how-i-got-here-what-its-like-and-what-im-doing-2/.

Ahmed, Sara. 2010. "Feminist Killjoys (and Other Willful Subjects)." *The Scholar and Feminist Online* 8, no. 3. http://sfonline.barnard.edu/polyphonic/print_ahmed .htm.

Alexander, Leigh. 2012. "It's Raining." *leighalexander.net*. Jan. 23. http://leighalex ander.net/its-raining/.

Altice, Nathan. 2013. "The Art of Erasure." *Memory Insufficient: Hardware*. Issue 5. 10–15.

———. 2015. *I Am Error: The Nintendo Family Computer/Entertainment System Platform*. Cambridge, Mass.: MIT Press.

Anthropy, Anna. 2008. "mario vs. airman." *auntie pixelante*. Nov. 14. http://www .auntiepixelante.com/?p=322.

———. 2012. "indie game: the movie." *auntie pixelante*. Mar. 25. http://auntiepixel ante.com/?p=1556.

Apple. 2009. "Magic Mouse." Apple.com. n.d. https://www.apple.com/magicmouse/.

Arcangel, Cory. 2005. "The Making of Super Mario Clouds." In *Cory Arcangel: Beige*, edited by Raphael Gygax and Heike Munder, 105–15. Zurih: Migros Museum für Gegenwartskunst.

Ashcraft, Brian. 2010. "Why Are Consoles Banned in China?" *Kotaku*. July 15. http:// kotaku.com/5587577/why-are-consoles-banned-in-china.

Augustine, Josh. 2010. "Riot Games' Dev Counter-Files 'DotA' Trademark." Aug. 16. *PC Gamer*. www.pcgamer.com/riot-games-dev-counter-files-dota-trademark/.

Baio, Andy. 2011. "Metagames: Games About Games." *Waxy.org*. Feb. 1. http://waxy .org/2011/02/mctagames_games_about_games/.

Baker, Chris. 2015. "Fans Have Dropped $77M on This Guy's Buggy, Half-Built Game." *Vice*. Mar. 31. www.wired.com/2015/03/fans-dropped-77m-guys-buggy -half-built-game/.

Barlet, Mark C. and Steve D. Spohn. 2012. *Includification: A Practical Guide to Game Accessibility*, ed. Alicia Drumgoole and Jay Taylor Mason. The AbleGamers Foundation. http://www.includification.com/AbleGamers_Includification.pdf.

Barret, Victoria. 2005. "It's A Mod, Mod Underworld." *Forbes*. Dec. 12. http://www .forbes.com/forbes/2005/1212/064.html.

Beauchamp, Travis. 2011. "The Smash Brothers Series—Production." *Kickstarter*. Sept. 1. https://www.kickstarter.com/projects/eastpointpictures/the-smash -brothers-series-production.

Beller, Jonathan. 2006. *The Cinematic Mode of Production: Attention Economy and the Society of the Spectacle*. Hanover, N.H.: Dartmouth College Press.

Birnbaum, Phil. 2014. "A Guide to Sabermetric Research: Asking the Right Questions." *Society for American Baseball Research*. n.d. http://sabr.org/sabermetrics.

Bissell, Tom. 2010. *Extra Lives: Why Video Games Matter*. New York: Pantheon Books.

Blair, Clay Jr. 1957. "Passing of a Great Mind." *LIFE Magazine*. Feb. 25. 89–104.

Blizzard Entertainment. 2013. "World Editor." *Battle.net*. n.d. http://classic.battle .net/war3/faq/worldeditor.shtml.

Bogost, Ian. 2006. *Unit Operations: An Approach to Videogame Criticism*. Cambridge, Mass.: MIT Press.

———. 2009. "Videogames are a Mess." *Bogost.com*. Sept. 3. http://bogost.com/writ ing/videogames_are_a_mess/.

———. 2012. *Alien Phenomenology*. Minneapolis, Minn.: University of Minnesota Press.

Bolter, J. David and Richard Grusin. 1999. *Remediation: Understanding New Media*. Cambridge, Mass.: MIT Press, 1999.

Boluk, Stephanie. 2014. "Serial Death and the Zombie: The Networked Necronomics of *Left 4 Dead*." In *Birthing the Monster of Tomorrow: Unnatural Reproductions*, ed. Brandy Shillace and Andrea Wood, 159–87. Amherst, N.Y.: Cambria Press.

Boluk, Stephanie and Patrick LeMieux. 2009. "Eccentric Spaces and Filmic Traces: Portals in Aperture Science and New York City." *After Media: Embodiment and Context—Proceedings of the 8th Digital Arts and Culture Conference*. Irvine, Calif. http://www.escholarship.org/uc/item/95b6t1cm.

———. 2013. "Dwarven Epitaphs: Procedural Histories in Dwarf Fortress." In *Comparative Textual Media: Transforming the Humanities in the Postprint Era*, ed. N. Katherine Hayles and Jessica Pressman, 125–54. Minneapolis, Minn.: University of Minnesota Press.

Borges, Jorge L. 1998. "On Exactitude in Science." In *Collected Fictions*. Trans. Andrew Hurley, 325. New York: Penguin Books.

Brand, Stewart. 1972. "Spacewar: Fantastic Life and Symbolic Death among the Computer Bums." *Rolling Stone* (Dec. 7, no. 123): 50–58.

Brecht, Bertolt. 2002. "Emphasis on Sport." In *Cultural Resistance Reader*, ed. Stephen Duncombe, 183–85. New York: Verso.

Bryant, Levi. 2010. "Flat Ontology." *Larval Subjects*. Feb. 24. http://larvalsubjects .wordpress.com/2010/02/24/flat-ontology-2/.

Cage, John. 1961. *Silence*. Middletown, Conn.: Wesleyan University Press.

Caillois, Roger. 2001. *Man, Play, and Games.* Trans. Meyer Barash. Chicago: University of Illinois Press.

Calvino, Italo. 1986. *The Uses of Literature: Essays.* San Diego: Harcourt Brace Jovanovich.

Cameron, Phill. 2013. "How to Make a Living Selling Virtual Hats." *IGN.* April 16. http://ign.com/articles/2013/04/16/how-to-make-a-living-selling-virtual-hats.

Carlucci, Bruno. 2013. "Dota 2 Replay Parser—Bruno's Enhanced Edition." *Cyborgmatt's Blog.* Jan. 18. http://www.cyborgmatt.com/2013/01/dota-2-replay-parser -bruno.

Carter, Marcus, Martin Gibbs, and Mitchell Harrop. 2012. "Metagames, Paragames and Orthogames: A New Vocabulary." In *Proceedings of the International Conference on the Foundations of Digital Games (FDG '12),* 11–17. New York: ACM.

Cayley, John. 1996. "Pressing the 'Reveal Code' Key." *EJournal* 36, no. 1 (March). www.ucalgary.ca/ejournal/archive/ej-6-1.txt.

CCP Games. 2014. "Find Your Path in the Sandbox." *Eve Online.* n.d. http://www .eveonline.com/sandbox/.

Chien, Irene. (Forthcoming). "Journey into the Techno-Primitive Desert." In *Identity Matters: Race, Gender, and Sexuality in Video Game Studies,* ed. Jen Malkowski and Trea Andrea Russworm. Bloomington: Indiana University Press.

Chun, Wendy. 2004. "On Software, or the Persistence of Visual Knowledge." *Grey Room* 18 (Winter 2004): 26–51.

Clark, Andy and David J. Chalmers. 1998. "The Extended Mind." *Analysis* 58: 7–19.

Clark, Liat. 2013. "China May Lift Decade-Long Ban on Games Consoles." *Wired UK.* http://www.wired.co.uk/news/archive/2013–01/28/china-game-console-ban-lif.

Clinton, Hillary Rodham. 2012. "Remarks at the Transfer of Remains Ceremony to Honor Those Lost in Attacks in Benghazi, Libya." *U.S. Department of State.* Sept. 14. http://www.state.gov/secretary/20092013clinton/rm/2012/09/197780.htm.

Condis, Megan. 2014. "Trolling Gender Trouble." *Avidly.* Sept. 12. http://avidly .lareviewofbooks.org/2014/09/12/trolling-gender-trouble/.

Connor, Steven. 2011. *A Philosophy of Sport.* London, England: Reaktion Books.

Consalvo, Mia. 2007. *Cheating Gaining Advantage in Videogames.* Cambridge, Mass.: MIT Press.

———. 2009. "There Is No Magic Circle." *Games and Culture* 4, no. 4: 408–17.

coolcwer2. 2006. "Can Someone Please Help Me with OoT?" *Speed Demos Archive.* Oct. 22. https://forum.speeddemosarchive.com/post/can_someone_please_ help_me_with_oot45.html#can_someone_please_help_me_with_oot45.

Coover, Robert. 1968. *The Universal Baseball Association, Inc., J. Henry Waugh, Prop.* New York: Penguin.

Costikyan, Greg. 2013. *Uncertainty in Games.* Cambridge, Mass.: MIT Press.

CtChocula. 2011. "A History of Dota: Part 1: From Aeon of Strife to 6.27." *Gosu Gamers.* Aug. 10. https://web.archive.org/web/20140110201700/http://www.gosugam ers.net/forums/topic/802775-a-history-of-dota-part-1/.

Damisch, Hubert. 1995. *The Origin of Perspective.* Trans. John Goodman. Cambridge, Mass.: MIT Press.

Davis, Lennard J. 2006. "Constructing Normalcy: The Bell Curve, the Novel, and the Invention 3 of the Disabled Body in the Nineteenth Century." In *The Disability Studies Reader, Second Edition,* ed. Lennard J. Davis, 3–16. New York: Routledge.

Deacon, Terrence. 2012. *Incomplete Nature: How Mind Emerged from Matter.* New York: W. W. Norton & Co.

DeCarlo, Matthew. 2013. "PC Game Sales Hit $20 Billion Last Year, No Signs of Slow-ing." *TechSpot.* Mar. 27. http://www.techspot.com/news/52070-pc-game-sales-hit-20-billion-last-year-no-signs-of-slowing.html.

DeLanda, Manuel. 1997. *A Thousand Years of Nonlinear History.* New York: Zone Books.

———. 2002. *Intensive Science and Virtual Philosophy.* New York: Continuum.

DeLeon, Chris. 2013. "Rules in Computer Games Compared to Rules in Tradi-tional Games." *Proceedings of DiGRA 2013: DeFragging Game Studies.* DiGRA. Atlanta, Ga. http://www.digra.org/digital-library/publications/rules-in-computer-games-compared-to-rules-in-traditional-games/.

Deleuze, Gilles. 1986. *Cinema 1: The Movement-Image.* Trans. Hugh Tomlinson and Barbara Habberjam. Minneapolis, Minn.: University of Minnesota Press.

———. 1994. *Difference and Repetition.* New York: Columbia University Press.

Denson, Shane and Andreas Jahn-Sudmann. 2013. "Digital Seriality: On the Serial Aesthetics and Practice of Digital Games." *Eludamos: Journal for Computer Game Culture* 7.1, 1–32.

Dimirti [Skyl3lazer]. 2013. "Dota 2: A History Lesson." *The Mittani.* July 22. http://themittani.com/features/dota-2-history-lesson.

Dockery, Stephen. 2011. "Ken Yankelevitz Builds 30 Years of Quadriplegic Video Games." *Huffington Post.* Nov. 6. http://www.huffingtonpost.com/2011/06/12/ken-yankelevitz-quadriplegic-video-games_n_875521.html.

Doree, Adam. 2008. "Hideo Kiojima: The Kikizo Interview." *Kikizo.* Aug. 24. http://archive.videogamesdaily.com/features/hideo-kojima-interview-2008-p1.asp.

Dugan, Patrick. "ROM CHECK FAIL: There Is No More Filament." *Play This Thing!* http://playthisthing.com/romcheck-fail.

Dulin, Ron. 1998. "Half-Life Review." *Gamespot.* Nov. 20. http://gamespot.com/reviews/half-life-review/1900-2537398/.

Dyer-Witheford, Nick, and Greig De Peuter. 2009. *Games of Empire: Global Capital-ism and Video Games.* Minneapolis, Minn.: University of Minnesota Press.

East Point Pictures. 2013a. *The Smash Brothers: Episode 1—Show Me Your Moves.* YouTube. Oct 11. http://www.youtube.com/watch?v=6tgWH-qXpv8.

———. 2013b. *The Smash Brothers: Episode 7—The Robot.* YouTube. Oct. 11. https://www.youtube.com/watch?v=pKZmZfiIsto.

Edge. 2003. "Hideo Kojima vs. The Big Robots." *Edge Magazine* 136 (May): 68–75.

Edwards, Cliff. 2013. "Valve Lines Up Console Partners in Challenge to Microsoft, Sony." *Bloomberg.* Nov. 4. http://www.bloomberg.com/news/2013–11–04/valve-lines-up-console-partners-in-challenge-to-microsoft-sony.html.

Elias, George Skaff, Richard Garfield, and K. Robert Gutschera. 2012. *Characteris-tics of Games.* Cambridge, Mass.: MIT Press.

Eyestone, Sean, Christopher Johns, and Jackie Tan. 2013. *KP Alert!* Episode 2. June 6. http://www.kjp.konami.jp/gs/hideoblog_e/2013/06/000271.html.

Fabizak, Chris. 2013. *Team Ben: A Year as a Professional Gamer. Smashwords.* https://www.smashwords.com/books/view/348106.

Feak, Stephen [Ginsoo] and Steve [Pendragon] Mescon. 2009. "Postmortem: Defense of the Ancients." *Gamasutra.* Mar. 19. http://www.gamasutra.com/view/feature/132358/postmortem_defense_of_the_ancients.php.

Federici, Silvia. 2012. *Revolution at Point Zero: Housework, Reproduction, and Fem-inist Struggle.* Oakland, Calif.: PM Press.

flagitious. 2005. "Bigame Movies." *TAS Videos Forum.* May 28. http://tasvideos.org/forum/viewtopic.php?t=2385.

Flanagan, Mary. 2006a. "[giantJoystick]." *MaryFlanagan.com*. n.d. http://www .maryflanagan.com/giant-joystick.

———. 2006b. "Politicizing Playculture." In *Game/Play*, ed. Giles Askham, Louise Clements, Ruth Catlaw, Marc Garrett, and Corrado Morgana, 10–11. London: HTTP Gallery.

———. 2009. *Critical Play: Radical Game Design*. Cambridge, Mass.: MIT Press.

FluxWaveZ. 2013. "Is Joakim Mogren CG?" *Giant Bomb*. March. http://www.giant bomb.com/metal-gear-solid-v-ground-zeroes/3030-39575/forums/is -joakim-mogren-cg-1428893/.

FODA. 2004. "Crazy Idea: NES Pinball Competition!!! (It's Really Crazy)." *TAS Videos Forum*. May 12. http://tasvideos.org/forum/viewtopic.php?t=1490.

Foddy, Bennett. 2014. "IndieCade East 2014: State of the Union." Feb. 25. *YouTube*. https://www.youtube.com/watch?v=7XfCT3jhEC0.

Friedberg, Anne. 2005. *The Virtual Window: From Alberti to Microsoft*. Cambridge, Mass.: MIT Press, 2006.

Fuchs, Christian. 2012. "Dallas Smythe Today—The Audience Commodity, the Digital Labour Debate, Marxist Political Economy and Critical Theory. Prolegomena to a Digital Labour Theory of Value." *tripleC* 10, no. 2: 692–740.

Funkhouser, C. T. 2007. *Prehistoric Digital Poetry: An Archaeology of Forms, 1959–1995*. Tuscaloosa, Al.: University of Alabama Press.

Gaiman, Neil. 1993. "Distant Mirrors: Ramadan." *The Sandman*. June. New York: DC Comics.

Galloway, Alexander. 2006. *Gaming: Essays on Algorithmic Culture*. Minneapolis, Minn.: University of Minnesota Press.

———. 2012. "Does the Whatever Speak?" In *Race After the Internet*, ed. Peter Chow-White and Lisa Nakamura, 111–27. New York: Routledge.

Garda, Maria B. and Paweł Grabarczyk. 2016. "Is Every Indie Game Independent? Towards the Concept of Independent Game." *Game Studies* 16, no. 1. http:// gamestudies.org/1601/articles/gardagrabarczyk.

Gardikis, Andrew. 2007. "Can Someone Please Help Me with OoT?" *Speed Demos Archive*. July 30. https://forum.speeddemosarchive.com/post/can_someone_ please_help_me_with_oot305.html#can_someone_please_help_me_with_ oot305.

Garfield, Richard. 1993. "Shahrazad." *Magic: The Gathering*. Seattle, Wash.: Wizards of the Coast.

———. 1995. "Lost in the Shuffle: Games Within Games." *The Duelist: The Official Deckmaster Magazine*. Spring. 86–88.

———. 2000a. "Metagames." *GDC 2000 Proceedings Archive*. Mar. 8–12. https://web. archive.org/web/20081221121908/http://www.gamasutra.com/features/gdcar chive/2000/garfield.doc.

———. 2000b. "Metagames." In *Horseman of the Apocalypse: Essays on Roleplaying*, ed. Jim Dietz, 14–21. Charleston, Ill.: Jolly Roger Games.

———. 2002. "The Making of *Arabian Nights*." *Wizards of the Coast*. Aug. 5. http:// archive.wizards.com/Magic/magazine/article.aspx?x=mtgcom/feature/78.

Garland-Thomson, Rosemarie. 1997. *Extraordinary Bodies: Figuring Physical Disability in American Culture and Literature*. New York: Columbia University Press.

GGBeyond. 2014. "Top 100 Highest Overall Earnings." e-Sports Earnings. n.d. http:// www.esportsearnings.com/players.

Gianturco, Alex [The Mitanni]. 2012. "RIP: Vile Rat." *The Mittani*. September 12. http://themittani.com/news/rip-vile-rat.

Gibbs, Martin, Marcus Carter, and Jori Mori. 2013. "Vile Rat: Spontaneous Shrines in EVE Online." *Workshop Proceedings of the 8th International Conference on the Foundations of Digital Games.* May 14–17. Chania, Crete, Greece.

Gilbert, Henry. 2010. "Super Mario Crossover Kicks Your Balls into Next Week with Awesomeness." *GamesRadar.* Apr. 28. http://www.gamesradar.com/wii/wii/news/super-mario-crossoverkicks-your-balls-into-next-week-with-awesomeness/a-20100428142237272009/g-20060308165433320026.

Goldman, Alex and PJ Vogt. 2014. "#11—RIP Vile Rat." *TLDR.* Jan. 22. http://www.onthemedia.org/story/11-rip-vile-rat/.

Columbia, David. 2009. "Games without Play." *New Literary History* 40: 179–204.

Graser, Marc. 2014. "How the 'EVE Online' TV Series Could Become the Next 'Game of Thrones.'" *Variety.* Feb. 5. http://variety.com/2014/digital/news/how-the-eve-online-tv-series-could-become-the-next-game-of-thrones-1201088301/.

Grayson, Nathan. 2016. "One of the World's Best Speedrunners Can't Speed-run Anymore." *Kotaku.* Jan. 11. http://kotaku.com/one-of-the-worlds-best-speedrunners-cant-speedrun-anymo-1752274907.

Greenberg, Clement. 1990. "Modernist Painting." In *20th Century Theories of Art,* ed. James M. Thomson, 94–101. Ottawa, Ont.: Carleton University Press.

Guiberu. 2013. "Okay, TeamCG. Come Own Up to Your Foolishness. #trolljima." *NeoGAF.* Mar. 15. http://www.neogaf.com/forum/showpost.php?p=50273070&postcount=1192.

Guins, Raiford. 2014. *Game After: A Cultural Study of Video Game Afterlife.* Cambridge, Mass.: MIT Press.

Gunning, Tom. 1986. "The Cinema of Attraction: Early Film, Its Spectator and the Avant-Garde." *Wide Angle* 8, no. 3/4: 63–70.

Hacking, Ian. 2006. *The Emergence of Probability: A Philosophical Study of Early Ideas about Probability, Induction and Statistical Inference.* Cambridge, Mass.: Cambridge University Press.

Hadley, Bree. 2014. *Disability Public Space Performance and Spectatorship: Unconscious Performers.* London: Palgrave Macmillan.

Hansen, Mark B. N. 2006a. "Media Theory." *Theory, Culture & Society* 23. no. 2–3: 297–306.

———. 2006b. *New Philosophy for New Media.* Cambridge, Mass.: MIT Press.

———. 2015. *Feed-Forward: On the Future of Twenty-First-Century Media.* Chicago, Ill.: University of Chicago Press.

Harman, Graham. 2002. *Tool-Being: Heidegger and the Metaphysics of Objects.* Chicago, Ill.: Open Court.

Harpold, Terry. 2009. *Ex-foliations Reading Machines and the Upgrade Path.* Minneapolis, Minn.: University of Minnesota Press.

Harrison, Charles. 2003. *Essays on Art and Language.* Cambridge, Mass.: MIT Press.

Hart, Vaughan and Joe Robson. 1999. "Hans Holbein's 'The Ambassadors' (1533): A Computer View of Renaissance Perspective Illusion." *Computers and the History of Art* 8, no. 2: 1–13.

Hayashi, Yoichi. 1995. "Recording Medium, Method of Loading Games Program Code Means, and Games Machine." U.S. Patent No. 5,718,632. Washington, D.C.: U.S.

Hayles, N. Katherine. 2002. *Writing Machines.* Cambridge, Mass.: MIT Press.

———. 2012. *How We Think: Digital Media and Contemporary Technogenesis.* Chicago, Ill.: The University of Chicago Press.

Hayles, N. Katherine, Patrick Jagoda, and Patrick LeMieux. "Speculation: Financial Games and Derivative Worlding in a Transmedia Era." In *Comics & Media: A Special Issue of Critical Inquiry,* ed. Patrick Jagoda and Hillary Chute, 220–36. Chicago, Ill.: University of Chicago Press.

Hayles, N. Katherine and Jessica Pressman. 2013. *Comparative Textual Media: Transforming the Humanities in the Postprint Era.* Minneapolis: University of Minnesota Press.

Henderson, Linda Dalrymple. 1984. "The Fourth Dimension and Non-Euclidean Geometry in Modern Art: Conclusion." *Leonardo* 17, no. 3: 205–10.

Hernandez, Patricia. 2015. "Creator of 'Hardest Super Mario World Level Ever' Says Copyright Crackdown Gutted His YouTube Channel." *Kotaku.* Sept. 9. http://kotaku.com/creator-of-hardest-super-mario-world-level-ever-says-co-1729624158.

Hitaro. 2006. "Can Someone Please Help Me with OoT?" *Speed Demos Archive.* Oct. 20. https://forum.speeddemosarchive.com/post/can_someone_please_help_me_with_oot2.html#can_someone_please_help_me_with_oot2.

Hofstadter, Douglas. 1999. *Gödel, Escher, Bach: An Eternal Golden Braid.* New York: Basic Books.

Howard, Nigel. 1971. *Paradoxes of Rationality: Theory of Metagames and Political Behavior.* Cambridge, Mass.: MIT Press.

Huhtamo, Erikki. 2005. "Slots of Fun, Slots of Trouble: An Archaeology of Arcade Gaming." In *Handbook of Computer Games Studies,* ed. J. Raessens and J. Goldstein, 3–21. Cambridge, Mass.: MIT Press.

Huizinga, Johan. 1949. *Homo Ludens: A Study of the Play-Element in Culture.* London: Routledge & Kegan Paul.

IceFrog. 2009a. "Q&A Session #2." *Play Dota.* Feb. 3. http://www.playdota.com/forums/blog.php?b=62.

———. 2009b. "Great News for DotA Fans." *Play Dota.* Oct. 5. http://www.playdota.com/forums/blog.php?b=264.

———. 2010. "Q&A Session #4." *Play Dota.* Apr. 30. http://www.playdota.com/forums/blog.php?b=892.

Iwabuchi, Kōichi. 2002. *Recentering Globalization.* Durham, N. Car.: Duke University Press.

Iwata, Satoru. 2011. "Iwata Asks: Super Mario Galaxy. Vol. 4: Shigeru Miyamoto." *Wii.com.* n.d. http://us.wii.com/soft_smg.jsp.

Iwata, Satoru and Masahiro Sakurai. 2008a. "E3 2005—A Beginning." *Iwata Asks.* n.d. http://www.nintendo.co.uk/Iwata-Asks/Iwata-Asks-Super-Smash-Bros-Brawl/Volume-1-E3-2005-A-Beginning/1-Iwata-Asks-His-Former-Employee/1-Iwata-Asks-His-Former-Employee-212640.html.

———. 2008b. "Dragon King: The Fighting Game." *Iwata Asks.* n.d. http://www.nintendo.co.uk/Iwata-Asks/Iwata-Asks-Super-Smash-Bros-Brawl/Volume-7-Once-in-a-Lifetime-Experience/1-Dragon-King-The-Fighting-Game/1-Dragon-King-The-Fighting-Game-226141.html.

———. 2008c. "For First-Time Players." *Iwata Asks.* n.d. http://www.nintendo.co.uk/Iwata-Asks/Iwata-Asks-Super-Smash-Bros-Brawl/Volume-7-Once-in-a-Lifetime-Experience/1-Dragon-King-The-Fighting-Game/1-Dragon-King-The-Fighting-Game-226141.html.

Jagoda, Patrick. 2013. "Fabulously Procedural: *Braid,* Historical Processing, and the Videogame Sensorium." *American Literature* 18, no. 4: 745–79.

———. 2016. *Network Aesthetics.* Chicago, Ill.: University of Chicago Press.

Jay, Martin. 1988. "Scopic Regimes of Modernity." In *Vision and Visuality,* ed. Hal Foster, 3–23. Seattle, Wash.: Bay Press.

Jenkins, Ria. 2014. "Metal Gear Solid: Ground Zeroes Fails to Portray Sexual Violence meaningfully." *The Guardian.* Apr. 9. http://www.theguardian.com/technology/2014/apr/09/metal-gear-solid-ground-zeroes-sexual-violence.

Jerz, Dennis. 2007. "Somewhere Nearby is Colossal Cave: Examining Will Crowther's Original 'Adventure' in Code and in Kentucky." *Digital Humanities Quarterly* 1, no. 2: http://www.digitalhumanities.org/dhq/vol/001/2/000009/000009.html.

Johnston, Casey. 2014. "The Death of the 'Gamers' and the Women Who 'Killed' Them." *Ars Technica.* Aug. 28. http://arstechnica.com/gaming/2014/08/the-death-of-the-gamers-and-the-women-who-killed-them/.

Kafer, Alison. 2013. *Feminist, Queer, Crip.* Bloomington: Indiana University Press.

Kent, Steven. 1999. "Hideo Kojima: Game Guru, Movie Maniac." *Metal Gear Solid: The Unofficial Site.* http://www.metalgearsolid.net/features/hideo-kojima-game-guru-movie-maniac.

Kirschenbaum, Matthew. 2008. *Mechanisms: New Media and the Forensic Imagination.* Cambridge, Mass.: MIT Press.

———. 2011. "War. What is it Good For? Learning from Wargaming." *Play the Past.* Aug. 16. http://www.playthepast.org/?p=1819.

Kirsh, David and Paul Maglio. 1994. "On Distinguishing Epistemic from Pragmatic Action." *Cognitive Science* 18, no. 4: 513–49.

Kleege, Georgina. 2006a. *Blind Rage: Letters to Helen Keller.* Washington, D.C.: Gallaudet University Press.

———. 2006b. "Blindness and Visual Culture: An Eyewitness Account." In *The Disability Studies Reader, Second Edition,* ed. Lennard J. Davis, 391–98. New York: Routledge.

Kohler, Chris. 2006. *Retro Gaming Hacks: Tips & Tools for Playing the Classics.* Cambridge, Mass.: O'Reilly.

Kojima, Hideo et al. 2013. "Photorealism Through the Eyes of a FOX: The Core of Metal Gear Solid Ground Zeroes." *GDC Vault.* Mar. 27. http://www.gdcvault.com/play/1018086/Photorealism-Through-the-Eyes-of.

Kolhatkar, Sheelah. 2014. "The Gaming Industry's Greatest Adversary Is Just Getting Started." *Bloomberg Business.* Nov. 26. http://www.bloomberg.com/bw/articles/2014-11-26/anita-sarkeesian-battles-sexism-in-games-gamergate-harassment.

Korean Culture and Information Service. 2012. "South Korea, the Mecca of e-Sports." *Korea.net.* June 4. http://www.korea.net/NewsFocus/Sci-Tech/view?articleId=100629.

Kosuth, Joseph. 1991. *Art After Philosophy and After: Collected Writings, 1966–1990,* ed. Gabriele Guercio. Cambridge, Mass.: MIT Press.

Kow, Yong Ming, Timothy Young, and Katie Salen Tekinbaş. 2014. *Crafting the Metagame: Connected Learning in the StarCraft II Community.* Irvine, Calif.: Digital Media and Learning Research Hub.

Lacan, Jacques. 1998. *The Four Fundamental Concepts of Psychoanalysis: The Seminar of Jacques Lacan Book IV,* ed. Jacques-Alain Miller; Trans. Alan Sheridan. New York: W. W. Norton & Company.

LeMieux, Patrick. 2014a. "From NES-4021 to moSMB3. wmv: Speedrunning the Serial Interface." *Eludamos: Journal for Computer Game Culture* 8, no. 1: 7–31.

———. 2014b. "Histories of the Future." *Electronic Book Review*. Mar. 1. http://elec
tronicbookreview.com/thread/electropoetics/Historicizing.

Lenoir, Tim. "All but War is Simulation: The Military-Entertainment Complex."
Configurations 2000, no. 8: 289–335.

Lenoir, Tim and Henry Lowood. 2005. "Theaters of War: The Military-Entertainment
Complex." In *Collection, Laboratory, Theater: Scenes of Knowledge in the 17th
Century*, ed. Helmar Schramm, Ludger Schwarte, Jan Lazardzig, 427–56. Berlin:
Walter de Gruyter.

Leodavinci. 2014. "I Used to Run the Largest Alliance in *Eve Online*—AMA." *Reddit*.
Jan. 28. http://www.reddit.com/r/Games/comments/1weo82/i_used_to_run_the
_largest_alliance_in_eve_online/cfla4qf.

Lewis, Michael. 2003. *Moneyball: The Art of Winning an Unfair Game*. New York:
W. W. Norton.

Li, Roland. 2014. "Making Money as a Zelda Speed Runner." *Polygon*. Jan. 09. http://
www.polygon.com/features/2014/1/9/5280786/making-money-zelda-speed
-runner.

Lien, Tracey. 2013. "The Story of How Two StarCraft Commentators Became Stars."
Polygon. July 16. http://www.polygon.com/features/2013/7/16/4503412/starcraft
-commentators-tastosis.

"List of Best Selling Videogames." *Wikipedia*. Last modified February 3, 2016. http://
en.wikipedia.org/wiki/List_of_best-selling_video_games.

Lobosco, Katie. 2013. "China to Lift 13-Year Ban on Video Game Consoles."
CNNMoney. July 10. http://money.cnn.com/2013/07/10/technology/china-video
-games/index.html.

Lowood, Henry and Michael Nitsche. 2011. *The Machinimal Reader*. Cambridge,
Mass.: MIT Press.

Major League Baseball. 2013. "Official Baseball Rules, 2013 Edition." *Major League
Baseball*. n.d. http://mlb.mlb.com/mlb/downloads/y2013/official_baseball_rules
.pdf.

Malabou, Catherine. 2008. *What Should We Do with Our Brain?* Trans. Sebastian
Rand. New York: Fordham University Press.

Marx, Karl. 1990. *Capital: A Critique of Political Economy, Volume I*. Trans. Ben
Fowkes. London: Penguin Books.

McClure, Andi. 2008. "Super Mario World vs. the Many-Worlds Interpretation of
Quantum Physics." *Run Hello*. http://msm.runhello.com/?p=20.

McCormick, Rich. "E3 2011: Our John Carmack Video Interview Covers Rage, the
PC, and Gamma Corrected Anti-Aliasing." *PC Gamer*. June 8. http://www
.pcgamer.com/2011/06/08/e3–2011-our-john-carmack-interview-covers-rage-the
-pc-and-gamma-corrected-anti-aliasing/.

McGonigal, Jane. 2011. *Reality Is Broken: Why Games Make Us Better and How They
Can Change the World*. New York: Penguin Press.

McJobless. 2014. "Re: #gamergate Megathread." *Blockland Forums*. Sept. 24. http://
forum.blockland.us/index.php?PHPSESSID=s2rn1qkuidu17rdmkhh6bp9sm0&
topic=267442.msg7889691#msg7889691.

McLuhan, Marshall. 1962. *The Gutenberg Galaxy: The Making of Typographic Man*.
Toronto, Ont.: University of Toronto Press.

McNew, Bradley Seth. 2014. "China's Online Gaming Market Is Reportedly up
246% in 2013." *The Motley Fool*. Apr. 10. http://www.fool.com/investing/gen
eral/2014/02/11/chinas-online-gaming-market-is-reportedly-up-246-i.aspx.

Meillassoux, Quentin. 2008. *After Finitude: An Essay on the Necessity of Contingency.* New York: Continuum.

Mellor, Lee. 2013. *Rampage Canadian: Mass Murder and Spree Killing.* Toronto: Dundurn.

Mielke, James. 2013. "BitSummit: The Secret World of Independent Japanese Game Development and Supporting Its Future." *Gamasutra: The Art & Business of Making Games.* Feb. 14. http://www.gamasutra.com/blogs/JamesMielke/20130214/186632/BitSummit_the_secret_world_of_independent_Japanese_game_development_and_supporting_its_future.php.

Miller, Patrick. 2012. "GDC2012: How Valve made *Team Fortress 2* Free-to-Play." *Gamasutra.* Mar. 7. http://gamasutra.com/view/news/164922/GDC_2012_How_Valve_made_Team_Fortress_2_freetoplay.php.

Mirzoeff, Nicholas. 1997. "Blindness and Art." In *The Disability Studies Reader, Second Edition,* ed. Lennard J. Davis, 182–200. New York: Routledge.

———. 2011. "The Right to Look." *Critical Inquiry* 37, no. 3: 473–96.

Mitchell, William J. 1994. *Reconfigured Eye: Visual Truth in the Post-Photographic Era.* Cambridge, Mass.: MIT Press, 1994.

Mitchell, W. J. T. 1986. *Iconology: Image, Text, Ideology.* Chicago: University of Chicago Press.

———. 1994. *Picture Theory: Essays on Verbal and Visual Representation.* Chicago: University of Chicago Press.

———. 2012. "Image X Text." In *The Future of Text and Image: Collected Essays on Literary and Visual Conjunctures,* ed. Ofra Amihay and Lauren Walsh, 1–11. Newcastle upon Tyne, U.K.: Cambridge Scholars Publishing.

Mogren, Joakim. 2012. "The Phantom Pain [HD]—VGA 2012 Debut Trailer. Dec. 10." *YouTube.* https://www.youtube.com/watch?v=_Kav2t0spyE.

Montfort, Nick. 2005. *Twisty Little Passages: An Approach to Interactive Fiction.* Cambridge, Mass.: MIT Press.

Montfort, Nick and Ian Bogost. 2009. *Racing the Beam: The Atari Video Computer System.* Cambridge, Mass.: MIT Press.

Montfort, Nick and Noah Wardrip-Fruin, eds. 2003. *The New Media Reader.* Cambridge, Mass.: The MIT Press.

MormaPope. 2013. "Okay, TeamCG. Come Own Up to Your Foolishness. #trolljima." *NeoGAF.* Mar. 15. http://neogaf.com/forum/showthread.php?t=524364.

Myerson, Roger B. 1991. *Game Theory: Analysis of Conflict.* Cambridge, Mass.: Harvard University Press.

NaCl. 2013. "That Joakim Mogren Interview WAS THE FOX Engine." *GameFAQs.* Mar. 21. http://www.gamefaqs.com/boards/691087-playstation-4/65754605.

Nakamura, Lisa. 2009. "The Socioalgorithmics of Race: Sorting It Out in Jihad Worlds." In *The New Media of Surveillance,* ed. Kelly Gates and Shoshana Magnet, 149–61. London: Routledge.

———. 2013. "Don't Hate the Player, Hate the Game: The Racialization of Labor in *World of Warcraft.*" In *Digital Labor: The Internet as Playground and Factory,* ed. Trebor Scholz, 187–204. New York: Routledge.

NASA. 2004. "Accidental Art." *NASA.gov.* Mar. 4. http://mars.jpl.nasa.gov/mer/gallery/press/spirit/20040304a.html.

———. 2012. "A Piece of New Mexico on Mars." *NASA.gov.* Sept. 17. http://www.nasa.gov/mission_pages/msl/multimedia/pia16136.html.

Neugebauer, Cimaron. 2014. "Terror Threat against Feminist Anita Sarkeesian at USU." *Standard-Examiner.* Oct. 15. www.standard.net/Police/2014/10/14/Utah-State-University-student-threatens-act-of-terror-if-feminist.html.

Newell, Gabe. 2013. "On Productivity, Economics, Political Institutions and the Future of Corporations: Reflections of a Video Game Maker." Lyndon B. Johnson Graduate School of Public Affairs, University of Texas. Austin, TX. Jan. 30 https://www.youtube.com/watch?v=t8QEOBgLBQU.

Nideffer, Robert. 2007. "Game Engines as Embedded Systems." *Database Aesthetics: Art in the Age of Information Overflow,* ed. Victoria Vesna, 211–42. Minneapolis, Minn.: University of Minnesota Press.

Nooney, Laine. 2013. "A Pedestal, A Table, A Love Letter: Archaeologies of Gender in Videogame History." *Game Studies* 13, no. 2. http://gamestudies.org/1302/articles/nooney.

Nutt, Christian. 2011. "The Valve Way: Gabe Newell and Erik Johnson Speak." *Gamasutra.* Aug. 29. http://www.gamasutra.com/view/feature/134839/the_valve_way_gabe_newell_and_.php?page=3.

Oliver, Julian. 2009. "levelHead." *Selectparks.net.* http://selectparks.net/~julian/levelhead/.

Óskarsson, Pétur Jóhannes [CCP Xhagen]. 2012. "A Tribute to Sean 'Vile Rat' Smith." *Eve Online.* Sept. 13. http://community.eveonline.com/news/dev-blogs/73406.

Oxford English Dictionary. 2014a. "meta, adj., adv., and n.3." *OED Online.* June 1. http://www.oed.com/view/Entry/117149?rskey=wTBNSz&result=3&isAdvanced=false#eid.

———. 2014b. "meta-, prefix." *OED Online.* June 1. http://www.oed.com/view/Entry/117150?rskey=wTBNSz&result=4&isAdvanced=false#eid.

Ozick, Cynthia. 2003. "What Helen Keller Saw." *The New Yorker.* June 16. http://www.newyorker.com/magazine/2003/06/16/what-helen-keller-saw.

PAADA. 2013. "Auction EF Pink War Dog_(191, 78, 123) with b/o." *Reddit.* Nov. 6. http://www.reddit.com/r/Dota2Trade/comments/1q0kxp/auction_ef_pink_war_dog_191_78_123_with_bo/.

Pajot, Lisanne and James Swirsky. 2012a. "About." *Indie Game: The Movie.* n.d. http://www.indiegamethemovie.com/about/.

———. 2012b. *Indie Game: The Movie.* Orlando, Fla.: Flutter Media.

Panofsky, Erwin. 1996. *Perspective as Symbolic Form.* Trans. Christopher S. Wood. Cambridge, Mass.: Zone Books (MIT Press).

Parish, Jeremy. 2012. Anatomy of a Game: *The Legend of Zelda 1.*" *The Anatomy of Games.* Sept. 4. http://www.anatomyofgames.com/2012/09/04/anatomy-of-a-game-the-legend-of-zelda-i/.

Parkin, Simon. 2012. "Hideo Kojima: Video Game Drop-out Interview." *The Guardian.* May 23. http://www.theguardian.com/technology/gamesblog/2012/may/23/hideo-kojima-interview-part-1.

———. 2014. "The Guilt of the Video-Game Millionaires." *The New Yorker Blogs.* Apr. 3. http://www.newyorker.com/online/blogs/elements/2014/04/the-guilt-of-the-video-game-millionaires.html.

———. 2015. "The Sometimes Fatal Attraction of Video Games." *The Guardian.* August 9. www.theguardian.com/technology/2015/aug/09/who-killed-the-video-gamers-simon-parkin-taiwan.

Parsons, Amy. 2013. "'A Careful Disorderliness': Transnational Labors in Melville's *Moby-Dick.*" *ESQ: A Journal of the American Renaissance* 58, no. 1 (2012): 71–101.

Pasquinelli, Matteo. 2009. "Google's PageRank Algorithm: A Diagram of Cognitive Capitalism and the Rentier of the Common Intellect." In *Deep Search,* ed. Konrad Becker and Felix Stalder, 152–62. London: Transaction Publishers.

Paumgarten, Nick. 2010. "Master of Play: The Many Worlds of a Video-Game Artist." *New Yorker.* Dec. 20. http://www.newyorker.com/magazine/2010/12/20/master-of-play?currentPage=all.

Pedercini, Paolo. 2014. "Videogames and the Spirit of Capitalism." *Molle Industria.* Feb. 14. www.molleindustria.org/blog/videogames-and-the-spirit-of-capitalism/.

Peterson, Jon. 2012. *Playing at the World: A History of Simulating Wars, People and Fantastic Adventure, from Chess to Role-Playing Games.* San Diego, Calif.: Unreason Press.

Pinckard, Jane. 2002. "Sex in Games: Rez + Vibrator." *Game Girl Advance.* Oct. 26. http://www.gamegirladvance.com/2002/10/sex-in-games-rezvibrator.html.

Plato. 1892. *The Dialogues of Plato.* Trans. B. Jowett. New York: Oxford University Press.

Pliny, the Elder. *The Natural History* (Bk. 35, Ch. 43), ed. John Bostock, Henry T. Riley, and Karl Friedrich Theodor Mayhoff. Somerville, Mass.: Perseus Digital Library. http://www.perseus.tufts.edu/cgi-bin/ptext?lookup=Plin.+Nat.+toc.

Plott, Sean [Day[9]]. 2009. "Building Triggers and the Imaginary Player." *Team Liquid.* Mar. 16. http://www.teamliquid.net/forum/bw-strategy/89581-day-podcasts-e14-tvz-on-heartbreak-ridge.

———. 2010. "Day[9] Daily #100—My Life of *StarCraft.*" *Day[9]TV.* http://day9.tv/d/Day9/day9-daily-100-my-life-of-starcraft/.

———. 2011. "E-Sports Manifesto." *Day[9]TV.* June 21. http://day9.tv/manifesto/.

Plunkett, Luke. 2010. "Before *StarCraft,* There Were Space Marines." *Kotaku.* July 22. http://kotaku.com/5591285/before-starcraft-there-was-warhammer-40k.

———. 2012. "Blizzard and Valve Go to War over DOTA Name." *Kotaku.* Feb. 10. http://kotaku.com/5883938/blizzard-and-valve-go-to-war-over-dota-name.

———. 2015. "Pro *Counter-Strike* Player: 'We Were All on Adderall.'" *Kotaku.* July 14. http://kotaku.com/pro-counter-strike-player-we-were-all-on-adderall-1717849428.

Polytron Corporation. 2013. "Fez Sells a Million." *Polytron Corporation.* Dec. 9. http://polytroncorporation.com/fez-sells-a-million.

Poundstone, William. 1992. *Prisoner's Dilemma: John von Neumann, Game Theory, and the Puzzle of the Bomb.* New York: Doubleday.

Pratt, Charles. 2013. "Why You Should Love the Fighting Game Community." *Polygon.* July 17. http://www.polygon.com/2013/7/17/4531320/opinion-why-you-should-love-the-fighting-game-community.

Pring, Kindra. 2015. "Well, Most of Us Just Want to Go On with Our Actual Purpose . . ." *HitFix.* Feb. 13. http://www.hitfix.com/motion-captured/why-law-order-svu-did-more-harm-than-good-with-their-gamergate-episode#comment-1852916028.

Puar, Jasbir K. 2010. "Prognosis time: Towards a Geopolitics of Affect, Debility, and Capacity." *Women & Performance: a Journal of Feminist Theory* 19, no. 2: 161–72.

Radio Lab. 2011. "The Rules Can Set You Free." *WNYC.* Aug. 24. http://www.radiolab.org/story/153799-games/.

Reinhardt, Ad. 1946. "How to Look at Low (Surrealist) Art." *PM.* Mar. 24.

———. 1991. *Art-as-Art: The Selected Writings of Ad Reinhardt,* ed. Barbara Rose. Berkeley, Calif.: University of California Press.

riptide. 2013. "All Pick: Wong Hock Chuan." *Team Liquid.* May 1. http://www.teamliquid.net/forum/viewmessage.php?topic_id=410435.

riptide and Marc [SirJolt] McEntegart. 2012. "All Pick: Danil 'Dendi' Ishutin." *Team Liquid.* Aug. 31. http://www.teamliquid.net/forum/viewmessage.php?topic_id=364641.

Rossignol, Jim. 2008. "The Great War." *Rock, Paper, Shotgun.* Sept. 9. http://www
.rockpapershotgun.com/2008/09/09/the-great-war/.

Ryan, Marie-Laure. 2006. *Avatars of Story.* Minneapolis: University of Minnesota Press.

Salen Tekinbaş, Katie, and Eric Zimmerman. 2004. *Rules of Play: Game Design Fundamentals.* Cambridge, Mass.: MIT Press.

Samyn, Michaël. 2010. "Not a Manifesto." *Notgames.* Mar. 19. http://notgames.org/
blog/2010/03/19/not-a-manifesto/.

Sandifer, Phil. 2006. "Player Epsilon: Demoing a New Hermeneutic for Games." *Proceedings of the 2006 UF Game Studies Conference.* June 21. http://www.gameol
ogy.org/essays/player_epsilon_demoing_a_new_hermeneutic_for_games.

Sarkeesian, Anita. 2012a. "Tropes vs. Women in Video Games." *Kickstarter.* May 17.
https://www.kickstarter.com/projects/566429325/tropes-vs-women-in-video
-games/description.

———. 2012b. "OMG! 1000 Backers! (And About That Harassment Stuff)." *Kickstarter.* June 7. https://www.kickstarter.com/projects/566429325/tropes-vs-women
-in-video-games/posts/242547.

———. 2015. "'What I Couldn't Say' Panel at All About Women." *Feminist Frequency.* Mar. 21. http://feministfrequency.com/2015/03/21/what-i-couldnt-say
-panel-at-all-about-women/.

Sarkeesian, Anita and Jonathan McIntosh. 2013. "Damsel in Distress (Part 1): Tropes
vs Women." *Feminist Frequency.* Mar. 7. http://feministfrequency.com/2013/03/07/
damsel-in-distress-part-1/.

Sartre, Jean-Paul. 2004. *Critique of Dialectical Reason.* New York: Verso.

Seaman, Bill. 1993. "Notes and Observations on Artificial Games." *BillSeaman.com.*
N.d. http://billseaman.trinity.duke.edu/pdf/artificialGames.pdf.

———. 2000. "Motioning Toward the Emergent Definition of E-phany Physics." *Art,
Technology, Consciousness Mind@large,* ed. Roy Ascott. Bristol, U.K.; Portland,
Ore.: Intellect Ltd.

Seiff, Abby. 2008. "The Super Mario Multiverse." *Popular Science.* Mar. 18. http://
www.popsci.com/entertainment-gaming/article/2008-03/super-mario
-multiverse.

Shannon, Claude. 1948. "A Mathematical Theory of Information." *Bell Labs.* http://
cm.bell-labs.com/cm/ms/what/shannonday/shannon1948.pdf.

Shapiro, Joseph P. 1993. *No Pity: People with Disabilities Forging a New Civil Rights
Movement.* New York: Times Books.

Shaviro, Steven. 2003. *Connected, or, What It Means to Live in the Network Society.*
Minneapolis, Minn.: University of Minnesota Press.

Shaw, Adrienne. 2013. "How Do You Say Gamer in Hindi?: Exploratory Research on
the Indian Digital Game Industry and Culture." In *Gaming Globally: Production,
Play, and Place,* ed. Nina B. Huntemann and Ben Aslinger, 183–202. New York:
Palgrave Macmillan.

Sheff, David. 1993. *Game Over: How Nintendo Zapped an American Industry, Captured Your Dollars, and Enslaved Your Children.* New York: Random House.

Sherman, William H. 2008. "☞: Toward a History of the Manicule." *Used Books:
Marking Readers in Renaissance England,* 25–52. Philadelphia: University of
Pennsylvania Press.

Siebers, Tobin. 2008. *Disability Theory.* Ann Arbor, Mich.: University of Michigan
Press.

Sitsky, Larry. 2002. *Music of the Twentieth-Century Avant-Garde: A Biocritical
Sourcebook.* Westport, Conn.: Greenwood Press.

Sobchack, Vivian. 2008. "The Line and the Animorph, or 'Travel is More than Just A to B'." *Animation: An Interdisciplinary Arts Journal* 3, no. 3: 251–65.

———. 2010. "Living a 'Phantom Limb': On the Phenomenology of Bodily Integrity." *Body & Society* 16, no. 3: 51–67.

Sontag, Susan. 1977. *On Photography.* New York: Farrar, Straus and Giroux.

Sony Computer Entertainment Inc. 2008. "Echochrome Official Trailer." *YouTube.* Oct. 3. https://www.youtube.com/watch?v=GybxIwfU4rI.

Speed Demos Archive. 2013. "Rules." *Internet Archive.* Sept. 11. https://web.archive .org/web/20130911001928/http://speeddemosarchive.com/lang/rules_en.html.

Speed Runs Live. 2014. "FAQ." *Speed Runs Live.* n.d. http://speedrunslive.com/ faq/.

Spicer, John. 2013. "Is the Compendium the Best Thing to Happen to eSports?" *Team Dignitas.* July 28. http://www.team-dignitas.org/articles/blogs/DotA-2/3625/ Is-the-Compendium-the-best-thing-to-happen-to-eSports/.

Squeaky Wheel. 2014. "TechARTS for Girls." *Squeaky Wheel.* n.d. http://www .squeaky.org/techarts.

Steinberg, Marc. 2003. "Characterizing a New Seriality: Murakami Takashi's DOB Project." *Parachute: Contemporary Art Magazine* 110 (April–June): 90–109.

Stemkoski, Daniel [Artosis]. 2012. "Mapping out the Metagame." *SC Dojo.* Oct. 25. http://scdojo.tumblr.com/post/34233737871/mapping-out-the-metagame.

Stiegler, Bernard. 1998. *Technics and Time: The Fault of Epimetheus.* Trans. Richard Beardsworth and George Collins. Stanford, Calif.: Stanford University Press.

———. 2010. *For a New Critique of Political Economy.* Cambridge, Mass.: Polity.

Suits, Bernard. 2005. *The Grasshopper: Games, Life and Utopia.* Peterborough, Ont.: Broadview Press.

Swink, Steve. 2009. *Game Feel: A Game Designer's Guide to Virtual Sensation.* Amsterdam: Morgan Kaufmann Publishers.

TASVideos. 2007. "NES Mega Man 3, 4, 5 & 6 (USA) in 39:06.92 by Lennart W. (Baxter) & Yashar Nasirian (AngerFist)." *TAS Videos.* May 23. http://tasvideos. org/871M.html.

Taylor, T.L. 2012. *Raising the Stakes: E-Sports and the Professionalization of Computer Gaming.* Cambridge, Mass.: MIT Press.

Team Meat [SuperMeatBoy]. "Fun Fact: Super Meat Boy Past the Million Sales Mark Last Month! PLATINUM BABY." *Twitter.* Jan. 3. https://twitter.com/Super MeatBoy/status/154091784929161217.

ten Bosch, Marc. 2011. "Miegakure: A Puzzle-Platformer in Four Dimensions." *Marctenbosch.com.* http://marctenbosch.com/miegakure/.

Terrell, Richard. 2010. "An Examination of Skill Pt. 1." *Critical-Gaming Network.* Mar. 31. http://critical-gaming.com/blog/2010/3/31/an-examination-of-skill-pt1 .html.

———. 2011a. "Appraising the Art of Combat Pt. 10." *Critical-Gaming Network.* Jan. 24. http://critical-gaming.squarespace.com/blog/2011/1/24/appraising-the-art -of-combat-pt10.html.

———. 2011b. "Metagame Meditations Pt. 4." *Critical-Gaming Network.* Jan. 30. http://critical-gaming.com/blog/2011/1/30/metagame-meditations-pt3.html.

———. 2011c. "Metagame Meditations Pt. 4." *Critical-Gaming Network.* Feb. 1. http://critical-gaming.com/blog/2011/2/1/metagame-meditations-pt4.html.

———. 2011d. "Project M-etagame." Critical-Gaming Network. March 3. http://criti cal-gaming.com/blog/2011/3/3/project-m-etagame.html.

Thacker, Eugene. 2010. *After Life.* Chicago, Ill.: University of Chicago Press.

Thorn, Benjamin. 2002. In *Music of the Twentieth-Century Avant-Garde: A Bio-critical Sourcebook,* ed. Larry Sitsky, 415–19. Westport, Conn.: Greenwood Press.

Thursten, Chris. 2013. "Hero's Journey." *PC Gamer UK.* 254, July 2013: 36–47.

Trudeau, Justin. 2015. "Up for Debate: Justin Trudeau (English)." *YouTube.* Oct. 1. https://www.youtube.com/watch?v=KLYCcoCAT_Y.

Tufnell, Nicholas. 2011. "Interview: Gabe Newell." Nov. 24. *The Cambridge Student.* http://tcs.cam.ac.uk/interviews/0012301-interview-gabe-newell.html.

Turkle, Sherry. 2011. *Alone Together: Why We Expect More from Technology and Less from Each Other.* New York: Basic Books.

Twain, Mark. 1917. *Mark Twain's Letters, Vol. II,* ed. Albert Bigelow Paine. New York: Harper & Brothers Publishers.

Twitch Interactive. 2013. "Twitch 2013 Retrospective." *Twitch TV.* http://www.twitch.tv/year/2013.

Ulmer, Gregory L. 2005. *Electronic Monuments.* Minneapolis, Minn.: University of Minnesota Press.

Ungerleider, Neal. 2014. "Meet The Alan Greenspan of Virtual Currency in 'EVE Online.'" *Fast Company.* Jan. 6. http://www.fastcompany.com/3024392/meet-the-alan-greenspan-of-virtual-currency-in-eve-online.

Valve Corporation. 2012a. "Foam Fingers!" *Dota 2 Official Blog.* Aug. 23. http://blog.dota2.com/2012/08/foam-fingers/.

———. 2012b. "iG vs Na`Vi—Game 1, Winner Bracket Semifinals." *YouTube.* Sept. 1. https://www.youtube.com/watch?v=OTcgVD0wRYA.

———. 2012c. "iG vs Na`Vi—Game 2, Winner Bracket Semifinals." *YouTube.* Sept. 1. https://www.youtube.com/watch?v=La—egn0MrU.

———. 2012d. "Na`Vi vs DK—Game 3, Winner Bracket Quarter Finals." *YouTube.* Sept. 1. https://www.youtube.com/watch?v=yWGVPWeyPhQ.

———. 2012e. "EHOME vs iG—Loser Bracket Round 4, Game 1." *YouTube.* Sept 1. https://www.youtube.com/watch?v=bZdc1lyccds.

———. 2012f. "TF vs EG—Loser Bracket Quarter Finals." *YouTube.* Sept 1. https://www.youtube.com/watch?v=Biw3SdR9xu0.

———. 2012g. "The 2012 International." *Dota 2 Official Blog.* Sept. 7. http://blog.dota2.com/2012/09/the-2012-international/.

———. 2012h. *Handbook for New Employees.* Steamworks. http://media.steampowered.com/apps/valve/Valve_NewEmployeeHandbook.pdf.

———. 2013a. "Interactive Compendium." *Dota 2: Official Blog.* Feb. 22. 2013. http://www.dota2.com/international/compendium.

———. 2013b. "The Beta is Over!" *Dota 2 Official Blog.* July 9. http://blog.dota2.com/2013/07/the-beta-is-over/.

van Inwagen, Peter. 2013. "Metaphysics." *The Stanford Encyclopedia of Philosophy* (Winter 2013 Edition). http://plato.stanford.edu/archives/win2013/entries/metaphysics/.

Various. 2005. "Introduction to Hacking." ROMhacking.net. http://datacrystal.romhacking.net/wiki/Introduction_to_Hacking.

Varoufakis, Yanis. 2013. "Confessions of an Erratic Marxist in the Midst of a Repugnant European Crisis." *Yanis Varoufakis: Thoughts for the Post-2008 World.* Dec. 10. http://yanisvaroufakis.eu/2013/12/10/confessions-of-an-erratic-marxist-in-the-midst-of-a-repugnant-european-crisis/.

Verner, Jordan. 2006. "Can Someone Please Help Me with OoT?" *Speed Demos Archive.* Oct. 20. https://forum.speeddemosarchive.com/post/can_someone_please_help_me_with_oot.html.

Verner, Jordan et al. 2006–2009. "MasterScript.txt." Unpublished.

von Neumann, John, and Oskar Morgenstern. 1953. *Theory of Games and Economic Behavior.* Princeton, N.J.: Princeton University Press.

Wardrip-Fruin, Noah, and Nick Montfort, eds. 2003. *The New Media Reader.* Cambridge, Mass.: MIT Press.

Wark, McKenzie. 2004. *A Hacker Manifesto.* Cambridge, Mass.: Harvard University Press.

———. 2007. *Gamer Theory.* Cambridge, Mass.: Harvard University Press.

———. 2012. *Telesthesia: Communication, Culture, and Class.* Cambridge, U.K.: Polity.

———. 2013. "Accelerationism." *Public Seminar* 1, no. 1: http://www.publicseminar.org/2013/11/accelerationism/.

Weir, Andy. 2002. "Gug." *Galactanet.com.* n.d. http://galactanet.com/gug.htm.

Weise, Matthew. 2010. "The Decline of Anti-Americanism in Metal Gear." *Outside Your Heaven.* April 10. http://outsideyourheaven.blogspot.com/2012/04/decline-of-anti-americanism-in-metal.html.

———. 2012. "One Paragraph Review—Metal Gear Solid 3: Snake Eater." *Outside Your Heaven.* Dec. 31. http://outsideyourheaven.blogspot.com/2012/12/one-paragraph-review-metal-gear-solid-3.html.

Wendell, Susan. 2006. "Toward a Feminist Theory of Disability." In *The Disability Studies Reader, Second Edition,* ed. Lennard J. Davis, 243–56. New York: Routledge.

Werner, Nicholas. 2012. "All Your History: DOTA Part 1: The Pebble that Started the Avalanche." *YouTube.* Jan. 2. https://www.youtube.com/watch?v=AnQfdSEqGDA.

Wilson, Douglas. 2016. "A Tale of Two Jousts: Multimedia, Game Feel, and Imagination." *YouTube.* Oct. 31. https://www.youtube.com/watch?v=JkbCNMAS0qI.

Wilson, Douglas and Miguel Sicart. 2010. "Now It's Personal: On Abusive Game Design." In *Proceedings of the International Academic Conference on the Future of Game Design and Technology* (Futureplay '10), 40–47. ACM, New York, USA.

Wizards of the Coast. 2014. "Magic: The Gathering Comprehensive Rules." *Wizards of the Coast.* June 1. http://media.wizards.com/images/magic/tcg/resources/rules/MagicCompRules_20140601.pdf.

Woods, Jarrad "Farbs." 2008. "ROM CHECK FAIL Press Kit." *Farbs.com.* March 25. http://farbs.org/press/sheet.php?p=rom_check_fail.

Woods, Stewart. 2012. *Eurogames: The Design, Culture and Play of Modern European Board Games.* Jefferson, N. Car.: McFarland & Company, Inc.

Wright, Narcissa. 2012. "Welcome to Ocarina of Time." *YouTube.* Dec. 20. https://www.youtube.com/watch?v=xOrRRdAOU-4.

———. 2013a. "*Ocarina of Time*—Speedrunning & Version Differences." *Cosmo's Blog.* Aug. 13. http://blog.cosmowright.com/?p=33.

———. 2013b. "Why Speedrunning is Meaningful for Me." *YouTube.* Feb. 8. https://www.youtube.com/watch?v=xT6hOfLthS4.

———. 2013c. "Cosmo's List of Speedrun Progress." *Pastebin.* Sept. 19. http://pastebin.com/FsUEBVyh.

———. 2013d. "Speedrun Leaderboards Discussion Topic (SRL)." *Speed Demos Archive Forum.* Aug. 14. https://forum.speeddemosarchive.com/post/srl_leaderboards_discussion_topic_46.html#srl_leaderboards_discussion_topic_46.

———. 2013e. "*The Legend of Zelda: Ocarina of Time* Speedrun by Cosmo, Live at SGDQ." *YouTube.* Aug. 5. https://www.youtube.com/watch?v=7mp0uHr2X6U.

———. 2015. "all the categories are arbitrary." *YouTube*. Dec 17. https://www.you tube.com/watch?v=EHAlqxsLH-0.

Wyatt, Patrick. 2012a. "The Inside Story of the Making of *Warcraft*, Part 1." *Kotaku*. July 26. http://kotaku.com/5929157/the-making-of-warcraft-part-1.

———. 2012b. "*StarCraft*: Orcs in Space Go Down in Flames." *Code of Honor*. Sept. 27. http://www.codeofhonor.com/blog/starcraft-orcs-in-space-go-down-in-flames.

Zimmerman, Eric. 2011. "Secret History of the Metagame." *Being Playful*. Feb. 18. http://ericzimmerman.wordpress.com/2011/02/18/secret-history-of-the -metagame/.

———. 2012. "Jerked Around by the Magic Circle—Clearing the Air Ten Years Later." *Gamasutra*. Feb. 7. www.gamasutra.com/view/feature/135063/jerked_ around_by_the_magic_circle_.php.

———. 2013. "Manifesto for a Ludic Century." *Being Playful*. Sept. 9. https://ericzim merman.wordpress.com/2013/09/09/manifesto-for-a-ludic-century/.

Zurreco. 2006. "Can Someone Please Help Me with OoT?" *Speed Demos Archive*. Oct. 22. https://forum.speeddemosarchive.com/post/can_someone_please_ help_me_with_oot50.html#can_someone_please_help_me_with_oot50.

Gameography

4:32. Browser. Developed by Jesper Juul. Jesper Juul, 2010. http://www.jesperjuul .net/4.32/.

4 Minutes and 33 Seconds of Uniqueness. Microsoft Windows. Developed by Petri Purho. Petri Purho, 2009. http://www.kloonigames.com/blog/games/4mins 33secs.

Achievement Unlocked. Browser. Developed by John Cooney. Armor Games, 2008. http://armorgames.com/play/2893/achievement-unlocked.

Adventure. Atari 2600. Developed by Atari, Inc. (Warren Robinett). Atari, Inc., 1980.

Adventures of Lolo. Nintendo Entertainment System. Developed by HAL Laboratory. HAL America, 1989.

Aeon of Strife. Windows, Macintosh OS. Developed by Aeon64. Blizzard Entertainment (Battle.net) ~2002.

Afternoon, A Story. Macintosh and Windows. Developed by Michael Joyce. Eastgate Systems, 1987.

Alien Hominid. PlayStation 2 and Nintendo GameCube. Developed by The Behemoth. O3 Entertainment and Zoo Digital Publishing, 2004.

America's Army. Windows. Developed by United States Army. United States Army, 2002.

Amnesia: The Dark Descent. Microsoft Windows, Macintosh OS X, and Linux. Developed by Frictional Games. Frictional Games, 2010.

Angry Birds. iOS. Developed by Rovio Entertainment. Chillingo/Clickgamer, Rovio Entertainment, 2009.

Antichamber. Microsoft Windows, Macintosh OS X, Linux. Developed by Alexander Bruce. Alexander Bruce, 2013.

Asteroids. Arcade. Developed by Atari, Inc. (Lyle Rains and Ed Logg). Atari, Inc., 1979.

AudioQuake. PC. Developed by Ω, Matthew Tylee Nintendo., Sabahattin Gucukoglu, et al. The AGRIP Project, 2003–present.

Audiosurf. Microsoft Windows. Developed by Dylan Fitterer. Steam, 2008.

Awesomenauts. PlayStation 3, Xbox 360, Windows, OS X, Linux (2013), PlayStation 4 (2014). Developed by Ronimo Games. dtp Entertainment, 2012.

Basho's Frogger. Java. Developed by Neil Hennessy. *Electronic Literature Collection, Volume 2,* 2000.

Battlefield 1942. Microsoft Windows and OS X. Developed by EA Digital Illusions CE. Electronic Arts, 2002.

The Beast. ARG. Developed by Microsoft. Warner Bros., 2001.

Beat Up Anita Sarkeesian. Flash. Developed by Benjamin Spurr. Benjamin Spurr, 2012.

BECOME A GREAT ARTIST IN JUST 10 SECONDS. Mac, Windows, and Linux. Developed by Michael Brough and Andi McClure. Run Hello, 2013. http://ludumdare.com/compo/ludum-dare-27/?action=preview&uid=4987.

The Binding of Isaac. Microsoft Windows, Macintosh OS X, and Linux. Developed by Edmund McMillen and Florian Himsl. Headup Games, 2011.

Bit.Trip Runner. WiiWare. Developed by Gaijin Games. Aksys Games and Gaijin Games, 2010.

Blaster Master. Nintendo Entertainment System. Developed by Sunsoft. Sunsoft, 1988.

Blinx: The Time Sweeper. Xbox. Developed by Artoon. Microsoft Game Studios, 2002.

Boktai: The Sun is in Your Hand. Game Boy Advance. Developed by Konami Computer Entertainment Japan. Konami, 2003.

Braid. Xbox Live Arcade. Developed by Jonathan Blow. Microsoft Game Studios, 2008.

Breakout. Arcade. Developed by Atari, Inc. (Nolan Bushnell, Steve Bristow, and Steve Wozniak) Atari, Inc., 1976.

Bubble Bobble. Arcade. Developed by Taito. Taito and Romstar, 1986.

Call of Duty. Microsoft Windows. Developed by Infinity Ward. Activision, 2003.

Candy Box. Browser. Developed by aniwey. aniwey, 2013. http://candies.aniwey.net/.

Candy Crush Saga. Facebook, iOS, Android, Windows Phone. Developed by King. King, 2012.

Captain Toad: Treasure Tracker. Nintendo Wii U. Developed by 1-UP Studio, Nintendo EAD. Nintendo, 2014.

Castle Crashers. Xbox 360. Developed by The Behemoth. Microsoft Game Studios, 2008.

Castlevania. Nintendo Entertainment System. Developed by Konami. Konami, 1986.

Castlevania II: Simon's Quest. Nintendo Entertainment System. Developed by Konami. Konami, 1987.

Castlevania: Symphony of the Night. PlayStation. Developed by Konami Computer Entertainment Japan. Konami, 1997.

Cave Story. Microsoft Windows. Developed by Daisuke Amaya. Studio Pixel, 2004.

Centipede. Arcade. Developed by Atari, Inc. (Ed Logg and Dona Bailey). Atari, Inc., 1981.

Chronotron. Flash. Developed by Scarybug Games. Scarybug Games, 2008.

Circus Atari. Arcade. Developed by Edward Valeau and Howell Ivey. Exidy, 1980.

Close Range. Browser. Developed by The Onion. The Onion, 2009.

Closure. PlayStation 3, Microsoft Windows, Mac, and Linux. Developed by Eyebrow Interactive. Eyebrow Interactive.

Colossal Cave Adventure. PDP-10. Developed by Will Crowther. CRL, 1975.

Contra. Nintendo Entertainment System. Developed by Konami. Konami, 1987.

Contrast. PlayStation 4, PlayStation 3, Xbox One, Xbox 360, Windows. Developed by Compulsion Games. Focus Home Interactive, 2013.

Cookie Clicker. Browser. Developed by Julien [Orteil] Thiennot. Julien Thiennot, 2013. http:///orteil.dashnet.org/cookieclicker/.

Counter-Strike. Developed by Valve Corporation. Valve Corporation and Sierra Entertainment, 1999. Windows.

Cow Clicker. Browser. Developed by Ian Bogost. Facebook, 2010. https://apps.facebook.com/cowclicker/.

Crush. PlayStation Portable. Developed by Zoë Mode. Sega, 2007.

Cursor*10. Flash. Developed by Yoshio Ishii. Nekogames, 2008.

Dark Souls. PlayStation3 and Xbox 360. Developed by From Software. From Software and Namco Bandai Games, 2011.

Day of Defeat. Windows. Developed by Valve Corporation. Activision, 2003.

DefeatMe. Browser. Developed by Kenta Cho. Kenta Cho, 2009.

Defender. Arcade. Developed by Williams Electronics (Eugene Jarvis and Larry DeMar). Williams Electronics, 1981.

Defense of the Ancients. Windows, Macintosh OS X. Developed by Eul. Blizzard Entertainment (Battle.net), 2003.

Demigod. Windows. Developed by Gas Powered Games. Stardock, 2009.

"Desert Bus" in *Penn and Teller's Smoke and Mirrors.* Sega CD. Developed by Imagineering. Absolute Entertainment, 1995.

Destiny. PlayStation 3, PlayStation 4, Xbox 360, Xbox One. Developed by Bungie. Activision, 2014.

Diablo III. Microsoft Windows, OS X. Developed by Blizzard Entertainment. Blizzard Entertainment, 2012.

Diplomacy. Print. Developed by Alan B. Calhamer. Self-published, 1959.

Donkey Kong. Arcade. Developed by Nintendo R&D1. Nintendo, 1981.

Donkey Kong Game & Watch. Hand held. Developed by Nintendo R&D1. Nintendo, 1981.

Do Not Push the Red Button. Flash. Developed by fancylad. I Am Bored, 2005. http://www.i-am-bored.com/bored_link.cfm?link_id=9644.

Don't Shoot the Puppy. Browser. Developed by Serious Sandbox LLC. Serious Sandbox LLC, 2006. http://www.rrrrthats5rs.com/games/dont-shoot-the-puppy/.

Doom. MS-DOS. Developed by id Software. id Software, 1993.

Doom 64. Nintendo 64. Developed by Midway Games and id Software. Nintendo, 1997.

DotA Allstars 1.0. Windows, Macintosh OS X. Developed by Meian and Ragn0r et al. Blizzard Entertainment (Battle.net.), 2004.

DotA Allstars 2.0. Windows, Macintosh OS X. Developed by Stephen [Guinsoo] Feak et al. Blizzard Entertainment (Battle.net.), 2004.

DotA Allstars 6.0. Windows, Macintosh OS X. Developed by IceFrog and Neichus et al. Blizzard Entertainment (Battle.net.), 2005.

DotA Allstars 6.1. Windows, Macintosh OS X. Developed by IceFrog et al. Blizzard Entertainment (Battle.net.), 2005.

DotA Allstars 6.12 (Chinese Translation). Windows, Macintosh OS X. Developed by Heintje et al. Blizzard Entertainment (Battle.net.), 2005.

DotA: Thirst for Gamma. Windows, Macintosh OS X. Developed by Eul. Blizzard Entertainment (Battle.net.), 2003.

Dota 2. Microsoft Windows, Macintosh OS X, Linux. Developed by Valve Corporation. Valve Corporation, Perfect World (China), Nexon Co. LTD. (Korea and Japan), 2013.

Dune 2: Building a Dynasty. Developed by Westwood Studios. Virgin Interactive, 1992. MS-DOS, Amiga (1993), Sega Mega Drive/Genesis (1993).

Dungeons & Dragons. Print and mixed media. Developed by Gary Gygax and Dave Arneson. TSR, Inc, 1974.

Dwarf Fortress. Windows, Macintosh OS X Linux. Developed by Tarn Adams. Bay 12 Games.

Dys4ia. Browser. Developed by Anna Anthropy. Newgrounds, 2012.

EarthBound. SNES. Developed by Ape and HAL Laboratory. Nintendo, 1994.

Echochrome. PlayStation 3. Developed by Game Yarouze and JAPAN Studio. Sony Computer Entertainment, 2008.

Echochrome II. PlayStation 3. Developed by JAPAN Studio. Sony Computer Entertainment, 2010.

Echoshift. PlayStation Portable. Developed by Artoon. SCE, 2009.

The Elder Scrolls V: Skyrim. Microsoft Windows, PlayStation 3, Xbox 360. Developed by Bethesda Game Studios. Bethesda Softworks, 2011.

E.T. the Extra-Terrestrial. Atari 2600. Developed by Atari, Inc. (Howard Scott Warshaw). Atari, Inc, 1982.

EVE Online. Microsoft Windows, Macintosh OS X, Linux. Developed by CCP Games. CCP Games, 2003.

EverQuest. Windows, Macintosh OS X (2003). Developed by Sony Online Entertainment. Sony Online Entertainment.

Evoland 2. Microsoft Windows, OS X. Developed by Shiro Games. Shiro Games, 2015.

Extra Mario Bros. Nintendo Entertainment System. Developed by ATA, 2005. http://www.romhacking.net/hacks/369/.

Fallout 3. Microsoft Windows, PlayStation 3, Xbox 360. Developed by Bethesda Game Studios. Bethesda Softworks, 2008.

Fallout 4. Microsoft Windows, PlayStation 4, Xbox One. Developed by Bethesda Game Studios. Bethesda Softworks, 2015.

FarmVille. Browser. Developed by Zynga. Facebook, 2009.

Fez. Xbox Live Arcade. Developed by Polytron Corporation. Microsoft Game Studios, 2012.

Final Fantasy. Nintendo Entertainment System. Developed by Square. Square, 1987.

Final Fantasy VII. PlayStation. Developed by Square. Square, Sony Computer Entertainment, 1997.

Frog Fractions 2. Developed by Twinbeard. Forthcoming.

F-Zero. Super Family Computer/SNES. Developed by Nintendo EAD. Nintendo, 1990.

Game Dev Story. Microsoft Windows, iOS, and Android. Developed by Kairosoft. Kairosoft, 2010.

GameMaker. Microsoft Windows. Developed by Mark Overmars and YoYo Games. YoYo Games, 1999.

Garry Kitchen's Game Maker. Commodore 64, Apple II, IBM PC. Developed by Garry Kitchen. Activision, 1985.

Ghosts n' Goblins. Arcade and Nintendo Entertainment System. Developed by Capcom. Capcom and Taito America Corp, 1985.

A Good Hunch. Flash. Developed by Marckus Mundjar and Philipp Seifried. Arcade Town, 2007.

Grand Unified Game. Developed by Andy Weir. Andy Weir, 2003. http://www.galactanet.com/gug.htm.

The Graveyard. Windows and Mac. Developed by Tale of Tales (Auriea Harvey and Michaël Samyn). Tale of Tales, 2008.

Gravitar. Arcade. Developed by Atari, Inc. (Mike Hally and Rich Adam). Atari, Inc., 1983.

Guardians of Middle-Earth. PlayStation 3, Xbox 360, Windows (2013). Developed by Monolith Productions. Warner Bros. Interactive Entertainment, 2012.

Guru Meditation. Atari VCS, iPhone. Developed by Ian Bogost. Ian Bogost, 2009.

Half-Life. Windows PC. Developed by Valve Corporation. Sierra Entertainment, 1998.

Halo: Combat Evolved. Xbox. Developed by Bungie. Microsoft Game Studios, 2001.

Halo 2. Xbox. Developed by Bungie. Microsoft Game Studios, 2004.

Hard Relay Mario. Nintendo Entertainment System. Developed by Mana, Rei, SnowArrow, Quark, U1, 79. 2004. http://tasvideos.org/4347S.html.

The Helen Keller Simulator. Browser. Developer Unknown. c2005–.

Heroes of Newerth. Windows, Macintosh OS X, Linux. Developed by S2 Games. S2 Games, Garena (Russia and Southeast Asia), Ntreev Soft (Korea), 2010.

Heroes of the Storm. Windows, OS X. Developed by Blizzard Entertainment. Blizzard Entertainment, 2014.

Herzog Zwei. Sega Mega Drive/Genesis. Developed by Technosoft. Technosoft, 1989.

Ico. PlayStation 2. Developed by Team Ico. Sony Computer Entertainment, 2001.

I Love Bees. ARG. Developed by 42 Entertainment. Microsoft, 2008.

Infinite Crisis. Windows. Developed by Turbine. Warner Bros. Interactive Entertainment, 2015.

Infinite Mario Bros. Browser. Developed by Markus [Notch] Perssons. Mojang, 2006.

I Wanna Be the Guy: The Movie: The Game. Microsoft Windows. Developed by Michael [Kayin] O'Reilly. 2007. http://kayin.moe/iwbtg/.

Johann Sebastian Joust. PlayStation 3, PlayStation 4. Developed by Die Gute Fabrik (Douglas Wilson). Die Gute Fabrik, 2014.

Journey. PlayStation 3. Developed by Thatgamecompany. Sony Computer Entertainment, 2012.

Jumpman. Mac, Windows, and Linux. Developed by Andi McClure. Run Hello. 2008. https://runhello.com/p/24.

Kaizo Mario World. Super Nintendo Entertainment System. Developed by T. Takemoto. T. Takemoto, 2007.

Kingdom Hearts. PlayStation 2. Developed by Square. Square, 2002.

Kirby's Adventure. Nintendo Entertainment System. Developed by HAL Laboratory. Nintendo, 1993.

Kirby's Dream Land. Game Boy. Developed by HAL Laboratory. Nintendo, 1992.

League of Legends. Windows, OS X. Developed by Riot Games. Riot Games, Tencent Holdings LTD. (China), Garena (Southeast Asia), 2009.

The Legend of Zelda. Nintendo Entertainment System. Developed by Nintendo R&D4. Nintendo, 1986.

The Legend of Zelda: A Link to the Past. Nintendo. Super Nintendo Entertainment System. Developed by Nintendo EAD. Nintendo, 1991.

The Legend of Zelda: Ocarina of Time. Nintendo 64, Nintendo GameCube (2002), iQue Player (2003). Developed by Nintendo EAD, 1998. Nintendo, 1998.

The Legend of Zelda: The Wind Waker. Nintendo GameCube. Developed by Nintendo EAD. Nintendo, 2002.

levelHead. Linux. Developed by Julian Oliver. 2008. http://julianoliver.com/level head/.

Limbo. Xbox Live Arcade. Developed by Playdead. Microsoft Studios, 2010.

Line Wobbler. Arduino. Developed by Robin Baumgarten. Robin Baumgarten, 2014.

Lode Runner. Multiple Platforms. Developed by Douglas E. Smith. Brøderbund, 1983.

Lost in Shadow. Nintendo Wii. Developed by Hudson Soft. Hudson Soft, Konami, Mindscape, 2010.

Magic: The Gathering. Collectable card game. Developed by Richard Garfield. Wizards of the Coast, 1993.

Mari0. Windows. Developed by Stabyourself.net (Maurice Guégan and Raicuparta). Stabyourself.net, 2012. http://stabyourself.net/mari0/.

Mario Golf. Nintendo 64. Developed by Camelot. Nintendo, 1999.

Mario Paint. Super Nintendo Entertainment System. Developed by Nintendo R&D1 and Intelligent Systems. Nintendo, 1992.

Mario Tennis. Nintendo 64. Developed by Camelot. Nintendo, 2000.

Mario vs. Airman. Nintendo Entertainment System. Developed by ATA. 2008. http://smbarchives.run.buttobi.net/.

The Marriage. Microsoft Windows. Developed by Rod Humble. http://rodvik.com/ rodgames/marriage.html.

Max Payne. Developed by Remedy Entertainment. Microsoft Windows, PlayStation 2, and Xbox. Gathering and 3D Realms, 2001.

Meat Boy. Browser. Developed by Edmund McMillen and Jonathan McEntee. Newgrounds, 2008. http://www.newgrounds.com/portal/view/463.

Medal of Honor. PlayStation. Developed by DreamWorks Interactive. Electronic Arts, 1999.

Mega Man. Nintendo Entertainment System. Developed by Capcom. Capcom, 1987.

Mega Man 2. Nintendo Entertainment System. Developed by Capcom. Capcom, 1988.

Mega Man 3. Nintendo Entertainment System. Developed by Capcom. Capcom, 1990.

Mega Man 4. Nintendo Entertainment System. Developed by Capcom. Capcom, 1991.

Mega Man 5. Nintendo Entertainment System. Developed by Capcom. Capcom, 1992.

Mega Man 6. Nintendo Entertainment System. Developed by Capcom. Capcom, 1993.

Mega Man 9. Wii. Developed by Capcom and Inti Creates. Capcom, 2008.

Mega Man 9. Wii. Developed by Capcom and Inti Creates. Capcom, 2010.

Mega Man X. Super Nintendo Entertainment System. Developed by Capcom. Capcom, 1993.

Mega Man X2. Super Nintendo Entertainment System. Developed by Capcom. Capcom, 1994.

Mega Man X3. Super Nintendo Entertainment System. Developed by Capcom. Capcom, 1995.

Metal Gear. Developed by Konami. Konami, 1987. MSX2.

Metal Gear Rising: Revengeance. PlayStation 3, Xbox 360, Windows, OS X. Developed by Platinum Games, Kojima Productions, TransGaming. Konami, 2010.

Metal Gear Solid. PlayStation. Developed by Konami Computer Entertainment Japan. Konami, 1998.

Metal Gear Solid 2: Sons of Liberty. PlayStation 2. Developed by Konami Computer Entertainment Japan. Konami, 2001.

Metal Gear Solid 3: Snake Eater. PlayStation 2. Developed by Konami Computer Entertainment Japan. Konami, 2004.

Metal Gear Solid 4: Guns of the Patriots. PlayStation 3. Developed by Kojima Productions. Konami, 2008.

Metal Gear Solid V: Ground Zeroes. PlayStation 4, Xbox One, PlayStation 3, Xbox 360, Windows. Developed by Kojima Productions. Konami, 2014.

Metal Gear Solid V: The Phantom Pain. PlayStation 4, PlayStation 3, Xbox One, Xbox 360, Microsoft Windows. Developed by Kojima Productions. Konami, 2015.

Metal Gear Solid: Peace Walker. PlayStation Portable. Developed by Kojima Productions. Konami, 2010.

Metroid. Famicom/NES. Developed by Nintendo R&D1 and Intelligent Systems. Nintendo, 1986.

Miegakure. Developed by Marc ten Bosch. Forthcoming. http://miegakure.com.

Mighty Bomb Jack. Arcade. Developed by Tecmo. Tecmo, 1986.

Mighty Jill Off. Microsoft Windows and Macintosh OS X. Developed by Anna Anthropy. Anna Anthropy, 2008.

Mike Tyson's Punch Out!! NES/Famicom/PlayChoice-10. Developed by Nintendo R&D3. Nintendo, 1987.

Minecraft. Microsoft Windows, Macintosh OS X, Linux. Developed by Mojang. Mojang, 2011.

The Misadventures of P.B. Winterbottom. Xbox 360, Microsoft Windows. Developed by The Odd Gentlemen. 2K Play and Valve, 2010.

Missile Command. Arcade. Developed by Atari, Inc. (Dave Theurer). Atari, Inc., 1980.

Monument Valley. Android, iOS, Windows Phone. Developed by Ustwo. Ustwo, 2014.

Mother. Famicom. Developed by Nintendo and Ape. Nintendo, 1989.

Museum of Simulation Technology. Microsoft Windows, Macintosh OS X, Linux. Developed by Pillow Castle. Pillow Castle, forthcoming.

Mystery House. Apple II. Developed by Ken Williams and Roberta Williams. On-Line Systems, 1980.

N. Adobe Flash. Developed by Metanet Software (Raigan Burns and Mare Sheppard). Metanet Software, 2005.

Narbacular Drop. Windows. Developed by Nuclear Monkey Software. DigiPen Institute of Technology, 2005.

NES Remix. Wii U, Nintendo 3DS. Developed by Nintendo EAD Tokyo and indieszero. Nintendo, 2013.

NES Remix 2. Wii U/Nintendo 3DS. Developed by Nintendo EAD Tokyo and indieszero. Nintendo, 2014.

New Super Mario Bros. Nintendo DS. Developed by Nintendo EAD. Nintendo, 2006.

New Super Mario Bros U. Nintendo DS. Developed by Nintendo EAD. Nintendo, 2012.

Ninja Gaiden. Arcade and Nintendo Entertainment System. Developed by Tecmo. Tecmo and Nintendo, 1988.

Onore no Shinzuru Michi wo Yuke. PlayStation Portable. Developed by Silicon Studio. From Software, 2009.

The Orange Box. Microsoft Windows, PlayStation3, Xbox 360, Macintosh OS X, Linux. Developed by Valve Corporation. Steam and Electronic Arts, 2007.

Pac-Man. Arcade. Developed by Namco (Tōru Iwatani). Namco and Midway, 1980.

Pang. 1989. Arcade. Developed by Mitchell (Toshihiko Uda). Mitchell and Capcom, 1983.

Papa Sangre. iOS. Developed by Somethin' Else. Somethin' Else, 2010.

Parallax. Microsoft Windows, Macintosh OS X, Linux. Developed by Toasty Games. Toasty Games, 2015.

Passage. Jason Rohrer. Windows, Macintosh OS X and GNU/Linux. Developed by Jason Rohrer. Rohrer, 2007.

The Path. Windows and Mac. Developed by Tale of Tales (Auriea Harvey and Michaël Samyn). Tale of Tales, 2009.

Perspective. Microsoft Windows. Developed by DigiPen Institute of Technology. DigiPen Institute of Technology, 2012.

Pinball. Nintendo Entertainment System. Developed by Nintendo R&D1. Nintendo, 1984.

Pokémon Blue/Red. Game Boy. Developed by Game Freak. Nintendo, 1996.

Policenauts. PC-9821 (1994); 3DO, PlayStation, and Sega Saturn (1995). Developed by Konami. Konami, 1994.

Pong. Arcade. Developed by Atari, Inc. (Allan Alcorn). Atari, Inc., 1972.

pongpongpongpongpongpongpongpong. Mac, Windows, and Linux. Developed by Andi McClure. Run Hello. https://runhello.com/p/481.

Portal. Windows, Xbox 360, and PlayStation 3. Developed by Valve Corporation. Valve Corporation and Microsoft Game Studios, 2007.

Portal 2. Microsoft Windows, Macintosh OS X, Linux, PlayStation 3, Xbox 360. Developed by Valve Corporation. Valve Corporation, 2011.

Potato Fool's Day ARG. ARG. Developed by Valve Corporation. Steam, 2011.

Prince of Persia: The Sands of Time. PlayStation 2, GameCube, Microsoft Windows, and Xbox. Developed by Ubisoft Montreal. Ubisoft, 2003.

Progress Quest. Microsoft Windows, Linux. Developed by Eric Fredricksen. Eric Fredricksen, 2002.

Quake. MS-DOS, Macintosh OS (1997). Developed by id Software. id Software, 1996.

Quantum Conundrum. Microsoft Windows, PlayStation 3, Xbox 360. Developed by Airtight Games. Square Enix, 2012.

Q.U.B.E. Microsoft Windows, Macintosh OS X, iOS PlayStation 3, PlayStation 4. Developed by Toxic Games. Toxic Games, 2011.

Quest for the Crown. Browser. Developed by Lance and Eskimo and Chef Elf. 2005. http://www.lanceandeskimo.com/flash/quest.html.

Qix. Arcade. Developed by Taito (Randy Pfeiffer and Sandy Pfeiffer). Taito, 1981.

Ratchet and Clank: A Crack in Time. PlayStation 3. Developed by Insomnia Games. Sony Computer Entertainment, 2009.

Real Sound: Kaze no Regret. Saturn. Developed by WARP, Inc. Sega, 1997.

RealSports Volleyball. Atari 2600. Developed by Atari, Inc. (Alan Murphy and Bob Polaro). Atari, Inc., 1982.

Rez. Developed by United Game Artists. Dreamcast and PlayStation 2. Sega, 2001.

The Road Less Taken. rrrrthat's5rs.com. Developed by Serious Sandbox LLC. Serious Sandbox LLC, 2007. http://www.rrrrthats5rs.com/games/the-road-less -taken/.

ROM CHECK FAIL. Browser. Developed by Jarrad [Farbs] Woods. Jarrad Woods, 2008. http://www.farbs.org/romcheckfail.php.

ROM CHECK GO! PC. Developed by Jarrad "Farbs" Woods. Farbs. 2016. http:// farbs.org/ROMCHECKGO.v0.1.zip.

ROM CHECK YOURSELF. Python. Developed by Jarrad "Farbs" Woods. Farbs. 2011. http://farbs.org/rom-check-yourself.

RPG Maker 2000. Microsoft Windows. Developed by ASCII and Enterbrain. ASCII, 2000.

Scale. Microsoft Windows, Macintosh OS X, Linux. Developed by CubeHeart Games. CubeHeart Games, Forthcoming.

Sea Wolf. Arcade. Developed by Dave Nutting Associates. Midway, 1976.

Second Life. Microsoft Windows and Macintosh OS X. Developed by Linden Research, Inc. Linden Research Inc., 2003.

Segagaga. Dreamcast. Developed by Hitmaker. Sega, 2001.

Shades of Doom. Microsoft Windows. Developed by GMA Games. GMA Games, 2001.

SOD. JODI. Microsoft Windows and Macintosh OS9. Developed by JODI (Joan Heemskerk and Dirk Paesmans). JODI, 2001.

Soulcalibur IV. PlayStation 3, Xbox 360. Developed by Project Soul. Namco Bandai and Ubisoft, 2008.

Space Invaders. Arcade. Developed by Taito. Taito, 1978.

Space War! PDP-1. Developed by Steve Russell, Martin Graetz, and Wayne Wii-tanen. 1962.

Speculation. ARG. N. Developed by Katherine Hayles, Patrick Jagoda, Patrick LeMieux. Greater than Games Lab. Duke University, 2012–14.

Spelunky. Microsoft Windows. Developed by Derek Yu. Mossmouth, 2009.

Spy Hunter. Arcade. Developed by Bally Midway (George Gomez). Bally Midway.

Star Citizen. Microsoft Windows and Linux. Developed by Cloud Imperium Games. Cloud Imperium Games, Forthcoming (2012—).

StarCraft. Microsoft Windows, Macintosh OS. Developed by Blizzard Entertain-ment. Blizzard Entertainment, 1998.

StarCraft: Brood War. Windows, Macintosh OS (1999). Developed by Blizzard Entertainment and Saffire. Blizzard Entertainment and Sierra Entertainment, 1998.

StarCraft II: Heart of the Swarm. Windows, Macintosh OS X. Developed by Blizzard Entertainment. Blizzard Entertainment, 2013.

StarCraft II: Wings of Liberty. Microsoft Windows, Macintosh OS. Developed by Blizzard Entertainment. Blizzard Entertainment, 2010.

Star Fox. Super Nintendo Entertainment System. Developed by Nintendo EAD. Nintendo, 1993.

Street Fighter. Arcade. Developed by Capcom. Capcom, 1987.

Super Columbine Massacre RPG! Microsoft Windows. Developed by Danny Ledonne. 2005. http://www.columbinegame.com/.

Super Mario Bros. Nintendo Entertainment System. Developed by Nintendo R&D4. Nintendo, 1985.

Super Mario Bros. 2. Nintendo Entertainment System. Developed by Nintendo R&D4. Nintendo, 1987.

Super Mario Bros. 3. Nintendo Entertainment System. Developed by Nintendo R&D4. Nintendo, 1988.

Super Mario Bros. Crossover. Flash. Developed by Jay Pavlina. Exploding Rabbit, 2010.

Super Mario Bros.: The Lost Levels. Famicom. Developed by Nintendo R&D4. Nintendo, 1986.

Super Mario Clouds. Nintendo. Developed by Cory Arcangel. Cory Arcangel, 2002.

Super Mario Galaxy. Wii. Developed by Nintendo EAD. Nintendo, 2007.

Super Mario Galaxy 2. Wii. Developed by Nintendo EAD. Nintendo, 2009.

Super Mario Kart. Super Nintendo Entertainment System. Developed by Nintendo EAD. Nintendo, 1992.

Super Mario Land. Game Boy. Developed by Nintendo R&D1. Nintendo, 1989.

Super Mario Maker. Nintendo Wii U. Developed by Nintendo EAD Group No. 4. Nintendo, 2015.

Super Mario RPG: Legend of the Seven Stars. Super Famicom/SNES. Developed by Square. Nintendo, 1996.

Super Mario 64. Nintendo 64, iQue Player (2003), Wii Virtual Console (2006). Developed by Nintendo EAD. Nintendo, 1996.

Super Mario Sunshine. GameCube. Developed by Nintendo EAD. Nintendo, 2002.

Super Mario 3D World. Wii U. Developed by Nintendo EAD Tokyo. Nintendo, 2013.

Super Mario World. Super Nintendo Entertainment System. Developed by Nintendo EAD. Nintendo, 1990.

Super Meat Boy. Xbox Live Arcade. Developed by Team Meat. Microsoft Game Studios, 2010.

Super Monday Night Combat. Windows. Developed by Uber Entertainment. Uber Entertainment, 2012.

Super Paper Mario. Nintendo Wii. Developed by Intelligent Systems. Nintendo, 2007.

Super Smash Bros. Nintendo 64, iQue Player (2003), Wii Virtual Console (2009). Developed by HAL Laboratory. Nintendo, 1999.

Super Smash Bros. Brawl. Nintendo Wii. Developed by Nintendo, Game Arts, Sora Ltd., et al. Nintendo 2008.

Super Smash Bros. for Wii U. Nintendo. Nintendo Wii U. Developed by Sora Ltd. and Bandai Namco Games. Nintendo, 2014.

Super Smash Bros. Melee. Nintendo GameCube. Developed by HAL Laboratory. Nintendo, 2001.

Super Smash Bros.: Project M. Wii. Developed by Project M Development Team. 2011.

Super Time Force. Xbox One, Xbox 360. Developed by Capybara Games. Capybara Games. 2014.

Surgeon Simulator 2013. Microsoft Windows, OS, Linux. Developed by Bossa Studios. Bossa Studios, 2013.

Swamp. Windows. Developed by Jeremy [Aprone] Kaldobsky. Jeremy Kaldobsky, 2011.

Syobon Action. Microsoft Windows. Developed by ちく(Chiku). 2007. http://www
.geocities.jp/z_gundam_tanosii/home/Main.html.

Tatsunoko vs. Capcom: Ultimate All-Stars. Arcade. Developed by Eighting. Capcom, 2008.

Team Fortress Classic. Windows. Developed by Valve Corporation. Sierra On-Line and Valve Corporation, 1999.

Team Fortress 2. Microsoft Windows. Developed by Valve Corporation. Valve Corporation, 2007.

Tennis for Two. Analog Computer and Oscilloscope. Developed by William Higinbotham. William Higinbotham, 1958.

Tetris. Nintendo Entertainment System. Developed by Alexy Pajitnov. Nintendo, 1984.

Timebot. Flash. Developed by David Durham. David Durham, 2007.

Time Donkey. Browser. Developed by Flashbang Studios. Blurst, 2009.

Tokimeki Memorial. PC Engine. Developed by Konami. Konami, 1994.

TowerFall. Ouya. Developed by Matt Thorson. Matt Thorson, 2013.

Trackmania Sunrise. Microsoft Windows. Developed by Nadeo. Enlight Software, 2005.

Transformice. Browser. Developed by Mélanie Christin and Jean-Baptiste Lemarchand. Atelier 801, 2010.

Trials Evolution. Xbox 360. Developed by RedLynx. Microsoft Studios, 2012.

Tuper Tario Tros. Browser. Developed by SwingSwing. Newgrounds, 2009.

Ultimate NES Remix. Will U, Nintendo 3DS. Developed by Nintendo EAD Tokyo and indieszero. Nintendo, 2014.

Undertale. Microsoft Windows, OS X. Developed by tobyfox. tobyfox, 2015.

The Unfinished Swan. PlayStation 3. Developed by Giant Sparrow. Sony Computer Entertainment, 2012.

Unreal Tournament '99. Windows. Developed by Epic Games and Digital Extremes. GT Interactive, 1999.

Unreal Tournament 2004. Windows, Macintosh OS X, Linux. Developed by Epic Games and Digital Extremes. Atari, Inc. (Windows/Linux), MacSoft (Macintosh OS X), and Midway, 2004.

Untitled Game. Microsoft Windows and Macintosh OS9. Developed by JODI (Joan Heemskerk and Dirk Paesmans). JODI, 1996–2002.

Upgrade Complete. Browser. Developed by That's Tony. Armor Games, 2009. http://armorgames.com/play/3955/upgrade-complete.

Velvet Strike. Windows. Developed by Anne-Marie Schleiner, Joan Leandre, and Brody Condon. 2002.

VVVVVV. Windows and OS X. Developed by Terry Cavanagh. Terry Cavanagh and Nicalis, Inc., 2010.

Warcraft: Orcs & Humans. MS-DOS, Macintosh OS (1996). Developed by Blizzard Entertainment. Blizzard Entertainment and Interplay Entertainment, 1994.

Warcraft II: Tides of Darkness. MS-DOS, Macintosh OS. Developed by Blizzard Entertainment. Blizzard Entertainment, 1995.

Warcraft III: Reign of Chaos. Windows, Macintosh OS, Macintosh OS X. Developed by Blizzard Entertainment. Blizzard Entertainment, Sierra Entertainment, and Capcom (Japan), 2002.

Warcraft III: The Frozen Throne. Windows, Macintosh OS, Macintosh OS X. Developed by Blizzard Entertainment. Blizzard Entertainment, Sierra Entertainment,

Capcom (Japan), and Sonokong (Korea), 2003. Windows, Macintosh OS, Macintosh OS X.

Warhammer 40,000. Print and mixed media. Developed by Games Workshop. Games Workshop, 1987.

Warhammer Fantasy Battle. Print and mixed media. Developed by Games Workshop. Games Workshop, 1983.

Watch Dogs. Microsoft Windows, PlayStation 3, PlayStation 4. Xbox 360, Xbox One, Wii U. Ubisoft Montreal. Ubisoft, 2014.

World of Goo. Microsoft Windows and WiiWare. Developed by 2D Boy. 2D Boy, 2008.

World of Warcraft. Windows, Macintosh OS X. Developed by Blizzard Entertainment. Blizzard Entertainment, 2004.

Yar's Revenge. Atari 2600. Developed by Atari, Inc. (Howard Scott Warshaw). Atari, Inc., 1981.

Year Zero. ARG. Developed by 42 Entertainment and Nine Inch Nails. Interscope, 2007.

You Have to Burn the Rope. Browser. Developed by Kian Bashiri. Adobe Flash, 2008. http://www.kongregate.com/games/Mazapan/you-have-to-burn-the-rope/.

You Only Live Once. Flash. Developed by Raitendo. Kongregate, 2009. http://www.kongregate.com/games/raitendo/you-only-live-once.

Yume Kōjō: Doki Doki Panic. Nintendo Entertainment System. Developed by Nintendo R&D4. Nintendo, 1987.

Zeno of Elea. Browser. Developed by Darius Kazemi. Darius Kazemi, 2013. http://tinysubversions.com/game/zeno/.

Zero Wing. Arcade. Developed by Toaplan. Taito, 1989.

Zone of the Enders. PlayStation 2. Developed by KCEJ. Konami, 2001.

ZZT. Developed by Tim Sweeney. MS-DOS. Epic MegaGames, 1991.

Index

(continued from p. ii)

ELECTRONIC MEDIATIONS

STEPHANIE BOLUK is assistant professor in the English department and Cinema and Digital Media Program at University of California, Davis.

PATRICK LEMIEUX is an artist, game designer, and assistant professor in the Cinema and Digital Media Program at University of California, Davis.